VALUATION

MEASURING AND MANAGING THE VALUE OF COMPANIES

WILEY FRONTIERS IN FINANCE

VALUATION

MEASURING AND MANAGING THE VALUE OF COMPANIES, SECOND EDITION

Tom Copeland
Tim Koller
Jack Murrin

McKinsey & Company, Inc.

JOHN WILEY & SONS, INC.

New York • Chichester • Brisbane • Toronto • Singapore

Copyright© 1995, 1996 by McKinsey & Company, Inc.
Published by John Wiley & Sons, Inc.
All rights reserved.
Published simultaneously in Canada.

Library of Congress Cataloging-in-Publication Data:

Copeland, Thomas E., 1946–
    Valuation : measuring and managing the value of companies / Tom Copeland, Tim Koller, Jack Murrin. — 2nd ed.
        p.   cm. — (Wiley Frontiers in Finance Series)
    ISSN 0733-8945)
    Includes bibliographical references and index.
    ISBN 0-471-08627-4 (paperback)
    ISBN 0-471-00993-8 (cloth—acid free paper)
    ISBN 0-471-00994-6 (cloth with disk—acid free paper)
    ISBN 0-471-01313-7 (disk alone)
    1. Corporations—Valuation—Handbooks, manuals, etc.   I. Koller, Tim.   II. Murrin, Jack.   III. Title.   IV. Series.
    HG4028.V3C67   1994
    658.15—dc20   94-8304

10   9

This book is dedicated to our parents to thank them for their loving support through the years: George and Irene Copeland, David and Jeanette Koller, and John and Wilma Murrin.

About the Authors

TOM COPELAND is a partner in the New York office of McKinsey & Co., Inc., and a co-leader of the firm's corporate finance practice. Previously, he was a professor of finance at UCLA's Anderson Graduate School of Management, where he served as chairman of the Finance Department and vice chairman of the Graduate School of Management. He is coauthor with J. Fred Weston of *Financial Theory and Corporate Policy* and *Managerial Finance*. He received his PhD in applied economics from the University of Pennsylvania.

TIM KOLLER is a partner at McKinsey & Co., Inc., and a co-leader of the firm's corporate finance practice. He has served a broad range of clients on restructuring, mergers and acquisitions, and corporate strategy. He was formerly a vice president at Stern Stewart & Co., a financial consulting firm, and a senior financial analyst with Mobil Corporation. He received his MBA from the University of Chicago.

JACK MURRIN, a former partner and leader of the corporate finance practice at McKinsey's New York office, is Senior Vice President, Travelers, Inc., in New York. He is a Certified Public Accountant and was previously with Arthur Andersen & Co. He received his MBA from Stanford University.

Preface

This is an unusual book. It is intended to be at once a guide to doing valuations of companies rigorously and well, a treatment of some special issues in valuation (for example, how to value financial institutions), and a perspective on how the corporate environment—and, therefore, the challenge for corporate managers—has changed. Value and valuation are more important than ever. This book is about how to reckon true value.

We hope it is a book you will use again and again. If we have done our job well, it will soon be full of underlinings, marginal notations, and highlighting. This is no coffee-table book. It is a tool, to be deployed in the pursuit of value.

In the last decade, two separate streams of thinking and activity—corporate finance and corporate strategy—have come together with a resounding crash. Corporate finance is no longer the exclusive preserve of financiers. Corporate strategy is no longer a separate realm ruled by CEOs. The link between strategy and finance has become very close and clear. Participants in the financial markets are increasingly involved in business operations through leveraged buyouts, hostile takeovers, and proxy contests. At the same time, chief executives have led their companies to become increasingly active players in the financial markets through self-generated restructurings, leveraged recapitalizations, leveraged buyouts, share repurchases, and the like. Financing and investment are now inextricably linked. Around the globe, privatization and the necessity of corporate efficiency in the face of international competition reinforce this theme.

This new reality presents a challenge to business managers: the need to *manage value*. They need to focus as never before on the value their corporate and business-level strategies are creating. In the quest for value, they find that they must consider such radical alternatives as selling the "crown jewels" or completely restructuring operations. And they need more systematic and reliable ways to look for opportunities in the turbulence resulting from the confluence of strategy and finance. For instance, as a result of restructurings, companies face unprecedented opportunities to acquire assets and businesses that may be worth more to them than to their original owners.

WHY THIS BOOK?

Our firm, McKinsey & Company, Inc., works with hundreds of companies each year on strategies to make lasting improvements in their performance. Often this work has a significant financial component, such as counsel on potential restructurings, acquisition programs, merger transactions, divestitures, and international ventures. At McKinsey, then, finance is not simply a specialized practice area, but an integral part of our overall service to clients.

This book grew out of a special research project in our Corporate Finance Practice aimed at developing approaches to valuation and financial thinking that effectively link finance to strategy. We have drawn on leading-edge academic thinking as well as our own research to devise clear and sound ways to calibrate value in a variety of contexts that we encounter frequently in our work with clients. These include valuing single-business companies; assessing the value creation and restructuring potential in multibusiness companies; implementing value-based management; evaluating acquisitions; analyzing international and multinational business opportunities; and using option-pricing methods to value strategies based on the flexibility they give.

Our primary goal in this book is to *demystify* the field of valuation. We hope that value-based thinking and the application of sophisticated valuation approaches will soon become commonplace. We believe that clear thinking about valuation and skill in using valuation to guide business decisions are prerequisites for success in today's competitive environment. Value needs to be understood clearly by CEOs, business managers, and financial managers alike. Heretofore, valuation has been left to "experts" and used in special situations. Too often, it has been viewed as a specialized discipline unto itself, rather than as a key tool for running businesses better. But valuation is not a rarefied art or arcane science.

In this book, we hope to lift the veil on valuation by explaining, step by step, how to do it well. We spell out valuation frameworks that we use in our consulting work, and we bring these frameworks to life with detailed case studies that highlight the practical judgments involved in developing and using valuations. Most important, we discuss how to use valuation to make decisions about courses of action for a company.

WHAT'S NEW ABOUT THE SECOND EDITION

When we sat down to write the first edition at the end of the 1980s, the market for corporate control was exerting strong external pressure on management in the United States due to hostile takeover activity and leveraged buyouts. "Raider" economics was an easy theme and an obvious reason for wanting to manage for value creation—for incumbent management to achieve the greatest value for shareholders. But we have learned that the reason for managing value is much broader, and although the market for corporate control is important, it is not the only, or even the best, motivating force—especially outside of the United States. Therefore, the top-management perspective in the second edition is much more global in outlook. For example, Chapter 1, entitled "Why Value Value," provides the theoretical basis (supported by empirical evidence) for maximizing shareholder value in any free economy, particularly outside of the United States; and Chapter 13 discusses "Valuations Outside of the United States."

Additionally, we have gained broad experience in the practical aspects of using value-based management (VBM) as a high-impact way of transitioning from current accounting-based performance systems to value-based systems, as well as for providing an on-going method for using operational value drivers at the front line of management to attain continual performance improvements in income statement as well as balance sheet management. Chapter 4 is new to the second edition and covers value-based management from a top-management perspective. VBM concepts are also woven through the other chapters where appropriate.

The hardback second edition also contains a computer disk with Excel and Lotus 1-2-3 versions of our valuation spreadsheets. The model is appropriate for most U.S. nonfinancial companies that use GAAP accounting. Practitioners will find the model easy to use in a variety of situations: mergers and acquisitions, valuing business units for restructuring or value-based management, or testing the implications of major strategic decisions on the value of their company. Of course, we accept no responsibility whatsoever for any decisions based on your inputs to the model.

WHO SHOULD USE IT?

This book began as a guide for McKinsey consultants. By publishing it, we hope to reach and help a wider audience.

- *Students of finance and corporate trainers.* One of the best ways to learn about valuation is to do it. Consequently, this book has served as a useful primer for thousands of business students at universities around the world. This version has end-of-chapter problems, questions, and exercises to challenge your thinking and help you to test your understanding of the material.

- *Business managers.* Now more than ever, leaders at the corporate and business-unit levels need to know how to assess the value of alternative strategies. They need to know how much value they can create through restructurings and other major transactions. Beyond this, they need to instill a managing value mindset throughout their organizations.

- *Corporate finance practitioners.* Valuation approaches and the linkage between finance and strategy are important to chief financial officers, merger and acquisition specialists, corporate financial professionals within companies and on Wall Street, and corporate development managers and strategists. Value—how to assess it, create it, and communicate it—lies at the core of their roles and responsibilities.

- *Investors, portfolio managers, and security analysts.* These professionals should find this volume a useful guide to applying cash flow valuation approaches. This is the purest form of fundamental security analysis, since it links the value of the company directly to the economic returns it can generate from its businesses and assets.

Moreover, while many of our case examples and illustrations are geared toward U.S. situations, the fundamental principles of valuation and the valuation approaches described here are applicable in any country. With minor adjustment, they can be used in Europe and the Far East. This is the subject of Chapter 13. Market conditions and the availability of information differ from country to country, but the techniques themselves are a bedrock on which managers and investors can build their assessments of value.

WHEN TO USE IT

First and foremost, this book is written for those who want to improve their ability to create value of the stakeholders in their business. It will be of most use when a need exists to do the following:

- *Estimate the value of alternative corporate and business strategies* and the value of specific programs within those strategies. These strategies include such initiatives as new product introductions, capital expenditures, joint venture agreements, and new market entries.
- *Assess major transactions* such as mergers, acquisitions, divestitures, recapitalizations, and share repurchases.
- *Use value-based management* to review and target the performance of business operations. It is essential to know whether and to what extent a business, as currently performing and configured, is creating value. Equally important is the need to understand which operating measures have the greatest prospects for enhancing value.
- *Communicate with key stakeholders,* especially stockholders, about the value of the business. Our fundamental premise is that the value of a company derives from its ability to generate cash flows and cash flow based returns on investment. In

our view, many companies could do a much better job than they now do of communicating with the market and other players about the value of their plans and strategies. But first they need to become value managers themselves and understand what value they are creating and why.

STRUCTURE OF THE BOOK

This book is organized into three clusters of chapters. In the first cluster—Chapters 1 through 4—we discuss the link between business strategies and value. In Chapter 1, we make the case that *managing shareholder value* is a central role and challenge for senior managers today. By comparing companies in Europe, North America, and Japan we show that winning companies do so by increasing shareholder value, productivity, and employment over the long run. There is no evidence to support allegations of a conflict between employment and maximizing shareholders' wealth. These objectives are, in the long run, complements not substitutes. In Chapter 2, we develop a picture of what it means to be a value manager. We do this through a detailed case study based on the actual experiences of a CEO who needed to restructure his company and build a new managing-value philosophy throughout it. Chapter 3 reviews our fundamental premise that managing value effectively means focusing on *cash flows* and cash flow rates of return from business activities. We make the case that traditional accounting measures can be useful tools for understanding cash flow returns but are no substitute for these more direct indicators of value. Chapter 4 rounds out the section on managing value by introducing value-based management and economic profit (EP). It describes client situations where value-based decision making completely changed top management's course of action and shows how to implement VBM.

The next group of chapters—Chapters 5 through 10—is a self-contained handbook for doing valuations of single-business companies. In it we describe, step by step, a general approach to discounted cash flow valuation and how to implement it. This includes how to analyze historical performance, forecast free cash flows, estimate the appropriate opportunity cost of capital, identify sources of value, and interpret results. As a further aid to the practitioner, we walk through the valuation of an actual company (Preston Corporation) from the outside, using publicly available information.

The final block of chapters—Chapters 11 through 16—is devoted to valuation in more complex situations. We have included a chapter on valuing multibusiness companies that shows how to estimate the value of each part of the portfolio, the corporate center, and so forth. There is a chapter on valuation of multinational companies, and another on valuations outside of the United States. Chapter 14 covers our thinking about the management of acquisitions, mergers, divestitures, and joint ventures. We explore the application of option-pricing theory to corporate assets and liabilities (such as convertible debt) in Chapter 15. And in Chapter 16 we discuss the principles of valuation applicable to financial intermediaries such as banks, an exceedingly intricate area that is growing in importance with the wave of bank mergers, S&L failures, and international financial combinations.

INTELLECTUAL FOUNDATIONS

One of us was asked by the editor of *Le Figaro* in Paris, "what is new about your approach?" As far as the methodology is concerned, the answer is, "practically nothing." Valuation is an age-old methodology in finance with its intellectual origins in the present value method of capital budgeting and in the valuation approach developed by Professors Merton Miller and Franco Modigliani (both Nobel laureates) in their 1963 *Journal of Business* article entitled "Dividend Policy, Growth and the Valuation of Shares." Our intellectual debt is primarily to them, but others have gone far to popularize their approach. In particular, Professor Al Rappaport of Northwestern (cofounder of ALCAR) and Joel Stern (of Stern Stewart & Co.) were among the first to extend the Miller-Modigliani entity valuation formula to real-world applications and to develop and market computer tools for making this an easy task for companies.

There is another answer, however, to the question, "what's new about your approach?" The advent of personal computers has largely demystified spreadsheet valuation and made it easily accessible to management for practical applications like mergers and acquisitions, restructuring, and value-based management. What's new is that valuation has become a useful tool that links strategic decisions at the board level all the way down to operational value drivers used by frontline managers. This helps to develop a correct, common language based on maximizing shareholder wealth throughout the organization.

Acknowledgments

No book is solely the effort of its authors. This book is certainly no exception, especially since it grew out of the collective work of McKinsey's corporate finance practice and the experiences of consultants throughout our Firm. The second edition has benefited greatly from the help of a new list of friends whose names are added to those who helped with the first edition.

For their guidance and encouragement, we would especially like to thank Ennius Bergsma and Fred Gluck.

For help in developing the original drafts of this book as an internal guide for our consultants, we owe a special debt to Dave Furer. Mimi James provided analytical support for many portions of this book and was instrumental in developing both the valuation model for industrial companies and the banking model. Ahmed Taha, Phil Kholos, Ali Asghar, and Perry Moilinoff deserve special mention for their contributions to the case materials and the valuation models. The chapter on "Why Value Value" extends the productivity work done at the McKinsey Global Institute under the direction of Bill Lewis. We thank Bill Fallon, David Rothschild, and Kurt Losert for their help with the chapter on "Value-Based

Management." The chapter on acquisitions and joint ventures benefited from work undertaken by our Corporate Leadership Center, whose key contributors were John Patience, Steve Coley, and Jack Welch; and from *Collaborating to Compete* co-authored by David Ernst and Joel Bleeke. Shyanjaw Kuo provided extensive help on option-pricing applications, based on knowledge developed in an ongoing McKinsey research project in collaboration with Alo Ghosh, Jon Weiner, and Juan Ocampo.

We are also grateful to the large number of finance-savvy consultants and specialists around our Firm who provided input to our efforts. Several people in particular must be mentioned: Buford Alexander, Peter Bisson, Dan Bergman, Johan Depraetere, Mikel Dodd, Pat Anslinger, Frank Richter, Silvia Stefini, Keiko Honda, Will Draper, Russ Fradin, Bill Barnett, Bill Trent, Konrad Stiglbrunner, Carlos Abad, David Willensky, Bill Pursche, Mike Murray, and Christian von Drathen.

For their help in preparing the manuscript and exhibits, we owe our thanks to Lenora Cannegieter and Tricia Hennessey. John Donovan and the rest of the visual aids team in New York did their usual terrific job.

Gene Zelazny worked his magic with visual communications in the book while Vera Deutsche added her design touch to the exhibits and cover.

Last, but not least, we want to thank Stuart Flack for serving as a sounding board and for expertly crafting syntheses of our earlier drafts into readable form.

The Wiley editorial, marketing and production teams also did a great job: Myles Thompson, Jacqueline Urinyi, and the people at Impressions.

Finally, our warmest thanks to those who stood by us enduring late nights, weekends, and parts of "vacations" that were consumed to produce this book. Maggie Queen and Melissa Koller, your support and encouragement are truly appreciated.

TOM COPELAND
TIM KOLLER

Contents

Part I

Company Value and the Manager's Mission

1

Why Value Value?

This book is not only about how to value companies. It's also about how to use valuation as a tool for better decision making. Beneath the techniques and methods we present lies the belief that maximizing shareholder value is or ought to be the fundamental goal of all businesses. In this chapter, we attempt to show why we hold value so dear and hope to convince the reader why he or she should care about managing value.

This topic is either commonplace or controversial depending on where you sit. In the United States, there is an established tradition. Top management is expected to maximize shareholder value. Failure to do so results in pressure from the board of directors, activist shareholders, or even a hostile takeover. Around the world though, other societies make far different implicit tradeoffs among a variety of stakeholders. In continental Europe and Japan intricate weightings are given to the interests of customers, suppliers, workers, the government, debt providers, equity holders and even society at large. In those quarters, maximizing shareholder value is often seen as shortsighted, inefficient, simplistic, and perhaps antisocial. To support this view, proponents of the balanced-stakeholders approach point to the high standards of living and rapid economic growth in Europe and Japan, and to the success of Japanese auto and consumer electronics companies.

Yet there is mounting evidence to the contrary. A U.S.-style system based on maximizing shareholder value, accompanied by broad ownership of debt and equity and an open market for corporate control, appears to be closely linked with: a higher standard of living, greater overall productivity and competitiveness, and a better functioning equity market. If countries whose economic systems are not based on maximizing shareholder value give investors lower returns on capital than those who do, they will slowly be starved for capital, as capital markets continue to globalize, falling farther and farther behind in global competition. A value-based system becomes ever more important as capital becomes ever more mobile.

The first step to understanding the value of value begins with a discussion of the differences in ownership and control across the triad—Germany, Japan, and the United States. We'll then forge the link between maximizing shareholder value, here calculated as market value added (MVA), and other indisputable economic and social goods: GDP per capita, a proxy for standard of living; high productivity, a proxy for international competitiveness; and employment growth, a proxy for labor's claim. Shareholder wealth creation does not come at the expense of other stakeholders. Quite the opposite. Winning companies, when compared to their competitors, have greater productivity, greater increases in shareholder's wealth, and higher employment. Shareholder wealth maximization may be an explicitly stated goal, as for many companies in the U.S., or it may be implicitly the result of other correct decisions, as with many companies in Europe or especially in Japan. Either way, it cannot be ignored. Managers must measure and manage the value of their companies.

OWNERSHIP AND CONTROL ACROSS THE TRIAD

European and Asian managers often tell us that they do not and should not maximize shareholder value as the exclusive goal of their company. Instead, they place a much greater weight on the value of other claims, especially labor. The reasons behind this point of view have to do partly with the composition of ownership and control and partly with the roles and responsibilities that corporations play in society.

European countries balance stakeholder claims differently than in the United States. For example, Exhibit 1.1 illustrates the co-determination structure in Germany. Employees have specific rights to share decision making and elect half of the supervisory board representatives directly. Furthermore, the workers council, composed of non-executive employees, has decision-sharing power in

Exhibit 1.1 **CO-DETERMINATION STRUCTURE IN GERMANY**

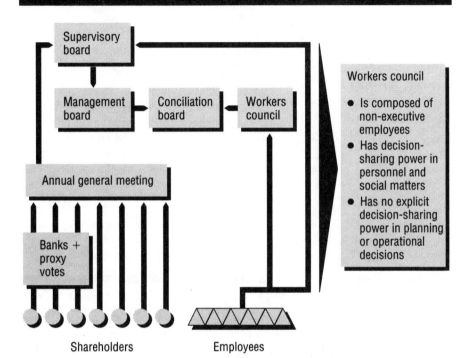

Source: Klaus Chmielewiez, "Codetermination," in *Handbook of German Business Management* (Poeschel Verlag, Stuttgart: 1990).

personnel and social matters, although it has no explicit decision-sharing power in planning or operational decisions. Exhibit 1.2 gives some indication of employee power across Europe. Clearly employees have a greater say in the management process in Europe than in the United States.

Another clear difference between the U.S. and Europe is the concentration of the ownership and control of sources of capital. German debt is dominated by institutional, not market sources. Exhibit 1.3 shows that debt provides roughly 85 percent of all external capital. But it is mostly privately placed debt with banks. There is virtually no use of commercial paper, a common publicly held source of short-term debt financing in the United States. And publicly traded corporate bonds make up only 0.14 percent of outstanding German bonds. In Exhibit 1.4 we see that German banks

Exhibit 1.2 **EMPLOYEE POWER ACROSS EUROPE**

Country	Employee power
Germany	• Emplyees have up to 50% of seats on supervisory board • Employees have decision-sharing power in personnel and social matters
Netherlands	• The workers council has a right to information and consultation, and the right to grant or withhold approval of certain decisions • Veto on appointment of directors
Belgium	• CEO must provide the workers council with detailed data • Workers council gives opinion and suggestions in some areas
France	• Two employee representatives may attend board meetings but have no voting rights • Trade unions and workers council have right to be consulted about certain activities but have no veto right
U.K.	• Management has no obligation to consult or involve employees in decision making
Denmark	• Employees have statutory right to co-determination

Sources: Data from Julian Franks and Colin Mayer, "Capital Markets and Corporate Control: A Study of France, Germany, and the UK," *Economic Policy* 5 (April 1990): 189–231; Eberhard Duelfer, "Public Limited Company," in *Handbook of German Business Management* (Poeschel Verlag, Stuttgart: 1990); *Juridisch Zakboekje* 63 (Wolters Kluwer, Amsterdam: June 1990); Commission of the European Communities–Directorate General for Employment, Industrial Relations, and Social Affairs, "First Report on the Application of the Community Charter of the Fundamental Social Rights of Workers," Luxembourg, 1992.

administer approximately 50 percent of proxy voting rights, although they own only 8.2 percent of all equity shares for their own account.

The situation is not dissimilar in Japan. Exhibit 1.5 indicates that the lion's share of external funding is provided by borrowing from private financial institutions. Publicly traded corporate bonds provided only 2.8 percent of external capital and equity issues only 8.9 percent. According to Hodder and Tschoegl, the major security holders in Japan hold shares to maintain business relationships and do very little trading.[1] The major institutional holders (banks, insurance companies, and nonfinancial business corporations)

[1] J. Hodder and A. Tschoegl, "Some Aspects of Japanese Corporate Finance," in E. Elton and M. Gruber, eds., *Japanese Capital Markets* (New York: Harper & Row, 1990), 57–80.

Exhibit 1.3 **SOURCES OF GERMAN DEBT**

Loans as % of total external
funds for Germany

Outstanding commercial paper as %
of bank credit to non-financial
companies for U.S. and Germany

Percent

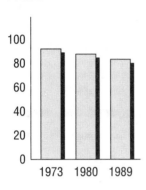

Percent

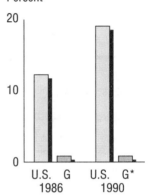

Outstanding German bonds, May 1992

100% = 2,042 billion DM

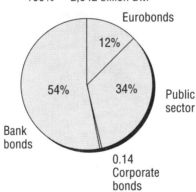

Sources: "Statistisches Bundesamt-Lange Reihe zur Wirtschaftsentwicklung," *Deutsche Bundesbank;* Mark Bex and Peter Praet, paper in *Europe, Revue de la Banque* 3 (Kluwer Editorial: 1992): 112–113; Reiner Bach, article in *1992 Guide to European Domestic Bondmarkets* (Euromoney Publications: 1992): 25.

*Domestic DM commercial paper only allowed since 1991.

Exhibit 1.4 **VOTING POWER OF GERMAN BANKS, 1989**

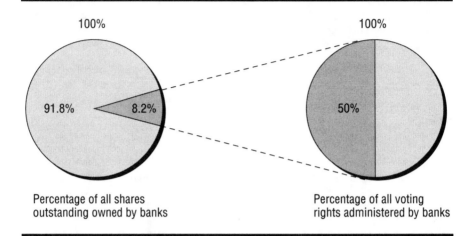

100%   100%

91.8% 8.2%   50%

Percentage of all shares   Percentage of all voting
outstanding owned by banks   rights administered by banks

Source: Nicholas Kochan and Michel Syrett, "New Directions in Corporate Governance," report no. 2137 (London, Business International Limited: 1991).

Exhibit 1.5 **JAPAN, 1982, NET SUPPLY OF EXTERNAL INDUSTRIAL FUNDS BY SOURCE**

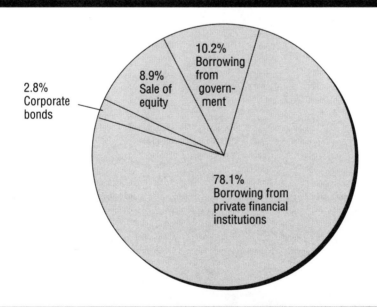

10.2%
Borrowing
from
govern-
ment

8.9%
Sale of
equity

2.8%
Corporate
bonds

78.1%
Borrowing from
private financial
institutions

Source: Hodder and Tschoegl.

collectively held 61.2 percent of listed shares in 1983, but engaged in only 10.7 percent of trades. Most of the institutional share-holding is within the large business groups, the Keiretsu. Thus, Okumura concludes that cross-holding acts as a barrier to hostile takeovers and mergers.[2]

What are the consequences for an economy without widely distributed ownership and control? One is that the demand for publicly available information is much lower where capital is closely held. Less publicly available information usually implies that capital markets are less efficient and that, consequently, capital is less likely to flow quickly toward new productive uses. A second consequence is that managers are less likely to focus on value creation—a long-term performance metric, because market prices of shares are less likely to reflect good information, at least from the perspective of informed management. Therefore, the market price of equity is commonly disregarded as the best indicator of management performance. A third consequence is that there is a strong market for corporate control only in the U.S. Interlocking ownership in Germany and Japan prevents hostile takeovers. These facts seem to affect management's focus on shareholder value creation. Not only are market prices unlikely to reflect good information, there is also no strong incentive to shepherd value creation opportunities.

SHAREHOLDER WEALTH AND ECONOMIC PERFORMANCE

The unique combination of features that make up the capital markets of the U.S., Germany, and Japan in turn affect each nation's economy in unique ways. We begin to see these effects by looking at Gross Domestic Product (GDP), productivity, and job creation across the triad. All consumption, savings, and investment in an economy is captured by GDP. If GDP per capita of one economy remains higher than another over a long period of time, the population is generally better off in terms of their material needs (although environmentalists have argued that GDP does not capture the quality of life). Exhibit 1.6 gives GDP per capita, with currencies converted at 1990 rates using Organization for Economic Cooperation and Development (OECD) purchasing power parity

---

[2] H. Okumura, "Interfirm Relations in an Enterprise Group: The Case of Mitsubishi," *Japanese Economic Studies* 6 (1982): 53–82.

Exhibit 1.6 **GDP PER CAPITA, 1950–90,** PERCENT

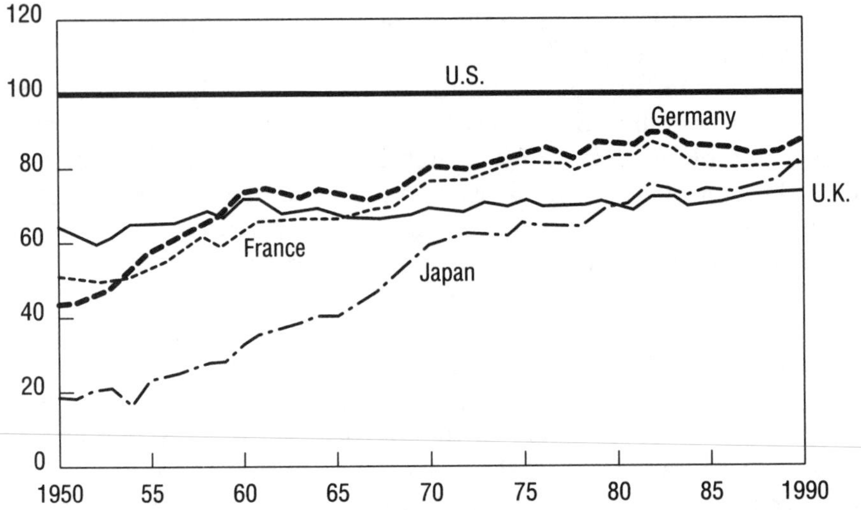

Source: OECD National Accounts, 1978–1990, Vol. 1, Paris: OECD, 1992; A. Maddison, *Dynamic Forces in Capitalist Development* (London: Oxford University Press, 1991).

estimates, for five countries from 1950 to 1990. The United States is set at 100. Until 1980 the other countries had been closing the gap. However, since then only Japan has been catching up. The U.S., with shareholder value focus, remains the GDP leader.

Two recent studies by the McKinsey Global Institute shed light on the productivity part of the picture.[3] The first study examined productivity across the triad in five service industries: airlines, telecommunications, retail banking, general merchandise retailing, and restaurants. As shown in Exhibit 1.7, the service sector has played an increasingly important role in developed economies so that by 1987 it represented 55 percent of employment in Germany, 58 percent in Japan, and 63 percent in the United States.

Labor productivity was calculated as revenues minus materials and energy costs, divided by the number of hours worked. All productivity measures were converted to dollars using an industry purchasing power parity (PPP) concept in order to avoid the large

[3] McKinsey Global Institute, *Service Sector Productivity,* Washington D.C., October, 1992; and *Manufacturing Productivity,* Washington D.C., October 1993.

Exhibit 1.7 **STRUCTURE OF EMPLOYMENT, 1870, 1950, AND 1987,** PERCENT

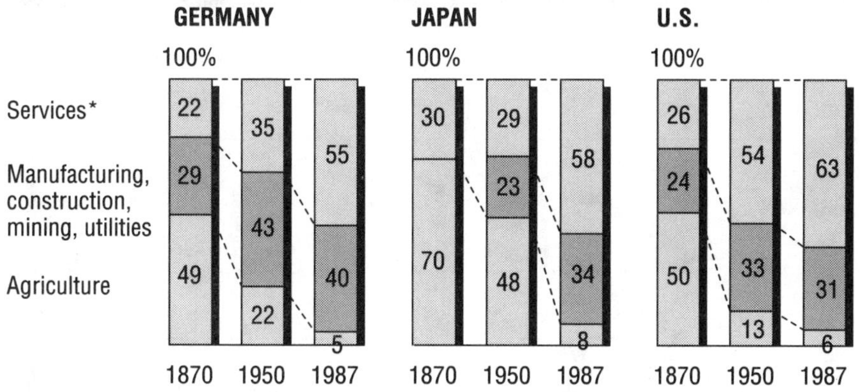

	GERMANY	JAPAN	U.S.

Source: A. Maddison, *Dynamic Forces in Capitalist Development* (London: Oxford University Press, 1991).

*Including government.

swings in spot foreign exchange rates. Comparable quality products produced in a given industry in all three countries were priced, and the relative prices went into the industry PPP index. When there were several products in the same industry, their individual PPPs were weighted to construct an average PPP exchange rate for the industry as a whole. The labor productivity results are shown in Exhibit 1.8. The United States is more productive in every service industry studied, except for restaurants in France.

The second study examined nine industries in the manufacturing sector: auto assembly, auto parts, metal working, steel, computers, consumer electronics, soaps and detergents, and processed food. As shown in Exhibit 1.9, the United States is equal to Germany in steel and metal working but ahead in all other industries. Japan is ahead of the United States in auto assembly, auto parts, metal working, steel, and consumer electronics. Overall, however, Japan has lower productivity. The reason is that a relatively greater percentage of Japanese employment is located in the lower productivity industries, especially food processing. This is illustrated in Exhibit 1.10.

The productivity gaps can largely be explained by the extent that an industry is globalized. Exhibit 1.11 relates an index of productivity in nine manufacturing industries relative to the industry leader

Exhibit 1.8 **SERVICE SECTOR LABOR PRODUCTIVITY COMPARISON***,
U.S. PRODUCTIVITY = 100

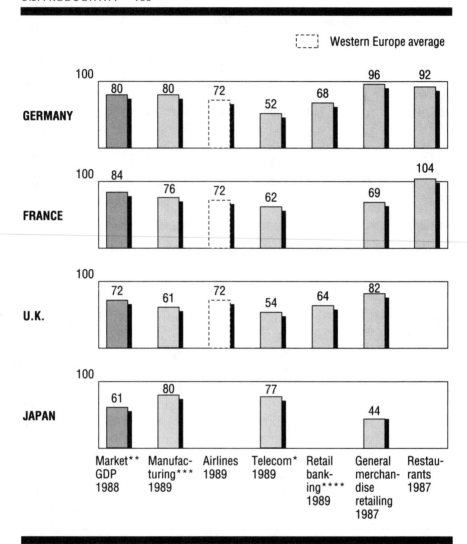

* Total factor productivity shown for telecommunications.
** GDP excluding government, education, health, and real estate.
*** Estimates by van Ark and Pilat for International Comparisons of Output and
Productivity (ICDP) Project, Groningen, NL.
**** In retail banking, productivity was measured using physical output by function.

Exhibit 1.9 **MANUFACTURING SECTOR, LABOR PRODUCTIVITY COMPARISON, VALUE ADDED PER HOUR WORKED AT INDUSTRY PPP,** U.S. PRODUCTIVITY = 100

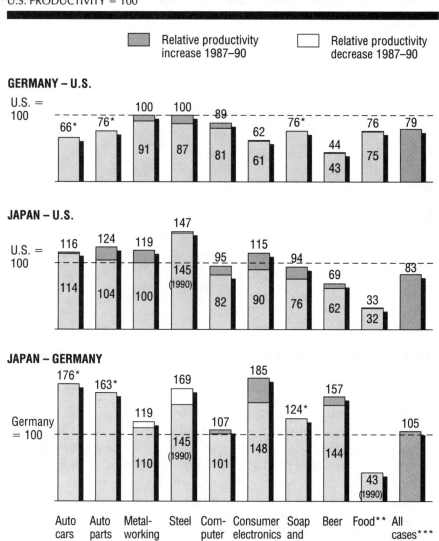

Source: McKinsey analysis.

* Only 1990.
** Based on shipment.
*** Weighted by employment.

Exhibit 1.10 **RELATIVE PRODUCTIVITY LEVELS AND EMPLOYMENT SHARE IN JAPAN 1990, NINE CASE STUDIES,** U.S. PRODUCTIVITY = 100

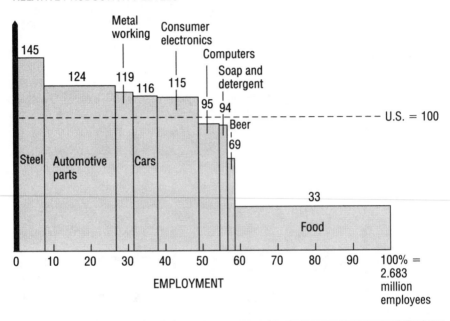

Source: McKinsey analysis.

versus an index that measures the extent to which an industry is globalized. The relationship is clear. Globalization reduces the differences in productivity among companies in an industry. If your company is not a leader in productivity, and if your industry is becoming more global, you will need to increase productivity to survive.

The link between material well-being and productivity is unmistakable. If you want to consume, you need to produce. The U.S. maintains its overall lead in GDP per capita because of its overall lead in productivity.

Next we need to examine how MVA, the best indicator of shareholder value creation in each of the three countries, is correlated to both productivity and GDP.[4] The change in MVA is the

---

[4] To the best of our knowledge, MVA is a term coined by Stern, Stewart and Co., for example, see G. Bennett Stewart II, *The Quest for Value*, New York: HarperCollins Publishers, 1991.

Exhibit 1.11 **GLOBALIZATION VS. RELATIVE PRODUCTIVITY*:
TRANSPLANT, TRANSPLANT EXPOSURE, AND TRADE**

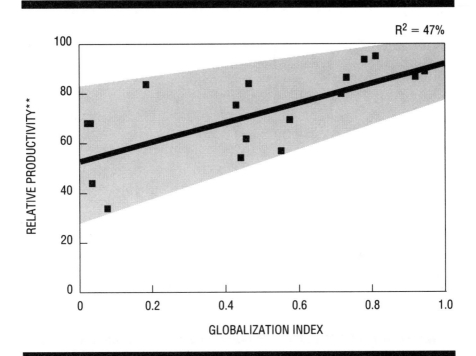

Source: McKinsey analysis.

* Data points are nine case study industries in countries without productivity leading edge.
** Relative to industry leader at 100.

measure of value creation that we use. Exhibit 1.12 shows this measure for AT&T—it is the change in the market value of capital (debt and equity) minus the change in the book value of invested capital. Because the book value of debt is embedded in both the market value of total capital as well as the book value of invested capital (since debt is a source of funds for invested capital), the change in MVA is the change in the difference between the market and book value of equity over a given period of time. In this case, between 1988 and 1992, AT&T added $23.4 billion for its shareholders.

To study the change in MVA across the triad, we chose the time interval 1983 to 1991. We started in 1983 because it was the first year available on the Standard & Poor's Global Vantage database. We went through 1991 to be sure that we covered the stock market crashes in all 3 triad countries. The NYSE, DAX, and Nikkei indices

Exhibit 1.12 **MARKET VALUE ADDED, AT&T, 1988–92,** $ BILLIONS

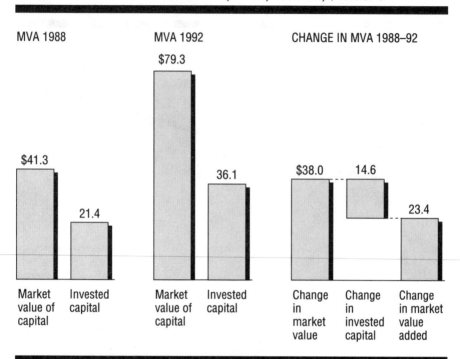

Source: Compustat, McKinsey analysis.

are graphed in Exhibit 1.13, with 1983 set equal to 100 for all three. Since the three indices performed similarly between 1983 and 1991, the results that follow are not driven by unusual stock market movements.

We calculated the change in MVA for the largest companies ranked by 1991 sales in the United States, Japan, and Germany. To be included in our final data set, each company had to be listed on an exchange in 1983 and 1991 and have its financials on the Global Vantage database. As shown in Exhibit 1.14, the top ten value creating companies in the United States created $438 billion, $276 billion more than was destroyed by the bottom ten. The median company created $408 million. In Japan the median value created was $717 million, and the top ten companies created $132 billion. The bottom ten destroyed $41 billion. In Germany, where only 125 companies entered our data set, the top ten created $13 billion in value, while the bottom ten destroyed $29 billion. The median company created

Exhibit 1.13 **STOCK MARKET INDICES, 1983–91,** JANUARY 1983 = 100

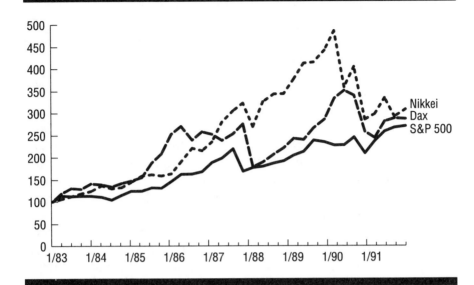

Source: Bloomberg, McKinsey analysis.

Exhibit 1.14 **CHANGE IN MVA 1983–91 FOR TOP AND BOTTOM TEN COMPANIES,** $ BILLIONS

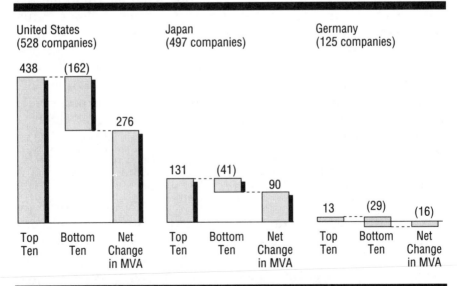

Source: Global Vantage, McKinsey analysis.

$6 million. Although interesting in their own right, these statistics do little more than confirm that Germany, with its overall lower productivity, also created less shareholder value.

To study the relationship between productivity and the change in MVA we compared industries across the triad. The prior work of the McKinsey Global Institute provided estimates of labor productivity. Ideally, we would have used productivity estimates for both 1983 and 1991, but only the more recent estimate was available. The change in MVA for all publicly traded companies was computed using the Global Vantage data set. In order to scale the change in MVA, it was divided by the company's 1991 sales revenue. The results stayed the same when the change in MVA was scaled by the book value of equity and equity equivalents. Finally, in order to create an industry MVA for each country, each company's scaled MVA change was weighted by its sales revenue to create an industry weighted average estimate of the scaled change in MVA.

For manufacturing, the strong positive relationship between productivity and the change in MVA is graphed in Exhibit 1.15. Five out of five industries for which we had adequate data confirm that high productivity is associated with high value added for shareholders. If our initial belief assumes a 50/50 chance of observing a positive relationship, the five for five result has only a 3.1 percent chance of happening. Therefore, a simple binomial test confirms that our results are statistically significant. Some industries were good to be in. The beer industry, for one, did well in all three countries. The lowest scaled MVA was Germany whose beer industry experienced a 33 percent increase in MVA relative to sales in spite of labor productivity that were only 44 percent of the U.S. standard. Japan with 69 percent relative productivity experienced a 76 percent MVA increase as a percent of 1991 sales. And the U.S., whose productivity is scaled to equal 100, had an 82 percent MVA increase. Other industries, steel for example, did not do as well. Only Japan, with productivity 45 percent higher than Germany and the U.S., had an MVA increase (32 percent).

Lack of data made it difficult to compute MVA for most of the service industries. For example, many of the airlines and telecommunications companies are government owned—perhaps an explanation for their low productivity. Therefore, our results in services are limited to retail as shown in Exhibit 1.16. Again, we see the positive relationship between productivity and the change in MVA. The Japanese retail industry, for example, had only 44 percent

Exhibit 1.15 **LABOR PRODUCTIVITY VS. THE CHANGE IN MVA MANUFACTURING, 1983–91,** U.S. PRODUCTIVITY = 100

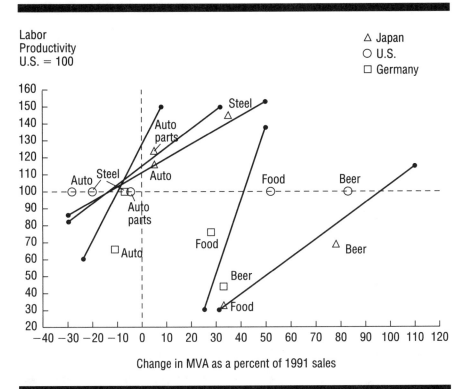

Change in MVA as a percent of 1991 sales

Source: Global Vantage, McKinsey analysis.

productivity relative to the U.S. and a –8 percent change in MVA (as a percent of 1991 sales).

It is always possible that productivity increases and the associated increases in MVA are achieved at the expense of labor. However, our hypothesis is that the most productive companies in an industry gain market share, and consequently they are able to benefit labor as well as sources of capital in the long run. In other words, winning companies have higher productivity, higher market share, higher employment growth, and higher changes in MVA.

To study this issue we used the Global Vantage database to collect employment data at the company level for 1983 and 1991 in order to correlate growth in employment with the change in MVA as a percent of sales. Exhibit 1.17 shows there is no evidence that

Exhibit 1.16 **LABOR PRODUCTIVITY VS. THE CHANGE IN MVA, SERVICE,**
1983–91, U.S. PRODUCTIVITY = 100

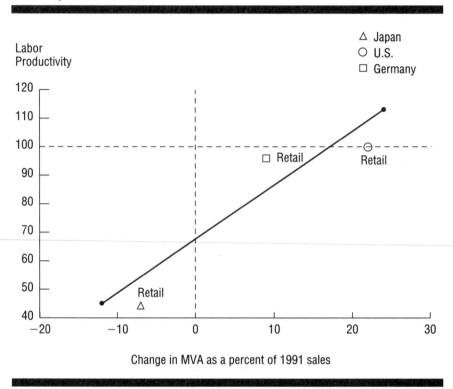

Source: Global Vantage, McKinsey analysis.

labor suffers to benefit shareholders. Within an industry, and in the long run, companies that are winners are more productive, create more shareholder wealth, and experience higher growth in employment. In the auto assembly industry all countries experienced growth in employment, but the Japanese who were the most productive—had the greatest growth in employment. Similarly in steel, an industry with over capacity and shrinking employment due to technological change, Germany had greater change in MVA and better employment results than the U.S. In the short run, increases in productivity may be accompanied by decreases in employment, however, the winners within each industry are the companies that are the first to increase productivity. In the long run, they have greater employment than laggard competitors and greater increases in shareholder wealth. This result suggests that

Exhibit 1.17 **EMPLOYMENT GROWTH VS. THE CHANGE IN MVA,**
1983–91, PERCENT

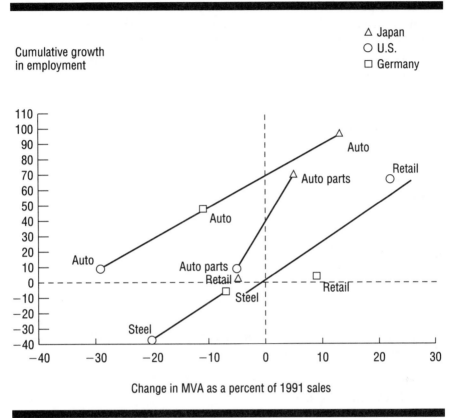

Source: Global Vantage, McKinsey analysis.

protectionist government policies that delay productivity increases, especially in globally competitive industries, might
worsen employment in the long run. A better government strategy
would be to focus on retraining and relocating labor as well as supporting labor during transitions.

Thus, when the cross national scorecard is in, the results
strongly suggest a link between GDP per capita, productivity, and
value creation. Furthermore, there is no evidence that higher productivity hurts labor. Productivity is the ratio of output produced
relative to the costs of the inputs needed to produce it. The objective is always to produce more output with less input. When, in the
long run, this result is achieved, value is created. In a competitive

environment, productivity growth is not merely the source of increased value, it is the key to survival. Companies that cannot match the productivity increases of rivals will find themselves losing market share. Countries that cannot match the productivity of competitors will suffer a flight of capital, emigration of skilled human resources, and a standard of living that declines relative to more productive countries.

WHY VALUE VALUE?

Empirical evidence indicates that increasing shareholder value does not conflict with the long-run interests of other stakeholders. Winning companies seem to create relatively greater value for all stakeholders: customers, labor, the government (via taxes paid), and suppliers of capital. Yet, there are additional reasons—more conceptual in nature, but equally compelling—to adopt a system that emphasizes shareholder value. First, value is the best metric for performance that we know. Second, shareholders are the only stakeholders of a corporation who simultaneously maximize everyone's claim in seeking to maximize their own. And finally, companies that do not perform will find that capital flows toward their competitors.

Value Is the Best Metric

Value (discounted cash flows) is best because it is the only measure that requires complete information. To understand value creation one must use a long-term point of view, manage all cash flows on both the income statement and the balance sheet, and understand how to compare cash flows from different time periods on a risk-adjusted basis. It is nearly impossible to make good decisions without complete information, and no other performance metric uses complete information. In Chapter 4, on value-based management, we provide a number of examples in which a shift to decision making based on value resulted in completely different decisions for major corporations.

There are other measures of corporate performance, but none are as comprehensive as value. As we shall unequivocally demonstrate later in this book, an extremely strong correlation exists between the market value of a company and its discounted cash flows. Value cannot be short-term, but other measures can be. Earnings per share or return on equity are usually used in a myopic way—requiring information about only the next few years at best. Furthermore, earnings tends to focus mainly on managing the income statement and places low weight on the actual amount and timing of cash flows. Even the spread between the return on invested capital (ROIC) and the cost of capital can be a bad metric if used only for the short term and because it encourages underinvestment (harvesting the business to increase ROIC). If the value manager does the job well, the results are reflected in MVA. Other performance measures, such as the growth in earnings, return on equity, and the spread between the return on capital and the cost of capital are less comprehensive than value creation and less well correlated with the actual market value of companies.

If you adopt the perspective of managing value, you will make better decisions and tradeoffs, regardless of your social context or emphasis. All systems, whether European, American, or Japanese make trade-offs between stakeholders. Value, as the best metric, allows more transparent, accurate trade-offs, because *any* stakeholder claim can be valued. Take labor for example. The value of labor's claim on a company is the discounted present value of all of the cash flows that labor expects to receive from the company now and in the future. Value is not myopic. It requires a multiperiod point of view. It requires complete information.

Exhibit 1.18 shows pro forma income statements and balance sheets forecasted forward in time. They represent the basic building blocks of information needed to value the claims that various stakeholders have on the company. For example, the value to customers is the present value of the difference between what they would be willing to pay for the company's goods and services minus what the company receives as revenues. Economists call this consumer's surplus. If the company increases its prices, and nothing else changes, the value of consumer's surplus decreases, and the value of equity increases. Of course, price increases often result in lower sales volume, so that the value impact on customers and equity holders depends heavily on the price-quantity relationship embedded in the demand curve for the product.

Exhibit 1.18 also makes it clear that real trade-offs among the various stakeholders of companies can be made explicit using a value-based approach. Too often these trade-offs are made on an emotional or political basis without any attempt to bring the facts

Exhibit 1.18 **PRO FORMA FINANCIALS,** $ MILLIONS

	Today	Distant Future	Present Value of
Value to customers	1,100 ...	4,400	
Income Statement			➤ Consumer's Surplus
Sales revenue	1,000 ...	4,000	
— Labor costs	(400) ...	(1,600)	➤ Labor's Claim
— Cost of goods and services	(300) ...	(1,200)	➤ Supplier's Claim
— Depreciation	(100) ...	(400)	
Operating income	200 ...	800	
— Interest expenses	(50) ...	(200)	➤ Debt Claim
Taxable income	150 ...	600	
— Taxes	(75) ...	(300)	➤ Government Claim
Net income	75 ...	300	
— Retained Earnings	(40) ...	(160)	
Dividends	35 ...	140	➤ Equity Claim

Balance Sheet

Assets

	Today	Distant Future	Present Value of
Cash	50 ...	200	
Accounts Receivable	200 ...	800	➤ Uses of Working Capital
Inventories	250 ...	1000	
Net Property, Plant, Equip.	1,000 ...	4,000	➤ Uses of Physical Capital
Total Assets	1,500 ...	6,000	

Liabilities

	Today	Distant Future	Present Value of
Accounts Payable	100 ...	400	➤ Sources of Working Capital
Accruals	150 ...	600	
Debt	500 ...	2000	➤ Sources of Debt
Retained Earnings	500 ...	2000	➤ Sources of Equity
Common Equity	250 ...	1000	
Total Liabilities	1500 ...	6000	

to the table. The balance among claimants often determines the structure of the organization. Consider the difference between the claims on companies of varying capital intensity (excluding consumer's surplus, which is very difficult to estimate). Because the value of labor at public accounting firms is so large relative to other claims, they are often organized as partnerships with a small "equity" claim owned by each partner. For them, managing the value of labor's claim is clearly the key to success. At the opposite extreme are capital intensive companies like telecommunications, electric utilities, or pulp and paper. The relative importance of the labor component is lower and the need for capital supplied by debt and equity holders becomes much more important. These companies need to balance capital and labor claims, but cannot survive unless they provide an adequate return in the long run to suppliers of capital as well as providing competitive compensation for laborers.

Performance measures other than value are less complete uses of information and are therefore worse for decision making. Managers are often confronted with a wide variety of choices. Often their orientation is short-term, such as growth in operating income next year, or over the next three years. Additionally, many of them completely ignore, or under emphasize management of resources on the balance sheet. For example, a company that can significantly improve its working capital management will immediately free up cash flow, but will have only a marginal impact on the income statement. Chapter 3 is dedicated to showing why valuation is a superior measure of corporate performance.

The value approach illustrated in Exhibit 1.18 makes it clear that value-based decision making is not shortsighted. For example, a regulatory body that holds energy prices down in the short run but raises them later on, may actually decrease the present value of consumer's surplus. A labor union that is successful in winning abnormally high wages and benefits in the short run may actually decrease the value of labor's claim on the company if the company is forced out of business or loses market share in the long run. A company that pays below market wages in the short run will lose productive laborers and end up worse off in the long run. A company that milks the market with high product prices in the near term may destroy shareholder value in the long term if the high prices accelerate the entry of strong new competitors into the market. Trade-offs between current and future cash flows are never easy, but are absolutely necessary for good decision making.

Shareholders Increase the Value of All Claims

Not all stakeholders need to use complete information in order to make decisions for their own benefit. Employees, for example, do not need, nor do they seek, complete information concerning all other claims on the company when making their decisions.

This is not the case with equity holders who are the *residual* claimants on the cash flows of a company. They need to consider all revenues and all payments to other stakeholders when they make decisions that affect their claim. They take the greatest risk, but even more important, they are the only claimants who need information concerning all other claims in order to make good decisions on their own behalf. Consumers, for example, only need to know product (or service) attributes and the product price in order to make their decisions. They don't need to know whether an automobile manufacturer is productive or profitable when they buy a new car. If consumers were assigned managerial control of a company, they might be tempted to maximize the value of their claim, consumer's surplus, at the expense of other claimants. Shareholders are at the opposite extreme. To understand the effect of a decision on their claim, they need to know prices and sales volumes; the cost of goods sold, which includes labor, materials, and energy costs; interest costs on debt; and taxes. Shareholders require complete information.

But why should control be handed over to shareholders? To answer this we need to ask why are corporations organized the way they are? Why aren't they organized as Athenian pure democracies where all stakeholders have an equal vote on all critical decisions? Or, why aren't they dictatorships with a single individual having complete unconstrained control over all stakeholder claims? The reason is that neither of these extremes represents the optimal form of organization in a competitive environment.

If a group of people needs to organize to perform a task in the face of competition for scarce resources, what arrangement will they make among themselves? Some will choose to perform specialized tasks requiring limited information about the goings on of the entire company in return for relatively fixed compensation and protection by employment contracts. If capital is needed, some of it will be provided in return for a high priority senior claim on cash flows and will be protected with covenants that constrain the actions the organization can take. The remaining, or residual, capital accepts the greatest risk, but is given decision-making authority. This is the equity claim.

Equity holders have the strongest incentive to manage the labor and capital resources of the company to win over the long run in competition with other companies. Their actions are constrained by their contracts with labor and with providers of debt, but given these constraints they organize the scarce resources under the control that is given to them by the other claimants. They have strong incentives to maximize the (constrained) value of their claim and need to use complete information to do so. Their role as residual claimant is crucial. All claimants benefit when shareholders (or their agents) use complete information and their decision-making authority to maximize the value of their own claim. The alignment of information and incentives within the equity claim is what makes this form of organization (the modern corporation) the best competitive mechanism. Shareholders maximize the value of other claims in the attempt to maximize their own value.

Capital Flows Toward Returns

Regardless of what you think about the merit of stakeholder claims relative to each other, one thing is certain: if suppliers of capital do not receive a fair return to compensate them for the risk they are taking, they will move their capital across national borders in search of better returns. If they are prohibited by law from moving their capital, they will consume more and invest less. Either way, nations who don't provide global investors with adequate returns on invested capital are doomed to fall farther behind in the race for global competitiveness and suffer a stagnating or decreasing standard of living.

It's easy to see how capital flows when we look at the world from an investor's point of view. If ROIC is less than zero, a company cannot generate enough cash to stay in business and will either go bankrupt or require government support. If the ROIC is greater than zero but less than its weighted average cost of capital (WACC) the company may be "profitable" but it will not provide an adequate return to the suppliers of capital. From their perspective, the company is destroying value. If this persists, the company will not be able to obtain capital and is not sustainable in the long run. Most companies in a competitive economy can be found in a third category. On average, across business cycles, their return on invested capital should equal the cost of capital. Across long enough periods of time, we might expect half of the companies in a society to earn more and half to earn less than their WACC. This is a sustainable equilibrium, because suppliers of capital can expect, on average, to earn a fair return. Some companies, not many, earn a rate of return in excess of their cost of capital over a long period of time. Usually their competitive advantage is controlled by society in one way or another. For example, patents and trademarks are protected internationally, and local monopolies are regulated by government. The challenge for management is to create value by earning more than the company's cost of capital in the long run. When capital is not earning the required rate of return, the market decreases its value until the rate of return reaches competitive levels. Value is destroyed.

THE MANAGEMENT CHALLENGE

The link between productivity and shareholder value maximization is too strong to ignore. If more output is produced with fewer inputs then the residual, the shareholder's value, is greater. But in the long run all claims, including the employment of labor, benefit when a company is a winner in its industry. Modern corporations give (constrained) control over decision making to shareholders (or their agents), because shareholders are the only claimants that require complete information to make decisions in their self interest. They have the incentive to make their companies into winners.

The challenges for management differ for each triad country. In the U.S., pressure is ever present from hostile takeovers and activist investors. In Europe, low productivity will hamper the promised retirement income of the aging population. And in Japan, with its dual economy, the sectors with low productivity provide inertia that is difficult to overcome.

The consequences of failing to maximize shareholder's value differ between the U.S., Japan and Europe mainly in their pace. In the U.S., things happen quickly. Hostile takeovers force out under-performing management and increase productivity. Investor activism is on the rise. Pension and mutual funds own 53 percent of all U.S. stock outstanding and are beginning to use their clout. For example, in March of 1993 the $73 billion Calpers pension fund announced plans to spend nearly $1 billion on large stakes in companies whose managers are not measuring up, with a view to demanding better financial results. Recent targets were General Motors, Westinghouse, Sears Roebuck, and Kodak. The chairman and CEO of McDonnell Douglas stepped down in the face of pressure from the New York City Employee's Retirement System. And the Securities and Exchange Commission is sympathetic. It has relaxed rules that previously limited communications among large activist shareholders.

In Europe, chronic uncompetitiveness results in slow change—for the worse. Productivity is lower than in the U.S. and Japan. Employee absentee rates are far higher than elsewhere and so is its pay-for-time-not-worked and the social charges borne by employers. According to Fassbender and Cooper-Hedegaard

> The typical pay-as-you-go pension systems of Europe, in which today's workers directly fund the benefits for today's retirees, are now faced with a grotesque demographic mismatch that will grow worse with every year that passes. If the trend persists, German public pension payments could alone account for over 14 percent of the country's GDP by the end of the century, swelling to nearly one quarter of the total economic output by 2030.[5]

Unless Europe increases productivity by managing value better, it may hemorrhage and collapse. Promises of a better social system will become empty.

In Japan, globally competitive management is already very productive and is creating tremendous shareholder value, although that is not the stated objective. Those portions of the economy that are not competitive, however, serve as a sea anchor, holding back the entire economy. They need to be reorganized to create more value.

The rest of this book is about how to measure and manage the value of your company. We show that discounted cash flow valuation corresponds better to the actual market value of companies than any other measure. This is a necessary starting point because without the right measure of performance you cannot make value creating decisions. Even more important though, is showing how valuation is used as a decision-making tool for creating value. And why create value? What happens if you don't? All stakeholders lose in local, industry wide, and global competition.

---

[5] H. Fassbender and S. Cooper-Hedegaard, "The Ticking Bomb at the Core of Europe," *McKinsey Quarterly* 3 (1993): 127–142.

REVIEW QUESTIONS

1. Explain the key differences in the ownership and control of Japanese, U.S., and German firms.

2. What are the economic consequences of each country's ownership and control style?

3. The value framework provides a metric for all of a firm's stakeholders. Explain how.

4. How do differing preferences for risk and return evolve multiple opportunities for funding a single operational entity?

5. Why should equityholders have the most decision-making power in the firm?

6. How can a fair return follow from the competitive use of capital?

7. What is management's challenge in creating value in the U.S., Europe, and Japan?

2

The Value Manager

In Chapter 1, we argued that value creation is the ultimate measure of performance for a management team. This chapter explains, primarily through a case example, what it means to manage for maximum value creation, in other words, to be a value manager.

BECOMING A VALUE MANAGER

Becoming a value manager is not a mysterious process open only to a few. It does require, however, a different perspective from that taken by many managers. It requires a focus on long-run cash flow returns, not quarter-to-quarter changes in earnings per share. It also requires a willingness to adopt a dispassionate, value-oriented view of corporate activities that recognizes businesses for what they are—investments in productive capacity that either earn a return above their opportunity cost of capital or do not. The value manager's perspective is characterized by an ability to adopt an outsider's view of the business and by a willingness to act on opportunities to create incremental value. Finally, and most important, it includes the need to develop and institutionalize a managing value philosophy throughout the organization. Focusing on shareholder value is not a one-time task to be done only when outside pressure from shareholders emerges or potential acquirers emerge. It is an ongoing initiative.

In essence, the process of becoming value-oriented has two distinct aspects. The first involves a restructuring that unleashes value trapped within the company. The immediate results from such actions can range from moderate to spectacular: for example, share prices that double or triple in a matter of months. At the same time, the price to be paid for such results can be high. It can involve divestitures and layoffs. Management can avoid the need for cataclysmic change in the future by embracing the second aspect of the managing value process: developing a value-oriented approach to leading and managing their companies after the restructuring. This involves establishing priorities based on value creation; gearing planning, performance measurement, and incentive compensation systems toward shareholder value; and communicating with investors in terms of value creation.

By taking these steps to ensure that managing value becomes a routine part of decision making and operations, management can keep the gap narrow between potential and actual value-creation performance. Consequently, the need for major restructuring that goes with large performance gaps will be less likely to arise. Those who manage value well can guide their companies in a series of smaller steps to the higher levels of performance that even the most comprehensive of restructurings cannot match.

In the balance of this chapter, we illustrate the integrated application of value management principles by presenting a case example distilled from the real-world experiences of client executives we have worked with. Our purpose is to show the process of transforming a company in terms of value to shareholders and management philosophy. The case serves as an overview of and framework for the application of the more detailed valuation approaches developed in the main body of this book.

THE CASE OF EG CORPORATION, PART 1: SITUATION

In early 1993, Ralph Demsky took the helm of EG Corporation as chairman and CEO. For the prior ten years, Ralph was president of Consumerco, EG Corporation's largest division. Consumerco had been the original business of EG before it entered other lines of business through acquisition. Unfortunately, EG had recently become the subject of vocal dissatisfaction from major institutional shareholders.

The EG Businesses

EG Corporation had sales of just over $3.5 billion in 1992. The company was in three main lines of business—consumer products, food service, and furniture—with its Consumerco, Foodco, and Woodco divisions.

Consumerco manufactured consumer products and sold them via a direct sales force to grocery and drug stores throughout the United States. It had a dominant market share (over 40 percent) in the majority of its product lines, all of which had a strong branded consumer franchise.

Woodco was a mid-sized competitor in the highly fragmented furniture business. Woodco had been created through acquisition and consisted of eight separate smaller companies acquired over a period of ten years. All served the mid- to lower-priced end of the market with complementary product lines. The Woodco companies sold their products under their original brand names. As of early 1993, the companies were still operated as autonomous units, but EG had begun to implement a plan to combine the companies into one unit, consolidating separate administration, sales, and production functions to the extent feasible. They also planned to establish an "umbrella brand" to tie together the wide range of Woodco product offerings and establish a base for adding new lines.

Thus far, the Woodco businesses had turned in uneven financial results. Management capability in the eight businesses varied widely. Moreover, Woodco's business performance was to varying degrees dependent on keeping up with the latest in furniture styling and fashion. Some of the companies were very skilled in this area, but the disastrous consequences of missing the trends had been brought home over the years by their uneven performance. Despite this, Woodco's management was convinced that EG could build a large and successful business over the next few years. They believed consolidation would reduce Woodco's operating costs significantly and strengthen the company's management control over the businesses. They thought the new common sales and marketing thrust would lead to increased volumes and higher margins. The Woodco management's convictions were lent some credence by the existence of several other players in the industry that earned consistently high returns, achieved in part by rationalizing less-efficient companies they had acquired.

Foodco, EG's third main division, was in the food service business. Foodco operated a small chain of fast food restaurants, as well as providing food service under contract to major corporations and other institutions around the country. It had been built up from internal growth plus a few small acquisitions over the last five years. The former CEO had viewed Foodco as a major growth vehicle for EG and had backed aggressive expansion plans and the associated capital spending. As of early 1993, EG's Foodco unit was earning a profit but was still in the early stages of its development plan. It was a small player in the restaurant business and had only a few institutional food service accounts. In both businesses it faced formidable competition, but management believed that its operating approach and EG Corporation's Consumerco name recognition, which was being used as the branding proposition for Foodco, would establish Foodco as a major factor in the industry.

Beyond Consumerco, Foodco, and Woodco, EG Corporation owned a few other smaller businesses: a property development company (Propco), a small consumer finance company (Finco), and several small newspapers (Newsco). No one currently employed by EG could recall why EG had acquired these businesses. They had been added to the portfolio in the 1960s. All were earning a profit, although these businesses were small by comparison with EG's three main divisions. (See Exhibit 2.1.)

EG's Financial Performance

Overall, EG Corporation's financial performance had been mediocre for the last five years. Earnings growth had not kept pace with inflation, and return on equity hovered around 10 percent. Part of the problem was that EG had been hit with unfavorable "extraordinary items," which had depressed bottom line results. Beyond this, though, the company had failed to deliver on overall commitments for growth and operating earnings in its businesses for the last few years.

From an investor's standpoint, the company's stock price had lagged the market for the last several years. Analysts bemoaned the company's lackluster performance, especially in view of its strong brand position in Consumerco. They were disenchanted with the slow progress in building profits in other parts of the company. Some security analysts had gone so far as to speculate that

Exhibit 2.1 **THE EG CORP. BUSINESSES, 1992,** $ MILLIONS

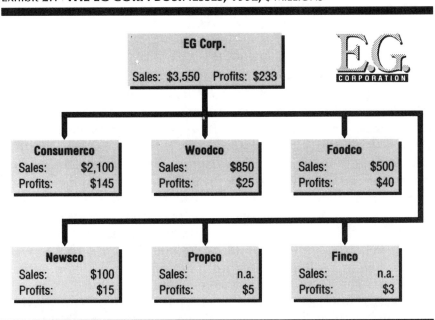

EG would make a good breakup play. EG Corporation's board and senior management were frustrated by their inability to convince the market that EG should be more highly valued.

Ralph Demsky's Ingoing Perspective

Ralph Demsky was very familiar with EG's worrisome corporate situation, and he had been a vocal advocate of a sharper focus on shareholder value for EG for several years. Ralph was convinced that great opportunities existed for EG to boost its value. Upon retirement of the previous chairman and CEO, the board had tapped Ralph to lead EG because of his controversial ideas and his strong operating track record leading Consumerco.

Ralph knew he needed to act fast. His plan was first to uncover and act on any immediate restructuring opportunities within EG. Then for the longer term he would put in place management systems and approaches to ensure EG did not pass up such opportunities in the future.

THE CASE OF EG CORPORATION,
PART 2: RALPH AS RESTRUCTURER

During the first week of his tenure as CEO, Ralph initiated a project to assess restructuring opportunities within EG. He wanted to take action soon to build value for EG's shareholders and to convince the market that EG could be worth more than its current market value.

To carry out the project, he structured a task force with himself as chairman, the chief financial officer, and the other heads of the businesses. Analysts from the finance staff provided support for the valuation work, while each business-unit head was responsible for getting the work on his or her business done. The team met twice a week to review progress, develop conclusions, and—importantly—keep up the tempo of the work. Ralph expected the project to provide actionable recommendations within six to eight weeks.

Ralph had thought long and hard about doing the review with a smaller team, perhaps consisting of himself, the CFO, and several financial analysts, to maintain secrecy and speed up the process. He rejected this alternative for several reasons. First, he wanted to draw on the best judgment of his senior managers about the prospects for their businesses. Second, because they would play a key role in carrying out the business improvements that were sure to be identified, he wanted to involve them from the outset. Finally, he wanted them to learn the process by doing it, since he planned to undertake a similar thorough review annually from then on.

As an analytical framework, Ralph envisioned investigating the value of EG's existing businesses along five dimensions, which he thought of as forming a restructuring pentagon (see Exhibit 2.2). The pentagon analysis would start with a thorough understanding of EG's current market value. Then the team would assess the "as is" and potential values of EG's businesses with internal improvements based on expected cash flows, the external sale values of the businesses and the opportunities to increase value through financial engineering. All of these values would be tied back to EG's value in the stock market to estimate the potential gain to EG's shareholders from a thorough restructuring. The comparison would also help to identify gaps in perceptions between investors and EG management about prospects for the businesses. When their analysis was complete, Ralph and his team would have a thorough, fact-based perspective on the condition of EG's portfolio and their options for building value.

Exhibit 2.2 **PENTAGON FRAMEWORK FOR ASSESSING RESTRUCTURING OPPORTUNITIES**

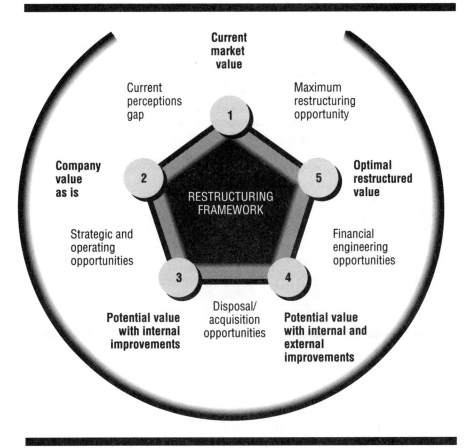

Current Valuation

The first thing Ralph did was to review EG's performance from the standpoint of its stockholders. He already knew EG had not performed particularly well for its shareholders in recent times and operating returns had not been as good as everyone had hoped. But Ralph wanted to be more systematic in his review of the market's perspective, so his team set about analyzing EG's market situation using the framework detailed in Exhibit 2.3.

What Ralph found was disturbing—and revealing. EG's return to investors had indeed been below the market overall and below the returns for a roughly assembled set of "comparable" companies

---

Exhibit 2.3 **ANALYTIC FRAMEWORK FOR DIAGNOSING MARKET PERFORMANCE**

1. Review market performance

- Determine returns to shareholders compared with other investments

2. Analyze comparative corporate performance

- Develop initial picture of company performance that underlies market performance

3. Understand corporate cash flow

- Identify where the corporation has been generating and investing cash and the return this investment is generating

4. Synthesize market views

- Identify assumptions that form basis for current market value

---

(see Exhibit 2.4). What also stood out from the analysis were a couple of events that had knocked down the value of EG relative to the market. In the period 1986 to 1991, EG had made several acquisitions to establish and build the Woodco furniture businesses. Ralph noticed a decline in EG's share price relative to comparables and the market around the date of each acquisition. In fact, when the team calculated the impact of these declines on EG's total value, they realized that the decline in EG's total value was about equal to the dollar amount of the premiums over market price EG had paid to acquire the companies. Evidently, the stock market did not believe EG would add any value to the acquired businesses. It had viewed the acquisition premiums EG had paid as a damaging transfer of value from EG investors to the selling shareholders in the acquired companies.

Ralph thought this made sense. Since EG had not in fact done anything to these companies after they were purchased, there was no reason for them to be worth any more than their preacquisition value. It didn't seem to matter that the deals had been carefully

Exhibit 2.4 **EG CORP., COMPARATIVE SHAREHOLDER PERFORMANCE**

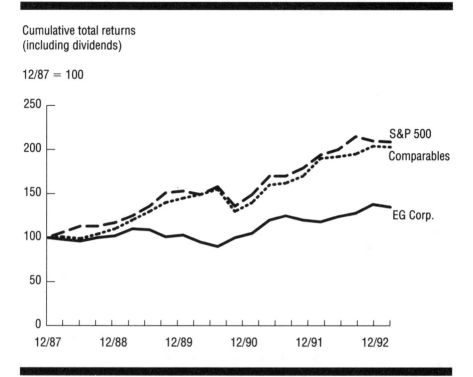

Cumulative total returns
(including dividends)

12/87 = 100

structured and financed in part with debt to avoid diluting EG's earnings per share. The market had seen through those gimmicks.

Looking next at the financial results of each of EG's businesses, the team noted that Consumerco had generated high, stable returns on capital (35+ percent) for the last five years. However, the businesses' earnings base was only growing at the pace of inflation. Meanwhile, EG's Woodco business had suffered steadily declining returns. The Foodco business's earnings, on the other hand, were growing, but returns on investment were low due to high capital investment requirements in the restaurants. All of these factors had conspired to hold overall EG returns on capital down and hamper growth in profits.

One investment analysis Ralph found especially intriguing was a cash flow map of EG based on information for the last five years (see Exhibit 2.5). What it showed was that EG had been generating substantial discretionary or free cash flow in the

Exhibit 2.5 **EG CORP., CUMULATIVE CASH FLOWS, 5 YEARS ENDED DECEMBER 31, 1992,** $ MILLIONS

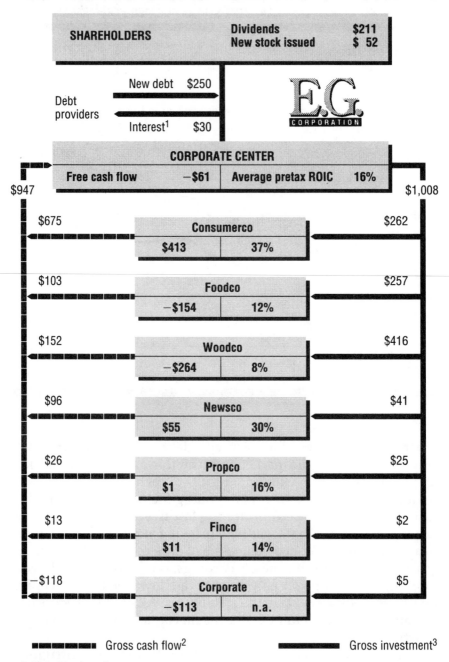

1. Net of tax benefit.
2. Equals after-tax operating profits plus depreciation.
3. Equals capital expenditures, acquisitions, increases in working capital, and other assets.

Consumerco business, a large portion of which had been sunk into Woodco and Foodco. Relatively little had been reinvested in Consumerco. Moreover, little of the cash had found its way back to EG's shareholders. In fact, on a five-year basis, EG had in effect been borrowing to pay dividends to shareholders. Since Ralph believed that shareholder value derived from the cash flow returns EG could generate, he became increasingly suspicious that EG had taken the cash Consumerco had generated and reinvested it in businesses that might not generate an adequate return for shareholders.

To round out his perspective on EG's valuation by the stock market, Ralph spent a day reading all the reports security analysts had written recently about the company. He then went to visit several of the leading analysts who followed EG's stock, to gain their perspective on the company's situation. He was surprised at the favorable reception he received. Evidently, the previous CEO had little regard for security analysts. He had never met with them individually to understand their views. When he did meet with them, it was always to tell them why the stock should be more highly valued, never to listen to what they thought about EG.

What Ralph heard about EG was disturbing but agreed with his views. The analysts thought EG had been complacent for the last five years or more and had pursued new businesses with little regard for the returns to be generated. Moreover, they felt EG would remain an unattractive investment candidate unless Demsky took actions to demonstrate more commitment to creating value for shareholders. However, management would need to see this potential and act on it. They thought some real synergies were possible with strategic acquirers for some EG businesses, but the real problem at EG had been a management that was not really serious about generating value for shareholders.

EG's "As Is" Value

Ralph's team turned their attention next to assessing the value of each component of EG's portfolio on the basis of projected future cash flows. To do this they developed cash flow models for each business and then set to work assembling key inputs for the projections, many of which were available from each unit's business plan. They needed to know projected sales growth, margins, working capital and capital expenditure needs, and the like. The finance staff meanwhile developed estimates of the cost of capital for each division.

When they had the inputs assembled, they ran two sets of discounted cash flow valuations as preliminary benchmarks. The first was based on simple extrapolations of the operating results for each business from recent historical performance; in this case, they chose the last three years. They used these projections to estimate the gross value of each EG business, as well as the cost of corporate headquarters activities and the value of nonoperating investments. Exhibit 2.6 shows the "value buildup" the team used to compare the total value to EG's market value. They noticed several points immediately. First, the total value based on history was substantially below the value of EG in the marketplace. Second, the Foodco food service/restaurant business would be worth far less than the capital EG had invested in it over the last few years, unless performance improved dramatically. Third, the vast majority of EG's value was represented by the cash flow generated by Consumerco. Finally, the corporate headquarters costs, when viewed on a value basis, were a very large drag on overall EG value—almost 25 percent.

After reviewing the disturbing results of the historical extrapolations, Ralph asked the team to look at the value of EG assuming

Exhibit 2.6 **EG CORP., VALUE BUILDUP COMPARISON, JANUARY 1993,** $ MILLIONS

E.G CORPORATION	Historical extrapolation	Business plans	% difference
Consumerco	$1,750	$2,115	+21%
Foodco	300	275	−8
Woodco	200	600	+200
Newsco	175	200	+14
Propco	125	150	+20
Finco	25	35	+40
Corporate overhead	−425	−425	0
Total	$2,150	$2,950	+37%
Debt	−300	−300	
Equity value	**$1,850**	**$2,650**	**+43%**
Stock market value	2,400	2,400	
Value gap	**−$550**	**+$250**	
% of stock market value	−23%	+10%	

the performance estimates in the business plans were achieved. The results, shown in Exhibit 2.6, were also less than comforting. The total value of EG would be above its market value if the plans came true, but only by about 10 percent. On the face of it this was good news, but Ralph knew that the plans were very aggressive, at least by normal EG standards. He especially did not like the idea that they would need to do all the hard work implied by the plans just to stand still from their shareholders' perspective. Apparently the market took for granted that EG would either improve its performance on its own, or someone would take it over soon and make the needed improvement. Ralph was beginning to think that EG would need to come up with some big ideas in order to create the impact on the value of his shareholders' investment that he was seeking during his tenure as CEO.

Ralph was interested also to note the change in value of the individual businesses projected by the plans. For example, Consumerco's plan performance would increase its value by about 20 percent over its value based on recent performance, which would have a large impact on EG given Consumerco's large size. Foodco's value, on the other hand, would actually decline despite the fact that their plan involved substantial growth in the number of outlets and overall sales and earnings. To Ralph this could mean only one thing—as he had suspected, the returns on investment in the business were too low. Foodco management was more focused on growth than returns. In contrast, the Woodco consolidation looked set to improve the value of the furniture businesses dramatically, while the newspaper, finance, and property businesses would improve somewhat too.

At this stage, Ralph drew a few preliminary conclusions. First, Consumerco would have to do even better, given its large impact on the company. Second, Foodco would need to revamp its strategy to make sure it built value, not simply bulk. Third, Woodco's consolidation was far more important than he had thought and would need to succeed to maintain EG's value. Finally, EG would need to run pretty hard just to maintain shareholder value, and any missteps could precipitate a collapse in the share price.

EG's Potential Value with Internal Improvements

After looking at EG's value "as is," Ralph's team tried to assess how much each business might be worth under more aggressive plans and strategies. Their first step was to identify the key value drivers for each business. They estimated the impact on the value of each business of increasing sales growth by 1 percent, boosting margins by a point, and reducing capital intensity, while holding other factors in constant proportion. The results, shown in Exhibit 2.7, indicated the key factors varied by business. Foodco, as Ralph

Exhibit 2.7 **EG CORP., VALUE DRIVERS: IMPACT OF CHANGES IN KEY OPERATING MEASURES,** PERCENT

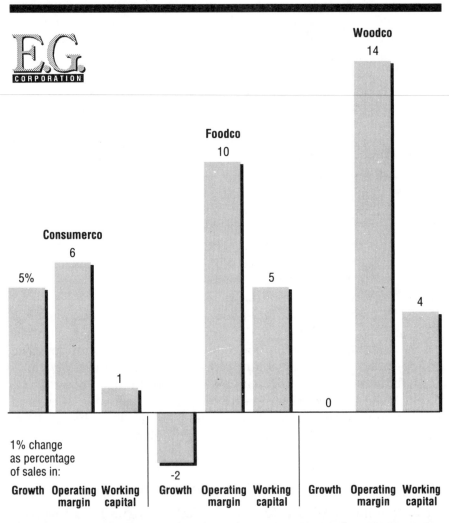

suspected, was most sensitive to reductions in capital intensity and increased margins. Woodco was most sensitive to improvements in operating margin, which he hoped would come about as a result of the consolidation of the companies. Consumerco, interestingly enough, was most sensitive to sales growth. Because of Consumerco's high margin and outstanding capital utilization, each dollar of sales generated large profits and cash flows.

The team next set about assessing the prospects for each business to improve its performance. One approach they used was simply to compare each EG business with similar companies to gauge relative operating performance. They also broke down each of EG's businesses into a "business system" that allowed them to compare —step by step—relative costs, productivity, and investment for EG versus the competition, based on observations and analyses provided by operating managers in each of the divisions. These analyses, coupled with the financial comparisons, showed it was reasonable to assume that some of EG's businesses could indeed be made to perform at much higher levels.

Consumerco, despite its already high operating margin, seemed to have room to increase revenue significantly while simultaneously earning ever higher margins.

- The team discovered that Consumerco had been holding down research and development (R&D) and advertising spending to generate cash for EG's diversification efforts and to buffer the impact of EG's poor performance in other parts of its portfolio. Ralph's team believed that increased spending in the short term would lead to higher sales volumes of existing products, as well as the introduction of additional high-margin products to the marketplace.

- Despite Consumerco's dominant position in its market categories, Consumerco's prices were lower than less popular brands. The team's research showed that most category leaders were able to charge higher prices. The team estimated that the value created by price increases would more than offset expected volume losses.

- Consumerco's sales force was analyzed and the team found it was less than half as productive as the sales forces at other companies selling through the same channels. Ralph had suspected opportunities here, and the analysis confirmed that actions had to be taken to improve sales force productivity.

- Finally, the team determined that cost of goods sold, particularly purchases and inventory management, held additional opportunities. The cost of sales could easily be reduced by one percentage point.

When the team factored in these improvements, they found that Consumerco's value could conservatively be increased by 25 percent as shown in Exhibit 2.8.

Woodco, the furniture division, also had the potential to improve its performance beyond plan by a large margin, if it could transform itself and perform at the levels of other top companies in its industry. However, this would likely require a change in Woodco's strategy after the consolidation to focus less on growth and more on developing higher margins. To do this, Woodco would need to build management information and control systems

Exhibit 2.8 **EG CORP., IMPACT OF POTENTIAL CONSUMERCO BUSINESS INITIATIVES,** $ MILLIONS

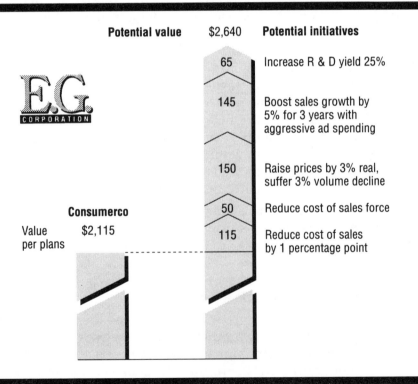

	Potential value	$2,640	Potential initiatives
		65	Increase R & D yield 25%
		145	Boost sales growth by 5% for 3 years with aggressive ad spending
		150	Raise prices by 3% real, suffer 3% volume decline
Consumerco		50	Reduce cost of sales force
Value per plans	$2,115	115	Reduce cost of sales by 1 percentage point

that would allow Woodco management to keep a tight rein on its potentially volatile businesses. Woodco would also need to consider sticking more to the basic, mass-market segment of the business where strong operating skills would provide an advantage. This would probably involve abandoning plans to move the business more "up market" although prices were higher and the potential rewards great, design skills were of utmost importance in this segment. Woodco would be better off sticking to its strong core in the mass-market basic-furniture segments and seeking to maximize its advantage and returns there. Competitors' performance bore this out. Companies with the highest returns had either a strong operational focus in higher-volume segments or downplayed manufacturing and won with innovative design. Companies who strayed into the middle ground—and there were many of them—turned in only marginal results.

On the other hand, Foodco, EG's restaurant business, looked like it would continue to be a poor performer. The industry was extremely competitive. A few large players were earning respectable returns, but even they were struggling to maintain momentum. Moreover, Foodco appeared to have no advantages to build on. The Consumerco brand, which Foodco was using, was of little or no real value in building the business. Foodco would be unable to develop significant scale economies, at least for the foreseeable future. To make matters worse, Foodco had a voracious appetite for capital to build facilities but was not generating a return on new investment sufficient to cover the opportunity cost of the capital. The team reckoned that the best strategy for Foodco almost certainly would involve cutting back to only its profitable locations and being much more circumspect about growth targets. Even then, it would be necessary to find some way to reduce the cost of capital employed in the Foodco business, either through franchising/management-contract approaches or substantially higher financial leverage. Otherwise, Foodco would likely remain an insignificant contributor to building EG's value.

Similar reviews were carried out for the smaller EG businesses. The team also looked critically at EG's corporate overhead situation and concluded that opportunities existed to reduce costs substantially. Over the years, EG's staff had grown at the corporate level. The divisions too had added staff to the point where they were functioning largely as freestanding operations. Ralph believed that 50 percent of the corporate costs could be eliminated.

Putting it all together, Ralph concluded that the potential internal value of EG's businesses was at least $3.6 billion, which would be 50 percent above its current market value (see Exhibit 2.9). This was before considering any incremental value that might be garnered through the sale of particular EG businesses to owners who might do more with them, as might be the case with the relatively unattractive Foodco business.

Ralph and his team were beginning to feel better about their chances for turning EG into a high-performance company. They were anxious to get on to the next step, which was to look at the value of EG as a breakup candidate. They thought too that they would uncover more ideas for improvement to undertake on behalf of their shareholders.

EG's Potential Value with External Improvements

Ralph's team decided to investigate the external value of EG's businesses under four different scenarios: sale to a strategic buyer

Exhibit 2.9 **EG CORP., POTENTIAL VALUE VS. PLAN VALUE, JANUARY 1993,** $ MILLIONS

	Historical extrapo- lation	Business plans	Potential value	% difference
Consumerco	$1,750	$2,115	$2,640	+25%
Foodco	300	275	300	+9
Woodco	200	600	800	+33
Newsco	175	200	215	+8
Propco	125	150	160	+7
Finco	25	35	35	0
Corporate overhead	−425	−425	−225	−47
Total	$2,150	$2,950	$3,925	+33%
Debt	−300	−300	−300	
Equity value	**$1,850**	**$2,650**	**$3,625**	**+37%**
Stock market value	2,400	2,400	2,400	
Value gap	**−$550**	**+$250**	**+1,225**	
% of stock market value	−23%	+10%	+51%	

(another company that could realize operating and strategic synergies); a flotation or spin-off; leveraged buyout by management or a third party; and liquidation.

The team started with the easiest values to estimate: what the EG businesses would trade for in the market if spun off as independent companies. To estimate these values, they identified a set of publicly traded companies comparable to each EG business. They used current stock market valuation data (for example, price-to-earnings, market-to-book, market-to-sales ratios) to estimate the value of the EG businesses as freestanding entities. They found that a simple breakup into separate, publicly traded companies would not, at current market prices, provide any gain overall for EG shareholders. Some benefit would result from reduced corporate overhead burden, but the freely traded sum of the parts was less than the current share price of EG.

Likewise, estimates of the value of the businesses as leveraged-buyout candidates did not suggest that EG as a whole would be worth more in parts, especially after taking into account the taxes EG would have to pay on the sale of the units. The Consumerco business with its strong, stable cash flow was a natural buyout candidate, but the other businesses were not.

The final financially oriented valuation Ralph's team considered was a complete or partial liquidation or decapitalization of the businesses. The only EG business of the three larger ones for which this might have made sense was the Foodco business, because of the real estate it encompassed. The restaurant property might be sold off piecemeal and the Foodco restaurant division shut down. To Ralph's team, a number of the units did appear to be worth more for their alternative real estate value than in their current incarnation as restaurants. However, this did not hold true for Foodco as a whole; the company was worth more as a going concern than in liquidation. The review of Foodco's properties *did* suggest to management, though, that they incorporate into their plans for Foodco the possibility of closing and selling some of those units, including some that were profitable.

One business the team found might be worth more liquidated than operated was EG's small consumer finance company. The business had become so competitive that the spread between its borrowing costs and the rates it earned on the new loans it booked did not cover its operating costs of generating and processing new business. The team discovered that the existing loan portfolio might be sold for more than the entire business was worth, even given management's plans going forward. In effect, each year's new business was dissipating some of the value inherent in the existing portfolio of loans. The team was sure also that it would be relatively easy to sell the portfolio and exit the business altogether. A number of financial companies might buy the loans. Moreover, no links between the finance company and any of the other EG businesses would need to be untangled. Of course, EG would also consider the possibility of selling the entire business and searching for ways to make the company more viable, but it seemed likely that it would end up going out of business.

Reflecting on the values generated by a financially driven dismemberment of EG, Ralph saw clearly that the gains to be gotten from pure financial maneuvering would be limited. The best combination of financial plays for each business did not generate an increment over EG's current market value.

Finally, Ralph reviewed the team's findings on the value of EG's parts to strategic buyers—potential owners who would be able to make the improvements required to increase the value of the businesses. From these analyses, it was evident that Consumerco, EG's largest business, might be worth much more in the hands of another owner than it was now to EG and might still be worth more to them even after Ralph achieved the potential value he had identified earlier. A strategic buyer might see several sources of value in Consumerco. First was the ability to make the improvements to the growth and returns in the business Ralph's team had identified earlier. It was clear to Ralph that these opportunities were evident to any potential acquirer who looked at Consumerco, even using publicly available data. Important too was the potential for cost savings between the consumer businesses of certain potential buyers and Consumerco. For instance, sales forces could be combined and much of Consumerco's direct sales force eliminated. Potential savings could also be realized in the management of Consumerco itself, since it might be merged into an existing management structure at another consumer products company.

In addition to cost savings, an acquirer might believe it could improve Consumerco's business by injecting more vigorous marketing know-how into the business and improving its new product development activities. Ralph believed that these areas, while difficult to quantify, needed improvement at Consumerco, which was not known for the strength of its marketing team. It had grown accustomed to the high returns its dominant and essentially un-challenged brand recognition provided to its range of products. All these factors together suggested Consumerco might be worth over $3.2 billion to a strategic buyer, which was much more than it was currently worth as run by EG (around $2 billion). It was also more than the $2.6 billion potential value of Consumerco to EG that Ralph's team had estimated previously as the best EG could do with the business. Since Consumerco was a large portion of EG's value, the whole company was at risk of a takeover by a buyer interested in getting its hands on Consumerco.

Potential strategic buyers existed for the other EG businesses too, and Ralph's team did their best to estimate the value of the EG businesses to each company. They thought Foodco would be attractive to another more established restaurant company who might follow one of two courses of action. On the one hand, they could accelerate Foodco's development and leverage their own management skills to improve the profitability of the Foodco units. Alternatively, they could convert the Foodco sites over to their own restaurant concept. Foodco did have quite a few reasonably good locations. In fact, it looked as though EG would be better off to sell Foodco if the potential prices were likely to be realized, since even after paying tax on the proceeds the Foodco business was unlikely to be worth as much under EG's plans.

The Woodco business, which was in the process of being consolidated, might be attractive to one of several other companies in the industry who had earned a reputation for buying and improving smaller furniture companies. However, it made little sense to sell Woodco when it was in the midst of the consolidation. Any potential buyer would not be willing to take the risk of having the business fall apart completely in the transition to new ownership. For all practical purposes, the Woodco business would not be salable for 12 to 18 months at anything other than a distressed sale price. By the end of 18 months, though, EG would be in a good position to evaluate a sale. The business would be streamlined and Ralph would have a better idea about the ability of Woodco's management to improve performance to approach that of the industry leaders. If Woodco could perform that well on its own, EG would be better off to retain it and perhaps use it as a base for making additional furniture company acquisitions. If Woodco did not look able to reach higher performance levels, it could be sold at that time to another player in the industry and for a much better price than today.

Exhibit 2.10 **EG CORP., COMPARISON OF EXTERNAL VALUE ESTIMATES BY BUSINESS, JANUARY 1993,** $ MILLIONS

E.G. CORPORATION	Consumerco	Foodco	Woodco	Propco	Finco	Newsco
LBO	$2,500	290	n.a.	n.a.	n.a.	180
Spin-off	2,000	280	55	n.a.	25	140
Liquidation	n.a.	260	25	130	50	n.a.
Strategic buyer	3,250	350	155	175	35	190
Highest value	**3,250**	**350**	**155**	**175**	**50**	**190**

Exhibit 2.10 shows the conclusions the team drew about estimated values for the EG businesses under the different scenarios. In total, they concluded that, even allowing for difficulty in selling Woodco at this time, EG could be worth substantially more than its current stock price if sold piece by piece to the best potential owners of each business.

Potential Value of Financial Engineering

Ralph also urged his CFO to look hard at EG's financial structure and come up with an aggressive plan to take advantage of the tax advantages of debt financing. EG had heretofore had a policy of maintaining an AA rating from Standard & Poor's and liked to think of itself as a strong "investment grade" company. However, Ralph knew that many companies had taken on much higher debt levels and performed very well. In fact, the performance of many had been spectacular, as managers thought harder about how to generate additional cash flow and looked more critically at investment requirements and so-called fixed expenses.

EG had sizable and stable free cash flows that could support much higher debt. The Consumerco business, which generated the bulk of the cash, was recession-resistant. Ralph also knew he did not need much reserve financial capacity given the relative maturity of EG's core business and its limited need for capital. He also believed EG would be able to get access to the funding it needed for a major expansion or acquisition, if it made economic sense. Otherwise, it was probably a poor investment in the first place.

By the CFO's calculations, EG could indeed carry a lot more debt than it did currently, depending on the interest coverage Ralph wished to maintain. Moreover, as the financial performance of the EG businesses improved, EG would be able to carry an even higher debt load comfortably. Ralph figured that at a minimum, EG could raise $500 million in new debt in the next six months and use the proceeds to repurchase shares or pay a special dividend. This debt would provide a more tax-efficient capital structure for EG, which would be worth about $200 million in present value to EG's shareholders, assuming a combined federal and state marginal tax rate of about 40 percent.

EG's Restructuring Plan

Ralph's team had analyzed EG's value from multiple perspectives, both internal and external. Having done so, it was in a good position to develop an overall restructuring plan for the company. As shown in Exhibit 2.11, the team identified, business area by business area, the actions Ralph and his management could take. Ralph's plan would produce a large gain for EG shareholders, if he

Exhibit 2.11 **EG CORP., SUMMARY OF RESTRUCTURING ACTIONS**

E.G. CORPORATION

Area	Action
Consumerco	Cut cost of sales Reorganize sales force Increase advertising, R&D Build marketing skills
Foodco	Sell
Woodco	Keep and consolidate; sell if in two years management cannot reach next level of performance
Propco	Sell
Finco	Liquidate
Newsco	Sell
Corporate	Cut by 50%; decentralize remainder
Financing	Set leverage to maintain BBB rating to capture tax benefits

Exhibit 2.12 **EG CORP., VALUE CREATED THROUGH RESTRUCTURING, JANUARY 1993,** $ MILLIONS

	Historical extrapolation	Restructuring action	% difference	
Consumerco	$1,750	$2,900	+66%	Improvements
Foodco	300	350	+17	Sale
Woodco	200	800	+300	Consol./sale
Newsco	175	190	+9	Sale
Propco	125	160	+28	Sale
Finco	25	45	+80	Liquidation
Corporate overhead	−425	−225	−47	Cuts
Debt tax benefit	n.a.	200	n.a.	
Total	$2,150	$4,420	+106%	
Debt	−300	−300		
Equity value	**$1,850**	**$4,120**	+122%	
Stock market value	2,400	2,400		
Value gap	**− $550**	**+ $1,720**		
% of stock market value	− 23%	+ 72%		

were successful in executing it. Exhibit 2.12 and 2.13 show the projected sources of increase in the value of EG's stock and the increment over EG's recent share value in the market. In a nutshell, Ralph's restructuring plan would entail these moves:

- Making improvements in the Consumerco business aimed at doubling its already high value: increasing prices, investing more in advertising and new products, rationalizing the large direct sales force to boost productivity, hiring several top-flight marketing executives from leading consumer companies, cutting back on staff functions that had been allowed to grow unchecked.

- Accelerating the consolidation of the Woodco companies and reorienting plans for its direction after the consolidation to focus on boosting returns in basic furniture markets rather than expanding into more upscale segments.

- Stopping further expansion in Foodco and putting the company up for sale.

Exhibit 2.13 **EG CORP., VALUE BUILDUP, JANUARY 1993,** $ MILLIONS

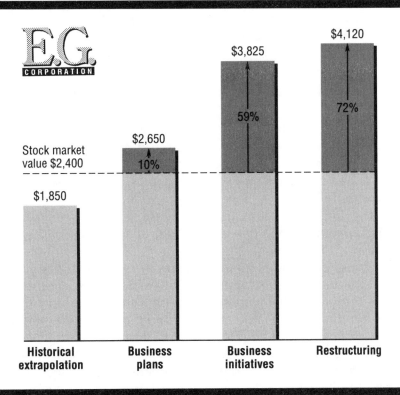

- Putting the finance company portfolio up for sale, and taking steps to wind down the rest of its business activities.
- Selling the newspaper and property development companies—valuable properties, but needless distractions for EG.
- Launching a review of corporate overhead, starting from the premise that EG could operate with only a handful of people by moving to a holding-company type structure, with staff functions pushed down into the divisions.
- Recapitalizing the company by borrowing $500 million and targeting a BBB rating for EG going forward, rather than its historically conservative AA rating.
- Developing a strategy for communicating with the investment markets about the restructuring plan and its potential impact on the value of EG.

Ralph and his team were confident their plan would work well. Since they could take immediate steps, they also expected to get a quick and favorable response to the program.

THE CASE OF EG CORPORATION, PART 3: RALPH AS VALUE MANAGER

EG's restructuring plan did in fact result in an increase in the price of its shares. When the plan was announced, EG's price jumped immediately. Then, when investors saw that EG was in fact taking the actions it had promised, the stock price rose further. Over the first six months of 1993, EG's shares increased over 40 percentage points above the stock market average increase. The analysts who followed EG dropped their talk of takeovers and applauded the transformation of the company.

Needless to say, Ralph and his team were feeling pleased with the results. Ralph regretted having to reduce the corporate staff and sell some of EG's businesses, but took some comfort from the knowledge that he did it in a more orderly and humane way than an outsider would have. Despite his successes, though, Ralph knew he had a lot more work ahead to see his restructuring plan through to completion. Furthermore, he knew he needed to begin the job of building an orientation toward managing value into the company's ongoing activities. Otherwise, he feared that people throughout the company would soon become complacent about EG's performance, and the accumulation of untapped value potential would begin anew. He wanted to build on the fragile momentum he had established.

Ralph planned to take six steps to build EG's ability to manage value:

1. Focus planning and business performance reviews around value creation.

2. Develop value oriented targets and performance measurement.

3. Restructure EG's compensation system to foster an emphasis on creating shareholder value.

4. Evaluate strategic investment decisions explicitly in terms of their impact on value.

5. Begin communicating more clearly with investors and analysts about the value of EG's plans.

6. Reshape the role of EG's CFO.

Ralph's plans and thinking in each of these areas are set out in the following paragraphs. The first three of these ideas are developed into a comprehensive value-based management approach in Chapter 4.

Put Value into Planning

Ralph was convinced that one of the main reasons EG Corporation had gotten into the position it had was a lack of focus on value creation in developing corporate-level and business-unit plans. Likewise, evaluations of the performance of the businesses had only a vague focus on value. Ralph firmly believed it was the responsibility of all senior managers to focus on value creation. Going forward, Ralph would ensure that company plans included a thorough analysis of the value of each of the businesses under alternative scenarios. He would also make sure that EG used the restructuring pentagon approach on an annual basis to identify any restructuring opportunities within EG's portfolio.

This new focus on value would also require some changes in the way EG thought about its corporate strategy. For the next year or so, EG clearly would need to focus on carrying out its restructuring. In effect, EG's corporate strategy for the next year would be to restructure itself. However, beyond that, Ralph would need to develop a plan for sustaining EG's advantage in the market for corporate control. To do this, he would need to get clear about the company's real skills and assets and in which businesses they would be most valuable. Most important, he would ensure that the value of these skills could be identified in terms of higher margins, growth rates, and the like before building action plans around them. Too often in the past, Ralph was convinced, EG had done a perfunctory analysis of its capabilities and entered businesses without a clear idea of how and why EG would be a better owner and able to create value for its shareholders. As a first step, later in the year Ralph would establish a task force to begin inventorying and analyzing EG's skills and assets compared with competition, as well as ideas for new businesses EG might enter.

At the business level, EG's new focus on value would require some changes too. The restructuring review had pointed out a number of specific strategic and operating actions that the various business managers would need to take. Beyond this, management in the business units would need to think differently about their operations. They would need to focus on what was driving the value of their businesses—whether it was volume growth, margins, or capital utilization. Everyone had been used to focusing on growth in earnings, but what would matter going forward would be growth in value and economic returns on investment. Sometimes this would mean foregoing growth in the business that would have been accepted in years gone by. At other times, managers would have to get more comfortable with the idea of reporting lower earnings when investment in research and development or advertising with a longer-term payoff made economic sense. Ralph knew that these changes would be difficult for his management group, because they had not been encouraged to think this way in the past. To help bring about change, he decided to share with them the results of the overall corporate restructuring analysis and to develop a series of training seminars for senior division management about shareholder value.

Develop Value Oriented Targets and Performance Measures

Ralph knew that his managers needed clear targets and performance measures to track their progress. While the stock price performance was the ultimate measure, he needed something more concrete and directly manageable by his managers, particularly his business-unit managers. He also knew that traditional accounting measures like net income ignored the opportunity cost of the capital tied up to generate earnings. Return on invested capital, on the other hand, ignored value creating growth. So he turned to a measure that incorporated both growth and ROIC called economic profit. Economic profit is the spread between the return on capital and its opportunity cost times the quantity of invested capital:

$$\text{Economic Profit} = \text{Invested Capital} \times (\text{ROIC} - \text{Opportunity Cost of Capital})$$

Ralph chose this measure because he knew that the discounted value of future economic profit (plus the current amount of invested capital) would equal the discounted cash flow (DCF) value.

In other words, EG could maximize its DCF value by maximizing economic profit. Ralph asked that all strategic plans and budgets include economic profit targets for each of the business units.

Knowing that lower level managers also needed targets and performance measures they could directly influence, he asked his business-unit managers to translate their economic profit targets into specific operational performance measures for their operating managers. For example, the manufacturing manager might be measured by cost per unit, quality, and meeting delivery schedules. Sales might be measured by sales growth, price realizations, and selling costs as a percent of revenues.

This new integrated system of target setting and performance measurement required a new mindset for Ralph's accounting group, which was used to just dealing with accounting results. They resisted, but Ralph convinced them of the benefits of integrating financial results with operating measures and of moving toward more economically relevant financial measures.

Tie Compensation to Value

Ralph believed that one of the most powerful levers he could use in building a value-creation focus throughout EG was the compensation system. At present, the package contained relatively little performance-based incentive for top managers. They did receive a bonus, but it was a relatively modest proportion of total compensation. They also received stock options, but few viewed these as significant in terms of their ability to build capital for doing a good job. It was also clear to Ralph that the top-management incentives did not focus on value creation. Bonus payouts were geared toward achievement of earnings-per-share targets, which he knew did not always correlate well with creating value. In addition, the compensation of business-unit managers was tied more closely to the performance of EG as a whole than it was to the fortunes of their particular business unit.

Ralph figured that several schemes were potentially capable of meeting his objectives. He asked his human resources executives to consider plans involving phantom stock for each of the divisions, a deferred compensation program structured around the economic profit targets that the businesses were adopting, and a more operationally focused plan using the attainment of goals on particular value drivers over time as a basis for compensation awards. Ralph was confident that through these plans he would be able to devise one that would suit EG's situation.

Assess Value of Strategic Investments

Injecting a value-creation focus into EG's planning and performance review process would make a big difference. However, Ralph knew he needed to make changes in the way the company looked at major spending proposals in the areas of capital expenditures and acquisitions.

To evaluate capital expenditures, EG had been using discounted cash flow analysis for at least five years, as had most other companies. This was fine and good, but Ralph saw two problems. First, capital expenditures were not linked tightly enough to the strategic and operating plans for the businesses. Because of this, capital expenditure proposals were very difficult to evaluate; they were out of context. Second, EG had been using a corporate-wide hurdle rate to assess capital investment proposals. From his restructuring review of EG, Ralph knew that each of the EG businesses involved a different degree of risk, so the hurdle rates for assessing capital investments should be different too. To make matters worse, the hurdle rate was much too high, having been set in an attempt to smoke out unrealistic operating projections. The result was an ineffective capital expenditure process. Ralph figured that many investments that earned above their cost of capital were being passed up because they did not meet EG's extremely high hurdle rate.

On the other hand, major capital investments were not evaluated as closely as they should be since the whole process had degenerated into a numbers game about assumptions. In the future, Ralph intended to tie in closely the capital expenditure cycle with the strategic and operating plans to ensure that evaluation of capital spending was done in a realistic, fact-based way. He would also ensure that the finance staff developed appropriate hurdle rates, which would differ by division, to reflect the relevant opportunity cost of capital.

Ralph knew that one of EG's biggest problems in the past had been the evaluation of acquisitions. He knew they had paid way too much for Woodco acquisitions in the 1980s. In his restructuring review, he had seen the impact of paying too much for them on the company's share price. Fortunately, as CEO he would have direct control over the decision to pursue acquisitions. He would insist that when proposing an acquisition, the relevant operating manager and CFO do a thorough valuation analysis based on cash flow returns for the transaction. He would not make the mistake his predecessor had made of believing that just because he could make the accounting earnings and dilution figures look good in the first year or two of an acquisition, it made sense from a value standpoint.

To Ralph it was really quite simple. Either the cash flow value to EG's shareholders of an acquisition would be above the price EG would have to pay, or Ralph would not make the acquisition. And he believed that value could be assessed in a relatively systematic way—much more systematically than had been done in the past.

First, EG management would evaluate the target's business on an "as is" basis, just as they had done for EG. Next, they would use the restructuring pentagon approach to identify improvements that could be made to the value of the company on a stand-alone basis. The management of the target company might or might not be capable of making these improvements on their own. Likewise, Ralph would ensure that EG management knew whether they were capable of making the changes. Third, EG management would evaluate the potential for synergies with other EG businesses on a systematic basis. These synergies would be evaluated in concrete terms for their impact on value. Finally, EG management would think about the strategic options the acquisition would create. These would be difficult to value and evaluate, but could nevertheless be important. For example, an acquisition might give EG an option on a new technology in one of its businesses or access to a new market, both of which could have substantial value in the future under the right conditions.

Armed with this information, Ralph would be much better able to evaluate the value of any particular acquisition and much clearer than EG management had ever been in the past. He would know how much EG could afford to pay. Equally important, he would know more specifically what to do with the business after it had been acquired. Before entering negotiations, Ralph would also have his team assess the value of the target to other potential acquirers; in this way he could be sure he would not enter into a fruitless bidding contest or end up buying the company at a price higher than he needed to. He certainly did not want to fall into the trap of assigning all of the potential value of the candidate to the selling shareholders. After all, why should EG do all the work and the sellers receive all the rewards?

Acquisition proposals would also be subjected to a new test. EG management would no longer presume that the best way to pursue a new business idea was by acquisition. Ralph would ensure that they considered entering the business on their own or via joint venture as an alternative to the big bang acquisitions that always seem like a quick and easy solution at the time, but afterward cause endless problems for the company's performance.

Develop Investor Communications Strategy

Ralph planned to continue working hard to build the company's credibility with Wall Street analysts and investors. As a key part of this, it would be essential for EG to track analyst views on its performance and prospects on a regular basis. Ralph wanted to do this for two reasons. First, he would be able to ensure that the market had sufficient information to evaluate the company at all times. Second, Ralph knew the market was smart. He could learn a lot about the direction of his industry and competitors from the way investors evaluated his shares and those of other companies. He did not believe he could, nor would he try to, fool the market about EG. He was convinced, though, that it was sound strategy to treat investors and the investing community with the same care that the company showed its customers and employees. Had previous management taken the time to really understand what the market was saying about EG, the company might have been less likely to get into the difficult position it had fallen into.

In addition to tracking the analysts' opinions and meeting with them regularly, Ralph thought EG should be more active and clearer in communicating with the investors. Henceforth, his communications with the market at security analyst meetings and in press releases would focus on what EG was doing to build value for shareholders. He even thought it might be a good idea to have a section in the annual report entitled something like "Perspective on the Value of Your Company" that would discuss clearly and in some depth the company's strategies for creating value.

He thought EG could even go so far as to publish its estimates of the value of the company, as long as the assumptions were spelled out clearly. Ralph knew this communications strategy would be a break with the practices of many companies and with EG's recent past. However, he did not really think investors got much benefit from the mechanical—and usually vague—explanations of changes in year-to-year performance typically found in the annual reports of many companies. Likewise, the glossy photographs and glowing language in the front sections of many annual reports did little to give investors a clear sense of where a company was going and what the status of their investment was.

Reshape CFO's Role

Critical to the success of Ralph's efforts to build a value creation focus into EG was the need to upgrade the role of the CFO. It was clear to Ralph that the link between business strategy and financial strategy was becoming tighter; on top of this, corporate strategies, since they are designed to create an advantage in the market for corporate control and financial markets, are by definition intertwined with financial considerations. Furthermore, it was going to take a lot of work to make managing value a key element of EG's strategy and management approaches. Ralph would need a strong executive who would be able to help him push this through.

Historically, EG financial officers had been focused entirely on financial matters such as running the treasury operation, producing financial reports, and negotiating the occasional deal. Ralph needed much more, and since his current CFO was due to retire at the end of the year, he felt this was a perfect opportunity to redefine the role.

Ralph's concept was to create a new position that would blend corporate strategy and finance responsibilities. The officer would act as a bridge between the strategic/operating focus of the division heads and the financial requirements of the corporation and its investors. Ralph drafted a job description for this position, which in EG's case would carry the title of executive vice-president for corporate strategy and finance (EVP). This description is set out in Exhibit 2.14. Key responsibilities of the new role would be to act as a kind of "super CFO" and take the lead in developing a value-creating corporate strategy for EG, as well as to work with Ralph and the division heads to build a value-management capability throughout the organization.

The EVP would also be responsible for managing the normal financial affairs and financial reporting of the corporation, but his or her success would be measured mainly in terms of how well EG made the transition to a corporation that managed value in a superior way. For example, if the EVP were successful, in a year or so

---

Exhibit 2.14 **EG CORP., JOB DESCRIPTION: EXECUTIVE VICE PRESIDENT FOR CORPORATE STRATEGY AND FINANCE**

Job Concept

The EVP will act as key advisor to the CEO and division heads on major strategic and operational issues, and will manage EG's financial and planning functions. Responsibilities will include:

- Corporate strategy
- Financial strategy
- Budgeting and management control, and
- Financial management.

Corporate strategy   The EVP will take the lead role in coordinating the development of a value-maximizing overall corporate strategy for EG:

- Ensuring that plans are in place to create maximum value for EG from its current businesses.
  - Assessing the value creation potential of plans on an ongoing basis.
  - Ensuring that plans focus on key issues by (1) challenging key assumptions and the rationale for changes in performance, and (2) providing external reference points for value creation opportunities (for example, value of the businesses to alternative owners).
  - Acting as a sounding board for the CEO and division heads on critical proposals.
  - Establishing financial measurement standards and developing systems to monitor performance against goals.
- Supporting the development of corporate expansion strategies to create additional shareholder value.
  - Developing perspectives on market opportunities in businesses closely related to current businesses.
  - Assessing EG's skills and assets in place for pursuing opportunities and suggesting programs to build skills to fill gaps.
  - Conducting business and financial evaluations of specific proposals.
- Planning and executing major transactions required to implement EG's strategies.

Exhibit 2.14 Continued

Financial strategy   The EVP will have responsibility for developing, recommending, and executing an overall financial strategy for EG that supports its business strategies and captures maximum value for its shareholders:

- Developing value creating capital structure and dividend policy recommendations.
- Designing and managing a strategy for communicating the key elements of EG's plans and performance to investors and the financial community.
- Negotiating and executing all major financial transactions, including borrowing, share issuances, and share repurchases.

Budgeting and management control   The EVP will design and implement processes to ensure that EG managers have the right information to set goals, make decisions, and monitor performance:

- Coordinating preparation of short-term operating budgets.
- Developing key performance measures for each business unit.
- Ensuring that business units have adequate management controls in place.
- Evaluating business-unit performance in conjunction with the CEO and division heads.

Financial management   The EVP will ensure the effective and efficient management of EG's financial operations:

- Ensuring that all external reporting and compliance obligations are fulfilled.
- Establishing controls to safeguard EG's assets.
- Ensuring the integrity and efficiency of cash, receivables, and payables management.
- Filing and paying all tax obligations.
- Pursuing opportunities to reduce EG's tax burden.
- Maintaining strong day-to-day relationships with EG's banks.
- Managing EG's pension fund.
- Managing EG's risk management programs.

Exhibit 2.14 Continued

Success Criteria

If the EVP is successful:

One year from now

- A well-defined corporate strategy will have been created, and early phases of execution will have been completed.
- A clearly articulated financial strategy will have been developed and implementation will have begun.
- Division heads and key managers will think in terms of shareholder value creation when developing their plans and evaluating proposals.
- The financial management functions will be operating smoothly.
- Security analysts will understand EG's strategy and evaluate it as a strong operating company rather than a breakup candidate.

Three years from now

- EG will have provided shareholders with superior returns.
- EG will have begun pursuing several value creating expansion initiatives (most likely through internal investments).
- Security analysts will view EG as a leading-edge "value manager" of its businesses.

Major Resources

The EVP's staff will include the treasury, controller's, planning, and tax departments. In addition, the financial staffs of the operating units will have dotted-line reporting relationships to the EVP. The EVP will have broad discretion in organizing the staff.

Key Organizational Relationships

The EVP's integrating role will require close working relationships with all the other key executives at EG:

- *CEO*: The EVP will provide recommendations and analyses to the CEO on all major issues. The EVP will carry out the financial policy decisions made by the CEO.
- *Operating-Unit Heads*: The EVP will work with the operating-unit heads to ensure the smooth functioning of the planning, reporting,

Exhibit 2.14 Continued

and control systems, and to resolve conflicts between corporate and business-unit priorities. The EVP will also counsel the operating-unit heads on finance-related issues and provide analytical support for special projects.

The EVP and staff will manage the relationships with key outside groups, including:

- Investors, financial analysts, rating agencies, and the financial press;
- Financial institutions (banks and investment banks);
- External auditors; and
- Regulators and tax authorities

Critical Skills/Requirements for the Job

The EVP should bring a broad business perspective and should possess the following characteristics:

- Seasoned business judgment and superior analytical abilities, particularly in strategic business and financial analysis.
- Ability to take an independent stance and challenge the ideas of the CEO and operating managers while maintaining their respect and confidence.
- Presence to deal with the financial community.
- Ability to lead/orchestrate negotiations in major transactions.
- Strong administrative and people management skills.

In addition, the EVP should have familiarity with the following:

- Financial markets
- Financial and managerial accounting
- Treasury operations
- Taxation

EG would have a first-draft corporate strategy in place, a clearly articulated financial strategy that supported it, and division heads and key managers who were thinking and acting in terms of value creation when submitting plans and proposals. Security analysts would also have a much clearer understanding of EG's strategy and the reason why it would not make sense to view the company as a breakup candidate. Longer term, the EVP's success would be measured as part of a team that would provide shareholders with superior returns, assist in launching several new value-creating expansion opportunities, and establish EG with a reputation in the financial community as a leading-edge, value-managing company.

Ralph Demsky expected his six-part plan for building a sharper focus on value into EG could take as long as two years to become a well-accepted part of EG's management approach. It would require the recruitment of the new EVP and substantial time and attention from Ralph himself. Focusing planning and performance measurement on value creation, evaluating all major decisions in terms of impact on value, redesigning the compensation system for senior management, and communicating more clearly and consistently with the stock market would help to ensure that EG maintained an advantage in the market for corporate control and produced outstanding value for shareholders. Moreover, by following this much more integrated approach, it would be easier for EG to set corporate priorities in the future, since major decisions would be brought back to the common benchmark of their impact on the value of the company.

SUMMARY

The ability to manage value is an essential part of developing sound corporate and business strategies—strategies that create value for shareholders and maintain an advantage in the market for corporate control. As the case of EG Corporation shows, managing value is not a mysterious process. Valuation techniques and approaches can be complex in their details, but are relatively straightforward in their objectives and applications. Our objective in the balance of this book is to demystify the approaches needed to implement value management in most companies.

As in the EG case, managing value consists of taking three broad steps: first, *taking stock* of the value-creation situation within the company and identifying restructuring opportunities; second *acting* on those opportunities, which usually involves major transactions such as divestitures and acquisitions as well as reorganization of the company; and third, *instilling a value-creation philosophy* into the management approaches of the company.

It should be clear that a managing-value focus does not create value through financial manipulations. Rather, it creates value through developing sound strategic and operating plans for a company's businesses. The link between sound strategy and value creation is a tight one. As many CEOs have learned, financial manipulations on their own seldom work.

Many companies thankfully are not in as desperate a condition as we outlined for EG Corporation. Most companies, however, *would* benefit from a thorough review of restructuring opportunities. Despite this, we know of relatively few companies that have made the attempt to institutionalize a managing-value approach to their business. Perhaps it is because many companies that have gone through massive restructuring believe it will only happen once. However, restructuring and an active market for corporate control are now facts of corporate life. Consequently, managers need to ensure that they identify and act on value creation opportunities regularly—not just once when the raider is knocking at the door, but on an ongoing basis. This is best done through fundamental changes in the way their businesses are structured and operated. By acting now, value managers can avoid the need to react under duress later.

REVIEW QUESTIONS

1. Describe the relationships among the various divisions of EG Corporation upon Ralph Demsky's arrival as CEO.

2. How would divisional relationships and performance give rise to the concerns the financial markets had about EG Corporation?

3. What is the data Ralph Demsky gathered to perform his analysis of EG Corporation?

4. Describe the value pentagon and its interpretation of performance for one of EG Corporation's divisions.

5. Discuss the specific judgments that can be made about the divisions in terms of each of the five points of the pentagon.

6. Relate the judgments derived from the pentagon value analysis to specific decision alternatives that can be generated for the division.

7. What relationships exist between the operational alternatives available to Ralph for each division and the plans for overall corporate financial engineering of capital structure, credit rating, and investor communications?

8. Outline Ralph's steps to build EG's ability to manage value.

9. What problems at EG would be resolved with the new EVP of finance and strategy's position?

10. Describe the requisite materials, reasoning, and decisions in the three-step development of a value management philosophy.

3

Cash Is King

On October 1, 1974, *The Wall Street Journal* published an editorial lamenting the prevalent focus on earnings per share as an indicator of value:

> A lot of executives apparently believe that if they can figure out a way to boost reported earnings, their stock prices will go up even if the higher earnings do not represent any underlying economic change. In other words, the executives think they are smart and the market is dumb. . . .
>
> The market is smart. Apparently the dumb one is the corporate executive caught up in the earnings-per-share mystique.

Unfortunately, our experience shows that 20 years later many corporate managers still worship earnings per share, and thus are still betting that the market is dumb. Although earnings per share is useful for some situations, its simplicity allows managers to ignore other important factors that affect the value of a company. It can, therefore, lead or allow managers to make choices that destroy value in the long term, often without the short-term share price improvement they hoped for.

The key problem with maximizing accounting earnings can be demonstrated with an example of another common valuation approach. Cable television companies are sometimes valued by placing a monetary value on each subscriber, say $2,000 each. Using the number of subscribers as a comparable for share value suggests that the latter can be increased simply by signing up more subscribers.

But if that is accomplished by slashing subscriber fees, for instance, value actually might be destroyed rather than increased.

The essential problem with the cable television dollars-per-subscriber approach is that it does not value what directly matters to investors. Investors cannot buy a house or car with subscribers. Nor can they use subscribers to make additional investments. Only the cash flow generated by the business can be used for consumption or additional investment. The price-per-subscriber approach is useful only when the number of subscribers is a good proxy for cash flow. That occurs only when all cable systems generate the same cash flow per subscriber.

Similarly, accounting earnings is useful for valuation only when earnings is a good proxy for the expected long-term cash flow of the company. Not all companies generate the same cash flow for each dollar of earnings, however, so earnings approaches are generally only useful for very rough value approximations. They fail as a comprehensive management tool.

As *The Wall Street Journal* editorial goes on to say, "To us the lesson is clear: If the manager keeps his eye on the long-run health of the enterprise, the stock price will take care of itself." That message gives rise to a question: What valuation tool is most consistent with the goal of long-term value creation? We believe that the manager who is interested in maximizing share value should use discounted cash flow (DCF) analysis, not earnings per share, to make decisions. The DCF approach captures all the elements that affect the value of the company in a comprehensive yet straightforward manner. Furthermore, the DCF approach is strongly supported by research into how the stock markets actually value companies.

DCF CAPTURES ALL ELEMENTS OF VALUE

Either explicitly or implicitly, all management decisions are based on some valuation model. It is therefore to the manager's advantage to base his or her decisions on the model that most accurately reflects share value. We will show that the DCF approach—an economic model—provides a more sophisticated and reliable picture of a company's value than the accounting approach.

First, let's define the two competing valuation approaches that we will be comparing throughout this chapter.

- In the *accounting approach*, all that matters is the accounting earnings of the business. Value is simply earnings times some multiple (the price-earnings or P/E ratio). In its extreme form, the accounting approach says that only this year's or next year's earnings matter. A more complex form might discount the future stream of earnings at some rate.
- In the *DCF approach*, the value of a business is the future expected cash flow discounted at a rate that reflects the riskiness of the cash flow.

A simple example illustrates the difference between the two models. Exhibit 3.1 shows the projected income statements of two companies. Based on this accounting information, would you pay more for Longlife Company or Shortlife Company? Both the level and expected growth rates of earnings are identical, so most people would be inclined to pay the same price for both companies.

Exhibit 3.2 shows the projected cash flow statements for the two companies. Longlife Company uses manufacturing equipment that must be replaced every three years, while Shortlife Company

Exhibit 3.1 **PROJECTED INCOME OF LONGLIFE AND SHORTLIFE COMPANIES**

Longlife Company	Year 1	2	3	4	5	6
Sales	1,000	1,050	1,100	1,200	1,300	1,450
Cash expenses	(700)	(745)	(790)	(880)	(970)	(1,105)
Depreciation	(200)	(200)	(200)	(200)	(200)	(200)
Net income	100	105	110	120	130	145

Shortlife Company	Year 1	2	3	4	5	6
Sales	1,000	1,050	1,100	1,200	1,300	1,450
Cash expenses	(700)	(745)	(790)	(880)	(970)	(1,105)
Depreciation	(200)	(200)	(200)	(200)	(200)	(200)
Net income	100	105	110	120	130	145

Exhibit 3.2 **PROJECTED CASH FLOW OF LONGLIFE AND SHORTLIFE COMPANIES**

Longlife Company	Year 1	2	3	4	5	6	Cumu-lative
Net income	100	105	110	120	130	145	710
Depreciation	200	200	200	200	200	200	1,200
Capital ex-penditures	(600)	0	0	(600)	0	0	(1,200)
Incr in receivables	(250)	(13)	(13)	35	45	(23)	(219)
Cash to/(from) shareholders	(550)	292	297	(245)	375	322	491

Shortlife Company	Year 1	2	3	4	5	6	Cumu-lative
Net income	100	105	110	120	130	145	710
Depreciation	200	200	200	200	200	200	1,200
Capital ex-penditures	(200)	(200)	(200)	(200)	(200)	(200)	(1,200)
Incr in receivables	(150)	(8)	(8)	(15)	(15)	(23)	(219)
Cash to/(from) shareholders	(50)	97	102	105	115	122	491

uses equipment that must be replaced every year but costs one-third what Longlife's equipment costs. In addition, Shortlife does a better job of collecting its receivables.

Now which one would you pay more for? Most people would pay more for Shortlife, because most people prefer to have cash now rather than later. Note that the total cash flow over the entire six-year period is the same for both companies, although Shortlife shareholders get their cash earlier. In fact, if you discounted these cash flows to the beginning of year one at 10 percent, you would see that the present value of Shortlife's cash flow ($323) is about 50 percent larger than the present value of Longlife's cash flows ($212).

This example illustrates the accounting approach's main weakness: It does not consider the investment required to generate earnings or its timing. Longlife Company has less value than Shortlife because it invests more capital (or the same amount of capital earlier) to generate the same level of sales and earnings. The accounting approach ignores the difference by concentrating on the P/E ratio as a function of expected earnings growth.

The DCF model, however, comprehends the difference in value by factoring in the capital expenditures and other cash flows required to generate the earnings. This approach is widely used by companies to evaluate capital spending proposals. The DCF model applies this approach to entire businesses, which are effectively just collections of individual projects.

As we will demonstrate formally in Chapter 5, the DCF approach is based on the simple concept that an investment adds value if it generates a return on investment above the return that can be earned on investments of similar risk. In other words, for a given level of earnings, a company with higher returns on investment will need to invest less capital in the business and will, in turn, generate higher cash flows and higher value.

So why has the accounting approach persisted all these years? Like most things that stand the test of time, it works very well in certain situations. When earnings reflect cash flow (e.g., businesses with little capital), the accounting approach provides a reasonably good proxy for discounted cash flow. It is when earnings and cash flow diverge that the accounting approach comes up short.

For example, suppose Longlife Company has just figured out a way to increase its earnings each year by 10 percent by increasing invested capital commensurably. Both the accounting approach and DCF analysis would suggest that the value of Longlife should increase by 10 percent as well, because both earnings and cash flow increase by 10 percent each year. So the accounting approach would appear to be incrementally correct in this situation.

Now suppose that Longlife's controller has figured out a way to increase the first year's earnings by 10 percent by recording some revenues in year one that would otherwise appear in year two. The increase in year one's earnings is exactly offset by the decrease in year 2's. The most extreme accounting approach would say that the value of Longlife has increased by 10 percent. As we will see in the next section, it is possible to create a more sophisticated accounting model. This model would see higher year one earnings but a lower growth rate and reduce the P/E ratio accordingly so the increase in value would be lower. (But how do you figure out the right P/E ratio?) In any event, the DCF model would not be fooled. Cash flow has not changed, so Longlife's value would be unchanged in the DCF model.

A REFINED ACCOUNTING MODEL

Before maligning the accounting approach too much, we should show how to develop a more sophisticated accounting model that mimics the DCF model pretty well under some circumstances. This entails finding a way to incorporate the *quality* of earnings into the P/E ratio so that we can differentiate between companies with identical earnings but different cash flows or risks.

Let us construct another simple example, using Value Inc. and Volume Inc., as shown in Exhibit 3.3. Both companies have identical earnings once again, but Value Inc. has a larger cash flow. Let us value the companies using DCF analysis.

If we assume both companies have identical risk, we can discount their cash flows at the same discount rate, say 10 percent. Both companies also continue their respective earnings and cash flow growth rates forever. Using some algebra that helps us deal with growing perpetuities, we can compute the value of Value Inc. to be $1,500 and Volume Inc. to be $1,000. This also means that Value Inc. has a P/E ratio of 15 and Volume Inc. of 10.

Exhibit 3.3 **CASH FLOWS OF VALUE INC. AND VOLUME INC.**

Value Inc.	Year 1	2	3	4	5	. . .
Net income	100	105	110	116	122	. . .
Net investment	(25)	(26)	(28)	(29)	(30)	. . .
Cash to/(from) shareholders	75	79	83	87	91	. . .

Volume Inc.	Year 1	2	3	4	5	. . .
Net income	100	105	110	116	122	. . .
Net investment	(50)	(53)	(55)	(58)	(61)	. . .
Cash to/(from) shareholders	50	53	55	58	61	. . .

The key to Value Inc.'s larger cash flow and higher value is that it does not invest as much capital to generate additional earnings. For example, Value Inc. invests only $25 in the first year to generate $5 additional earnings the next year, while Volume Inc. invests $50 to generate the same incremental earnings. Value Inc. earns a return of 20 percent on its new capital, while Volume Inc. earns a return of only 10 percent on its new capital.

In this simplified world, we can develop a simple formula that allows us to predict the P/E ratios of the two companies.[1] That formula is as follows:

$$\text{P/E ratio} = \frac{1 - g/r}{k - g}.$$

where

g = the long-term growth rate in earnings and cash flow.

r = the rate of return earned on new investment.

k = the discount rate.

This formula correctly calculates the P/E ratios for Value Inc. and Volume Inc.

For Value Inc.:

$$\text{P/E} = \frac{1 - (5\%/20\%)}{10\% - 5\%} = 15.$$

For Volume Inc.:

$$\text{P/E} = \frac{1 - (5\%/10\%)}{10\% - 5\%} = 10.$$

This formula improves the performance of the accounting valuation approach by adding investment and risk to the equation. But it also highlights the shortcomings of the naive accounting model. For example, what is the impact on Value Inc.'s value if it can increase its growth rate from 5 percent to 8 percent, while the return on incremental capital declines from 20 percent to 10 percent? The basic

---

[1] See Chapter 9, "Estimating Continuing Value" and Appendix A for the derivation of this formula.

accounting model suggests that Value Inc.'s value will increase as a result of the higher earnings growth. Our formula, however, tells us that the new P/E ratio should be ten and the resulting value should be $1,000, a substantial decline in value. So higher growth in this situation will yield a decline in value, but only the refined accounting model leads us to the right conclusion.

While our refined accounting approach works pretty well in a simplified world, it begins to break down once we add real-world complications.

- Varying accounting treatments for inventories, depreciation, and other items make it difficult to measure the incremental return on investment consistently across companies.
- Inflation distorts the relationship of accounting earnings to cash flow.
- Cyclicality is not dealt with by the accounting model, which attempts to capture an entire cycle in a single P/E ratio.
- The pattern of investments and their returns is not so simple that investments are made in one year and earn constant returns in all succeeding years.
- The base level of earnings must be normalized to eliminate any nonrecurring items.

We could develop an extremely complex version of the accounting model to handle these and other considerations, but in most cases the DCF model is simpler to work with since it already explicitly incorporates key valuation parameters like investment and risk.

IS THE STOCK MARKET NAIVE?

We have shown that the DCF model is conceptually superior to the accounting model. To be useful, however, it must also reflect how the stock market actually behaves. We are often confronted by managers who suggest that even though they agree with the DCF model, the market just does not behave that way: the market naively responds only to short-term earnings fluctuations.

It is true that the market does respond to quarterly earnings reports. The market would be foolish not to, because these earnings reports often convey important information. For example, increases in quarterly earnings often signal higher levels of cash flow in the future. Therefore earnings reports also matter to the DCF model, but they are not the only thing that matters.

As *The Wall Street Journal* editorial from which we quoted earlier asserts, the market is not fooled by cosmetic earnings increases; only earnings increases that are associated with improved long-term cash flow will increase share prices. Substantial evidence supports the view that the market takes a sophisticated approach to assessing accounting earnings. This evidence can be grouped into three classes:

1. Evidence that accounting earnings are not very well correlated with share prices.
2. Evidence that earnings window dressing does not improve share prices.
3. Evidence that the market evaluates management decisions based on their expected long-term cash flow impact, not their short-term earnings impact.

Accounting Earnings Are Not Well Correlated with Share Prices

According to the accounting model, a strong correlation should exist between earnings-per-share (EPS) growth and shareholder returns. Exhibit 3.4 uses P/E ratios as a proxy for how investors value earnings growth to show that the actual correlation between P/E ratios and earnings growth for the nonfinancial companies in the S&P 500 index. (There are 420 companies in the index; this exhibit shows only the 263 companies with P/E ratios between 0 and 50 and with average EPS growth from 1987–1991 between −30 percent and 30 percent.) In fact, many of the companies on the chart have strong earnings growth but low P/E ratios. (Unfortunately, we can only observe historical growth not projected growth, but read on.)

A comparison of Albertson's and Giant Food, two major supermarket chains, highlights the weak correlation between earnings growth and shareholder returns. As you can see in Exhibit 3.5, the earnings-per-share growth of the two companies was about equal during the period 1979–87, but Giant's shareholders were three times as well off as Albertson's at the end of that period. One dollar invested in Albertson's in 1978 was worth $8 at the end of 1987

Exhibit 3.4 **LOW CORRELATION BETWEEN EPS GROWTH AND P/E RATIO FOR S&P NONFINANCIAL COMPANIES**

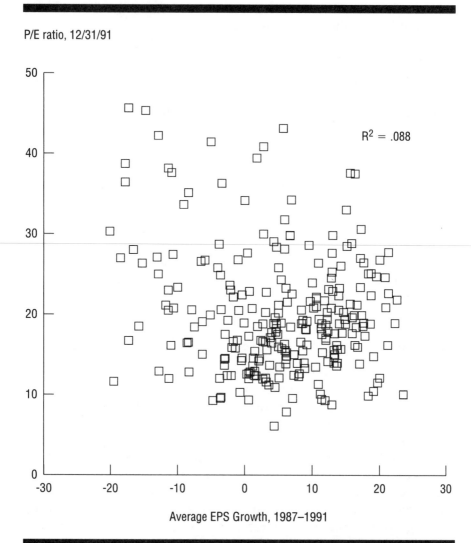

P/E ratio, 12/31/91

$R^2 = .088$

Average EPS Growth, 1987–1991

(including dividends), while the same amount invested in Giant was worth $25. This can be clearly explained by the companies' return on equity over the nine years. Albertson's return on equity declined steadily while Giant's improved substantially. These changes were due to fundamental business improvements by Giant relative to Albertson's.

Exhibit 3.5 **SHAREHOLDER VALUE AND EPS GROWTH, GIANT FOOD VS. ALBERTSON'S**

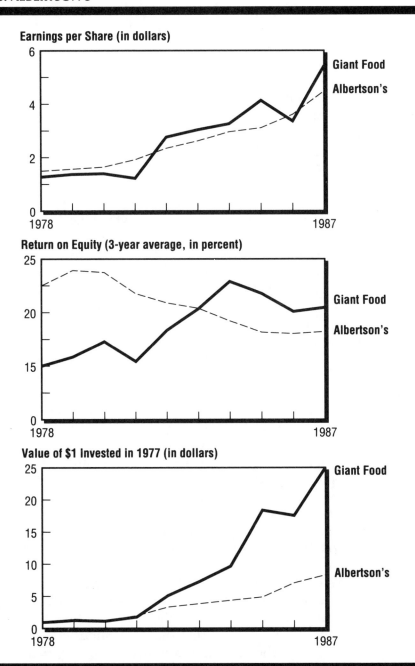

Earnings per Share (in dollars)

Giant Food

Albertson's

Return on Equity (3-year average, in percent)

Giant Food

Albertson's

Value of $1 Invested in 1977 (in dollars)

Giant Food

Albertson's

- Giant's operating margin improved; Albertson's declined. As a result, Albertson's sales had to grow faster to generate the same earnings growth.
- Giant's inventory turnover improved; Albertson's deteriorated.

So it is clear that earnings growth is a poor indicator of value creation. We stated earlier and will develop formally in Chapter 5, that companies create value when they earn a return on their investment in capital greater than their opportunity cost of capital. We would, therefore, expect companies that earn higher returns on capital relative to their cost of capital to have higher values. Unfortunately, return on invested capital by itself cannot explain company values for the same reason that growth alone does not determine value. Other factors matter. Consider two companies starting at the same point and with identical expected returns on capital over their cost of capital. However, one company plans to invest twice as much as the other. As a result, the company with higher investment and faster growth should have a higher value despite identical returns on capital. It follows that both growth and return on invested capital should drive value.

We tested this logic by measuring the market values of all the nonfinancial companies in the S&P 500 (a total of 420 companies) against their five-year growth in sales and five-year average spread in return on invested capital versus their opportunity cost of capital. The companies' market values were divided by their book values of equity to adjust for size differences. The results are shown in Exhibit 3.6. Each box represents a set of companies with sales growth and spread within a certain range. The number in each box is the average market-to-book ratio for the companies in each box.

The results are consistent with our expectations. Looking across any level of growth, companies with higher spreads have higher market-to-book ratios. Looking down for various spread levels, the picture is more complicated and not as clear-cut. When spreads are positive or near zero, higher growth generally results in higher market-to-book ratios. However, when spreads are negative, higher growth does not necessarily mean higher market-to-book values. This is consistent with our assertion that companies create value through growth only when they are earning a positive spread.

Exhibit 3.6 **RELATIONSHIP BETWEEN MARKET VALUES, SPREADS, AND GROWTH FOR S&P NONFINANCIAL COMPANIES, MARKET-TO-BOOK RATIOS**

1987–91 Average sales growth rate	1987–91 Average spread (ROIC−Cost of Capital)				
	<−5%	−5% to −2%	−2% to +2%	2% to 5%	>5%
<3%	1.5	1.8	1.7	(*)	(*)
3%–6%	1.7	1.6	2.1	1.9	(*)
6%–9%	1.5	1.6	2.0	2.9	3.6
9–12%	1.3	2.0	2.3	4.0	5.1
12–15%	1.8	1.8	2.8	(*)	5.5
>15%	(*)	1.7	3.1	3.6	5.3

(*) 5 or fewer companies.

One peculiar aspect of the chart is that the average market-to-book ratios are universally greater than one, even when spreads are negative. This is due to two factors:

• Market values are based on expectations not historical performance. If the market expects improving performance, then market-to-book ratios would be higher than expected.

- The market-to-book values were measured at the end of 1991 when the level of interest rates in the economy was almost 2 percent lower than it had been during the five-year period when spreads were estimated. This means that going forward, the cost of capital for these companies would be approximately 2 percent lower than it had been and, therefore, if they earned the same returns, spreads would increase by 2 percent.

These results are not scientific proof and, unfortunately, we cannot test our hypothesis more directly by measuring future growth and returns. The results do, however, provide another piece of evidence that it is cash flow, driven by the combination of growth and spreads, that drives value not just growth in earnings.

We also applied the DCF approach to 35 companies, using forecasts from the Value Line Investment Survey, and found very strong correlations with the companies' market values (Exhibit 3.7). While not scientific, these results are consistent with our experience that DCF is very good at explaining companies' market values.

Earnings Window Dressing Does Not Help Share Prices

The accounting model also suggests that the market might be fooled by accounting techniques that improve earnings. Academic studies have shown that the market is not deceived by accounting techniques. The most persuasive of these studies have focused either on inventory accounting or on techniques used to account for mergers and acquisitions.

Inventory accounting is one area where the U.S. tax authorities require that the method used for financial reporting also be used for calculating taxable income. As a result, the choice of accounting method affects both earnings and cash flow, but in opposite directions. In periods of rising prices (for as long as any of the authors can remember), the last-in-first-out (LIFO) inventory method results in lower earnings than the first-in-first-out (FIFO) method, because the cost of goods sold is based on the more recent higher costs. Lower earnings means lower income taxes. Since the pretax cash flow is the same regardless of the accounting method, LIFO accounting leads to a higher after-tax cash flow than FIFO accounting, despite the lower reported earnings.

Exhibit 3.7 **HIGH CORRELATION BETWEEN MARKET VALUE AND DCF VALUE FOR 35 COMPANIES**

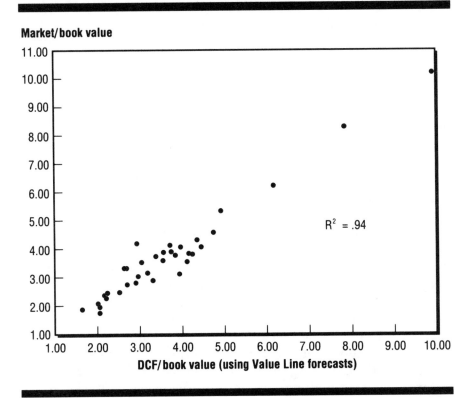

Market/book value

$R^2 = .94$

DCF/book value (using Value Line forecasts)

Source: McKinsey analysis.

A number of researchers have looked at the stock price reaction of companies that have switched from one accounting method to the other. The accounting model suggests that switching from FIFO to LIFO should result in a lower share price due to lower earnings, and vice versa.

Although the evidence is not entirely conclusive, some researchers have found, in fact, that switching from FIFO to LIFO results in a *higher* share price due to an increased cash flow, which is what the DCF model predicts. After adjusting for the market and other contemporaneous effects, firms switching to LIFO experienced significant share price increases, while firms switching to

FIFO saw their share price decline (see Exhibit 3.8). In fact, Biddle and Lindahl (1982) found that the larger the reduction in taxes resulting from the switch to LIFO was, the greater was the share price increase attributed to the change.[2]

Other studies that prove window dressing to be of little value involve mergers and acquisitions. A business combination that is accounted for as a purchase requires that the difference between the price paid for the target and the book value of its assets (with some adjustment) be recorded as an asset called goodwill and amortized over a period of generally 40 years. Under a pooling-of-interests accounting, on the other hand, the acquisition is reported at book value with no goodwill or amortization. Since goodwill amortization is not deductible for tax purposes, the company's cash flow is the same regardless of the accounting method. Reported earnings, however, are higher under pooling accounting, because there is no goodwill amortization.

The accounting model suggests that the market would react more favorably to pooling accounting than to purchase accounting because of the former's higher earnings. The DCF model suggests no difference, because cash flow would be the same. Hong, Kaplan, and Mandelker (1978) found no evidence that the market responds favorably to the higher earnings under a pooling-of-interests accounting.[3] Interestingly, companies using the purchase method performed better during the 12 months preceding the merger than companies using pooling. This is probably due to some self-selection bias. The poor performers are likely to attempt to improve their earnings through selective use of accounting techniques.

Sacrificing Long-Term Cash Flows for Short-Term Earnings Improvement Does Not Work

A lot of confusion about how the market evaluates accounting earnings has to do with the time frame of investors. Many managers believe the stock market focuses too narrowly on near-term earnings. They believe the market does not give credit for long-

---

[2] G. Biddle and F. Lindahl, "Stock Price Reactions to LIFO Adoptions: The Association Between Excess Returns and LIFO Tax Savings," *Journal of Accounting Research* (Autumn 1982): 551–548.

[3] H. Hong, R. Kaplan, and G. Mandelker, "Pooling vs. Purchase: The Effects of Accounting for Mergers on Stock Prices," *Accounting Review* Vol. 53 (1978): 31–47.

Exhibit 3.8 **EFFECT OF INVENTORY ACCOUNTING CHANGE
ON SHARE VALUE**

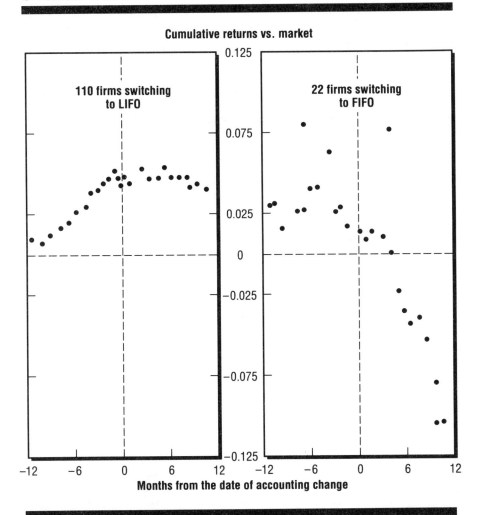

Cumulative returns vs. market

110 firms switching to LIFO

22 firms switching to FIFO

Months from the date of accounting change

Source: S. Sunder, "The Relationship Between Accounting Changes and Stock Prices: Problems of Measurement and Some Empirical Evidence," *Empirical Research in Accounting: Selected Studies* (1973): 18.

term investments. A quick look at the high values the stock market has placed on emerging biotechnology companies—without any earnings or even any products to sell in many cases—should be evidence enough that the market takes a long view, but we provide some systematic evidence as well.

We can perform a simple test of the time horizon of the stock market by examining how much of a company's current share price can be accounted for by its expected dividends over the next several years. For a random sample of 20 Fortune 500 companies, as shown in Exhibit 3.9, an average of only 11.8 percent of the total

Exhibit 3.9 **PRESENT VALUE OF EXPECTED DIVIDENDS VS. SHARE PRICE FOR 20 FORTUNE 500 COMPANIES, OCTOBER 1988**

Company	Share price	Present value of dividends expected over next 5 yrs.	Dividends as percentage of stock price
Aluminum Company of America	$55	$5.71	10.4%
Becton, Dickinson & Company	57	3.91	6.9
Bristol-Myers Company	45	8.10	18.0
Champion Spark Plug Company	13	1.03	7.9
Chesapeake Corp.	21	2.21	10.5
Coleman Company, Inc.	37	5.17	14.0
Esselte Business Systems, Inc.	33	3.79	11.5
Exxon Corporation	45	8.95	19.9
Fieldcrest Cannon, Inc.	22	2.56	11.6
Grumman Corp.	22	4.16	18.9
Jefferson Smurfit Corp.	27	1.92	7.1
Johnson Controls, Inc.	35	4.35	12.4
Lone Star Industries, Inc.	32	6.58	20.6
McDonnell Douglas Corporation	72	11.25	15.6
Medtronic, Inc.	80	5.30	6.6
Newmont Mining Corporation	36	2.61	7.2
Nucor Corp.	42	1.82	4.3
Reynolds Metals Company	54	4.08	7.6
Rohm and Haas Company	34	4.25	12.5
Westvaco Corp.	30	3.59	12.0
Average			11.8%

Source: Value Line; McKinsey analysis.

share value could be accounted for by dividends expected over the next five years. The largest percentage of value that the next five years' dividends could explain was 20.6 percent for Lone Star Industries. From this test, the market appears to take a long view. More rigorous analyses described in the following paragraphs also support this view.

We showed earlier that pure accounting manipulation does not fool the market. But managers can do other things to improve earnings at the expense of long-term cash flow. For example, they can reduce spending on research and development or capital goods. Reducing R&D spending will increase earnings (and cash flow) in the short run, potentially at the expense of developing profitable new products for the long run. Similarly, cutting back on value-adding capital spending will increase short-term profits because new capital projects often earn low profits in their earlier years.

A group of Securities and Exchange Commission economists examined the stock price reaction to announcements by 62 companies that they were embarking on R&D projects (Office of the Chief Economist, 1985).[4] As Exhibit 3.10 shows, the market had a significant positive reaction to these announcements.

To illustrate this, we looked at the R&D spending of six major pharmaceutical companies. R&D spending is generally treated as an expense in the year incurred, regardless of future benefits. Exhibit 3.11 shows that contrary to what the accounting model would suggest, the companies with the highest levels of spending on R&D tended to have the highest P/E ratios. While these results are not at all scientific, they do cast serious doubt on the view that the stock market penalizes companies that invest a lot in research and development.

The evidence on capital spending supports the DCF model as well. McConnell and Muscarella (1985) examined the stock market's reaction to announcements of increased capital expenditure levels.[5] They examined a sample of 349 such announcements, which contained no other company-specific information, by industrial firms from 1975 to 1981. On average, the stock market reacted

---

[4] Office of the Chief Economist, "Institutional Owners, Tender Offers, and Long-Term Investment," Washington D.C.: Securities and Exchange Commission, 1985.
[5] J. McConnell and C. Muscarella, "Corporate Capital Expenditure Decisions and the Market Value of the Firm," *Journal of Financial Economics* (March 1985): 399–422.

Exhibit 3.10 **STOCK MARKET REACTION TO RESEARCH AND DEVELOPMENT ANNOUNCEMENTS, AVERAGE OF 62 COMPANIES**

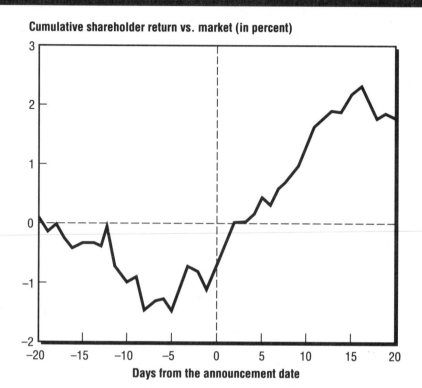

Source: Office of the Chief Economist, Securities and Exchange Commission (1985).

positively to spending increases and negatively to spending decreases for all industries except one. The results were the opposite for oil and gas exploration and development. Apparently, the market did not believe oil and gas exploration was a profitable investment at the time. Given the subsequent decline in oil prices and the high cost of exploration in the United States relative to other parts of the world, the market was probably right. In any case, it is clear that the market does not arbitrarily penalize companies for making long-term investments.

Conversely, the market also reacts favorably when companies write off bad investments, despite the negative short-term earnings impact. While the complex nature of write-offs prohibits compre-

Exhibit 3.11 **R&D SPENDING VS. P/E RATIOS FOR SIX MAJOR
PHARMACEUTICAL COMPANIES, OCTOBER 1988**

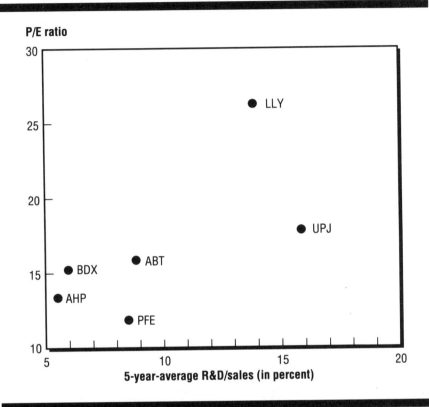

Source: Compustat, McKinsey analysis.

hensive statistical analysis, Mercer (1987) looked at 40 major write-offs from 1984 to 1986 and found that 60 percent of them resulted in share price increases. Furthermore, 75 percent of write-downs resulting from abandonment of entire businesses were associated with share price increases. The following summarizes the write-off experience of several companies.[6]

- Sohio's $163 million write-offs in 1984 of its Mukluk oil well in the Beaufort Sea led to a 6.5 percent increase in its share

[6] G. Mercer, "A Review of Major Corporate Writeoffs, 1984–86," unpublished manuscript, McKinsey & Co., 1987.

price around the announcement day. Poor drilling results had been announced previously and already were discounted in the share price. The write-off could be interpreted as good news if it meant that Sohio would no longer be committing cash to a losing effort.

- Beatrice took a $280 million write-off in 1983 as part of a long-term program to improve its future profitability, including write-downs of its Tropicana division, reserves for divestitures of 50 businesses, and a charge for the early retirement of some employees. Beatrice's share price increased 13 percent on the announcement. The announcement conveyed good news: management's realization of its past mistakes and its intention to avoid future mistakes.

- In contrast to the favorable reaction, Natomas suffered a 9 percent price decline following its $87 million write-off in 1982. In this case, however, the write-off resulted from a revised engineering survey indicating that oil reserves had been overestimated by six million barrels. The stock price decline is really attributable to the value lost in the future cash flow in the oil reserves rather than the accounting event itself.

Changes in leverage and the resulting impact on share prices and earnings per share provide another piece of evidence supporting the view that the market values cash not earnings. Copeland and Lee (1988) studied 161 exchange offers and stock swaps from 1962 to 1984.[7] The accounting model suggests that the earnings-per-share impact of the transaction determines the share price reaction. The study showed that the earnings-per-share EPS impact did not matter. What mattered was whether the transaction was leverage-increasing or leverage-decreasing. The average percentage changes in share value upon the announcement of the transactions relative to the changes in the market average were as follows:

	EPS-increasing transactions	EPS-decreasing transactions
Leverage-increasing transactions	3.77%	8.41
Leverage-decreasing transactions	−1.18	−0.41

[7] T. Copeland and W. H. Lee, "Exchange Offers and Stock Swaps—New Evidence," *Financial Management* 20, no. 3 (Autumn 1991): 34–48.

On average, leverage-decreasing transactions resulted in negative share price reactions, regardless of the earnings-per-share impact. Furthermore, Copeland and Lee concluded that the most likely explanation for the direction of the share price changes is that investors interpret these leverage-changing transactions as management's signals of future cash flow. For example, insiders could use leverage-increasing transactions to increase their ownership position and to exploit their superior knowledge regarding the future cash flows of their companies. Therefore, leverage-increasing transactions could signal strong cash flows in the future.

MARKET EFFICIENCY?

Sometimes managers point to evidence of inefficiencies in the stock market to justify their belief that the market behaves irrationally. These managers would argue that even financial academics are finding inefficiencies in the market, therefore any justification of the discounted cash flow approach does not square with the real world. While there is not much evidence against market efficiency, this argument ignores the time horizon of these supposed inefficiencies. We would argue that even if the market is inefficient for moderate periods of time, managers should make business decisions as if the market were efficient.

Ever since academics have suggested that the stock market behaves efficiently, researchers have been looking for anomalies to refute market efficiency. Market efficiency simply means that the market immediately incorporates all relevant, publicly available information about a company into its share price. In its weakest form, an efficient market is one in which patterns of historical prices cannot be used to earn excess returns. Recently, some researchers have used chaos theory borrowed from physics and advanced computer techniques to find market inefficiencies. They claim they can identify patterns in the way markets respond to new information and can use those patterns to earn excess returns through various investment strategies. These assertions remain untested in the academic literature. But let us assume that these researchers are correct. What are the implications for investors and corporate managers? For investors, this represents an opportunity to make money. Unfortunately, to exploit these inefficiencies requires massive computing power and minute-by-minute trading decisions. As is typical with most market inefficiencies, only the biggest and quickest investors are likely to benefit. Furthermore, once these inefficiencies become well known, they usually disappear and the search is on for new inefficiencies.

What about corporate managers? As long as your company's share price eventually gets back to its long run DCF value, you might as well use the DCF approach for strategic decisions and not worry about short-term anomalies that you cannot do much about. What should matter to you as a manager making business decisions is the long-term behavior of your company's share price, not whether it is 5 percent undervalued this week. Of course, if you can systematically identify when your company's stock is misvalued, you may try to use that information in determining when you sell more shares or buy back shares. But for strategic business decisions, the evidence we have presented strongly suggests that, over time, the market behaves more like it is using the DCF approach than the accounting approach.

SUMMARY

Managers who use the DCF approach to valuation, focusing on increasing long-term free cash flow, ultimately will be rewarded by higher share prices. The evidence from the market is conclusive. Naive attention to accounting earning will lead to value destroying decisions.

REVIEW QUESTIONS

1. Describe the accounting model of value. What elements of a comprehensive value management scheme would accounting earnings miss?

2. How does a discounted cash flow measurement make up for the shortcomings of the pure accounting approach?

3. Amend the accounting approach's use of P/E ratios to incorporate the quality of earnings. Under what circumstances does this model examine value in the same way as the DCF approach?

4. In what ways does the financial markets approach the question of valuing a firm's operations and use of assets?

5. What accounts for a positive correlation between sales growth and the return-on-invested-capital–cost-of-capital spread?

6. What support exists in the market for the view that investors take the long-term view of current managerial decisions?

7. R&D is treated by the accounting principle of conservatism as an expense in the first year. How does the market value R&D? Why would the market be justified?

8. Describe examples of earnings window dressing. Can any of these methods increase value? How might it be possible for these methods to destroy value?

9. What is market efficiency? Does market efficiency conflict with managerial determination of value?

10. Summarize the economic dimensions of cash flow valuation of management's decisions by markets.

4

Value-Based Management

In Chapter 2, Ralph Demsky used valuation analysis to develop a restructuring strategy to maximize the value of EG Corporation. That strategy included both actions to dispose of certain underperforming businesses as well as plans for refocusing the strategies of individual business units. Ralph realized though that this one-time restructuring was not sufficient for long-term value creation. He needed some way to transform his entire organization into a value maximizing one, and he found that way in value-based management (VBM).

VBM is based on the concepts discussed earlier. Company value is determined by its discounted future cash flows, and value is created only when companies invest capital at returns that exceed the cost of that capital. VBM takes these concepts further by focusing on how companies use them to make major strategic and everyday operating decisions. Properly executed, VBM is an approach to management whereby the company's overall aspirations, analytical techniques, and management processes are all aligned to help the company maximize its value by focusing management decision making on the key drivers of value.

VBM is very different from 1960s style planning systems. It is not a staff-driven exercise. It focuses on better decision making at all levels in an organization. It recognizes that top-down command-and-control style decision making cannot work well, especially in large multibusiness corporations. Consequently, frontline managers must learn to use value-based performance metrics for making better decisions. It requires managing the balance sheet as well as the income statement, and balancing long-term with short-term perspectives. When VBM is implemented well, the corporation receives tremendous benefit. It is like restructuring to achieve maximum value on a continuing basis. It works. It has high impact that can often be measured in improved economic performance, as illustrated in Exhibit 4.1.

Yet value-based management is not without pitfalls. Value-based management can become a staff-captured exercise that has no effect on operating managers at the front line or on the decisions that they make. Like 1960s style corporate planning, VBM can conjure images of a large corporate staff of specialists that has no line management experience, spends most of its time worrying about how to predict macroeconomic variables like GDP, and has little or no understanding of competitive strategy at the business-unit level. Instead of value-based management, a company in this situation simply has value veneering.

We saw an example of this a few years ago when the chief planning officer of a large western company invited us to attend a dry run of the presentation he and his planning staff intended to give to his chief financial officer and board of directors. For about two hours we listened to details on how each business unit had been valued—cash flow forecasts, cost of capital and a capital structure separately estimated for each business unit, and the assumptions that had gone into calculating continuing value. When the time came for us to comment, we had to say that the team deserved an A+ grade for their valuation skills. Their methodology was impeccable. But the team deserved an F for management content. None of the company's significant strategic or operating issues were on the table. The team had not even talked to any of the operating managers at the group or business-unit level. In short, the presentation was boring and of little interest to the real decision makers. It was a staff-captured exercise that would have little or no impact on how the company was run.

The lesson? Value-based management is an *integrative* process designed to improve strategic and operational decision making throughout an organization by focusing on the *key drivers of corporate value*. But the focus of VBM should not be on methodology. It should be on the why and how of changing your corporate culture.

Exhibit 4.1 **IMPACT OF VBM ON PERFORMANCE, EXAMPLES**

Business	Change in behavior	Impact
Retail household goods	• Shifted from broad national growth program to focus on building regional scale before expanding	• 30–40% potential value increase
Insurance	• Repositioned product portfolio to emphasize products most likely to create value	• 25% potential value increase
Oil production	• Used new planning and control process to help drive major change program; dramatic improvement in corporate-business dialogue	• Multimillion dollar reduction in planning function through streamlining • Acquisition that likely would not have otherwise happened • Exposed nonperforming managers
Bank	• Chose growth versus harvest strategy, even though five-year return on equity very similar	• 124% potential value increase

Telecommunications	• Generated ideas for value creation
	  – New service
	
	  – Premium pricing
	
	• Around 40% of planned developement projects in one business unit discontinued
	• Sales force expansion plans completely revised after discovering how much value expansion would destroy
		
		• 240% potential value increase in one unit
		• 246% potential value increase in one unit
		• n/a
		
		• n/a

A value-based manager is as interested in the subtleties of organizational behavior as in using valuation for a performance metric and decision-making tool.

In a well-functioning VBM organization, the management processes, such as planning and performance measurement, provide decision makers at all levels of the organization with the right information and incentives to make value creating decisions. For example, the manager of a business unit would have the information to quantify and compare the value of alternative business-unit strategies. He or she would then be encouraged to choose the value maximizing strategy because of specific financial targets set by senior management, because of evaluation and compensation systems that reinforce value creation, and probably—most importantly—because of the strategy review process with his or her superiors. The manager would also be evaluated based on long- and short-term targets that measure progress toward meeting the overall value creation objective.

VBM operates at other levels as well. Line managers and supervisors can have targets and performance measures tailored, to their particular circumstances, that are driven by the overall business-unit strategy. For example, the production manager might have targets set for cost per unit, quality, and turnaround time. The long- and short-term goals for each subunit or functional area can be set so that, when combined, they accomplish the business unit's overall goals. VBM also works at the very top of the organization. It informs the board of directors and corporate center about the value of their strategies and helps them to evaluate mergers, acquisitions and divestitures.

In addition, VBM can be a key component in improving organizational effectiveness, because it provides an unambiguous and precise performance metric—namely value—upon which to build an organization. In recent years, the press and business books have been full of new approaches for improving organizational performance via total quality management (TQM), flatter organizations, empowerment, continuous improvement, reengineering the organization, Kaizen, team-building, and so on. Although many of these have succeeded, quite a few have failed. In most cases, the failures have been due to a lack of clear performance targets or a misalignment between targets and the goal of creating shareholder value.

Consider total quality management. We have seen a number of companies set up sophisticated TQM programs only to abandon them after several years when they showed no results. These failed programs almost always lacked an underlying, meaningful performance objective. They would often measure their results in terms of inputs (i.e., the number of quality teams established) rather than bottom-line impact on the business (e.g., did customer turnaround time improve?) Lack of value-oriented performance targets and measures contributed to failure.

Recently Dichter, Gagnon and Alexander examined the efforts of more than 30 organizations to improve their performance and developed what they call the six "natural laws" of organizational transformation.[1] VBM plays a critical role in four of the crucial aspects of organizational change:

1. Performance is the objective. VBM helps define the specific financial performance objectives that companies should adopt.

2. Strategy and structure still matter. VBM helps companies decide between alternative strategies and helps them assess the resources necessary to achieve their selected strategies.

3. Teams are key building blocks. They need clear performance targets and follow-up measurement. VBM helps companies set these targets.

4. Focus is essential. Focus means trade-offs. By identifying key value drivers, VBM provides a way for companies to make trade-offs between competing objectives.

Value-based management can best be understood as a marriage between a value creation mindset and the management processes and systems that are necessary to translate that mindset into action. Taken alone, either element is insufficient. Taken together, they can have a huge and sustained impact:

- *A value creation mindset* ensures that members of senior management are clear among themselves that their ultimate financial objective is maximizing value, and they have clear rules for deciding when other objectives, such as employment or environmental goals, outweigh maximizing value. Furthermore, they have a solid analytical understanding of which performance variables drive the value of the company. For example, managers must know whether increasing revenue growth or improving margins will create more value, and they must ensure that the strategy in place focuses resources and attention on the key performance variables. VBM analytical tools, such as DCF valuation and value

[1] S. Dichter, C. Gagnon, and A. Alexander, "Memo to a CEO: Leading Organizational Transformations," *McKinsey Quarterly* 1 (1993): 89–106.

driver analysis, provide companies with the tools needed to make value creating decisions.

- *Management processes and systems* encourage managers and other employees to behave in a way that maximizes the value of the organization. They include the planning, target setting, performance measurement, and incentive systems that every company needs to run its business. These processes are working effectively when the communication within the organization during planning, budgeting, and other decision making sessions is tightly linked to value creation.

In the remainder of this chapter we will go into greater detail about what we mean by a value mindset—what to do—and the management process—how to do it. We'll also provide examples of the formidable challenges companies face in making the transition to full-fledged VBM. Like any large scale change effort, adopting a value-based orientation is a long and complex process that must balance soft organizational issues with complex strategic questions and the hard analytics of discounted cash flow valuation.

THE VALUE MINDSET

The first step in VBM is embracing value maximization as the ultimate *financial* objective for the company. Furthermore, senior management must know how this financial objective weighs in against other objectives.

In general, companies must have two sets of goals: financial goals, which guide senior management, and inspirational nonfinancial goals, which motivate the performance of the entire organization. In Chapter 3, we made the case that traditional financial performance measures, such as earnings or earnings growth, were not always good proxies for value creation, and that companies should focus more directly on creating value. This means that companies should set goals in terms of discounted cash flow values, the most direct measures of value creation. As we will see later in this chapter, DCF value targets also need to be translated into shorter term, more objective financial performance targets, such as economic profit.

In addition to financial objectives, companies need nonfinancial objectives to inspire and guide the behavior of employees, many of whom will not care about financial value creation. These may include goals about customer satisfaction, product innovation, and employee satisfaction, among others. We do not view these as contradicting value maximization. Usually the most financially successful companies are also the ones that excel in the areas of customer satisfaction, innovation, and employee satisfaction. Nonfinancial goals must, however, be carefully considered in light of the company's financial circumstances. For example, a defense contractor in the U.S., where shrinkage is a certainty, should not adopt a no layoff objective. The important element is to get everyone in the organization pointed in the same direction.

Objectives must also be tailored to the level of the organization. For the head of the business unit, this may mean explicit value creation measured in financial terms. For a functional manager, it may mean some combination of customer service, market share, product quality, or productivity. A manufacturing manager might focus on cost per unit, cycle time, or defect rate. Product development, on the other hand, might focus on the time it takes to develop a new product, the number of new products developed, and how those new products compare to the competition.

Focusing on financial goals for now, we see that managers are often confronted with many choices, for example, growth in earnings per share, maximizing the price-earnings ratio or the market-to-book ratio, and increasing the return on assets, to name a few. We strongly believe that value is the only correct performance objective. The next section explains why and gives a few examples of companies that drifted off course because they were making decision based on metrics other than value.

Value, Not Something Else

Exhibit 4.2 compares various measures of corporate performance along two dimensions: the need for taking a long-term point of view and the need to manage the company's balance sheet. Only discounted cash flow valuation (or multi-year economic profit) handles both adequately. Companies that focus on this year's net income or on return on sales take a myopic point of view and also tend to ignore major balance sheet opportunities, such as working

Exhibit 4.2 **KEY METRICS REQUIRED FOR DIFFERENT COMPANY SITUATIONS**

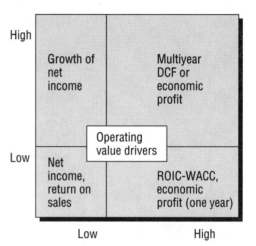

Need for long-term view

- High probability of significant industry change
  — Technology
  — Regulation
  — Competition
- Long life of investments
- Complexity of business portfolio

Capital intensity (need for balance sheet focus)

- Working capital
- Property, plant, and equipment

capital improvement or capital expenditure efficiency. Decision making can be heavily influenced by the choice of a performance metric. Shifting to a value mindset can make an enormous difference. The following cases provide real-life examples of how focusing on value, rather than other metrics of performance, can transform decision making.

Managing the balance sheet   Company X is a large consumer products company with about 50 business units. The performance of every business unit was measured by its operating margin or return on sales (ROS). Exhibit 4.3 shows that Company X was "doing better" than the average of its competitors because it was earning a 15.1 percent ROS versus only 14.3 percent for its average competitor. By the way, in this particular industry it was easy to find good comparables, i.e., companies that were very similar. But Company X had a problem. Its stock price was not performing well vis-a-vis its competitors. Management was dissatisfied and beginning to ask

Exhibit 4.3 **COMPANY X RETURN ON INVESTED CAPITAL VERSUS COMPETITOR'S AVERAGE,** PERCENT

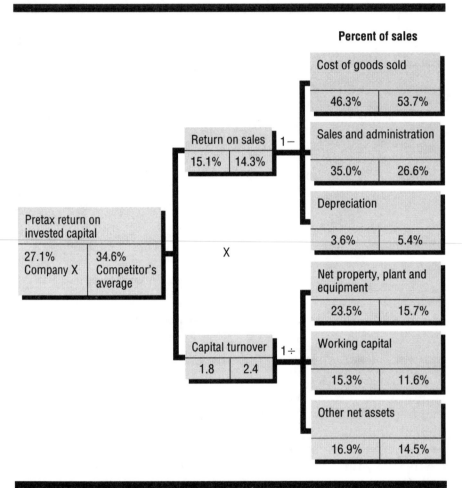

questions. No one could understand why the stock market "didn't appreciate" the company's success. Taking the analysis a little further, we see that Company X's ROIC (pretax) was 27.1 percent while competitors earned 34.6 percent. Company X was using the wrong performance metric. By using return on sales, it was completely ignoring balance sheet management. Consequently, its capital turnover (sales divided by invested capital) was only 1.8 versus 2.4 for its competitors.

All told, the impact of improvement in the balance sheet amounted to roughly $500 million. Of that total, $146 million was improved management of working capital, particularly inventories. Because of its emphasis on sales, Company X was overproducing and carrying excess inventories to minimize the probability of stockout. Periodic write-downs were required due to obsolete and outdated inventories. Inventory management was a shambles. An even larger value creation opportunity was found in consolidating manufacturing operations. Several plants in adjacent geographical areas were underutilized. When the least productive were closed and output shifted to the most productive facilities, two benefits emerged. First, less capital was employed to produce the same finished goods; and second, the product was produced more efficiently, causing operating margins to go up. The value of consolidating operations was about $364 million.

Company X was not managing its balance sheet because of its emphasis on the wrong performance metric—return on sales. When it moved to ROIC and to value creation, it discovered opportunities that were being missed completely.

Taking a long view   Company Y is a money center bank. One of its largest divisions, the retail bank, had been pursuing a "harvest strategy." It had been underinvesting and taking cash out of the business. Unfortunately, it had also been losing market share, albeit slowly over an extended period of time. The new chief operating officer of the retail bank wanted to spend roughly $100 million on a plan to recapture market share by refurbishing branch bank facilities, installing new automatic teller machines, training tellers for better customer satisfaction, and initiating a new aggressive advertising campaign. This alternative was called the "aggressive growth" strategy. The assumption was that this new program would allow the retail bank to recapture market share at the same slow rate at which it had been lost—a fairly conservative approach.

The bank's planning system required that all large programs be carefully documented. The crucial decision variable was return on equity (ROE) projected over the next three years, as shown in Exhibit 4.4. When the results were shown to the bank's CEO, his reaction was predictable. The ROE for the aggressive growth strategy was lower than the harvest strategy for the first year, about the same the second year, and only slightly higher in the third year. Initially, the CEO could not understand how the aggressive growth strategy could be better, but he changed his opinion when he saw

---

Exhibit 4.4 **FORECASTED RETURN ON EQUITY FOR A RETAIL BANK**

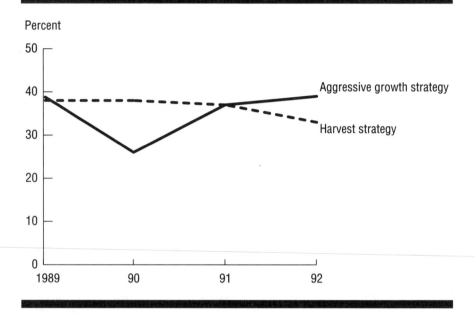

the value creation potential of the new strategy. It resulted in a 124 percent increase in value over the harvest strategy, worth better than $450 million. Why did the return on equity and the value creation performance metrics give such different answers in this case? The reason is that most of the assumed value creation potential of the project was beyond the three-year time frame that was used for making ROE comparisons at the bank. Valuation requires a long-run point of view, because the value of a strategy cannot be estimated without forecasting the cash flows over the long run.

FINDING THE VALUE DRIVERS

An important part of VBM is a deep understanding of what performance variables will actually drive the value of the business. We call them *key value drivers*. There are two reasons such an understanding is essential. First, the organization cannot act directly on value. It has to act on things it can influence, such as customer satisfaction, cost, capital expenditures, and so on. Second, it is through these drivers of value that senior management learns to understand the rest of the organization and to establish a dialogue about what it expects to be accomplished.

A value driver is simply any variable that affects the value of the company. To be useful, however, value drivers need to be organized so we can identify which have the greatest impact on value and assign responsibility for their performance to individuals who can help the organization meet its targets.

Value drivers must be developed down to the level of detail that aligns the value driver with the decision variables directly under the control of line management. Generic value drivers, such as sales growth, operating margins, and capital turns, apply equally well to nearly all business units, but lack specificity and cannot be used well at the grassroots level. Exhibit 4.5 shows that value drivers can be useful at three levels: the generic level, where operating margins and invested capital are combined to compute ROIC; the business-unit level, where variables such as customer mix are particularly relevant; and operating value drivers at the grassroots level, where great detail is needed to tie value drivers to specific decisions that frontline managers have under their control.

Exhibit 4.6 illustrates value drivers for the customer servicing function of a telecommunications company. Value driver trees like this one are usually linked into ROIC trees, which are, in turn, linked into multiperiod cash flows and valuation of the business unit. Total customer service expense, on the left-hand side of Exhibit 4.6, was an expense line item in the income statement of several business units. Efficiency improvements in this key function would, therefore, affect the value of many parts of the company. As you can see, five levels of detail were used to get down to useful operational value drivers. The "span of control," for example, was defined as the ratio of supervisors to workers. A small improvement in this ratio had a large impact on the value of the company without affecting the quality of customer service. Percent occupancy is the fraction of total work hours that are spent occupying an operator station. Relatively small changes here also have a major impact on value. What is important is the fact that these key value drivers, although only a small part of the total business system, have a significant impact on value, are measurable from month to month, and are clearly under the control of line management.

To illustrate how the numbers might work, consider a partial list of the value drivers for a hard goods retailer as shown in

Exhibit 4.5 **VARIOUS LEVELS OF VALUE DRIVER IDENTIFICATION**

LEVEL 1	LEVEL 2	LEVEL 3
	Examples	**Examples**

```
                                         Examples              Examples

                         Revenue    • Customer mix        • Percent
                                    • Sales force           accounts
              Margin                  productivity          revolving
                                      (expense:           • Dollars
                                      revenue)              per visit
                         Costs                             • Unit revenues

                                    • Fixed cost/         • Billable hours
                                      allocations           to total
                                    • Capacity             payroll hours
 ROIC                                 management         • Percent
                                    • Operational          capacity
                                      yield                utilized
                                                          • Cost per
                         Working                            delivery
                         capital
                                                          • Accounts
              Invested                                      receivable
              capital                                       terms &
                                                            timing
                         Fixed                            • Accounts
                         capital                            payable terms
                                                            & timing
```

Generic	Business-unit specific	Operating value drivers (grassroots level)

Exhibit 4.7. The value of the company is partially driven by gross margin, warehouse costs, and delivery costs. Gross margin, in turn, is determined by gross margin per transaction and the number of transactions. Gross margin per transaction and the number of transactions can be further disaggregated if necessary. Warehouse costs are a function of the number of retail stores per warehouse

Exhibit 4.6 CUSTOMER SERVICING—HUMAN EXPENSE FLOWCHART

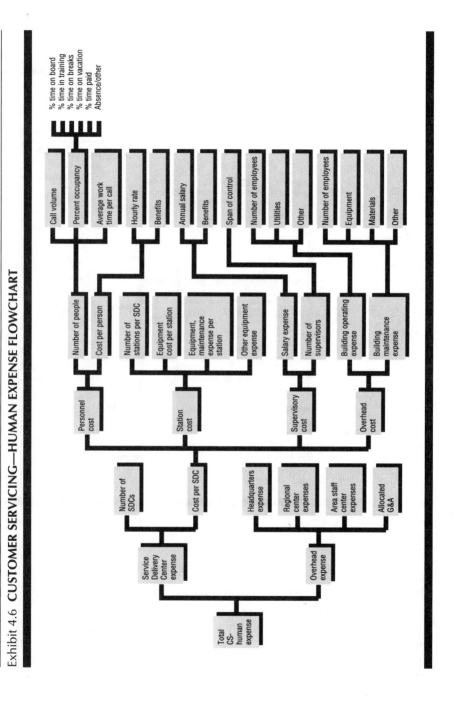

Exhibit 4.7 **VALUE DRIVERS FOR A HYPOTHETICAL HARD GOODS RETAILER**

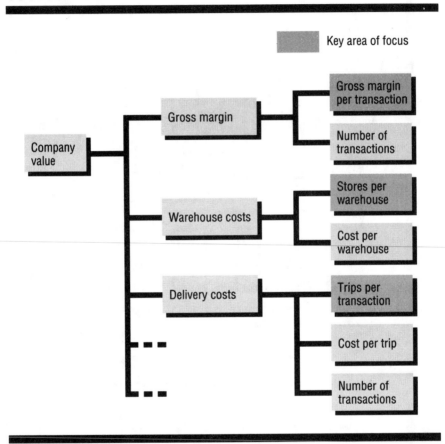

and the cost per warehouse. Finally, delivery costs are determined by the number of trips per transaction, the cost per trip, and the number of transactions.

Analysis of these variables showed that the number of stores per warehouse significantly affected the cost per transaction as there were substantial scale economies in the warehouse operation. The more stores that could be served out of one warehouse, the lower the warehouse costs relative to revenues. This effect was substantial enough to suggest that a strategy of growth through metropolitan concentration rather than a shotgun approach of opening stores scattered over many metropolitan areas would lead to much higher value. So, number of stores per warehouse became a strategic value driver for this organization because of its impact and its long-term nature.

Further analysis showed that the number of delivery trips per transaction was very high. As almost all the company's sales required delivery directly to the customer, delivery costs were a significant factor in the company's performance. Whenever there are errors in the order or if the goods are defective, multiple deliveries must be made to a single customer. This retailer found that on average it was making 1.5 trips per transaction versus a theoretical minimum of 1.0. Management believed this was high for the industry and that the number of trips per transaction should be reduced to 1.2. If it could achieve this performance, value would increase by 10 percent. This became an operating value driver as the company began to monitor its performance on a monthly basis.

Key value drivers are not static, they must be periodically reviewed. For example, once the retailer reaches its goal of 1.2 delivery trips per transaction it may find that it should shift its focus in the delivery area to cost per trip (while continuing to monitor trips per transaction to make sure it remains at its target). Identifying the key value drivers for a company can be difficult because it requires the company to think differently about its processes, and in many cases the company's reporting systems are not equipped to supply the necessary information.

Identifying key value drivers is also a creative process that requires much trial and error. Mechanical approaches based on existing information and purely financial approaches rarely identify the key value drivers. Aligning the value drivers with decisions is the key to organizing a value driver tree that is useful for decision making. For example, operating margins can be split up by product, geography, or consumer segment. If a company is struggling to match the skills of its sales force against customer segments, such a breakdown will be more useful than one that is geographic.

Nor can value drivers be considered in isolation from each other. For example, a price increase might, by itself, have a large impact on value—but not if it results in substantial loss of market share. For this reason we recommend that scenario analysis be employed to understand the interrelationships among value drivers. Scenarios represent the value impact of different sets of mutually consistent assumptions on the value of a company or business units within the company. They help top management to understand the relationship between strategy and value. For example, what might happen if there is a price war (perhaps the U.S.-based airlines should study this one), or what happens if additional capacity comes on-line in another country? Thinking about these issues helps keep management from getting caught off guard.

Value drivers and scenarios make VBM fact based by linking managerial actions to their effect on the value of the company. Together these aspects comprise the value-based mindset that is necessary for VBM. Next we turn to the management processes that are needed to stimulate and enforce the mindset pervasively throughout your company.

MANAGEMENT PROCESSES

Adopting a value-based mindset and finding the value drivers gets you only halfway home. Managers must also must establish processes that bring this value mindset to life in the daily activities and decision making of the company. Value-based thinking must be embraced by line management as an improved way of making decisions. And for VBM to stick, it must eventually involve all decision makers throughout the company.

There are four key management processes that collectively guide and govern the adopting of VBM in an organization:

1. Strategy development,
2. Target setting,
3. Action plans/budgeting, and
4. Performance measurement/incentive systems.

They are not necessarily sequential, but they are all necessary. First, a company or business unit develops a strategy to maximize company value. Second, the company translates the strategy into short-term and long-term performance targets defined in terms of the key value drivers. Third, action plans or budgets are developed to define the steps that will be taken over the next 12 or so months to achieve its targets. Finally, performance measurement and incentive systems are put in place to monitor performance against targets and to encourage employees to meet their goals.

These elements are also linked across the organization at the corporate, business-unit and functional/business process level. Clearly, strategies and performance targets must be consistent down through the organization if a company hopes to achieve its value creation goals.

Strategy Development

The strategy development process, particularly the measures that are used to evaluate strategies and the nature of the discussions between levels of management, must be based on maximizing value. However, implementation will vary by organizational level.

At the corporate level, strategy is primarily about deciding what businesses to be in, how to exploit potential synergies across business units and how to allocate resources across businesses. The restructuring framework described in Chapter 2 with the EG Corporation case highlights the key aspects of a VBM approach to corporate strategy. In a VBM context, senior management devises a corporate strategy that explicitly maximizes the overall value of the company, including buying and selling business units as appropriate. Often that strategy is built up from a thorough understanding of business-unit strategies.

At the business-unit level, strategy development generally requires the organization to identify alternative strategies, value the strategies, and choose the one with the highest value. Valuation is a powerful tool in helping business units analyze and decide upon the best strategy. Three examples illustrate this:

1. Earlier, when we discussed the need to focus on value creation not ROE, we saw that a bank reversed its harvest strategy for a more aggressive growth strategy when it found that the value of the aggressive growth strategy was 124 percent more than the old harvest strategy. The difference was so substantial that management decided to go for it despite a short-term reduction in return on equity—their old measure of performance.

2. A petrochemical company used valuation analysis to determine that the timing of expansion was probably the most critical determinant of long-term success in this cyclical industry. Hence the company moved to put more emphasis on doing a better job with the timing of capital expansions.

3. A consumer products company determined that a strategy of pursuing increased category growth had twice the potential value increase of a strategy to expand their brand into new products with only a fraction of the downside potential.

The strategy itself should first contain an explicit explanation of how the unit will achieve a competitive advantage that will permit it to create value. This should be grounded in a thorough analysis of the market, competitors, and the unit's existing assets and skills. See Chapter 7 for a discussion of some of the analyses that should support a strategy statement. Next, are the VBM elements of the strategy, including:

- Assessing the valuation results and key assumptions driving the value of the strategy. This facilitates discussions with senior management where key assumptions can be analyzed and challenged.
- Weighing the value of the alternative strategies that were discarded, along with reasons for discarding them.
- Stating resource requirements. VBM often focuses business-unit managers on the balance sheet for the first time. Human resource requirements should also be delineated.
- Summarizing the strategic plan projections, focusing on projections for the key value drivers. These should be supplemented by an analysis of the return on invested capital and its components over time and relative to competitors.
- Analyzing several alternative scenarios to identify the effect of competitive threats or opportunities.

The second key element of business-unit strategy is the process by which it is developed. The strategy development process does not have to become a bureaucratic time sink. We believe that companies can reengineer their planning processes at the same time they install VBM and actually reduce the time and costs associated with planning.

Target Setting

Once value maximizing strategies are agreed on, they must be translated into specific long- and short-term targets. Target setting is very subjective, yet its importance cannot be underestimated. Targets are the way management communicates what it expects to achieve. Without targets, organizations do not know where to go. Set targets too low, and they may be met, but performance will be mediocre. Set them at unattainable levels, and they will not provide any motivation.

Here are some general principles in applying VBM to target setting:

1. Targets should be based on the business unit's key value drivers and should include both financial and nonfinancial targets. Nonfinancial targets are important to prevent "gaming" of short-term financial targets. For example, an R&D intensive company could improve its short-term financial performance by deferring R&D expenditures to the long-run detriment of the company's ability to remain competitive. A way around this is to set a nonfinancial target, such as progress toward specific R&D objectives, that complements the financial targets.

2. Tailor the targets to the level of the organization. Senior business unit managers should have targets for overall financial performance and unit-wide nonfinancial objectives. Functional managers need targets tailored to their functions, such as cost per unit and quality.

3. Short-term targets must be linked to long-term targets. One company's approach that we particularly liked was to set linked performance targets for ten years, three years, and one year. The idea was that the ten-year targets expressed the company's aspirations. The three-year targets identified how much progress the company had to make within three years to have a chance of meeting its ten-year aspirations. The one-year target was a budget that managers worked towards.

For short-term financial performance targets, we recommend using economic profit. Ideally, you set targets in terms of value. But value is always based on long-term future cash flows. Since value is based on someone's assessment of the future, you need a shorter-term measure based on actual performance for a relatively short time period (i.e., one year). Economic profit is a short-term financial performance measure that is tightly linked to value creation as explained in detail in Chapter 5. Economic profit is defined as:

$$\begin{matrix} \text{Economic} \\ \text{Profit} \end{matrix} = \begin{matrix} \text{Invested capital} \times \text{(Return on invested capital} \\ - \text{Weighted average cost of capital).} \end{matrix}$$

Economic profit measures the gap between what a company earns during a period and the minimum it must earn to satisfy its investors. Maximizing economic profit over time will also maximize company value.

Action Plans/Budgets

Action plans translate the business-unit's strategy into the specific steps the organization will take to achieve its targets, particularly over the relatively short term. We have observed that many companies simply prepare short-term budgets expressed almost entirely in financial terms. Particularly for the short term, the company must identify specific steps it will take so the organization can pursue its goals in an organized manner.

Performance Measurement/Incentive Systems

Performance measurement and incentive systems track progress in achieving targets and encourage managers and other employees to achieve the targets. It is easy to dismiss performance measurement as something that accountants do, but we are always amazed at how carefully managers scrutinize the numbers on which they are evaluated. Unfortunately, in many organizations, the performance measurements are not linked to the company's or business unit's strategies, rendering them useless or, even worse, counterproductive. It is also amazing that front line supervisors and employees rarely have clear performance measures that are linked to the long-term strategy, if they have performance measures at all.

Performance measurement systems to support VBM may require significant changes from a company's traditional approach. In particular, performance measurement has to move away from being accounting driven to being management driven. In fact, if a company or business unit has established short- and long-term targets as described above and has a good understanding of its key value drivers, then developing a performance measurement system is relatively straightforward. Here are some key principles for performance measurement systems:

1. *Tailor performance measurement to the business unit.* This means that each business unit might have different performance measures—measures it can influence. Many multibusiness companies often try to use generic measures. As a result they end up with only financial measures, which may not tell senior management what is really going on. Furthermore, those financial measures may not be comparable across business units. For example, one unit may be capital intensive and have high margins, while another might have consumed little capital but have low margins. Headquarters often has difficulty understanding companies with different operating characteristics. But just because one unit earns only a 10 percent margin, while its sister units earn 20 percent does not mean it is performing poorly. Embracing different performance measurement approaches is essential if companies are to reap the benefits of VBM.

2. *Link performance measurement to the unit's short- and long-term targets.* This may seem obvious, but we often see performance measurement systems based almost solely on accounting results. For example, consider Company X, which measures overall performance based on its operating profits. This company is R&D intensive and the business-unit manager has significant discretion over short-term R&D spending. Unfortunately, the unit manager can slow down R&D spending in the short term to meet his performance target. A way around this is to measure performance on specific R&D progress goals as well as financial performance.

3. *Combine financial and operating measures based on the unit's key value drivers in the performance measurement.* Too often, the financial performance is reported separately from operating performance. As we discuss in the next section, managers would be better off with an integrated report.

4. *Identify performance measures that serve as early warning indicators.* Financial indicators measure only what has happened, when corrective actions may be too late. Early warning indicators might be simple items like market share or sales trends, or they might be more sophisticated like the results of focus group interviews.

Once performance measurements are established as part of your corporate culture and managers are familiar with using them, then you can revise your compensation system. We believe that changes in compensation should follow the implementation of a value-based management system, not lead it.

The first principle in compensation design is that it should provide the incentive to create value at all levels within the organization. Recent emphasis in the popular press on compensation for the chief executive officer is something of a red herring because the CEO is only one person. Exhibit 4.8 shows that managers' performance should be captured by a combination of metrics that reflect their organizational responsibilities and control over resources.

Exhibit 4.8 **MATCHING PERFORMANCE METRICS WITH MANAGERIAL ROLES**

Managerial role	Returns to shareholder	Economic profit	• EBIT • Capital utilization	Individual operating value drivers
CEO	X	X		
Corporate staff	X	X		X
Business-unit manager		X	X	
Functional manager			X	X
All other workers				X

Performance metric

At the CEO level, increases in the stock price of a publicly held company are directly observable, and therefore a CEO's bonus can take the form of stock options or stock appreciation rights. One of the drawbacks, of course, is that a large fraction of stock price changes are attributable to influences beyond the CEO's control, for instance, decreases in interest rates. Occasionally, stock appreciation plans have been adjusted to remove general market influences and, consequently, to focus more specifically on that portion of a company's performance that is directly attributable to the skill of top management.

Notice that the discounted cash flow of business units is not one of the performance metrics in the exhibit, and there is a good reason. DCF is the present value of *forecasted* cash flows. If compensation relied on DCF, it would be based on forecasts, not on results. Year-to-year changes in the DCF value of a business unit could be founded on changes in forecasts. This is not a good way to reward performance. However, we do recommend that economic profit and DCF be used together to establish benchmarks and reward performance at the business-unit level. Economic profit is a single-period, accounting-based performance metric that has the dual virtues of being tied to value creation and being easy to measure. However, the long-term perspective provided by DCF should often guide the establishment of economic profit benchmarks. Particularly for start-up or turn-around projects, economic profit can be negative during years of positive value creation. For example, embryonic rapid growth businesses often have negative economic profit in their early years because capital needs to be put into place before cash flows can be generated. The faster they grow, the greater their value creation is, but their economic profit is more negative. A compensation system that is too rigid, or one that fails to use DCF to apply appropriate adjustments to economic profit targets, can fail at the business-unit level.

Below the business-unit level there are rarely complete financial statements (income statements and balance sheets) to rely on. At the front line of management, operating value drivers are the key. They have to be detailed enough so that they can be tied to the actual operating decisions that managers have under their control.

FROM HERE TO THERE

Because true value-based management requires a change in mind-set for decision makers at all levels, it is a long and complex process, usually taking around two years to achieve. During the first year, managers are trained and learn to use the tools of VBM, especially value drivers. The second year solidifies their understanding, and when they become confident that value-based management tools really do work, they can accept a switch to value-based compensation systems.

The spider diagram, Exhibit 4.9, can help managers put the change process in perspective by helping them understand where their company is today in VBM terms. Six characteristics measure how deeply VBM informs an organization. To what extent is it:

- Performance driven?
- Value based?
- Managed bottom up and top down?
- Using two-way communications?
- Using self-reinforcing incentives?
- Low cost?

Together these characteristics capture both the hard and soft elements of VBM. The goal is to plot where your organization is on each of these parameters and then stretch to reach the outer limits of the hexagon. Few companies today have achieved this ultimate goal, but many are striving to do so. We will use a discussion of Company A, which implemented VBM, to illustrate how the spider chart can be helpful in understanding the challenges of adopting VBM.

Company A was already performance driven. The CEO spent a significant fraction of his time reviewing business-unit (BU) performance by benchmarking it against external competition and in terms of year-to-year improvements. A great deal of pressure was brought to bear on BU managers who slipped below promised performance levels, but few managers were fired. Instead, their careers were slowed or they were transferred.

Unfortunately, Company A was not using value-based decision making. Its entire focus was on meeting operating income targets. BU managers were often confronted with the dreaded fourth quarter demand to improve operating income for the fiscal year. Usually they could respond, of course, but they had to cut advertising or research and development during the fourth quarter and in so doing they threatened their long-term market position. Recognizing this problematic short-term focus, Company A

Exhibit 4.9 **SIX CONDITIONS FOR EXCELLENT VALUE-BASED MANAGEMENT**

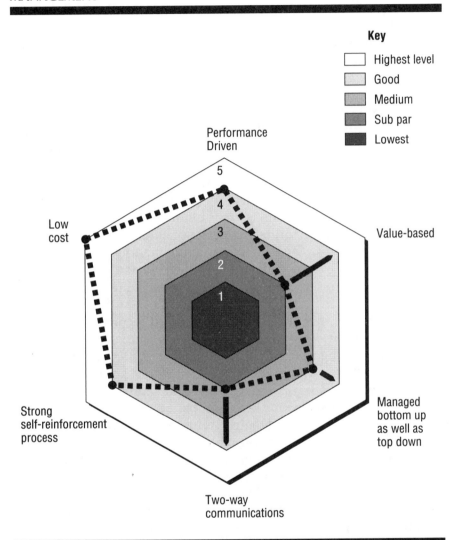

decided to implement VBM to embrace shareholder value as a superior performance metric. In do doing, it also recognized that VBM had to be performance-driven and implemented down to the level of grassroots decision making, which brings us to the third necessary condition.

Excellent VBM must be bottom up as well as top down. This means that frontline management has to understand which of the many operational decisions under its control have the greatest impact on the value of the company. These are the operational value drivers. It does not do much good for top management to understand that higher operating margins or better asset turnover create shareholder value. These value drivers are too generic. Top management cannot make the thousands of daily decisions that affect frontline value drivers. For example, at a pulp and paper company, the mill operators continually tried to establish high run rates in terms of feet of paper per second through the mill. When they focused on value creation instead, they realized that high run rates resulted in more frequent breakdowns and higher defect rates. Their value driver became feet of finished product per day. Company A realized that its current planning and budgeting system was too top-down for its business, so management tried to become more bottom-up by focusing on understanding value drivers at the grassroots level as well as at the BU level and above.

Two-way communication was a major challenge for Company A. Annual BU level plans were filled out and submitted to headquarters, but there was no feedback at all regarding the plans. Instead, headquarters waited until budgets were submitted later on before providing feedback. To cure this deficiency, VBM was implemented in a way that required relevant information in the management report which conveyed the BU plan, and explicit feedback on the plan between various levels of management. This helped to sharpen the focus of BU strategies and to establish a performance-driven ethic centered on value creation. Communication also improved dramatically. No longer was there a lack of commonality because one BU focused on market share, another on markup, and a third on return on equity. After implementing VBM, all units communicated in terms of the value impact of their strategies and operating decisions.

While Company A had a fairly strong self-reinforcing processes tied to executive compensation, it found that it needed to change to a value-based compensation scheme in order to reinforce the new mindset. The compensation change was implemented after managers had a year to work with and understand what value drivers to use and what it meant to maximize BU value.

Finally excellent VBM must be low cost. It should not be a staff-building or empire-building process. It should not result in a great deal more paperwork due to onerous reporting requirements. Company A already had a low-cost system in place and simply retrained people to implement VBM.

Key for Successful Implementation

Although putting a VBM system in place is a long and complex process, experience has taught us that successful efforts seem to share the ten traits listed in Exhibit 4.10. Some have already been touched on earlier in the chapter or are self-explanatory. Three, however, deserve a bit of elaboration.

First and foremost, it is absolutely necessary that top management understand and support the implementation of VBM. At one of our clients', the CEO and CFO created a videotape in which they expressed to employees their support, pledged that at the end of the first year the compensation policy would shift from earnings to economic profit, and gave examples of what VBM meant. For instance, the CFO remarked that all business units would be expected to earn their cost of capital. "If our cost of capital is 12 percent," he said, "a 12 percent rate of return on the capital that we have invested is not good enough. An 11 percent return destroys value, and a 13 percent return creates value. But a 14 percent rate of return creates twice as much value as a 13 percent return." Most managers had not thought about their business in these terms. The

---

Exhibit 4.10 **KEY FACTORS FOR SUCCESSFUL IMPLEMENTATION**

1. Establish explicit, visible top-management support.
2. Focus on better decision making for operating (not just financial) personnel.
3. Achieve critical mass by building skills in a wide cross section of the company.
4. Tightly integrate the VBM approach with all elements of planning.
5. Underemphasize methodological issues and focus on practical applications.
6. Use strategic issue analyses that are tailored to each business unit rather than a canned or generic approach to communicate concepts.
7. Ensure the availability of crucial data (e.g. business-unit balance sheets, external performance benchmarks).
8. Provide common, easy-to-use valuation templates and management report formats to facilitate the submission of management reports.
9. Tie incentives to value creation.
10. Require capital and human resource requests be value based.

videotape got their attention and helped them to get the message that top management supported the change that was under way.

Item three also deserves special note. If the objective is to achieve a critical mass of people who want to routinely use VBM, how should the program be rolled out? There are two extremes with any number of intermediate approaches between them. One extreme is to decide to implement broadly across all business units, within a relatively short period of time. As with any new idea, about one-third of the people will be opposed to it, another third will be relatively indifferent, and the remainder will be enthusiastic. If initial successes and top management support can sway the middle third, then the idea will stick and the transition to VBM will succeed. The other extreme is to experiment with a few carefully selected business units. The objective is to make these trial balloons into success stories, then leverage their success to convince the remaining business units to adopt VBM. Either approach has potential drawbacks. If the multi-unit rollout fails, there is no chance to make midstream correction, and a great deal of time and money will have been wasted for little result. On the other hand, the risk of rolling out VBM one unit at a time is that the initial units may not succeed, and this can block the way for others that may wish to try it. Either approach benefits from finding examples of decisions that might have been made differently without VBM, then broadcasting them widely within the company.

The fifth point deserves note because it is a bit counterintuitive. Valuation *methodology* should be underemphasized, particularly for line managers, during the rollout. Financial (not line) officers should be the gurus of the spreadsheet, and should fully understand the intricacies of valuation. Operating officers should have a good understanding of what free cash flow is and how it is discounted to obtain value estimates, but they need not understand the details. For example, during familiarization workshops, we often ask for crude estimates to the value of an idea—estimates that can be worked out on the back of an envelope. The process is simple. Line managers can estimate the effect of their idea on revenues and costs, then multiply the result times one minus the tax rate to get the after-tax effect on operating cash flows. This result is capitalized by dividing it by the cost of capital. Finally, any capital expenditures and increase in working capital are subtracted out. The final result is a very crude valuation, but it is usually good enough to rank-order projects in terms of their value creation potential and to demonstrate that value is a fairly simple concept. Once good value creating ideas have surfaced, they can be turned over to the staff experts for fine-tuned value estimates.

Making It Real

Most of the activity during the first year centers around modifying planning and reporting processes to support VBM, and building management support through business-unit specific training sessions. Exhibit 4.11 is a schematic that illustrates an approach that can be used for implementing VBM. After top management support is attained, the implementation team designs the approach.

The valuation template is a key part of the infrastructure. It must be easy to use on a personal computer. Ideally, it automatically provides all of the charts needed for the management report. Furthermore, it should be standardized across business units in a way that makes it easy to consolidate to the group or division level, and then up to the company level. And finally, it should not impose additional extensive data requirements, unless they are absolutely necessary. One of the early implementation hurdles is gaining the support of the financial officers at the business-unit level who are required to "feed the model" and to work with it. If it is cumbersome to use, or greatly increases their work load, they will find good reasons to be unsupportive. At the heart of communications and feedback is the design of a management report. It should contain all of the information that a senior manager, or a member of the board of directors, would like to know about a business unit in 25 pages or less. A list of typical management report requirements is given in Exhibit 4.12.

The valuation template, the content of the management report, and decisions about the depth and breadth of the training process are all elements of the first step—architecting the approach. The second step, modifying the systems, requires equally careful thought. It is shown in Exhibit 4.11. During this phase, the valuation templates are distributed to the business-unit financial officers in preparation for their training. The company's planning process itself is redesigned to reflect new reporting requirements and, therefore, a different schedule of events. Also, an infrastructure must be created to provide support for users of the model. For example, a hotline needs to be provided to answer urgent questions from users.

Exhibit 4.11 VALUE-BASED MANAGEMENT IMPLEMENTATION APPROACH

Value diagnostic

Top management decides to institutionalize approach

Architect VBM approach	Communicate and Institutionalize tools			Refine systems and establish ongoing capabilities
	Modify systems	Train staff	3-phase operating manager rollout	

- Enable better
  - Strategic analysis
  - Target setting
  - Frontline decision making
- Improve performance

Key activities

Architect VBM approach
- Develop VBM tools and materials
  - Preliminary valuation models
  - Valuation template
  - Management report format
- Determine breadth and depth of training
- Develop common set of assumptions
- Interview key managers

Modify systems
- Modify control and planning systems to support VBM
  - Disseminate models
  - Redesign planning process to reflect new requirements and timing
  - Ensure systems support is in place

Train staff
- Conduct staged training programs to
  - Introduce new processes and requirements
  - Introduce concepts
  - Familiarize staff with template use
  - Develop preliminary valuations

3-phase operating manager rollout
- Train managers in businesses
  - Develop business-specific analytics
    - Issue analyses
    - Valuations
    - Sensitivities/scenarios
    - Value drivers
  - Conduct business workshops
    - Valuation basics
    - Business-specific value driver and issues discussion
    - Value-enhancement brainstorming
  - Support management report development

Refine systems and establish ongoing capabilities
- Critique and refine VBM systems and training
- Lay groundwork for ongoing support efforts
- Aggregate business plans to surface corporate-level issues
- Provide coaching and feedback

126

Exhibit 4.12 **MANAGEMENT REPORT DESIGN**

Guiding principles	Management report structure	
	Section	**Contents**
• Illustrative linkages and relationships between industry structure, business strategy, and economic value	• Strategy summary	• Mission and strategic intent • Detailed market assessment • Key value drivers • Threats and opportunities • Key planning initiatives • Other
	• Valuation results	• Value • Key assumptions • Changes from previous submissions
• Encourage long-term time horizon on decision making	• Resource requirements	• Near- and long-term resource requirements • NPV of incremental investments • Human resource requirements
• Highlight value sensitivities and scenarios, not just "the answer"	• Plan forecast summary	• Financial overview of ten-year forecast—ROIC, revenue, market size and share, unit costs and revenue, operating income, capital turns
• Identify value drivers	• ROIC/ROE diagrams	• Business projections • Key competitor analogs
• Highlight cross-business-unit impacts	• Sensitivity and scenario analysis	• Value-driven sensitivities • Value impact of threats outlined above
	• Key performance metrics	• Metrics for ongoing tracking, i.e. operating value drivers • Projections for performance improvement • Proposed process for auditing performance
	• Cross-business issues	• Discussion of key issues and cross-elasticities between organizations
	• Detailed financial statements (appendix)	• Ten-year income statement, balance sheet, and cash flow statement

The first training phase of Exhibit 4.11 involves business-unit financial officers. When trained, they provide the knowledge base for the entire effort. Usually, they are very supportive and need little convincing that value-based management will provide for better decision making. They are also anxious to work closely with the top management team of their business unit to implement VBM. However, their commitment to the rollout, at least initially, involves spending extra time on training, on developing the management report for their business unit, and on identifying value drivers. Consequently, they are usually concerned about being overloaded. The timing of training has to be sensitive to this problem. During training, they are introduced to VBM as a management process; they are familiarized with the requirements of the management report; they learn how to operate the valuation template; and they develop preliminary valuations for their business units. Once the financial officers are well up the learning curve, implementation shifts to line management, the second training phase in Exhibit 4.11.

Value-based management cannot be implemented successfully unless line managers embrace it and use it on a daily basis for making better decisions. Their introduction to the concept must be very specific to their business and help them to surface new ideas for value creation, value their strategy, prioritize their initiatives, and improve daily management by focusing on value drivers. Consequently, the management training workshop should be tailored to the specific needs of the chief operating officer of the business unit. This requires careful preparation, weeks in advance. The financial officer should prepare the business-unit's management report, meet with the line managers to surface issues of concern, value the business unit, run scenarios, and identify value drivers. Once the preparation for the management workshop is completed, invitations should be sent to the "natural" management team. They are not only the top management of the business unit, but also managers of support functions (e.g., sales and marketing, if they are not already part of the business unit), critical managers from other parts of the company who supply goods or services, and managers from other parts of the company who are customers of this particular business unit.

By the time management workshops have been held at all business units, the VBM process has been launched. Top management needs to keep it going by using the tools—by asking business-unit managers what progress they are making on their value drivers, by going over their management reports with them, and by providing coaching and feedback. Staff at all levels provide the infrastructure. And corporate level staff integrate the business-unit plans in order to surface corporate level issues for the attention of the CEO. Very often, cross business-unit issues will require immediate resolution.

MAINTAINING VBM OVER TIME

Once VBM is part of your corporate culture, the very fact that it is used for decision making on a daily basis will do a lot to keep it fresh and alive. But one also needs to consider the organization and staffing of your planning function as well as the need for continuing education and support.

If value-based management (VBM) is your objective, your planning staff must be familiar with operations. Our favorite choice for chief planning officer is someone who has fairly extensive business experience, preferably as head of a business unit. He or she will have the respect of line management, will be head of planning for two to four years, and will then move on to another line management job. While filling the role of chief planning officer this individual will be capable of providing good feedback and coaching to those in line management about the viability of their strategy, their performance based on their value drivers, and the new initiatives they propose to undertake. At the same time, the chief planning officer will assist members of the top management team in making better decisions by keeping them fully informed about current and future competitive moves that the company can take—by highlighting the company's critical initiatives in terms of their value creation.

The planning staff at the corporate level should be kept as small as possible. Large multibusiness companies should push their planning capability down to the business-unit level. If business-unit performance is judged as if the unit were stand alone, then each BU should have its own planning capability.

Other than the chief planning officer, the corporate level staff could be professional staff who serve as a long-term memory for the organization, or they could be serving as planners on a rotating basis. In our opinion, a mixture of both models works best. Some companies use corporate planning as a training ground for bright young executives. After two or three years at corporate, they have a good overview of the company. They can then step out to accept jobs at the BU level and begin to work their way up the corporate ladder.

As the company grows and ages, an important human capital maintenance function must be served. As people change jobs, for instance, as new business-unit heads take over, they usually need to be briefed on the plans and on the operational value drivers of their business. At every level of the organization a continuing education effort is needed.

Because true value-based management requires a change in mindset for decision makers at all levels, it usually takes two years to achieve. During the first year, managers are trained and learn to use the tools of VBM, especially value drivers. The second year solidifies their understanding, and when they become confident that value-based management tools really do work, they can accept a switch to value-based compensation systems.

SUMMARY

Value-based management is the process of maximizing the value of your company on a continuing basis. It should guide decision making at all levels of the company from strategy at the board level to the daily operating decisions of frontline management. It should be designed to provide a value creation mindset based on management processes that focus on the key value drivers of the business. It should improve two-way communication based on a common language. It should be reinforced with a dialogue about performance on value drivers and with a value-based compensation system. Finally, it should be implemented at low cost.

REVIEW QUESTIONS

1. Compare and contrast value-based management with 1960s planning methods. What are the pitfalls of each approach?

2. What are the principal linkages between VBM and management processes of organizational change?

3. Identify the elements of the value mindset.

4. Trace how percent capacity utilized results in higher or lower levels of ROIC (level 3 of Exhibit 4.5).

5. In the human expense flowchart of Exhibit 4.6, trace how percentage time on training results in changes through the entire network of costs that result in total CS human expense. How does this reveal that training might or might not result in value creation for the whole firm?

6. Relate the four key management processes that guide VBM implementation to the value driver tree.

7. Describe six characteristics that measure how VBM works within an organization. Relate these conditions to Ralph Demsky's approach at EG.

8. Discuss the key factors for successful implementation of VBM practices. Highlight the ways in which line (operating) officers would implement VBM versus service (financial) officers.

9. Detail a project timeline for implementation of VBM in an organization. Specifically note the sensitivities of the project timeline to possible feed back and feed forward effects in the process.

10. Discuss the role of management report designs in the continuing improvement and education of the organization (see Exhibit 4.12).

Part II

Cash Flow Valuation: A Practitioner's Guide

5

Frameworks for Valuation

In Chapter 3, we presented evidence supporting the discounted cash flow approach to valuation. This chapter presents two DCF-based frameworks for valuing a business and for understanding what drives the value. These frameworks provide a practical approach to applying the DCF concept and will be followed by chapters that describe the detailed steps for using the frameworks.

To say that the value of a business equals the present value of its expected cash flows discounted at an appropriate discount rate leaves open many practical issues. How do you define cash flow? What is the right discount rate? Although a number of alternative frameworks for resolving these issues provide the same mathematical results, we recommend two that we will call the *entity DCF model* and the *economic profit model*. We favor these models for non-financial companies, because they are straightforward to use, and they provide insights into the underlying economics of the business being valued. Other models, which we will mention briefly at the end of this chapter, all have some feature that limits their usefulness.

THE ENTITY DCF MODEL

The entity DCF model values the equity of a company as the value of a company's operations (the entity value that is available to all investors) less the value of debt and other investor claims that are superior to common equity (such as preferred stock). The values of operations and debt are equal to their respective cash flows discounted at rates that reflect the riskiness of these cash flows. Exhibit 5.1 illustrates this model. As long as the discount rates are selected properly to reflect the riskiness of each cash flow stream,

Exhibit 5.1 **SIMPLE ENTITY VALUATION OF A SINGLE-BUSINESS COMPANY**

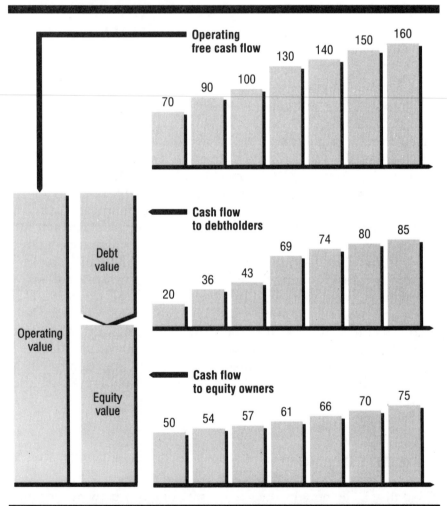

the entity approach will result in exactly the same equity value as if we directly discounted the cash flow to the shareholders.

The entity model is especially useful when extended to a multibusiness company, as shown in Exhibit 5.2. The equity value of the company equals the sum of the values of the individual operating units, plus cash-generating corporate assets, less the cost of operating the corporate center and the value of the company's debt and preferred stock. The exhibit helps to highlight the reasons for recommending the entity model, namely

- Valuing the components of the business that add up to the entity value, instead of just the equity, helps in identifying

Exhibit 5.2 **ENTITY VALUATION OF A MULTIBUSINESS COMPANY**

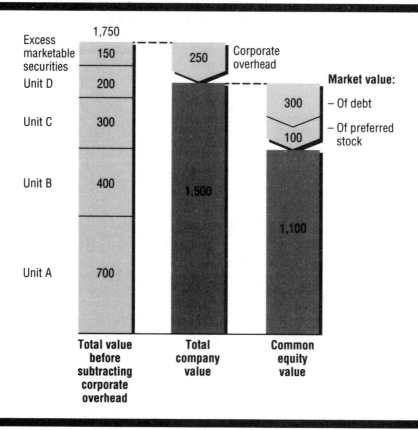

and understanding the separate investment and financing sources of value for the equity holders.

- This approach helps to pinpoint key leverage areas in the search for value creating ideas.
- It can be applied consistently at different levels of aggregation and is consistent with the capital budgeting process most companies are already familiar with.
- It is sophisticated enough to deal with the complexity of most situations, while at the same time it is easy to implement with simple personal computer tools.

Exhibit 5.3 is a simple valuation summary for the Hershey Foods Corporation.

Exhibit 5.3 **HERSHEY FOODS CORPORATION, FREE CASH FLOW VALUATION SUMMARY,** $ MILLIONS (EXCEPT PER SHARE)

Year	Free cash flow (FCF)	Discount factor @ 10%	Present value of FCF
1993	227	0.9091	206
1994	202	0.8264	167
1995	216	0.7513	163
1996	232	0.6830	159
1997	249	0.6209	155
1998	268	0.5645	151
1999	287	0.5132	147
2000	309	0.4665	144
2001	331	0.4241	141
2002	356	0.3855	137
Continuing value	6,604	0.3855	2,546
Value of operations			4,115
Value of nonoperating investments			207
Total entity value			4,322
Less: Value of debt			(560)
Equity value			3,762
Equity value per share			41.72

Value of Operations

The value of operations equals the discounted value of expected future free cash flow. Free cash flow is equal to the after-tax operating earnings of the company, plus noncash charges, less investments in operating working capital, property, plant and equipment, and other assets. It does not incorporate any financing-related cash flows such as interest expense or dividends. Exhibit 5.4 shows a summarized free cash flow calculation for the Hershey Foods Corporation. Free cash flow is the correct cash flow for this valuation model, because it reflects the cash flow that is generated by a company's operations and available to all the company's capital providers, both debt and equity. In fact, as you can see on Exhibit 5.4, free cash flow is also equal to the sum of the cash flows paid to or received from all the capital providers (interest, dividends, new borrowing, debt repayments, and so on).

For consistency with the cash flow definition, the discount rate applied to the free cash flow should reflect the opportunity cost to all the capital providers weighted by their relative contribution to the company's total capital. This is called the weighted average cost of capital (WACC). The opportunity cost to a class of investors equals the rate of return the investors could expect to earn on other investments of equivalent risk. The cost to the company equals the investors' costs less any tax benefits received by the company (for example, the tax shield provided by interest expense). Exhibit 5.5 shows a sample WACC calculation for Hershey Foods.

An additional issue in valuing a business is its indefinite life. One approach is to forecast the free cash flow for one hundred years and not worry about what comes after, because its discounted value will be tiny. Alternatively, you can make the problem tractable by separating the value of the business into two time periods, during and after an explicit forecast period. In this case,

$$\text{Value} = \begin{array}{c} \text{Present value of cash flow} \\ \textit{during} \text{ explicit forecast period} \end{array} + \begin{array}{c} \text{Present value of cash flow} \\ \textit{after} \text{ explicit forecast period.} \end{array}$$

The value after the explicit forecast period is referred to as the continuing value. Simple formulas can be used to estimate the continuing value without the need to forecast the company's cash flow in detail for an indefinite period. For example, one approach esti-

Exhibit 5.4 **HERSHEY FOODS CORPORATION, FREE CASH FLOW SUMMARY,** $ MILLIONS

Free cash flow	1991	1992	Forecast 1993	Forecast 1994	Forecast 1995
Earnings before interest and taxes (EBIT)	401	439	468	506	545
Cash taxes on EBIT	(137)	(138)	(153)	(166)	(178)
Net operating profits less adjusted taxes (NOPLAT)	264	302	315	341	366
Depreciation	73	84	97	105	115
Gross cash flow	337	386	412	445	482
Change in working capital	(46)	70	33	35	38
Capital expenditures	266	235	157	213	232
Increase in net other assets	(17)	(16)	(4)	(5)	(5)
Gross investment	204	289	186	244	265
Operating free cash flow	134	98	227	202	216
Cash flow from non-operating investments	0	(203)	228	0	0
Cash flow available to investors	134	(105)	455	202	216
Financing flow					
Net interest expense after-tax	16	17	29	12	8
Decrease/(increase) in net debt	(11)	(211)	326	80	88
Common dividends	83	91	99	110	120
Share repurchases/(issues)	45	(3)	0	0	0
Financing flow	134	(105)	455	202	216

Exhibit 5.5 **HERSHEY FOODS CORPORATION, WACC SUMMARY**

Source of capital	Proportion of total capital	Opportunity cost	Tax rate	After-tax cost	Contribution to weighted average
Debt	15.0%	7.5%	39.0%	4.6%	0.7%
Equity	85.0%	10.9%	–	10.9%	9.3%
WACC					10.0%

mates the continuing value using the following formula (Chapter 9 discusses more sophisticated continuing value approaches):

$$\text{Continuing value} = \frac{\text{Net operating profit less adjusted taxes}}{\text{Weighted average cost of capital}}.$$

Value of Debt

The value of the company's debt equals the present value of the cash flow to the debt holders, discounted at a rate that reflects the riskiness of that flow. The discount rate should equal the current market rate on similar-risk debt with comparable terms. In most cases, only the company's debt outstanding on the valuation date must be valued. Future borrowing can be assumed to have zero net present value, because the cash inflows from these borrowings will exactly equal the present value of the future repayments, discounted at the opportunity cost of the debt.

Value of Equity

The value of the company's equity is the value of its operations, less the value of its debt, and adjusted for any nonoperating assets or liabilities. In Hershey's case, as shown on Exhibit 5.3, the value of equity also includes the value of Hershey's investment in a company it attempted to purchase in 1992, which it was planning to sell in 1993.

WHAT DRIVES CASH FLOW AND VALUE

We could stop right here and say that once you have projected free cash flow and discounted it back at the WACC, the valuation is complete. You would not be satisfied, however, because you do not have a basis for evaluating the particular free cash flow projection you have developed. How does it compare to history? To other companies? What are the economics of the business expressed in a way that helps managers and others understand the business? What are the factors that could increase or decrease the value of the company? You need to step back and understand the underlying economic value drivers of the business.

Since value is based on discounted free cash flow, the underlying value drivers of the business must also be the drivers of free cash flow. There are two key drivers of free cash flow and ultimately value: the rate at which the company is growing its revenues, profits, and capital base; and the return on invested capital. These value drivers are consistent with common sense. A company that earns higher profits for every dollar invested in the business will be worth more than a similar company that earns less profits for every dollar of invested capital. Similarly, a faster growing company will be worth more than a slower growing company if they are both earning the same return on invested capital (and this return is high enough to satisfy the investors).

A simple model will demonstrate how growth and return on invested capital actually drive free cash flow. First, some definitions are needed. ROIC equals the operating profits of the company, divided by the amount of capital invested in the company.

$$\text{ROIC} = \frac{\text{NOPLAT}}{\text{Invested Capital}},$$

where

NOPLAT   = Net Operating Profits Less Adjusted Taxes.

Invested Capital = Operating working capital + net fixed assets + other assets. (All terms are defined in detail in Chapter 6.)

Earlier in this chapter (see Exhibit 5.4), we defined free cash flow as equal to gross cash flow (NOPLAT plus depreciation) minus gross investment (increases in working capital plus capital expenditures). To simplify the following examples, we will show free cash flow as NOPLAT less net investment, having subtracted depreciation from both gross cash flow and gross investment. In Year 1, Company A's NOPLAT equals $100, net investment equals $25, so free cash flow must equal $75.

Company A	Year 1
NOPLAT	$100.0
Net investment	25.0
Free cash flow	$ 75.0

Presumably, the purpose Company A invested $25 over and above depreciation was to earn additional profits. Assume Company A earns a 20 percent return on its new investment in Year 2 and every subsequent year. Year 2's NOPLAT would equal Year 1's NOPLAT ($100) plus 20 percent of Year 1's investment, or $5 ($25 × .20), for a total of $105. (We have also assumed that the operating profit on the base level of capital in place at the beginning of Year 1 does not change over time). Suppose the company reinvests the same percentage of its operating profits each year and earns the same return on new capital. Company A's free cash flow would look as follows:

Company A	Year 1	2	3	4
NOPLAT	$100.0	105.0	110.3	115.8
Net investment	25.0	26.2	27.6	29.0
Free cash flow	$75.0	78.8	82.7	86.8

Each year the company's operating profits and free cash flow grow at 5 percent and each year the company invests 25 percent of its cash flows into the business for future growth at a return of 20 percent. In fact, we can say that in this simple world, a company's growth rate is the product of its return on new capital and its investment rate (net investment divided by operating profits).

Growth rate = Return on new capital invested × Investment rate.

For Company A,

$$\text{Growth rate} = 20\% \times 25\%$$
$$= 5\%.$$

Now suppose that Company B wants to generate the same profit growth as Company A, 5 percent. It too earns $100 in Year 1. However, Company B earns only a 10 percent return on its capital. In order for Company B to increase its profits in Year 2 by $5, it must invest $50 in Year 1. Company B's free cash flow would look as follows:

Company B	Year 1	Year 2	Year 3	Year 4
NOPLAT	$100.0	105.0	110.3	115.8
Net investment	50.0	52.5	55.1	57.9
Free cash flow	$ 50.0	52.5	55.1	57.9

It is clear that a higher return on invested capital results in higher free cash flow, given the same desired growth rate in operating profits. As would be expected, Company A would be worth more than Company B, despite identical operating profits and growth rates.

Now let's look at how growth drives cash flow and value. Suppose Company A wants to increase its growth rate, and it can invest more capital at the same return. If A wants to grow at 8 percent instead of 5 percent, it must now invest 40 percent of its operating profits each year as shown in the following table. (We can use the formula we developed above to calculate the required investment rate.)

Company A	Year 1	Year 2	Year 3	Year 4
NOPLAT	$100.0	108.0	116.6	126.0
Net investment	40.0	43.2	46.6	50.4
Free cash flow	$ 60.0	64.8	70.0	75.6

Note that Company A's free cash flow is now lower in the years presented. In fact, at this new higher growth rate, Company A's free cash flow is lower than the first scenario until Year 9, but from then on the free cash flow becomes much larger (as shown in Exhibit 5.6). Which scenario results in a higher value? It turns out that as long as the return on invested capital is greater than the WACC used to discount the cash flow, higher growth will generate greater value. In these two scenarios, if we assume that the growth and return patterns continue forever, and that Company A's WACC is 12 percent, then the present value of the 5 percent growth scenario is $1,071, and the present value of the 8 percent growth scenario is $1,500. This means it is worthwhile for the investors to accept lower free cash flow in the earlier years.

Exhibit 5.7 shows a matrix of values for a hypothetical company over a range of projected growth and return on invested capital. As you can see, a given value can result from different combinations of growth and return. Assuming companies can't always have more of both, a table like this helps managers set targets for long-term performance improvement. This table also demonstrates what happens if the return on invested capital does not exceed the cost of capital. If the return exactly equals the WACC, then additional growth neither creates nor destroys value. It makes sense that in-

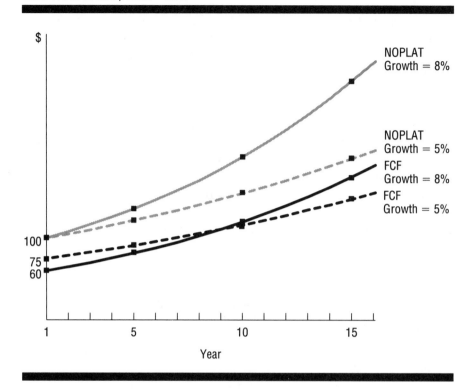

Exhibit 5.7 **HOW ROIC AND GROWTH DRIVE VALUE,*** WACC = 10%

	Return on invested capital				
Annual growth in operating profit	7.5%	10.0%	12.5%	15.0%	20.0%
3.0%	887	1,000	1,068	1,113	1,170
6.0%	706	1,000	1,177	1,295	1,442
9.0%	410	1,000	1,354	1,591	1,886

*Assumes starting NOPLAT = $100 and a 25 year horizon, after which ROIC = WACC.

145

vestors will not pay more for additional growth if they can earn the same returns elsewhere. Finally, if the return on invested capital is less than WACC, then additional growth actually destroys value. Investors would be better off investing the capital elsewhere.

These examples are quite simplistic. Companies do not grow at constant rates every year, they do not invest the same proportion of their profits, and they do not earn the same return on capital every year. However, the core idea—that the key drivers of value are return on invested capital (relative to WACC) and growth—is generally applicable for all companies over time. Exhibit 5.8 shows the calculation of Hershey's return on invested capital. Exhibit 5.9 shows Hershey's historical and projected performance in terms of growth and return on invested capital. These results are summarized in the following table.

Hershey Foods Corporation	1984–87	1988–92	Forecast 1993–2002
Average spread			
ROIC	19.2%	18.9%	19.3%
WACC	12.9	11.5	10.0
Spread	6.3%	7.4%	9.3%
Average annual growth			
Revenues	8.7%	5.8%	8.0%
NOPLAT	8.2	11.5	7.4
Invested capital	12.8	8.2	7.7

As you can see, Hershey has consistently earned a return on invested capital of approximately 19 percent (except for 1988), even while interest rates and its WACC have declined from 15.2 percent in 1984 to 10 percent in 1993. Thus, Hershey's spread has increased to an average of 7.4 percent over the 5 years, from 1988 to 1992. Returns on invested capital in this scenario are projected to remain essentially constant. Revenue growth is projected to be somewhat higher than in recent years and NOPLAT is projected to grow in line with revenues (in other words, margins are expected to remain constant). Managers can use information like this to assess a projection and set long-term performance targets.

In summary, return on invested capital (relative to WACC) and

Exhibit 5.8 **HERSHEY FOODS CORPORATION, RETURN ON INVESTED CAPITAL CALCULATION,** $ MILLIONS

NOPLAT	1991	1992	Forecast 1993	Forecast 1994	Forecast 1995
Revenues	2,899	3,220	3,477	3,756	4,056
Operating expenses	(2,498)	(2,781)	(3,009)	(3,249)	(3,511)
Earnings before interest and taxes (EBIT)	401	439	468	506	545
Cash taxes on EBIT	(137)	(138)	(153)	(166)	(178)
NOPLAT	264	302	315	341	366
Invested Capital					
Operating current assets	702	761	822	888	959
Noninterest bearing current liabilities	(363)	(352)	(380)	(410)	(443)
Operating working capital	340	409	442	477	516
Net property plant and equipment	1,146	1,296	1,356	1,465	1,582
Other assets net of other liabilities	(51)	(56)	(60)	(65)	(70)
Operating invested capital	1,434	1,649	1,738	1,877	2,027
ROIC					
Return on invested capital (beginning of year)	20.1%	21.0%	19.1%	19.6%	19.5
WACC	10.6%	10.5%	10.0%	10.0%	10.0%
Spread	9.5%	10.5%	9.1%	9.6%	9.5%

growth are the fundamental drivers of a company's value. To increase its value, a company must do one or more of the following:

- Increase the level of profits it earns on its existing capital in place (earn a higher return on invested capital).
- Increase the return on new capital investment.
- Increase its growth rate, but only as long as the return on new capital exceeds WACC.
- Reduce its cost of capital.

Exhibit 5.9 **HERSHEY FOODS CORPORATION, ROIC AND GROWTH TRENDS**

Percent

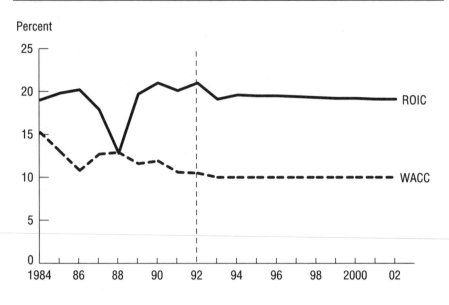

Growth Index
1992 = 100

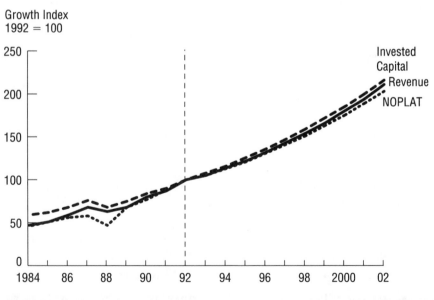

THE ECONOMIC PROFIT MODEL

Another framework for valuation is the economic profit model. In this model, the value of a company equals the amount of capital invested plus a premium equal to the present value of the value created each year going forward. The concept of economic profit dates back at least to the economist Alfred Marshall who wrote in 1890: "What remains of his [the owner or manager's] profits after deducting interest on his capital at the current rate may be called his earnings of undertaking or management."[1]

Marshall is saying that the value created by a company during any time period (its economic profit) must take into account not only the expenses recorded in its accounting records but also the opportunity cost of the capital employed in the business.

An advantage of the economic profit model over the DCF model is that economic profit is a useful measure for understanding a company's performance in any single year, while free cash flow is not. For example, you would not track a company's progress by comparing actual and projected free cash flow, because free cash flow in any year is determined by highly discretionary investments in fixed assets and working capital. Management could easily delay investments simply to improve free cash flow in a given year at the expense of long term value creation.

Economic profit measures the value created in a company in a single period of time and is defined as follows:

$$\text{Economic Profit} = \text{Invested capital} \times (\text{ROIC} - \text{WACC}).$$

In other words, economic profit equals the spread between the return on invested capital and the cost of capital, times the amount of invested capital. Company C has invested capital of $1,000, return on invested capital of 10 percent, and WACC of 8 percent. Its economic profit for the year is $20.

$$
\begin{aligned}
\text{Economic Profit} &= \$1,000 \times (10\% - 8\%), \\
&= \$1,000 \times 2\%, \\
&= \$20.
\end{aligned}
$$

---

[1] Alfred Marshall, *Principles of Economics, Vol. 1.* (New York: MacMillan & Co., 1890), p. 142.

Economic profit translates the value drivers discussed earlier, return on invested capital and growth, into a single dollar figure (growth is ultimately related to the amount of invested capital or the size of the company). Another way to define economic profit is as after-tax operating profits less a charge for the capital used by the company.

$$\text{Economic Profit} = \text{NOPLAT} - \text{Capital charge,}$$
$$= \text{NOPLAT} - (\text{Invested capital} \times \text{WACC}).$$

This alternative calculation generates the same value for economic profit.

$$\text{Economic Profit} = \$100 - (\$1,000 \times 8\%),$$
$$= \$100 - \$80,$$
$$= \$20.$$

This approach shows that economic profit is similar in concept to accounting net income, but where the company is explicitly charged for all its capital, not just the interest on its debt.

A simple example will illustrate how economic profit can be used for valuations. Assume that the same Company C invested $1,000 in working capital and fixed assets at the beginning of Period 1. Each year after that, it earns $100 in NOPLAT (a 10 percent ROIC). Its net investment is zero, so its free cash flow is also $100. Using the formula just mentioned, Company C's economic profit is $20 per year.

The economic profit approach says that the value of a company equals the amount of capital invested, plus a premium or discount equal to present value of its projected economic profit.

$$\text{Value} = \text{Invested capital} + \text{Present value of projected Economic Profit.}$$

The logic behind this is simple. If a company earned exactly its WACC every period, then the discounted value of its projected free cash flow should exactly equal its invested capital. In other words, the company is worth exactly what was originally invested. A company is worth more or less than its invested capital only to the extent it earns more or less than its WACC. So the premium or discount relative to invested capital must equal the present value of the company's future economic profit.

Company C earns $20 per year more than investors demand (its economic profit). Therefore the value of company C should equal $1,000 (its invested capital at the time of the valuation) plus the present value of its economic profit. In this case, since economic profit remains forever at $20 per year, we can use a perpetuity to calculate the present value of its economic profit.

$$\text{Present value of Economic Profit} = \frac{\$20}{8\%}$$
$$= \$250.$$

Overall, company C's value is $1,250. Now if you were to discount company C's free cash flow (FCF) you would also end up with a value for company C of $1,250. Company C's projected free cash flow is $100 per year.

$$\text{Present value of FCF} = \frac{\$100}{8\%}$$
$$= \$1,250.$$

Exhibits 5.10 and 5.11 show the economic profit and economic profit valuation of Hershey Foods. In 1992, Hershey generated economic profit of $151 million. In other words, Hershey generated $151 million of operating profit more than required by investors

Exhibit 5.10 **HERSHEY FOODS CORPORATION, ECONOMIC PROFIT CALCULATION,** $ MILLIONS

	1991	1992	Forecast 1993	Forecast 1994	Forecast 1995
Return on invested capital	20.1%	21.0%	19.1%	19.6%	19.5%
WACC	10.6%	10.5%	10.0%	10.0%	10.0%
Spread	9.5%	10.5%	9.1%	9.6%	9.5%
Invested capital (beginning of year)	1,319	1,434	1,649	1,738	1,877
Economic profit	125	151	151	167	179
NOPLAT	264	302	315	341	366
Capital charge	139	151	164	174	187
Economic profit	125	151	151	167	179

Exhibit 5.11 **HERSHEY FOODS CORPORATION, ECONOMIC PROFIT VALUATION SUMMARY,** $ MILLIONS (EXCEPT PER SHARE)

Year	Economic profit	Discount factor @ 10.0%	Present value of economic profit
1993	151	0.9091	137
1994	167	0.8264	138
1995	179	0.7513	135
1996	192	0.6830	131
1997	206	0.6209	128
1998	221	0.5645	124
1999	237	0.5132	121
2000	254	0.4665	118
2001	273	0.4241	115
2002	293	0.3855	112
Continuing value	3,130	0.3855	1,207
Present value of economic profit			2,465
Invested capital (beginning of forecast)			1,649
Value of operations			4,115
Value of nonoperating investments			207
Total entity value			4,322
Less: Value of debt			(560)
Equity value			3,762
Equity value per share			41.72

based on the returns available from alternative investments. Note that the economic profit value of Hershey exactly equals the discounted free cash flow value we calculated earlier in this chapter. Furthermore, as would be expected, the value of operations, $4.1 billion, exceeds the amount of invested capital (at the end of 1992) of $1.6 billion. In other words, in present value terms, Hershey has created $2.5 billion of value ($4.1 billion less $1.6 billion).

OTHER DISCOUNTED CASH FLOW FRAMEWORKS

Other discounted cash flow frameworks, if properly applied, will result in the same values for companies as the approaches we rec-

ommend. However, each has significant drawbacks, and their usefulness for practical applications is limited.

Direct Discounting of Equity Cash Flow

Valuing a company's equity by directly discounting the cash flow to
the equity holders (dividends and share repurchases) is intuitively
the most straightforward valuation technique. Unfortunately, except for financial institutions (see Chapter 16), this approach is not
as useful as the entity model. Discounting equity cash flow provides
less information about the sources of value creation and is not as
useful for identifying value creation opportunities. Furthermore, it
requires careful adjustments to ensure that changes in projected financing do not incorrectly affect the company's value.

For example, a common error in discounted equity valuations
is an inconsistency between the company's dividend policy and the
discount rate used. First, an analyst conducts a base valuation that
results in a value of, say, $15 per share. Next, the analyst increases
the dividend payout ratio while holding the projected operating
performance constant (in other words, no changes in revenues or
margins). Presto! The equity value has just increased because of the
higher dividend payments, despite the constant operating performance. The error here is that the discount rate was not changed.
Increasing the dividend payout ratio requires more use of debt.
More debt means riskier equity and a higher discount rate for the
equity.

Another shortcoming of the direct equity approach appears
when valuing business units. The direct equity approach requires
you to allocate debt and interest expense to each unit. This creates
extra work without any extra information being provided.

Using Real Instead of Nominal Cash Flow and Discount Rate

Another valuation approach is to project cash flow in real terms
(for example, in constant 1994 dollars) and discount this cash flow
at a real discount rate (for example, the nominal rate less expected
inflation). However, most managers think in terms of nominal
rather than real measures, so nominal measures are often easier to
communicate. Interest rates are generally quoted nominally rather
than in real terms (excluding expected inflation). Moreover, we
have found that since historical financial statements are stated in

nominal terms, projecting future statements in real terms is difficult and confusing.

A key difficulty occurs when calculating rates of return on invested capital. The historical statements are nominal, so historical returns on invested capital are nominal. But if the projections for the company are real rather than nominal, returns on new capital are also real. So, looking forward, projected returns on total capital (new and old) are a combination of nominal and real, which are impossible to interpret. The only way around this is to restate historical performance to a real basis, a complex and time consuming task. We have generally found that the extra insights from this effort are insignificant for most companies.

In high inflation countries, using real cash flows and WACCs (or those expressed in terms of a stable reference currency) is often the most practical way to go. Fortunately, in these countries, historical financial statements are also restated to a common currency, so the difficulties expressed above are somewhat mitigated.

Discounting Pretax Cash Flow Instead of After-Tax Cash Flow

The entity model we recommend uses after-tax cash flow and an after-tax discount rate. It is conceptually valid, though, to use pretax cash flow and a pretax discount rate, as the following example illustrates.

$$\text{Value} = \frac{\text{After-tax cash flow}}{\text{After-tax discount rate}}.$$

$$\text{After-tax cash flow} = \text{Pretax cash flow} \times (1-\text{tax rate}).$$

$$\text{After-tax discount rate} = \text{Pretax discount rate} \times (1-\text{tax rate}).$$

Substituting into the initial equation gives:

$$\text{Value} = \frac{\text{Pretax cash flow} \times (1-\text{tax rate})}{\text{Pretax discount rate} \times (1-\text{tax rate})}.$$

$$\text{Value} = \frac{\text{Pretax cash flow}}{\text{Pretax discount rate}}.$$

However, real-world after-tax cash flow is not simply pretax cash flow adjusted by the tax rate. Taxes are based on accrual accounting (for example, the tax benefit of purchasing a machine is received in a different period from when the machine is paid for), not cash flow. Therefore, after-tax free cash flow is not equal to pre-tax free cash flow times a tax rate. As a result, you cannot simply gross up the discount rate to a pretax rate and discount the pretax cash flow and get the same result as the recommended approach. It is virtually impossible to perform a valid real-world discounted cash flow analysis using the pretax approach.

Formula-Based DCF Approaches Instead of Explicit Discounted Cash Flow

Formula-based DCF approaches make simplifying assumptions about a business and its cash flow stream (for example, constant revenue growth and margins), so that the entire discounted cash flow can be captured in a concise formula. Unfortunately, these formulas are most often too simple for real-world problem solving, though they may serve as valuable communication tools.

The Miller-Modigliani (MM) formula, although simple, is particularly useful for communicating the sources of a company's value. The MM formula (1961) values a company as the sum of the value of the cash flow of its assets currently in place plus the value of its growth opportunities.[2] The formula is based on sound economic analysis, so it can be used to illustrate the key factors that will affect the value of the company. Unfortunately its simplifying assumptions (at least in the version given below) render it too inaccurate for precise valuations.

The MM formula is defined as follows:

$$\text{Value of entity} = \text{Value of assets in place} + \text{Value of growth,}$$

$$= \frac{\text{NOPLAT}}{\text{WACC}} + K(\text{NOPLAT})N\left[\frac{\text{ROIC} - \text{WACC}}{\text{WACC}(1 + \text{WACC})}\right],$$

where

NOPLAT = Expected level of net operating profits less adjusted taxes in the first projected period.

WACC = weighted average cost of capital.

ROIC = expected rate of return on invested capital.

---

[2] M. Miller, and F. Modigliani, "Dividend Policy, Growth and the Valuation of Shares," *Journal of Business* (September 1985) 1031–1051.

K   = investment rate, the percentage of NOPLAT invested for growth in new projects.

N   = expected number of years that the company will continue to invest in new projects and earn the projected ROIC, also called the interval of competitive advantage.

Option-Pricing Models

Option-pricing models are variations on standard discounted cash flow models, which adjust for the fact that management decisions can be modified in the future as more information becomes available. Option models hold particular promise for valuing strategic and operating flexibility, such as opening and closing plants, abandoning operations, or exploring and developing natural resources. Chapter 15 discusses how option-pricing might be used as the technology is further developed.

SUMMARY

This chapter introduced two valuation frameworks: the entity DCF model and the economic profit model. We explained the rationale for each model and discussed the economic drivers of a company's value. Chapters 6 through 10 will describe a step-by-step approach to valuing a company, as shown in Exhibit 5.12. These chapters explain both the technical details, such as how to calculate free cash flow from complex accounting statements, and how to interpret the valuation through careful financial analysis.

Exhibit 5.12 **STEPS IN A VALUATION**

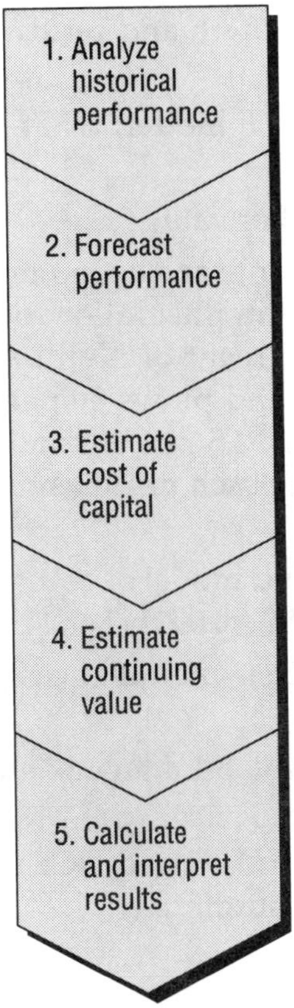

1. Analyze historical performance

- Calculate NOPLAT and invested capital
- Calculate value drivers
- Develop an integrated historical perspective
- Analyze financial health

2. Forecast performance

- Understand strategic position
- Develop performance scenarios
- Forecast individual line items
- Check overall forecast for reasonableness

3. Estimate cost of capital

- Develop target market value weights
- Estimate cost of nonequity financing
- Estimate cost of equity financing

4. Estimate continuing value

- Select appropriate technique
- Select forecast horizon
- Estimate the parameters
- Discount continuing value to present

5. Calculate and interpret results

- Calculate and test results
- Interpret results within decision context

REVIEW QUESTIONS

1. Describe the entity discounted cash flow model.
2. How is free cash flow driven by growth and return on invested capital?
3. According to the free cash flow DCF model, what must a company do to increase its value?
4. Describe the economic profit model of value.
5. Compare and contrast the free cash flow and economic profit models of value. Use three firms as an illustration: one firm earns 10 percent and plows 100 percent of NOPLAT into capital, another earns 12.5 percent and plows 80 percent of NOPLAT into capital, a third earns 12.5 percent and plows 200 percent of NOPLAT into capital; each firm has the same cost of capital.
6. Why doesn't the discounted dividend model of equity value always portray shareholders' wealth correctly?
7. When would managers use real versus nominal cash flows and rates to value entities?
8. Is there any difference between pre- and after-tax analyses of value?
9. Describe the Modigliani-Miller formula-based DCF calculation and its usefulness in valuation studies.
10. Outline the steps in a valuation.

6

Analyzing Historical
Performance

The first step in valuing a business is analyzing its historical performance. A sound understanding of the company's past performance provides an essential perspective for developing and evaluating forecasts of future performance.

Historical performance analysis should focus on the key value drivers discussed in Chapter 5. The rate of return on invested capital is the single most important value driver. As previously stated, a company creates value for its shareholders only when it earns rates of return on invested capital that exceed its cost of capital. ROIC and the proportion of its profits that the company invests for growth drive free cash flow, which in turn drives value. Economic profit is another way of looking at performance. Economic profit combines size and spread (ROIC less WACC) into a dollar estimate of periodic performance. The historical performance analysis considers all these elements.

The historical analysis should be developed in an integrated way. For example, in addition to ROIC itself, the key components of ROIC should be analyzed. The historical analysis should not be just a collection of ratios. Financial ratios that largely duplicate the core ratios or ratios that do not help to explain the core drivers should not be used. For example, the return on total assets (ROA) is not used because everything that can be learned from ROA is incorporated into the ROIC analysis.

The final step in the historical analysis is to explain the company's financial health from a credit perspective. Is the company generating or consuming cash? How much debt does the company employ relative to equity? What margin of safety does the company have with respect to its debt financing?

NOPLAT AND INVESTED CAPITAL

To review, the core value drivers are defined as follows:

$$\text{ROIC} = \frac{\text{NOPLAT}}{\text{Invested capital}}.$$

$$\text{Free cash flow} = \text{NOPLAT} - \text{Net investment}.$$

$$\text{Economic Profit} = \text{Invested capital} \times (\text{ROIC} - \text{WACC}).$$

As you can see, the value drivers are defined by the concepts NOPLAT and invested capital. Therefore, we must define NOPLAT and invested capital before moving on to the value drivers themselves.

Throughout this chapter, Hershey Foods Corporation will be used to demonstrate the calculation of the value drivers from Hershey's income statement (Exhibit 6.1) and balance sheet (Exhibit 6.2).

NOPLAT

Net operating profit less adjusted taxes represents the after-tax operating profits of the company after adjusting the taxes to a cash basis. Exhibit 6.3 shows the calculation of Hershey's NOPLAT and a reconciliation of NOPLAT to Hershey's accounting net income.

Earnings before interest and taxes (EBIT)   The NOPLAT calculation begins with EBIT, the pretax operating income that a company would have earned if it had no debt. It includes all types of operating income, including most revenues and expenses. Generally excluded are interest income, interest expense, the gain or loss from discontinued operations, extraordinary income or loss, and the investment income from nonoperating investments. Depreciation of fixed assets should be subtracted in calculating EBIT, but goodwill amortization should not. Goodwill and goodwill amortization will be given special treatment as described on the following pages.

Exhibit 6.1 **HERSHEY FOODS CORPORATION,**
HISTORICAL INCOME STATEMENT, $ MILLIONS

	1990	1991	1992
Net sales	2,715.6	2,899.2	3,219.8
Interest income	1.7	2.4	2.5
Total revenues	2,717.3	2,901.6	3,222.3
Cost of goods sold	(1,526.6)	(1,621.7)	(1,749.0)
Selling, general and administrative expenses	(765.7)	(803.5)	(947.2)
Depreciation expense	(61.7)	(72.7)	(84.4)
Amortization of goodwill	(11.0)	(11.0)	(11.0)
Interest expense	(26.3)	(29.3)	(29.7)
Total costs and expenses	(2,391.3)	(2,538.1)	(2,821.3)
Income before special items	326.0	363.5	401.0
Gain from business restructuring	35.5	0.0	0.0
Income before income taxes	361.5	363.5	401.0
Provision for income taxes	(145.6)	(143.9)	(158.4)
Net income	215.9	219.5	242.6
Statement of Retained Earnings			
Retained earnings, beginning of year	949.8	1,077.9	1,214.0
Net income	215.9	219.5	242.6
Dividends	(87.8)	(83.4)	(91.4)
Retained earnings, end of year	1,077.9	1,214.0	1,365.2

Taxes on EBIT   Taxes on EBIT represent the income taxes attributable to EBIT. They are the taxes the company would pay if it had no debt, excess marketable securities, or nonoperating income or expenses. Taxes on EBIT equal the total income tax provision (current and deferred) adjusted for the income taxes attributed to interest expense, interest income, and nonoperating items. For Hershey, 1992 taxes on EBIT are calculated as follows (in millions):

Total income tax provision from income statement	$158
+ Tax shield on interest expense	12
− Tax on interest income	(1)
− Tax on nonoperating income	0
= Taxes on EBIT	$169

Exhibit 6.2 **HERSHEY FOODS CORPORATION,
HISTORICAL BALANCE SHEET,** $ MILLIONS

Assets	1990	1991	1992
Operating cash	26.6	29.0	24.1
Excess marketable securities	0.0	42.1	0.0
Accounts receivable	143.0	159.8	173.6
Inventories	379.1	436.9	457.2
Other current assets	113.1	76.6	106.0
Total current assets	661.8	744.5	760.9
Gross property plant and equipment	1,323.6	1,581.3	1,797.4
Accumulated depreciation	(371.5)	(435.6)	(501.4)
Net property plant and equipment	952.1	1,145.7	1,296.0
Goodwill	417.6	421.7	399.8
Other assets	47.3	30.0	37.2
Investments	0.0	0.0	179.1
Total assets	2,078.8	2,341.8	2,672.9
Liabilities and Equity			
Short-term debt and current portion long-term debt	64.9	108.1	385.3
Accounts payable	87.1	114.4	105.2
Accrued liabilities	189.3	248.3	246.5
Total current liabilities	341.2	470.7	736.9
Long-term debt	273.4	282.9	174.3
Other long-term liabilities	66.2	80.9	92.9
Deferred income taxes	154.5	172.0	203.5
Common stock and paid-in-capital	139.4	94.8	97.6
Retained earnings	1,077.9	1,214.0	1,365.2
Cumulative translation adjustment	26.2	26.4	2.5
Total stockholders' equity	1,243.5	1,335.3	1,465.3
Total liabilities and equity	2,078.8	2,341.8	2,672.9

The taxes related to interest expense, interest income, and non-operating items are calculated by multiplying the marginal tax rate by the item (unless more specific tax information is available). The marginal tax rate is generally the statutory marginal rate, including state and local taxes. In Hershey's case, we estimated its marginal

Exhibit 6.3 **HERSHEY FOODS CORPORATION,**
NOPLAT CALCULATION, $ MILLIONS

NOPLAT	1990	1991	1992
Net sales	2,715.6	2,899.2	3,219.8
Cost of goods sold	(1,526.6)	(1,621.7)	(1,749.0)
Selling, general and administrative expenses	(765.7)	(803.5)	(947.2)
Depreciation expense	(61.7)	(72.7)	(84.4)
Operating earnings before interest and taxes (EBIT)	361.6	401.3	439.2
Taxes on EBIT	(141.4)	(154.4)	(169.0)
Change in deferred taxes	12.9	17.5	31.5
NOPLAT	233.1	264.4	301.7
Taxes on EBIT			
Provision for income taxes (from income statement)	145.6	143.9	158.4
Tax shield on interest expense (at 39%)	10.3	11.4	11.6
Tax on interest income (at 39%)	(0.7)	(0.9)	(1.0)
Tax on nonoperating income (at 39%)	(13.9)	0.0	0.0
Taxes on EBIT	141.4	154.4	169.0
Reconciliation to Net Income			
Net income	215.9	219.5	242.6
Add: Increase in deferred taxes	12.9	17.5	31.5
Add: Goodwill amortization	11.0	11.0	11.0
Adjusted net income	239.8	248.1	285.1
Add: Interest expense after-tax	16.1	17.9	18.1
Total income available to investors	255.9	265.9	303.2
Less: Interest income after-tax	(1.0)	(1.5)	(1.5)
Less: Nonoperating income after-tax	(21.7)	0.0	0.0
NOPLAT	233.1	264.4	301.7

tax rate to be 39 percent. (Companies with tax loss carry-forwards or those subject to the alternative minimum tax may have different marginal rates.)

Change in deferred taxes   For valuation and analytical purposes, income taxes should be stated on a cash basis. This is consistent with the principal that the mere accounting treatment of an item should not affect its treatment for financial analysis. In the case of income taxes, investors expect the company to continue to earn a return on the capital saved as a result of tax deferrals. Putting taxes on a cash basis is consistent with the treatment of deferred tax balances as capital on which investors expect to earn a return just as they do on all other capital.

The provision for income taxes in the income statement generally does not equal the actual taxes paid in cash by the company due to differences between financial accounting and tax accounting. The adjustment to a cash basis can generally be calculated from the change in accumulated deferred income taxes on the company's balance sheet (the net of long- and short-term deferred tax assets and long- and short-term deferred tax liabilities).

Reconciliation to net income   We generally also reconcile net income to NOPLAT, as shown on the bottom of Exhibit 6.3, to ensure that nothing is missed in the calculation of NOPLAT and to ensure a complete understanding of the company's financial statements.

Invested Capital

Invested capital represents the amount invested in the *operations* of the business. Invested capital is the sum of operating working capital; net property, plant, and equipment; and net other assets (net of noncurrent, noninterest-bearing liabilities). Invested capital, plus any nonoperating investments, measures the total amount invested by the company's investors, which we will call total investor funds. Total investor funds can also be calculated from the liability side of the balance sheet as the sum of all equity (plus quasi-equity items like deferred taxes) and interest-bearing debt. Exhibit 6.4 demonstrates the calculation of invested capital for Hershey.

From the asset side, specific line items include operating current assets; noninterest bearing current liabilities; net property plant and equipment; other operating assets, net of other liabilities; and nonoperating assets.

Operating current assets   Operating working capital equals operating current assets minus noninterest bearing current liabilities. Operating current assets include all current assets used in or necessary for the operations of the business, including some cash balances, trade accounts receivables, and inventories.

Exhibit 6.4 **HERSHEY FOODS CORPORATION, INVESTED CAPITAL CALCULATION,** $ MILLIONS

	1990	1991	1992
Operating current assets	661.8	702.3	760.9
Noninterest bearing current liabilities	(276.4)	(362.7)	(351.7)
Net working capital	385.4	339.7	409.2
Net property plant and equipment	952.1	1,145.7	1,296.0
Other operating assets, net of other liabilities	(18.9)	(50.9)	(55.8)
Operating invested capital	1,318.6	1,434.4	1,649.4
Excess marketable securities	0.0	42.1	0.0
Goodwill	417.6	421.7	399.8
Nonoperating investments	0.0	0.0	179.1
Total investor funds	1,736.3	1,898.3	2,228.3
Equity	1,243.5	1,335.3	1,465.3
Deferred income taxes	154.5	172.0	203.5
Adjusted equity	1,398.0	1,507.3	1,668.8
All interest bearing debt	338.3	391.0	559.5
Total investor funds	1,736.3	1,898.3	2,228.3

Specifically excluded are excess cash and marketable securities. Excess cash and marketable securities (we'll use "marketable securities" as short hand) generally represent temporary imbalances in the company's cash flow. For example, the company may build up cash while deciding how to invest or distribute it. These excess marketable securities are not generally related directly to the company's operations.

In addition, considering marketable securities as nonoperating makes valuation easier. Marketable securities are generally much less risky than the operations of the firm. As marketable securities grow or decline in relation to the size of the company, the company's overall level of risk and its cost of capital should rise or fall. Modeling the change in the cost of capital is complex. It is much easier to consider the value of a company as the sum of the value of its operating free cash flow plus the present value of the cash flow related to its excess marketable securities, where the risk of each component is relatively stable over time.

Excess cash and marketable securities are the short-term cash and investments that the company holds over and above its *target* cash balances to support operations. The target balances can be estimated by observing the variability in the company's cash and marketable security balances over time and by comparing these against similar companies. As a rule of thumb, we often consider any cash and marketable securities balances over 0.5 percent to 2.0 percent of revenues to be excess, depending on the industry. This is consistent with the practice of excluding interest income from the calculation of NOPLAT. By excluding interest and excess cash, we can get a better sense of how operating working capital has changed over time, relative to revenues, and how the company compares to competitors.

Recognize also that the investment in short-term marketable securities is a zero-net-present-value investment. (It could also be argued that they are negative NPV investments if the double taxation of corporate income is considered). The return on this investment just compensates for its risk. Therefore, the present value of the cash flow related to these marketable securities must equal the market value of the excess marketable securities on the company's books at the time of the valuation. Excess marketable securities is built into a company's value as a specific line item. Excluding excess marketable securities is important, because we have seen companies with cash balances that are clearly not needed to run the business, some as high as $5 billion. Excluding excess cash and securities gives us a cleaner view of the operations of the business.

Noninterest-bearing current liabilities   Noninterest bearing current liabilities, such as accounts payable and accrued expenses as well as other noninterest bearing liabilities, are subtracted to calculate operating working capital. The reason for subtracting these liabilities is to achieve consistency with the definition of NOPLAT. The implicit financing costs associated with these liabilities are included in the expenses that are deducted in calculating NOPLAT. For example, the implicit interest that companies incur when they pay their bills for goods or services in 30 days rather than paying on delivery is included in the cost of goods sold. Hence by subtracting the noninterest bearing liabilities in calculating capital, we achieve consistency with NOPLAT. Alternatively, we could add back the estimated financing cost associated with noninterest bearing liabilities and not subtract the liabilities from capital. However, this approach adds considerable complexity, without providing any additional insight into the economics of the business.

Any interest-bearing current liabilities, such as short-term debt and the current maturities of long-term debt, are not subtracted from invested capital since the financing cost associated with these liabilities is explicitly excluded from the NOPLAT calculation.

Net property plant and equipment   Net property plant and equipment is the book value of the company's fixed assets. Whether or not fixed assets should be revalued at market values or replacement costs will be discussed later.

Other operating assets, net of other liabilities   Any other assets or noninterest bearing liabilities that are related to the operations of the business, excluding special investments, are also included in invested capital. In deciding whether an item is operating or nonoperating, make sure the treatment of the asset is consistent with the treatment of any associated income or expense in calculating NOPLAT. Also, consider industry norms so that your calculation of ROIC is as consistent as possible with the company's peers.

Nonoperating assets   Any assets not included in operating invested capital should be added when calculating total investor funds, unless they are netted against equity or debt (e.g., deferred debt issuance costs).

From the liability side, the line items to include in total investor funds are equity, deferred income taxes, adjusted equity, and interest-bearing debt.

Equity   Equity should include the sum of all common equity accounts, such as paid-in-capital and retained earnings, as well as other equity accounts, such as preferred shares and the minority interest in consolidated subsidiaries (which may not be classified as equity in the company's accounts).

Deferred income taxes   Deferred income taxes are a quasi-equity account. For accounting purposes, they are treated like a liability. For economic analysis, they are more like equity. Until the taxes are paid to the government, the funds belong to the shareholders, and the shareholders expect to earn a return on these funds. Hence, treat them like equity. Recall that for consistency, income tax expense was also converted to a cash basis in the calculation of NOPLAT.

Adjusted equity   Adjusted equity is the sum of all the equity accounts plus any quasi-equity accounts (e.g., deferred taxes).

Interest-bearing debt   The other source of funds is interest-bearing debt. Interest-bearing debt includes long-term debt, short-term debt, current maturities of long-term debt, and capitalized leases.

As you can see from Exhibit 6.4, total investor funds must be the same whether calculated from the asset perspective or the sources of capital perspective.

CALCULATING THE VALUE DRIVERS

Now that NOPLAT and invested capital have been defined, we can turn to the value drivers themselves: return on invested capital, free cash flow, and economic profit. In addition, we will discuss some special items that may need to be taken into consideration.

Return on Invested Capital

ROIC is defined as follows:

$$\text{Return on invested capital} = \frac{\text{NOPLAT}}{\text{Invested capital}}.$$

Invested capital is generally measured at the beginning of the period or as an average of the beginning and end of the period. The most important aspect of calculating ROIC is to define the numerator and denominator consistently. In other words, if you include an asset in invested capital, the income related to that asset should be in NOPLAT. The definitions of NOPLAT and invested capital, which we have developed above, should ensure that consistency is achieved. Exhibit 6.5 shows the ROIC calculation for Hershey.

ROIC versus other return measures   ROIC is a better analytical tool for understanding the company's performance than other

Exhibit 6.5 **HERSHEY FOODS CORPORATION,**
ROIC CALCULATION, $ MILLIONS

	1990	1991	1992
NOPLAT	233.1	264.4	301.7
Operating invested capital (beginning of year)	1,110.7	1,318.6	1,434.4
ROIC	21.0%	20.1%	21.0%
ROIC (using average capital)	19.2%	19.2%	19.6%
ROIC (including goodwill)	15.7%	15.2%	16.3%

return measures, such as return on equity or return on assets, because it focuses on the true operating performance of the company. Return on equity mixes operating performance with financial structure, making peer group analysis or trend analysis less focused. The return on total assets is inadequate because it includes a number of inconsistencies between the numerator and the denominator. Noninterest-bearing liabilities are not deducted from the denominator, total assets. Yet the implicit financing cost of these liabilities is included in the expenses of the company and, therefore, deducted from the numerator.

Replacement cost or market value   While ROIC is the best single return measure, like other historical cost accounting measures, it can be distorted by inflation. Two options are typically suggested to remedy this distortion: using replacement cost or using market values for fixed assets. We disagree with using replacement cost and believe that market values should be used only in certain situations.

We disagree with using replacement cost for the simple reason that assets do not have to be and may never be replaced. It may be economically justifiable to continue to use an old asset even though the profits generated by that asset are not high enough to justify replacing that asset. Furthermore, a company with a plant built several years before its competitors (assuming the same productivity potential) at a lower cost than its competitors' plants has a real competitive advantage, which should be reflected in a higher

ROIC. This advantage is similar to that of a company with lower labor costs because its workers are nonunionized or of a company located in a low tax jurisdiction. These advantages must be reflected in a company's returns.

Using the market values of assets is appropriate when the realizable market value of the assets substantially exceeds the historical cost book value. However, you are only likely to find tangible assets with such high values in the case of assets that have general uses beyond the company's current use of the assets. Real estate and airplanes are good examples, where the realizable market values of the assets might exceed the book values. For most assets, such as equipment, computers, and fixtures, the market values for used assets are generally very low. For most companies, the proportion of assets with market values significantly higher than book values is low, so calculating ROIC based on book values does not introduce significant distortions.

If market values are used, however, NOPLAT must be adjusted to reflect the annual appreciation of the value of the assets. It would be inconsistent to write up the assets without reflecting the appreciation in profits. This is a common error that we see when analysts argue for using market values. They ignore the economic profit associated with the write-up.

It could be argued that the reason for writing up the assets and for not including the appreciation in profits is to get a sense of whether a company's assets would be better used some other way. For example, consider a retailer that owns valuable real estate. The retailer might earn less than its cost of capital if the market value of the real estate were used instead of its book value. While this is true, remember we are trying to analyze the company's actual performance, not whether it is making the best use of its assets. Companies should do both, measure actual performance and determine whether or not they are making the best use of their assets. In Chapter 2, we showed how a company should periodically evaluate alternative uses for its key assets to ensure that it is making the best use of them.

Goodwill   We explicitly excluded goodwill, both the asset and the amortization, from the calculation of ROIC. In most cases, however, ROIC should be calculated both with and without goodwill. ROIC excluding goodwill measures the operating performance of the company and is useful for comparing operating performance across companies and analyzing trends over time. It is not distorted by the price premiums paid for acquisitions made in building the company. ROIC including goodwill measures how well the company has used its investors' funds. Specifically, has the company earned its cost of capital, taking into consideration the premiums it paid for acquisitions?

It is not uncommon for companies to earn high returns on an operating basis while failing to earn their cost of capital when acquisition premiums are considered. Ann Taylor, the specialty retailer, was taken private in an LBO in the late 1980s. Its balance sheet included $342 million of goodwill at the end of 1992, out of total assets of $488 million. Ann Taylor's ROIC, with and without goodwill, are as follows:

	1990	1991	1992
ROIC excluding goodwill	45.3%	31.1%	31.0%
ROIC including goodwill	8.8	6.8	6.9

You can see that Ann Taylor is a very successful retailer from an operating perspective, but may not have been a good investment due to the high price that was paid.

On a technical note, the proper way to include goodwill in the ROIC calculation is to add to invested capital the total amount of goodwill before cumulative amortization and not to deduct from NOPLAT any goodwill amortization. In effect, this reverses the amortization of goodwill. The reason for not amortizing goodwill for economic analysis is that goodwill, unlike other fixed assets, does not wear out and is not replaced. For other assets, depreciation or amortization is a proxy for the physical deterioration of the asset with the recognition that the asset must be replaced if the company wishes to remain in business.

ROIC tree   A very useful way to organize an analysis of the rate of return is to develop a return-on-invested-capital tree. The ROIC tree disaggregates ROIC into its key components to provide more insights into the drivers of ROIC. The tree begins by dividing ROIC into its key components:

$$\text{ROIC} = \frac{\text{NOPLAT}}{\text{Invested capital}}.$$

Since NOPLAT can be expressed as EBIT × (1−Cash tax rate), ROIC can be expressed as a pretax ROIC (based on EBIT rather than NOPLAT) adjusted for taxes.

$$\text{ROIC} = \frac{\text{EBIT}}{\text{Invested capital}} \times (1 - \text{Cash tax rate}).$$

If we relate EBIT and invested capital to revenues, we get the equation:

$$\frac{\text{EBIT}}{\text{Invested capital}} = \frac{\text{EBIT}}{\text{Revenues}} \times \frac{\text{Revenues}}{\text{Invested Capital}}.$$

Pretax ROIC is thus disaggregated into two major components:

- Operating margin (EBIT/Revenues) measures how effectively the company converts revenues into profits
- Capital turnover (Revenues/Invested capital) measures how effectively the company employs its invested capital.

Each of these components can be further disaggregated into their components where the expense or capital items are compared to revenues. Exhibit 6.6 shows how the components can be organized into an ROIC tree for Hershey.

The component measures of the return on invested capital are industry- and company-specific. For example, wholesalers typically have slim margins and high turnover, while telephone companies have high margins and low capital turnover. These ratios may also reflect the company's operating strategy relative to its competitors. For example, higher margins might compensate for lower capital turnover (although the best companies often outperform their competitors on all measures).

Free Cash Flow

Free cash flow (FCF) is a company's true operating cash flow. It is the total after-tax cash flow generated by the company and available to all providers of the company's capital, both creditors and shareholders. It can be thought of as the after-tax cash flow that would be available to the company's shareholders if the company

EXHIBIT 6.6 HERSHEY FOODS CORPORATION, 1992 ROIC TREE
USING BEGINNING CAPITAL

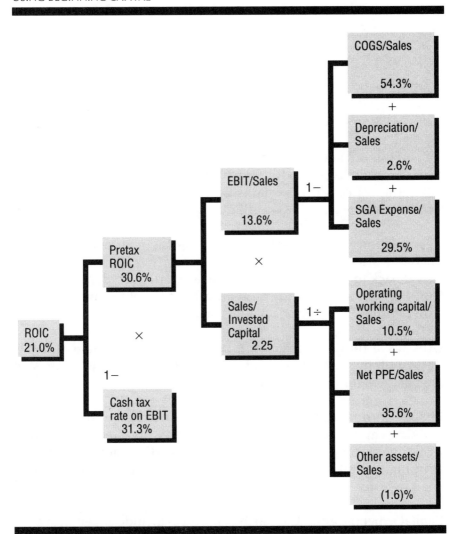

had no debt. Free cash flow is generally not affected by the company's financial structure, even though the financial structure may affect the company's weighted average cost of capital and therefore its value.

It is essential to define free cash flow properly to ensure consistency between the cash flow and the discount rate used to value the company. Free cash flow equals NOPLAT less net investment, where net investment is the change in invested capital. Adding depreciation to NOPLAT and net investment gives us gross cash flow and gross investment, which is how most free cash flow statements are presented.

FCF = NOPLAT − Net investment.

FCF = (NOPLAT + Depreciation) − (Net investment + Depreciation).

FCF = Gross cash flow − Gross investment.

Exhibit 6.7 shows the free cash flow calculation for Hershey and its reconciliation to total cash flow available to investors. The following list of terms explains the components of free cash flow that have not been defined earlier.

Depreciation   Depreciation includes all the noncash charges deducted from EBIT except goodwill amortization (which is not added back to NOPLAT, because it was not deducted in calculating NOPLAT). It also includes the amortization of intangible assets with definite lives, such as patents and franchises.

Gross cash flow   Gross cash flow represents the total cash flow thrown off by the company. It is the amount available to reinvest in the business for maintenance and growth.

Change in operating working capital   The change in operating working capital is the amount the company invested in operating working capital during the period. Use the definition of operating working capital described earlier in this chapter when we calculated invested capital.

Capital expenditures   Capital expenditures include expenditures on new and replacement property, plant, and equipment. Capital expenditures can be calculated from the balance sheet and income statement as the increase in *net* property, plant, and equipment plus depreciation expense for the period. (Technically, this calculation results in capital expenditures less the net book value of retired assets.)

Increase in other assets, net of liabilities   The increase in net other assets equals the expenditure on all other operating assets including capitalized intangibles (patents, trademarks), deferred expenses,

Exhibit 6.7 **HERSHEY FOODS CORPORATION, FREE CASH FLOW
CALCULATION,** $ MILLIONS

NOPLAT	1990	1991	1992
EBIT	361.6	401.3	439.2
Taxes on EBIT	(141.4)	(154.4)	(169.0)
Change in deferred taxes	12.9	17.5	31.5
NOPLAT	233.1	264.4	301.7
Depreciation expense	61.7	72.7	84.4
Gross cash flow	294.9	337.2	386.1
Increase in working capital	94.2	(45.7)	69.5
Capital expenditures	183.9	266.3	234.8
Increase in other assets, net of liabilities	(8.4)	(32.1)	(4.9)
Gross investment	269.7	188.5	299.4
Free cash flow before goodwill	25.2	148.7	86.7
Investment in goodwill	(55.2)	(15.0)	10.9
Free cash flow	(30.1)	133.6	97.6
Nonoperating cash flow	21.7	0.0	(179.1)
Foreign currency translation effect	(0.7)	0.2	(23.9)
Cash flow available to investors	(9.1)	133.8	(105.4)
Financing flow			
After-tax interest income	(1.0)	(1.5)	(1.5)
Increase/(decrease) in excess marketable securities	(28.3)	42.1	(42.1)
After tax-interest expense	16.1	17.9	18.1
Decrease/(increase) in debt	(84.5)	(52.7)	(168.5)
Dividends	87.8	83.4	91.4
Share repurchases/(issues)	1.0	44.6	(2.8)
Total financing flow	(9.1)	133.8	(105.4)

and net of increases in noncurrent, noninterest-bearing liabilities. These can be calculated directly from the change in the balance sheet accounts plus any amortization included in depreciation.

Gross investment   Gross investment is the sum of a company's expenditures for new capital, including working capital, capital expenditures, and other assets.

Investment in goodwill   The investment in goodwill equals the expenditures to acquire other companies in excess of the book value of their net assets. In any year, the investment in goodwill is best calculated as the net change in the goodwill account on the balance sheet plus the amortization of goodwill in that period. This ensures that goodwill amortization does not affect free cash flow in either gross cash flow or gross investment.

Nonoperating Cash Flow   Nonoperating cash flow represents the after-tax cash flow from items not related to operations. Free cash flow explicitly excludes nonoperating cash flow. Caution must be exercised, however, in considering an item to be nonoperating. Any nonoperating cash flow must be reflected in the value of the company explicitly. We do this by defining the total value of the company as the discounted present value of the company's free cash flow plus the value of its after-tax nonoperating cash flow.

Present value of company's free cash flow	+	Present value of after-tax nonoperating cash flow	=	Total value of company

Cash flow items that are sometimes considered nonoperating include cash flow from discontinued operations, extraordinary items, and the cash flow from investments in unrelated subsidiaries. Remember, though, that the present value of any nonoperating cash flow must be reflected in the total value of the company.

It is generally inadvisable to consider a recurring cash flow as nonoperating. The company's risk, and therefore its cost of capital, reflects all of its assets and its cash flow. Arbitrarily excluding items from free cash flow may violate the principle of consistency between free cash flow and cost of capital.

Financing cash flow   The sum of free cash flow and the nonoperating items just enumerated equals the total funds available to investors (or, if negative, the funds the investors must provide). These total funds available must equal the financing cash flows. That is, the total cash generated by the company's operations (plus nonoperating cash flow, if any) must equal the net payments to all the company's creditors and shareholders. Conversely, if free cash flow is negative, it must equal the net funds provided by the company's shareholders and creditors (for example, via new issues of debt or equity).

This equality between operating and financial flows helps ensure that the free cash flow calculation is correct. The complexity of some financial statements often leads to mistakes in FCF calculations. Errors can be minimized by always calculating the company's financial flow and ensuring that it equals the funds available to investors. The financing flow line items are

Change in excess marketable securities   Excess cash and marketable securities and related interest income were excluded from invested capital and NOPLAT. We generally treat them as financing cash flow since any excess marketable securities are effectively like negative debt.

After-tax interest income   The after-tax interest income on excess marketable securities equals the pretax income $\times$ 1 minus the appropriate marginal income tax rate.

Foreign currency translation effect   The change in the cumulative foreign currency translation gains or losses account is driven by the changes in translation rates applied to both assets and debt. As a practical matter, you generally cannot separate the asset and debt gains or losses without internal information. Therefore, treat these gains/losses as nonoperating cash flow in the free cash flow. If you have the information needed to separate the asset from the debt effects, treat the gains/losses on assets as adjustments to free cash flow and gains/losses on debt as financial cash flow.[1]

Change in debt   The change in debt represents the net borrowing or repayment on all the company's interest-bearing debt, including short-term debt and capitalized leases.

After-tax interest expense   The after-tax interest expense equals the pretax interest expense times 1 minus the company's marginal income tax rate. The marginal tax rate should be consistent with the rate used for the adjustment of taxes on EBIT.

[1] See Financial Accounting Standards Board Statement No. 52 for a complete discussion of foreign currency accounting.

Dividends   Dividends include all cash dividends on common and preferred shares. Dividends paid in stock have no cash effects and should be ignored.

Share issues/repurchases   Share issues/repurchases include both preferred and common shares and the effects of conversions of debt to equity. This figure can be calculated by taking the change in total equity plus dividends less net income.

Economic Profit

Economic profit measures the dollars of economic value created by a company in a single year and is defined as follows:

$$\text{Economic Profit} = \text{Invested capital} \times (\text{ROIC} - \text{WACC}).$$

Recall from Chapter 5 that economic profit can also be defined as:

$$\text{Economic Profit} = \text{NOPLAT} - \text{Capital charge}.$$

Where the capital charge equals invested capital times WACC:

$$\text{Economic Profit} = \text{NOPLAT} - (\text{Invested capital} \times \text{WACC}).$$

As a practical matter, we generally use invested capital measured at the beginning of the period or the average of beginning and ending capital. Technically, for the economic profit valuation to exactly equal the DCF valuation, you must use beginning capital. If you use average capital, the variance will generally be very small. Exhibit 6.8 shows the economic profit for Hershey.

Economic profit is an important measure because it combines size and ROIC into a single result. Too often companies focus on either size (often measured by earnings) or ROIC. Focusing on size (say earnings or earnings growth) could destroy value if returns on capital are too low. Conversely, earning a high ROIC on a low capital base may mean missed opportunities.

A question sometimes arises as to whether invested capital should be measured at book values, market values, or replacement costs. We recommend using book values, unless realizable market values are significantly higher for the same reasons that we outlined when discussing ROIC in the prior section of this chapter.

Exhibit 6.8 **HERSHEY FOODS CORPORATION, ECONOMIC PROFIT CALCULATION,** $ MILLIONS

	1990	1991	1992
Return on invested capital	21.0%	20.1%	21.0%
WACC	11.9%	10.6%	10.5%
Spread	9.1%	9.5%	10.5%
Invested capital (beginning of year)	1,110.7	1,318.6	1,434.4
Economic profit	101.0	124.7	151.1
NOPLAT	233.1	264.4	301.7
Capital charge	132.1	139.7	150.6
Economic profit	101.0	124.7	151.1

Finally, it is important not to confuse economic profit, which measures realized value creation, with the increase in the value of a company during the period. For example, in 1992, Hershey earned an economic profit of $151 million. However, during 1992 the market value of Hershey's shares increased by $377 million. Adding the dividends paid to Hershey's shareholders of $91 million in 1992, gives a total shareholder value creation of $418 million, substantially more than economic profit. The two concepts measure different aspects of value. The market value at any point in time measures perceived future value creation expectations, the increase in market value over a year equals economic profit (the realized value creation) plus the change in the value creation expectations. The change in market value will equal economic profit only if there is no change in expected future performance and if the WACC remains constant during the year.

Special Items in Calculating Value Drivers

A number of special items that were not discussed earlier may need to be reflected in the calculation of a company's value drivers.

Operating leases Operating leases are any lease obligations that the company has not capitalized. Operating leases represent a type of financing and, if material, should be treated as such in the calculation of the company's value drivers.

To do this, adjust the company's financial statements to treat operating leases as if they were capitalized. First, reclassify the implied interest expense portion of the lease payments from an operating expense (usually in cost of goods sold, or selling, general, and administrative expense) to an interest expense. This increases EBIT by the amount of implied interest. Do not forget to adjust the EBIT taxes as well. Second, add the implied principal amount of operating leases to invested capital and to debt. Finally, treat the principal amount as additional debt in the weighted average cost of capital calculation. This mimics the effects that would have occurred had the leases been capitalized.

To estimate the implied principal amount of the operating leases, a rule of thumb approach is to discount the future minimum lease payments (disclosed in the footnotes to U.S. audited statements) at the company's marginal borrowing rate. To estimate the implied interest expense, multiply the implied principal amount by the marginal borrowing rate.

Pensions   Adjusting for pension plans depends on whether the plan is over- or underfunded and whether any over- or underfunding is recorded on the financial statements. For fully funded plans, no adjustments are necessary. We will describe how to treat underfunded plans. The treatment of overfunded plans is the opposite.

For unfunded or underfunded plans, where the liability is recorded in the financial statements, follow these guidelines:

1. If the underfunding is not material to the financial analysis, treat the liability the same as other noninterest-bearing liabilities in calculating capital. No adjustment is needed for NOPLAT.

2. If the underfunding is material, treat the liability the same as interest-bearing debt in calculating invested capital and the cost of capital. For NOPLAT, estimate the implied interest expense on the liability for the year and reclassify a portion of operating expenses equal to this amount as interest expense. The footnotes to the financial statements generally provide enough information to do this. These adjustments ensure consistency between NOPLAT and invested capital

by treating them as if the company had borrowed the necessary money to fund the liability.

For unfunded and unrecorded pension liabilities that are significant, the proper procedure is to first adjust the financial statements to how they would appear if the liability were recorded. Then follow the procedure above for calculating NOPLAT and invested capital. Adjusting the financial statements involves reclassifying a portion of retained earnings as the pension liability and adjusting each year's earnings by the increase in the unfunded liability. To avoid enormous swings in ROIC due to large swings in the unfunded liability, consider smoothing the adjustments over time.

Minority interest   A minority interest occurs when a third party owns some percentage of one of the company's consolidated subsidiaries. If material, minority interest should be handled as follows:

1. Treat the balance sheet amount as a quasi-equity account.
2. Treat the earnings attributable to minority interest as a financing cost like interest expense, with an appropriate adjustment for income taxes.
3. Treat the associated cash flow to the minority investors as a financing flow. The cash flow can be estimated as the earnings attributable to the minority interest less the increase in the balance sheet account. This essentially equals the dividends paid to the minority investors less any contributions from them.

Post retirement medical benefits   Financial Accounting Statement 106 requires companies to record as a liability the present value of expected post retirement medical benefits for employees. These are conceptually similar to unfunded pension plans that are recorded on a company's financial statements and should be treated the same way.

AN INTEGRATED HISTORICAL PERSPECTIVE

Once you have calculated the historical value drivers, analyze the results by looking for trends and making comparisons with other companies in the same industry. Try to assemble this analysis into an integrated perspective, which combines the financial analysis with an analysis of the industry structure (opportunities for differentiation, entry/exit barriers, etc.) and a qualitative assessment of the company's strengths and vulnerabilities.

Developing this integrated perspective is not a mechanical process, so it is difficult to generalize, but we can provide some examples.

- For consumer products companies with strong brand names, like Hershey Foods, you are likely to find good ROICs. The key issues tend to be about growth (market share, new products, managing the distribution chain, etc.) and benchmarking performance against competitors (manufacturing costs, overhead, inventory management).

- For commodity companies, like paper or some chemical companies, you need to understand whether the company and the industry have been able to earn their cost of capital over time because in many cases they haven't. You then need to understand the short- and long-term supply/demand picture for the industry and evaluate competitor behavior. Try to identify where the industry is in its cycle and whether there are structural changes that will change the cycle permanently. Think about whether the company has any competitive advantages (technology, market access). Has the company been able to turn these advantages into higher returns than the industry average? How good a job has the company done at timing major capital expenditures?

While it is impossible to provide a comprehensive checklist for understanding a company's historical performance, here are some things to keep in mind:

- Look back in time as far as possible (at least ten years). This will help you to understand whether the company and the industry tend to revert to some normal level of performance over time and whether short term trends are likely to be permanent breaks from the past.

- Go as deep into the value drivers as you can, getting as close to operational performance measures as possible.

- If there are any radical changes in performance, identify the source of the change and determine whether it is real or perhaps just an accounting effect and whether any change is likely to be sustained.

FINANCIAL HEALTH FROM A CREDIT PERSPECTIVE

The final step in the historical analysis is understanding the financial health of the company from a credit perspective. Here we are not concerned with value creation itself, but with how the company has been financing its value creation. Specifically, is the company generating or consuming investors' cash? What proportion of invested capital comes from creditors rather than equity investors? How safe is this capital structure?

The best way to understand a company's financial health is to project its cash flows and develop a financing plan for a number of cash flow scenarios. However, as a first step, an analysis of historical performance provides some early insights. Since this book's focus is not credit analysis, we will just touch on some of the key measures we use to analyze financial health. Exhibit 6.9 shows an analysis of Hershey Foods' historical financial health.

Interest Coverage

Interest coverage, the amount of earnings available to pay interest expense, measures the company's financial cushion. It provides a sense of how far operating profits could fall before the company would have difficulty servicing its debt. We generally measure coverage as EBIT divided by interest expense and required preferred dividends. There are a number of variations for this measure, such as adding required lease payments to the denominator or adding depreciation back to the numerator. These may be helpful in some circumstances, particularly when you are trying to get a short-term perspective on the ability of the company to pay its creditors. For a long term perspective, however, we generally stick with the basic ratio.

Hershey's interest coverage ranged from 13.7 times to 14.8 times during the 1990 to 1992 period, which is extremely safe (thus accounting for Hershey's AA bond rating). In other words, Hershey's EBIT could fall to $\frac{1}{13}$ of its historical amount and its EBIT would still exceed its interest expense. Investment grade companies typically have coverage ratios exceeding 2 times interest expense.

Exhibit 6.9 **HERSHEY FOODS CORPORATION, FINANCING ANALYSIS,**
$ MILLIONS

	1990	1991	1992
Interest coverage			
EBIT	361.6	401.3	439.2
Interest expense	26.3	29.3	29.7
EBIT/Interest expense	13.7 ×	13.7 ×	14.8 ×
Capital structure			
Total interest bearing debt	338.3	391.0	559.5
Total investor funds	1,736.3	1,898.3	2,228.3
Debt/Total funds (book value)	19.5%	20.6%	25.1%
Debt/Total funds (market values)			15.0%
Investment rate			
Net investment	208.0	115.8	215.0
NOPLAT	233.1	264.4	301.7
Net investment rate	89.2%	43.8%	71.3%
Gross investment	269.7	188.5	299.4
Gross cash flow	294.9	337.2	386.1
Gross investment rate	91.5%	55.9%	77.6%
Dividend payout			
Common dividends	87.8	83.4	91.4
Net income available to common	215.9	219.5	242.6
Dividend payout ratio	40.7%	38.0%	37.7%
Financing flow analysis			
After-tax interest income	(1.0)	(1.5)	(1.5)
Increase/(decrease) in excess marketable securities	(28.3)	42.1	(42.1)
After-tax interest expense	16.1	17.9	18.1
Decrease/(increase) in debt	(84.5)	(52.7)	(168.5)
Dividends	87.8	83.4	91.4
Share repurchases/(issues)	1.0	44.6	(2.8)
Total financing flow	(9.1)	133.8	(105.4)

Debt/Total Investor Funds

Debt/investor funds measure the company's reliance on debt capital. While debt has tax advantages that will be outlined in Chapter 8, it also can reduce a company's flexibility, because debtholders expect to be paid on a set schedule, whereas the company has great flexibility in paying dividends to shareholders. We generally measure total interest-bearing debt to total investor funds, expressed both at book values and at market values. You may also consider subtracting excess cash and marketable securities from both the numerator and denominator, if the excess cash could be used to pay down debt.

At book values, which creditors often use, Hershey's debt to total investor funds ratio was 25 percent in 1992, slightly higher than in 1991 and 1990. Once again, this is fairly conservative.

Investment Rate

The investment rate is the ratio of investment to available funds. This can either be expressed on a net basis (net investment/NOPLAT) or gross basis (gross investment/gross cash flow). In either case, this measure tells you whether the company is consuming more funds than it is generating (investment rate greater than one) or generating extra cash flow that can be paid to investors as interest expense, dividends, debt reductions, share repurchases, and so on.

Dividend Payout Ratio

The dividend payout ratio is total common dividends divided by income available to common shareholders. In conjunction with our analysis of the investment rate, we can understand the company's financial situation by examining the financing flows of the company. If, for example, the company has a high dividend payout ratio and an investment rate greater than one, then it must be borrowing money to fund a negative free cash flow to pay interest and dividends. We might be concerned about how sustainable this is. On the other hand, a company with positive free cash flow and low dividend payout is probably paying down debt. If sustained over time, this company might be passing up the tax benefits of debt.

Hershey's gross investment rate was 78 percent in 1992, and has consistently been less than 100 percent. However, in 1992

Hershey invested about $180 million in the shares of a European company it wanted to take over. This resulted in a negative cash flow available to investors of $105 million. After paying dividends at 38 percent of earnings, paying interest expense, and adjusting for several smaller items, Hershey financed its negative cash flow by net borrowing of $169 million.

PRESTON CORPORATION

To wrap up this chapter and to provide examples at the ends of each of the next four chapters, we will illustrate the concepts we have developed with a comprehensive case: The Preston Corporation. Preston Corporation is a regional trucking company that transports freight by motor carrier. In 1987, the year before this valuation, Preston earned revenues of $505 million and had 8,300 employees. It carries truckload shipments, higher-fee less-than-truckload shipments, and special commodities. Less-than-truckload shipments account for 73.5 percent of its revenues. Preston competes with hundreds of other carriers throughout its areas of service, as well as with railroads, airlines, and shipper-operated trucks in some regions.

CALCULATE THE VALUE DRIVERS

Exhibits 6.10 through 6.19 show the calculation of the value drivers for Preston. Exhibits 6.10 and 6.11 present Preston's income statement and balance sheet for the years 1981 through 1987. Exhibits 6.12 through 6.14 show how to calculate Preston's NOPLAT, invested capital, and free cash flow for each year. Exhibit 6.15 summarizes Preston's ROIC and its growth rates, as well as several other key measures. Exhibit 6.16 shows the calculations of Preston's economic profit. The remainder of the exhibits show various backup calculations or ratios that will be used for forecasting.

The following highlights some key background information, derived from Preston's financial statement footnotes, that will be used in the valuation:

Consolidation

Preston Corporation has guaranteed the secured notes of its wholly owned subsidiaries, Reeves Transportation Company and Bowie Hall Trucking, Inc., as well as the unsecured note of its subsidiary Smalley Transportation Company. Because these subsidiaries are fully consolidated, we have

Exhibit 6.10 **PRESTON CORPORATION, HISTORICAL INCOME STATEMENT**, $ MILLIONS

	1981	1982	1983	1984	1985	1986	1987
Revenues	197.6	222.3	272.3	299.5	350.0	418.9	505.4
Operating expenses	(175.4)	(206.9)	(249.6)	(274.7)	(327.5)	(383.6)	(467.4)
Other expenses	0.0	0.0	0.0	0.0	0.0	0.0	0.0
Depreciation expense	(12.8)	(9.3)	(11.2)	(13.0)	(15.0)	(17.7)	(26.4)
Operating income	9.4	6.1	11.5	11.8	7.5	17.6	11.6
Amortization of goodwill	0.0	0.0	0.0	0.0	0.0	(0.1)	(0.6)
Nonoperating income	1.8	1.8	1.7	3.2	0.3	0.3	(0.5)
Interest income	0.0	0.0	0.0	0.0	0.9	0.7	0.6
Interest expense	(0.1)	(0.4)	(0.8)	(1.0)	(3.4)	(4.1)	(10.1)
Special items	0.0	0.0	0.0	0.0	0.0	0.0	0.0
Earnings before taxes	11.1	7.5	12.4	14.0	5.3	14.4	1.0
Income taxes	(5.3)	(2.4)	(5.8)	(5.2)	(1.0)	(7.1)	(0.7)
Minority interest	0.0	0.0	0.0	0.0	0.0	0.0	0.0
Income before extra items	5.8	5.1	6.6	8.8	4.3	7.3	0.3
Extraordinary items	0.0	0.0	0.0	0.0	0.0	0.0	0.0
Effect of accounting change	0.5	0.0	0.0	0.0	0.0	0.0	5.8
Net income	6.3	5.1	6.6	8.8	4.3	7.3	6.1
Statement of retained earnings							
Beginning retained earnings	60.6	64.8	67.8	70.0	76.0	78.2	82.6
Net income	6.3	5.1	6.6	8.8	4.3	7.3	6.1
Common dividends	(2.1)	(2.1)	(2.8)	(2.8)	(2.8)	(2.9)	(2.9)
Preferred dividends	0.0	0.0	0.0	0.0	0.0	0.0	0.0
Adjustment to retained earnings	(0.0)	(0.0)	(1.6)	0.0	0.7	0.0	0.0
Ending retained earnings	64.8	67.8	70.0	76.0	78.2	82.6	85.8

Exhibit 6.11 **PRESTON CORPORATION, HISTORICAL BALANCE SHEET,** $ MILLIONS

Assets	1981	1982	1983	1984	1985	1986	1987
Operating cash	4.0	4.4	5.4	6.0	6.0	8.4	10.1
Excess marketable securities	10.9	3.0	20.5	10.3	0.0	5.8	3.2
Accounts receivable	19.4	26.4	35.7	36.0	50.1	54.7	63.4
Inventories	1.9	2.1	2.8	2.5	9.0	10.9	11.9
Other current assets	4.3	5.1	5.3	6.0	2.4	4.4	5.0
Total current assets	40.5	41.0	69.7	60.8	67.5	84.2	93.6
Gross property, plant, and equipment	100.0	117.7	128.2	155.6	204.7	272.5	297.6
Accumulated depreciation	(37.7)	(42.3)	(48.7)	(56.5)	(71.9)	(86.9)	(103.4)
Net property, plant, and equipment	62.3	75.4	79.5	99.1	132.8	185.6	194.2
Goodwill	0.0	0.0	0.0	0.0	3.2	24.7	24.4
Other operating assets	0.5	1.2	1.2	3.1	3.4	6.2	8.3
Investments and advances	0.0	0.0	0.0	0.0	0.0	0.0	0.0
Total assets	103.3	117.6	150.4	163.0	206.9	300.7	320.5

Exhibit 6.11 Continued

	1981	1982	1983	1984	1985	1986	1987
Liabilities and equity							
Short-term debt	0.3	0.8	0.9	1.5	11.5	12.5	20.7
Accounts payable	7.3	11.0	11.9	10.5	14.2	16.2	18.9
Other current liabilities	13.9	13.5	18.2	18.5	21.4	27.8	28.8
Total current liabilities	21.5	25.3	31.0	30.5	47.1	56.5	68.4
Long term debt	3.7	8.6	13.2	17.4	38.4	112.9	122.4
Deferred income taxes	8.7	11.0	12.6	15.5	19.6	25.1	20.3
Other noninterest liabilities	0.0	0.0	0.0	0.0	0.0	0.0	0.0
Minority interest	0.0	0.0	0.0	0.0	0.0	0.0	0.0
Preferred stock	0.0	0.0	0.0	0.0	0.0	0.0	0.0
Common stock and paid-in capital	4.6	4.9	23.6	23.6	23.6	23.6	23.6
Retained earnings	64.8	67.8	70.0	76.0	78.2	82.6	85.8
Treasury stock	0.0	0.0	0.0	0.0	0.0	0.0	0.0
Cummulative translation and other adjustments	0.0	0.0	0.0	0.0	0.0	0.0	0.0
Total common equity	69.4	72.7	93.6	99.6	101.8	106.2	109.4
Total liabilities and equity	103.3	117.6	150.4	163.0	206.9	300.7	320.5

Exhibit 6.12 **PRESTON CORPORATION, HISTORICAL NOPLAT,** $ MILLIONS

	1982	1983	1984	1985	1986	1987
NOPLAT						
Net sales	222.3	272.3	299.5	350.0	418.9	505.4
Operating expenses	(206.9)	(249.6)	(274.7)	(327.5)	(383.6)	(487.4)
Other expenses	0.0	0.0	0.0	0.0	0.0	0.0
Depreciation expense	(9.3)	(11.2)	(13.0)	(15.0)	(17.7)	(26.4)
Adjustments for operating leases	0.8	0.9	1.0	1.1	1.2	1.2
EBIT	6.9	12.4	12.8	8.6	18.8	12.8
Taxes on EBIT	(2.1)	(5.8)	(4.6)	(2.6)	(9.2)	(5.7)
Change in deferred taxes	2.3	1.6	2.9	4.1	5.5	(4.8)
Deferred taxes accounting change	0.0	0.0	0.0	0.0	0.0	5.8
NOPLAT	7.1	8.2	11.1	10.1	15.1	8.1
Taxes on EBIT						
Provision for income taxes	2.4	5.8	5.2	1.0	7.1	0.7
Tax shield on interest expense	0.2	0.4	0.5	1.7	2.0	4.5
Tax shield on operating lease interest	0.4	0.4	0.5	0.5	0.6	0.5
Tax on interest income	0.0	0.0	0.0	(0.4)	(0.3)	(0.3)
Tax on nonoperating income	(0.9)	(0.8)	(1.6)	(0.1)	(0.1)	0.2
Taxes on EBIT	2.1	5.8	4.6	2.6	9.2	5.7

Exhibit 6.12 Continued

	1982	1983	1984	1985	1986	1987
Reconciliation to net income						
Net income	5.1	6.6	8.8	4.3	7.3	6.1
Add: Increase in deferred taxes	2.3	1.6	2.9	4.1	5.5	(4.8)
Add: Goodwill amortization	0.0	0.0	0.0	0.0	0.1	0.6
Add: Extraordinary items	0.0	0.0	0.0	0.0	0.0	0.0
Add: Special items after tax	0.0	0.0	0.0	0.0	0.0	0.0
Add: Minority interest	0.0	0.0	0.0	0.0	0.0	0.0
Adjusted net income	7.4	8.2	11.7	8.4	12.9	1.9
Add: Interest expense after tax	0.2	0.4	0.5	1.7	2.1	5.6
Add: Interest expense on operating leases	0.4	0.5	0.5	0.6	0.6	0.7
Total Income available to investors	8.0	9.1	12.7	10.7	15.6	8.1
Less: Interest income after tax	0.0	0.0	0.0	(0.5)	(0.4)	(0.3)
Less: Nonoperating income after tax	(0.9)	(0.9)	(1.6)	(0.2)	(0.2)	0.3
NOPLAT	7.1	8.2	11.1	10.1	15.1	8.1

Exhibit 6.13 **PRESTON CORPORATION, HISTORICAL INVESTED CAPITAL,** $ MILLIONS

	1981	1982	1983	1984	1985	1986	1987
Operating current assets	29.6	38.0	49.2	50.5	67.5	78.4	90.4
Noninterest bearing liabilities	(21.2)	(24.5)	(30.1)	(29.0)	(35.6)	(44.0)	(47.7)
Operating working capital	8.4	13.5	19.1	21.5	31.9	34.4	42.7
Net property plant and equipment	62.3	75.4	79.5	99.1	132.8	185.6	194.2
Other assets net of other liabilities	0.5	1.2	1.2	3.1	3.4	6.2	8.3
Value of operating leases	6.6	7.3	8.0	8.8	9.7	10.7	11.0
Operating invested capital	77.8	97.4	107.8	132.5	177.8	236.9	256.2
Excess marketable securities	10.9	3.0	20.5	10.3	0.0	5.8	3.2
Goodwill	0.0	0.0	0.0	0.0	3.2	24.7	24.4
Nonoperating investments	0.0	0.0	0.0	0.0	0.0	0.0	0.0
Total investor funds	88.7	100.4	128.3	142.8	181.0	267.4	283.8
Equity	69.4	72.7	93.6	99.6	101.8	106.2	109.4
Deferred income taxes	8.7	11.0	12.6	15.5	19.6	25.1	20.3
Adjusted equity	78.1	83.7	106.2	115.1	121.4	131.3	129.7
Interest bearing debt	4.0	9.4	14.1	18.9	49.9	125.4	143.1
Value of operating leases	6.6	7.3	8.0	8.8	9.7	10.7	11.0
Total investor funds	88.7	100.4	128.3	142.8	181.0	267.4	283.8

Exhibit 6.14 **PRESTON CORPORATION, HISTORICAL FREE CASH FLOW,** $ MILLIONS

	1982	1983	1984	1985	1986	1987
Free cash flow						
EBIT	6.9	12.4	12.8	8.6	18.8	12.8
Taxes on EBIT	(2.1)	(5.8)	(4.6)	(2.6)	(9.2)	(5.7)
Change in deferred taxes	2.3	1.6	2.9	4.1	5.5	1.0
NOPLAT	7.1	8.2	11.1	10.1	15.1	8.1
Depreciation	9.3	11.2	13.0	15.0	17.7	26.4
Gross cash flow	16.4	19.4	24.1	25.1	32.8	34.5
Increase in working capital	5.1	5.6	2.4	10.4	2.5	-8.3
Capital expenditures	22.4	15.3	32.6	48.7	70.5	35.0
Increase in other assets	0.7	0.0	1.9	0.3	2.8	2.1
Investment in operating leases	0.7	0.7	0.8	0.9	1.0	0.3
Gross investment	28.9	21.6	37.7	60.3	76.8	45.7
Free cash flow before goodwill	(12.5)	(2.2)	(13.6)	(35.2)	(44.0)	(11.3)
Investment in goodwill	0.0	0.0	0.0	(3.2)	(21.6)	(0.3)
Free cash flow	(12.5)	(2.2)	(13.6)	(38.4)	(65.6)	(11.6)
Nonoperating cash flow	0.9	0.9	1.6	0.2	0.2	(0.3)
Foreign currency translation effect	0.0	0.0	0.0	0.0	0.0	0.0
Cash flow available to investors	(11.6)	(1.4)	(12.0)	(38.2)	(65.4)	(11.8)

Exhibit 6.14 Continued

	1982	1983	1984	1985	1986	1987
Financing flow						
After-tax interest income	0.0	0.0	0.0	(0.5)	(0.4)	(0.3)
Increase/(Decrease) in excess marketable securities	(7.9)	17.5	(10.2)	(10.3)	5.8	(2.6)
After-tax interest expense	0.2	0.4	0.5	1.7	2.1	5.6
After-tax interest on operating leases	0.4	0.5	0.5	0.6	0.6	0.7
Decrease/(Increase) in debt	(5.4)	(4.7)	(4.8)	(31.0)	(75.5)	(17.7)
Decrease/(Increase) in operating leases	(0.7)	(0.7)	(0.8)	(0.9)	(1.0)	(0.3)
Minority interest	0.0	0.0	0.0	0.0	0.0	0.0
Common dividends	2.1	2.8	2.8	2.8	2.9	2.9
Preferred dividends	0.0	0.0	0.0	0.0	0.0	0.0
Decrease/(Increase) in preferred	0.0	0.0	0.0	0.0	0.0	0.0
Decrease/(Increase) in common	(0.3)	(17.1)	0.0	(0.7)	0.0	0.0
Total financing flow	(11.6)	(1.4)	(12.0)	(38.2)	(65.4)	(11.8)

Exhibit 6.15 **PRESTON CORPORATION, HISTORICAL OPERATING RATIOS**

	1982	1983	1984	1985	1986	1987
Return on invested capital (Beg. of yr.)						
All operating expenses/revenues	92.7%	91.3%	91.4%	93.3%	91.3%	92.2%
Depreciation/revenues	4.2%	4.1%	4.3%	4.3%	4.2%	5.2%
EBIT/revenues	3.1%	4.6%	4.3%	2.5%	4.5%	2.5%
Net PPE/revenues	28.0%	27.7%	26.5%	28.3%	31.7%	36.7%
Working capital/revenues	3.8%	5.0%	6.4%	6.1%	7.6%	6.8%
Net other assets/revenues	3.2%	3.1%	3.1%	3.4%	3.1%	3.3%
Revenues/invested capital	2.9	2.8	2.8	2.6	2.4	2.1
Pretax ROIC	8.9%	12.7%	11.9%	6.5%	10.6%	5.4%
Cash tax rate	−2.8%	33.9%	13.4%	−17.2%	19.7%	37.0%
After-tax ROIC	9.1%	8.4%	10.3%	7.6%	8.5%	3.4%
After-tax ROIC (including goodwill)	9.1%	8.4%	10.3%	7.6%	8.3%	3.1%
Return on invested capital (average)						
Net PPE/revenues	31.0%	28.4%	29.8%	33.1%	38.0%	37.6%
Working capital/revenues	4.9%	6.0%	6.8%	7.6%	7.9%	7.6%
Net other assets/revenues	0.4%	0.4%	0.7%	0.9%	1.1%	1.4%
Revenues/invested capital	2.5	2.7	2.5	2.3	2.0	2.0
Pretax ROIC	7.9%	12.1%	10.7%	5.5%	9.1%	5.2%
After-tax ROIC	8.1%	8.0%	9.2%	6.5%	7.3%	3.3%
After-tax ROIC (including goodwill)	8.1%	8.0%	9.2%	6.4%	6.8%	3.0%

Exhibit 6.15 Continued

	1982	1983	1984	1985	1986	1987
Growth rates						
Revenue growth rate	12.5%	22.5%	10.0%	16.9%	19.7%	20.6%
EBIT growth rate		79.7%	3.2%	−32.8%	118.6%	−31.9%
NOPLAT growth rate		15.6%	35.2%	−9.1%	49.7%	−46.6%
Invested capital growth rate	25.1%	10.7%	22.9%	34.2%	33.2%	8.2%
Investment rates						
Gross investment rate	176.1%	111.5%	156.5%	240.3%	234.1%	132.7%
Net investment rate	275.8%	127.2%	222.8%	449.1%	391.4%	239.7%
Financing						
Coverage (EBIT/interest)	17.3	15.5	12.8	2.5	4.6	1.3
Debt/total investor funds (book)	18.7%	19.1%	21.8%	36.9%	56.2%	58.5%
Average ROE	7.2%	7.9%	9.1%	4.3%	7.0%	5.7%

Exhibit 6.16 **PRESTON CORPORATION, HISTORICAL ECONOMIC PROFIT,** $ MILLIONS

	1982	1983	1984	1985	1986	1987
Return on invested capital	9.1%	8.4%	10.3%	7.6%	8.5%	3.4%
WACC	14.0%	12.1%	13.5%	11.6%	8.7%	9.4%
Spread	−4.9%	−3.7%	−3.2%	−4.0%	−0.2%	−6.0%
Invested capital (beginning of year)	77.8	97.4	107.8	132.5	177.8	236.9
Economic profit (before goodwill)	(3.8)	(3.6)	(3.5)	(5.3)	(0.4)	(14.2)
NOPLAT	7.1	8.2	11.1	10.1	15.1	8.1
Capital charge	(10.9)	(11.8)	(14.6)	(15.4)	(15.5)	(22.3)
Economic profit (before goodwill)	(3.8)	(3.6)	(3.5)	(5.3)	(0.4)	(14.2)

Exhibit 6.17 **PRESTON CORPORATION, OTHER RATIOS**

	1981	1982	1983	1984	1985	1986	1987
Operations							
Revenue growth		12.5%	22.5%	10.0%	16.9%	19.7%	20.6%
Operating expenses/revenues	88.8%	93.1%	91.7%	91.7%	93.6%	91.6%	92.5%
Other expenses/revenues	0.0%	0.0%	0.0%	0.0%	0.0%	0.0%	0.0%
EBDIT Margin	11.2%	6.9%	8.3%	8.3%	6.4%	8.4%	7.5%
Operating lease adjustments/revenues	0.0%	−0.4%	−0.3%	−0.3%	−0.3%	−0.3%	−0.2%
Depreciation/revenues	6.5%	4.2%	4.1%	4.3%	4.3%	4.2%	5.2%
Operating margin	4.8%	3.1%	4.6%	4.3%	2.5%	4.5%	2.5%
Working capital/revenues							
Operating cash	2.0%	2.0%	2.0%	2.0%	1.7%	2.0%	2.0%
Accounts receivable	9.8%	11.9%	13.1%	12.0%	14.3%	13.1%	12.5%
Inventories	1.0%	0.9%	1.0%	0.8%	2.6%	2.6%	2.4%
Other current assets	2.2%	2.3%	1.9%	2.0%	0.7%	1.1%	1.0%
Accounts payable	3.7%	4.9%	4.4%	3.5%	4.1%	3.9%	3.7%
Other current liabilities	7.0%	6.1%	6.7%	6.2%	6.1%	6.6%	5.7%
Net working capital	4.3%	6.1%	7.0%	7.2%	9.1%	8.2%	8.4%
Property, plant, and equipment							
Gross PPE/revenues	50.6%	52.9%	47.1%	52.0%	58.5%	65.1%	58.9%
NPPE/revenues	31.5%	33.9%	29.2%	33.1%	37.9%	44.3%	38.4%
CapX/revenues		10.1%	5.6%	10.9%	13.9%	16.8%	6.9%
Depreciation/last year's GPPE		9.3%	9.5%	10.1%	9.6%	8.6%	9.7%
Retirement/last year's GPPE		4.7%	4.1%	4.1%	−0.3%	1.3%	3.6%

Exhibit 6.18 **PRESTON CORPORATION, OTHER RATIOS**

	1981	1982	1983	1984	1985	1986	1987
Taxes							
EBIT tax rate		30.5%	46.8%	36.0%	30.4%	49.0%	44.8%
Marginal tax rate	49.0%	49.0%	49.0%	49.0%	49.0%	49.0%	45.0%
Increase in deferred tax/tax on EBIT		109.2%	27.6%	62.9%	156.7%	59.7%	17.4%
Financing							
Interest rate on existing debt		10.0%	8.5%	7.1%	18.0%	8.2%	8.1%
Dividend payout ratio	33.3%	41.2%	42.4%	31.8%	65.1%	39.7%	47.5%
Rate on operating leases		11.0%	11.2%	11.3%	11.3%	11.2%	10.9%
Other ratios							
Nonoperating income growth	0.0%	0.0%	−5.6%	88.2%	−90.6%	0.0%	−266.7%
Other assets/revenues	0.3%	0.5%	0.4%	1.0%	1.0%	1.5%	1.6%
Nonoperating assets growth rate	0.0%	0.0%	0.0%	0.0%	0.0%	0.0%	0.0%
Other liabilities/revenues	0.0%	0.0%	0.0%	0.0%	0.0%	0.0%	0.0%
Capitalized operating leases/revenues	3.4%	3.3%	2.9%	2.9%	2.8%	2.5%	2.2%

Exhibit 6.19 PRESTON CORPORATION, OTHER SUPPORTING DATA, $ MILLIONS

	1982	1983	1984	1985	1986	1987
Change in working capital						
Increase in operating cash	0.4	1.0	0.6	0.0	2.4	1.7
Increase in accounts receivable	7.0	9.3	0.3	14.1	4.6	8.7
Increase in inventories	0.2	0.7	(0.3)	6.5	1.9	1.0
Increase in other current assets	0.8	0.2	0.7	(3.6)	2.0	0.6
(Increase) in accounts payable	(3.7)	(0.9)	1.4	(3.7)	(2.0)	(2.7)
(Increase) other current liabilities	0.4	(4.7)	(0.3)	(2.9)	(6.4)	(1.0)
Net change in working capital	5.1	5.6	2.4	10.4	2.5	8.3
Capital expenditures						
Increase in net PPE	13.1	4.1	19.6	33.7	52.8	8.6
Depreciation	9.3	11.2	13.0	15.0	17.7	26.4
Capital expenditures (net of disposals)	22.4	15.3	32.6	48.7	70.5	35.0
Investment in goodwill						
Increase/(decrease) in balance sheet goodwill	0.0	0.0	0.0	3.2	21.5	(0.3)
Amortization of goodwill	0.0	0.0	0.0	0.0	0.1	0.6
Investment in goodwill	0.0	0.0	0.0	3.2	21.6	0.3
Nonoperating cash flow						
Extraordinary items	0.0	0.0	0.0	0.0	0.0	0.0
After-tax nonoperating income	0.9	0.9	1.6	0.2	0.2	(0.3)
Change in investments and advances	0.0	0.0	0.0	0.0	0.0	0.0
Nonoperating cash flow	0.9	0.9	1.6	0.2	0.2	(0.3)

already accounted for the effect of all loan guarantees on the parent. Were the subsidiaries not wholly owned, the loan guarantee would be an off-balance-sheet liability of the parent and would affect its cost of capital.

Taxes

Preston's marginal tax rate (for calculating the taxes related to interest expense and income) was assumed to be 49 percent through 1986: a 46 percent federal rate, plus 3 percent for state and local taxes, allowing for their deductibility from federal taxes. A 45 percent marginal tax rate was assumed for 1987, composed of a 40 percent federal rate, plus 5 percent for state and local taxes, again net of the federal benefit.

Acquisitions

Preston made several acquisitions in 1985 and 1986; therefore, the pre-1985 data are not entirely comparable with subsequent years' data. In our forecasts the later data should be given more weight than the earlier data.

Deferred Taxes

Beginning January 1, 1987, Preston reported its deferred income tax liability using the liability method, whereby the deferred tax liability is calculated using the tax rates that are expected to exist when the items that give rise to the deferred taxes reverse. Preston had previously calculated deferred taxes using the tax rates that existed when the deferral arose. The result of this change was to increase Preston's 1987 net income by $211,000, and its cumulative effect on prior years was to increase the 1987 net income by $5,752,000 ($1.00 per share). This is a one-time effect that should not affect the forecast.

Inventory Accounting

Because Preston is a service business, its inventory is much less than that of a company that sells a tangible product. However, Preston does carry inventories of fuel, operating supplies, and tires on equipment in service. Preston Corporation uses LIFO inventory accounting. This means that the book value of inventory is understated during and following inflationary periods. Often LIFO inventory reserves (the difference between inventories at current cost and their stated LIFO value) are referred to as off-balance-sheet assets. However, for each extra dollar of future increase in LIFO reserves, an extra dollar of expense accrues against future profits; consequently, the two items cancel each other out. The only valuation effect of LIFO is that it often permits earlier realization of tax shield, an effect that is already captured on the income statement.

Pension Plans

As of December 31, 1986, the date of the information used in this case study, Preston had an unfunded, unrecorded pension liability of approximately $8 million. Because this was not significant to the value driver analysis we did not adjust the NOPLAT and invested capital calculations. As a result, however, we will need to subtract the after-tax present value of these payments ($4.4 million) from the entity value estimates that we develop later in the valuation process.

Labor Contracts

As of December 1987, approximately 42 percent of Preston's employees were employed by its largest subsidiary, Preston Trucking, and were members of the International Brotherhood of Teamsters, Chauffeurs, Warehousemen, and Helpers of America. They were covered by a three-year contract with the industry that expired on April 1, 1988, and a new three-year contract commenced on that date. These were the only employees of Preston Corporation covered by a collective bargaining agreement during that time period.

Stock Options

As of December 31, 1987, Preston reported having 231,676 options outstanding with an average exercise price of $20.55 and stock appreciation rights equal to the income tax incurred by the exercise of the executive stock options outstanding. In addition, in February 1988, it issued 331,500 nonqualified stock options with similar stock appreciation rights. These options have an exercise price of $11.25, but they cannot be exercised unless the fair market value of Preston's stock is at least $21.25 per share. The total value of the outstanding executive options (estimated to be $4.5 million using an option pricing model) must be subtracted from the entity value to obtain a valuation of Preston's equity.

Preferred Stock

Although no preferred stock is outstanding, Preston is authorized to issue 2,500,000 no-par-value preferred shares. This provision in its charter allows the board of directors to issue additional shares without shareholder approval and thus may be intended to make a hostile takeover difficult.

Lawsuits and Government Actions

Preston states that no material legal or government actions are pending against it. If such actions were pending, the present value of their expected cost to Preston would have to be subtracted from our valuation.

DEVELOP AN INTEGRATED HISTORICAL PERSPECTIVE

The Motor Carrier Act of 1980 substantially deregulated the trucking industry leading to a long period of industry turmoil. This deregulation allowed a large number of smaller low-cost carriers, attracted by high industry profitability, to enter the industry. Substantial rate discounts resulted as companies competed for market share. This intense competition caused many carriers to leave the industry, and further price declines resulted as the remaining carriers sought to capture the market share held by the exiting carriers. Moreover, because they were not hampered by the restrictive work practices tolerated during the days of regulation, nonunion carriers were better positioned to take advantage of deregulation than were unionized carriers.

However, the industry outlook appears to be brightening. Recent rate increases have not been heavily discounted, and it appears that the industry has resolved to end the rate wars that have plagued its profitability. This price firming, in addition to recent increases in demand, has led to higher revenues and operating margins for Preston and for the rest of the industry. This trend may continue, but the decision of a major carrier or of several smaller carriers to attempt to gain market share by reducing rates could touch off further rate wars.

A large degree of consolidation has also occurred in the industry, and more consolidation is likely, although its pace may be slowed as the firming of rates retards potential bankruptcies. More takeovers seem possible in the future, and Preston has been regarded as a possible takeover target. (*Value Line* notes in its July 1, 1988, edition that "much of this [share price] rise is attributable to Preston's earnings improvement, but we suspect that with the stock trading below book value and the recent outbreak of takeover bids in the industry, buyout speculation is partly responsible.")

As would be expected given the state of the industry, Preston's performance over the past several years has been weak as strong growth was more than offset by low returns on capital. We estimated that revenue growth averaged just over 13 percent per year from 1982 to 1987 when you exclude the new revenues from its recent acquisition. Over the same period, EBIT increased by 12.6 percent per year, including the additional earnings from the acquisition. Unfortunately, this growth actually destroyed value as Preston's

ROIC averaged only 7.6 percent over the 1983 to 1987 period versus an average WACC of 11.1 percent. In fact, Preston destroyed value in each of the last 5 years with cumulative economic profit over the period of −$27 million.

In 1987 Preston's ROIC declined to a five-year low of 3.4 percent due to declines in both operating margins and capital turnover. Exhibit 6.20 (see page 200) shows how Preston's 1987 ROIC compared to six key competitors. On all measures, Preston underperformed its competitors. Preston's operating margin was the lowest of the six at 2.5 percent versus an average of 3.9 percent and capital turnover at 2.1 times also lagged the average of 2.5 times. Of course the overall performance of the industry was poor as the six companies earned an average ROIC in 1987 of only 6.9 percent.

To summarize, Preston is competing in an industry where none of the major competitors are earning adequate returns on capital, and Preston is underperforming all its important competitors.

FINANCIAL HEALTH FROM A CREDIT PERSPECTIVE

In 1983, Preston was conservatively financed with an EBIT/interest ratio of 15.5 times and debt-total investor funds ratio of only 19.1 percent on a book basis. By 1987, Preston's financial health was precarious. Due to a major acquisition, poor operating performance, and continued investment in the business (gross investment rates substantially higher than 100 percent for each of the last five years), Preston's debt-to-total investor funds ratio had increased to 58.1 percent (book basis) and EBIT/interest had declined to only 1.2 times. Any additional declines in performance could force Preston to default on its loans.

Exhibit 6.20 **COMPARISON OF RATES OF RETURN ON INVESTED CAPITAL, 1987**

Company	$1-\dfrac{\text{Operating expenses}}{\text{Revenue}}+\dfrac{\text{Depreciation}}{\text{Revenue}}=$		Operating margin
Roadway Services	91.0%	6.0%	3.0%
Carolina Freight	91.8	4.8	3.4
Consolidated Freightways	91.2	4.4	4.4
Arkansas Best	90.5	5.6	3.9
Yellow Freight	89.9	5.6	4.5
Viking Freight	90.8	4.8	4.4
Average	90.9%	5.2%	3.9%
Preston	92.3%	5.2%	2.5%

Company	$1\div\dfrac{\text{Working capital}}{\text{Revenue}}+\dfrac{\text{Net PPE}}{\text{Revenue}}+\dfrac{\text{Other assets}}{\text{Revenue}}=$			Capital turnover
Roadway Services	12.4%	28.6%	0.8%	2.4
Carolina Freight	5.2	33.2	1.0	2.5
Consolidated Freightways	7.2	26.0	1.1	2.9
Arkansas Best	5.6	32.0	2.1	2.5
Yellow Freight	5.2	36.9	1.1	2.6
Viking Freight	5.8	37.6	0.7	2.3
Average	6.0%	32.4%	1.1%	2.5
Preston	6.8%	36.7%	3.3%	2.1

Company	Operating margin	×	Capital turnover	×	Cash $1-$ tax rate	=	After-tax return on invested capital
Roadway Services	3.0%		2.4		72.1%		5.2%
Carolina Freight	3.4		2.5		86.1		7.4
Consolidated Freightways	4.4		2.4		61.5		6.5
Arkansas Best	3.9		2.5		67.0		6.6
Yellow Freight	4.5		2.6		77.0		9.0
Viking Freight	4.4		2.3		64.5		6.5
Average	3.9%		2.5		71.4%		6.9%
Preston	2.5%		2.1		63.0		3.4%

REVIEW QUESTIONS

1. Describe the data needed to analyze historical performance of a firm's value.
2. What are the starting points and ultimate goals of a comprehensive system for the analysis of historical performance?
3. What are the determinants of ROIC?
4. Why doesn't ROE or ROA adequately capture value-based movements for the analysis of historical performance?

Questions 5 through 10 refer to the historical data for Consolidated Freightways presented in the table that follows question 10.

5. Produce invested capital and NOPLAT statements from the Consolidated Freightways data supplied in the table.
6. Reconcile the NOPLAT statement to net income. Explain the utility of this exercise.
7. Produce a ROIC tree. Explain each of the successive decompositions of ROIC.
8. Develop a free cash flow statement.
9. Develop an economic profit statement. Assume a 11.1 percent weighted average cost of capital. Interpret the results from year to year.
10. Compare and contrast the free cash flow and economic profit statements.

Historical Data for Consolidated Freightways

	1992	1993
Current Assets	863	896
Current Liabilities	710	818
Debt in Current Liabilities	1	39
Long Term Debt	506	408
Total Assets	2,293	2,307
Capital Expenditures	111	117
Change in Deferred Taxes	(29)	(20)
Sales	4,056	4,192
Operating Expenses	3,307	3,408
General Expenses	562	528
Depreciation	139	136

Historical Data for Consolidated Freightways (Continued)

	1992	1993
Investment Income	5	6
Interest Expense	39	30
Miscellaneous Income, Net	(25)	(4)
Income Taxes	(7)	41

7

Forecasting
Performance

Once you've analyzed the company's historical performance, you can move on to forecasting its future performance. The key to projecting performance is to develop a point of view on how the company can or will perform on the key value drivers: growth and return on invested capital. Since growth and ROIC are not constant over time, a third dimension, time itself, must also be considered. While we cannot provide specific forecasting rules, here are some basic steps to consider when developing forecasts.

1. Evaluate the company's strategic position, considering both the industry characteristics as well as the company's competitive advantages or disadvantages. This will help you assess the company's growth potential and its ability to earn returns above its cost of capital.

2. Develop performance scenarios for the company and its industry that describe qualitatively how the company's performance will evolve and the critical events that are likely to impact that performance.

3. Forecast individual income-statement and balance-sheet line items based on the scenarios. These line items will then be aggregated to forecast free cash flow, ROIC, and the other key value drivers.

4. Check the overall forecast for reasonableness, particularly the key value drivers.

EVALUATE STRATEGIC POSITION

In order to earn returns on capital in excess of the opportunity cost of capital, companies must develop and exploit a competitive advantage. Without a competitive advantage, competition would force all the companies in the industry to earn only their cost of capital (or even less). Therefore, to develop a point of view about a company's ability to earn an attractive ROIC over time, we must identify the company's potential for generating competitive advantages, given the nature of the industry in which it competes and its own assets and capabilities.

Competitive advantages that translate into a positive ROIC versus WACC spread can be categorized into three types:

1. Providing superior value to the customer through a combination of price and product attributes that cannot be replicated by competitors. These attributes can be tangible (the fastest computer) or intangible (a strong relationship between salesperson and buyer).
2. Achieving lower costs than competitors.
3. Utilizing capital more productively than competitors.

A competitive advantage must ultimately be expressed in terms of one or more of these characteristics. Describing competitive advantages this way also helps to begin to shape the financial forecast.

Three techniques for identifying competitive advantages include customer segmentation analysis, competitive business system analysis, and industry structure analysis.

Customer Segmentation Analysis

The purpose of customer segmentation analysis is to help estimate potential market share by explicitly identifying why customers will choose one company's products over others. It also tells us how difficult it will be for a competitor to differentiate itself and helps to identify how profitable each type of customer is likely to be, based on their needs and cost to serve.

Customer segmentation analysis segments customers from two

perspectives: the customer and the producer. From the customer perspective, product attributes have different importance to different groups of customers. For example, after-sale service may be more important to a small manufacturing customer than a large customer with its own in-house maintenance staff. In addition, different competitors may include different attributes in their product offering and, therefore, deliver different benefits to customer groups.

A customer segment is a group of customers to whom similar product attributes provide similar benefits. Segmenting customers forces the analyst to understand why customers prefer one product over another, often despite the fact that the products appear very similar. This then helps to identify why competitive market share may differ across customer groups and to find opportunities for differentiation to segments. For example, in the overnight package delivery business, detailed billing information on each package is important to some customers, while others are content with summary data. Some customers want to be able to know instantaneously where a package is at any point in time, while other customers can wait for the information. So, while all customers receive the same overnight delivery, other less apparent attributes may also be important.

From the producer perspective, different customers have different costs to serve. For example, in the salt industry, distance to the customer has a major impact on the costs to serve because of salt's low value-to-weight characteristics. Accordingly, some customers may be simply too far away to serve if competitors are much closer. On the other hand, customers close by may be important to lock up because their proximity creates a major competitive advantage.

By segmenting customers according to both the customer and producer attributes, and then comparing a company's ability to satisfy those customers relative to competitors, you can begin to identify current or potential competitive advantages.

Competitive Business System Analysis

The business system is the way a company provides product attributes to the customer, as illustrated in Exhibit 7.1. The business system extends from product design to after-sales service. Analysis of the business system provides insight into how a company can

Exhibit 7.1 **BUSINESS SYSTEM ANALYSIS**

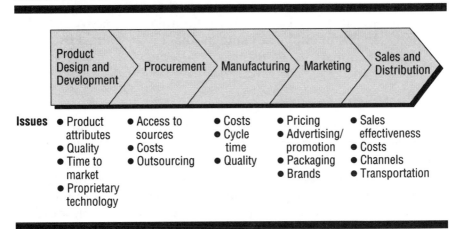

	Product Design and Development	Procurement	Manufacturing	Marketing	Sales and Distribution
Issues	• Product attributes • Quality • Time to market • Proprietary technology	• Access to sources • Costs • Outsourcing	• Costs • Cycle time • Quality	• Pricing • Advertising/ promotion • Packaging • Brands	• Sales effectiveness • Costs • Channels • Transportation

achieve a competitive advantage through lower costs, better capital utilization, or superior customer value. To do this, the analyst needs to lay out the business systems of the major competitors and identify:

- What product attributes does each competitor provide with its business system?
- What costs and capital are associated with providing these attributes? Ideally, this should be done for each component of the business system. In addition, linkages between the components should be considered.
- What are the reasons for differences in performance between competitors?

For example, a competitor may have a manufacturing cost advantage because its labor force is not unionized. In order to overcome this labor cost advantage, other competitors must achieve greater labor productivity or cost savings elsewhere in the business system, or provide a superior product to their customers.

Recently, a variation on this business system analysis has been introduced. It focuses on core processes rather than the functional orientation of the traditional business system. For example, a core process for a fast food chain might be site development (including site selection and construction), which might cut across many traditional functional areas, including marketing, real estate, construction, and finance. The advantage of this perspective is that it highlights the competitive advantages that can be gained from better cross-functional management.

Industry Structure Analysis

The third framework for assessing competitive advantages is industry structure analysis. Industry structure analysis looks outside the industry at the forces that will shape the industry's profitability. Michael Porter of Harvard is best known for having formalized industry structure models.[1] An approach to industry structure analysis is shown in Exhibit 7.2. In this model, four key external forces drive an industry's profit potential: substitute products, supplier bargaining power, customer bargaining power, and entry/exit barriers.

Exhibit 7.2 **INDUSTRY STRUCTURE MODEL**

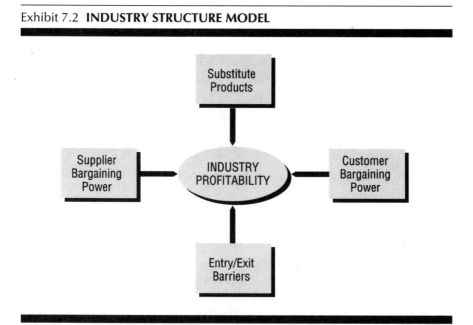

---

[1] Michael E. Porter, *Competitive Strategy: Techniques for Analyzing Industries and Competitors* (New York: Free Press, 1980).

The existence of substitute products can place significant limits on an industry. For example, railroads and trucks compete for the movement of freight. Rail movement is relatively cheap for large, long hauls but is not as flexible and inexpensive as truck movement for small, short hauls. However, for some shipments between the very long and very short, a shipper could use either rail or truck transportation and could try to create bidding competitions between them.

Entry and exit barriers determine the likelihood of new competitors entering the industry and old competitors leaving the industry. Entry barriers arise when there are skills or assets that only a few competitors can obtain. Access to capital is rarely an entry barrier because it is easy to obtain. Access to a new technology and patents, on the other hand, where only a handful of scientists can use the technology, can shut out new competitors. Exit barriers exist when competitors are better off staying in the industry, even though they are not earning their cost of capital. Exit barriers often arise in capital intensive industries where companies may be earning more than their marginal costs so they do not wish to exit, but the returns on capital are very low. Furthermore, managements may continue to invest capital in low return industries for long periods of time, because they do not wish to dismantle their organization or they are hoping someone else will leave first.

The bargaining power of suppliers determines what share of the total pool of customer revenues can be retained by the industry. If a company can increase its bargaining power, its share of the revenue will increase. Walmart, the discount retailer, has exploited its purchasing power and information technology about customer wants very successfully to obtain from its vendors lower prices and better service than its competitors. Attempts to extract value from suppliers do not always work. For example, many department stores have attempted to cut out the manufacturers altogether by developing their own house brands for which they design the products and contract out the manufacturing. Unfortunately, many of these retailers have found that their costs for design and manufacturing are not low enough to make up for the lower prices they generally have to charge.

The bargaining power of customers also affects the industry's share of revenues. For example, in carpet manufacturing, the major competitors have found ways to skip the wholesalers—who traditionally distributed their products to retailers—and deal directly

---

Exhibit 7.3 **STRUCTURE-CONDUCT-PERFORMANCE MODEL**

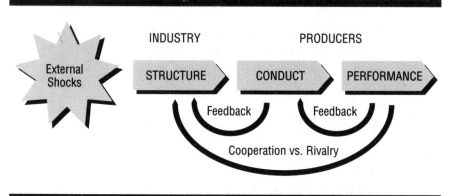

with the retail stores. They have thus been able to extract a significant share of the total revenue pool away from the wholesalers.

The Structure-Conduct-Performance model adds a dynamic element to industry structure analysis as illustrated in Exhibit 7.3. The S-C-P model adds external shocks to the system to analyze how external shocks will affect the structure, how competitors are likely to respond, and how the performance of the industry and competitors will be affected.

These three types of analyses (customer segmentation, business system, and industry structure) should provide insights into whether the industry as a whole is likely to earn returns exceeding the cost of capital and how the company being valued is positioned within the industry.

DEVELOP PERFORMANCE SCENARIOS

Once you have developed a point of view about the company's ability to achieve and sustain a competitive advantage, the next step is to develop performance scenarios. By using scenarios we acknowledge that forecasting financial performance is at best an educated guess. The best we can do is narrow down the range of likely future performance. Consider a high tech company that is developing a proprietary new product. If the company successfully develops the product, its competitive advantage will be a product that delivers superior value to customers. Accordingly, its growth and returns on capital are likely to be huge. If it fails to develop the product, it will likely go out of business. A scenario that projects moderate growth and returns is highly unlikely, even though it could be considered "most likely" from a statistical perspective. While this situation may be extreme, we strongly believe it is better to develop a number of scenarios for a company, and to understand the company's value under each scenario, than to build a single "most likely" forecast and value.

Once the scenarios are developed and valued, an overall value of the company can be estimated as a weighted average of the values of the independent scenarios, assigning probabilities to each scenario. The following table shows how we valued a steel company:

Scenario ($ millions)	Entity value	Debt	Equity value	Proba- bility	Weighted value
Business as usual	$2,662	$2,520	$142	15%	
Industry behavior improves slightly	3,694	2,520	1,174	65%	$1,228
Sustained improvement in industry behavior	4,736	2,520	2,216	20%	

Developing scenarios does not mean mechanically changing the sales growth rate by 10 percent. Instead, it means developing a comprehensive set of assumptions about how the future may evolve and how that is likely to affect industry profitability and the company's financial performance. For example, the industry may be characterized by rapid growth and few substitutes. One scenario may assume these conditions will continue for a certain time period after which the introduction of substitutes will slow growth (for example, the way personal computers have caused the demand for mainframes to decline). Here are two simple sample scenarios:

- *The company introduces a major new product line and sales take off.* The scenario should factor in how the competition would respond in terms of competing products and pricing. It should also deal with how the company would handle the strain of the higher sales level in areas like manufacturing and distribution.

- *A substitute product enters the market.* How would the company respond? Would it just lose sales, or would it retaliate? What organizational changes would be made to compete in the new environment?

In addition to the competitive advantage assessment just described, consider these shocks that could affect industry and company performance:

- The potential for new products or technological breakthroughs that would affect demand for the company's products.
- Potential changes in government policy or regulation, such as environmental laws or international trade barriers.
- Changes in consumer tastes or lifestyles, or other factors that may affect demand for the industry's products.
- The availability of key raw materials.
- Changes in the overall health of the domestic and world economy.

FORECAST INDIVIDUAL LINE ITEMS

Before forecasting individual line items you must decide on the structure of the forecast. The structure of the forecast is the order in which the variables are forecasted and the way in which they relate to each other. The best forecast structure begins with an integrated income statement and balance sheet forecast. The free cash flow and other value drivers can then be derived from them.

It is possible to forecast free cash flow directly rather than going through the income statement and balance sheet; however, we do not recommend it. If you forecast free cash flow first, you must still construct the balance sheet to properly evaluate the relationships between the cash flow or income statement items and the balance sheet accounts. If you do not construct the balance sheet, it is easy to lose sight of how all the pieces fit together. A recent experience provides an example. A team doing a valuation tried to simplify the forecasting process by ignoring the balance sheet. The company's history showed that it usually generated about two dollars in sales for each dollar of net fixed assets. By the end of the team's forecast, the company was generating five dollars in sales for each dollar of net fixed assets. The team had not intended this result and did not even know it was happening, because it had not constructed a balance sheet and supporting ratios. The balance sheet also helps to identify the financing implications of the forecast. It shows how much capital must be raised or how much excess cash will be available.

The most common approach to forecasting the income statement and balance sheet for nonfinancial companies is a demand-driven forecast. A demand-driven forecast starts with sales. Most other variables (expenses, working capital) are driven off the sales forecast. Use the ROIC tree to organize the forecast and as a consistency check.

Forecasts of individual line items should draw upon a careful analysis of industry structure and a company's internal capabilities. Analyzing the historical level of valuation variables is a useful starting point. Once these levels have been calculated, several questions will help you gain insight into the future level of each valuation variable.

- What characteristics of the industry have had the greatest impact on value drivers in the past?
- What company-specific capabilities have had the greatest impact on historical value drivers?
- Are industry characteristics and company capabilities expected to maintain historical patterns in the future? If not, what is expected to change?
- What must change in the industry or the company to cause a significant shift in the historical level of the company's value drivers?

While we will not talk about individual line items, two topics merit special mention: inflation and the length of the forecast.

Inflation

We recommend that financial forecasts and discount rates be estimated in nominal rather than real currency units as discussed in Chapter 5. *For consistency, both the free cash flow forecast and the discount rate must be based on the same expected general inflation rate.*

Individual line items, however, could have specific inflation rates that are higher or lower than the general rate, but they should still drive off the general rate. To provide a specific example, the revenue forecast should reflect the growth in units sold and the expected increase in unit prices. The increase in unit prices, in turn, should reflect the general expected level of inflation in the economy, plus or minus an inflation rate differential for that specific product. Suppose that general inflation is expected to be 4.0 percent and that unit prices for the company's products were expected to increase at 1 percent faster than general inflation. Overall, the company's prices would be expected to increase at 5.0 percent per year. Assuming a 3 percent annual increase in units sold would lead to a forecast of 8.2 percent annual revenue growth $(1.05 \times 1.03 - 1.00)$.

We can derive the expected general inflation rate that is consistent with the discount rate from the term structure of interest rates. The term structure is based on yields to maturity of U.S. government bonds. Nominal interest rates reflect lenders' expectations of future inflation. Lenders expect to be compensated for expected losses due to inflation as well as default and market risk. Exhibit 7.4 shows the term structure of interest rates at three points in time. Inflationary expectations are clearly reflected in each. In 1981, short-term interest rates were high, reflecting the market's belief at that time that future inflation would be lower than near-term inflation. In 1988, inflationary expectations were lower than in 1981, and the market believed long-term inflation would be higher than short-term inflation. In 1992, inflationary expectations were even lower.

The term structure of interest rates provides a market-based estimate of expected inflation over time. This should be the best estimate for valuation purposes, for these reasons:

- Most economists', or econometric, forecasts of inflation rarely extend beyond one or two years, far too short a period for valuation.

- Market-based estimates provide a broader consensus view (with investors' money at stake) than individual forecasts.

- Empirical analysis suggests that market-based estimates are the least biased.[2]

[2] See E. Fama and M. Gibbons, "A Comparison of Inflation Forecasts," *Journal of Monetary Economics* (May 1984): 327–348; or G. Hardouvelis, "The Predictive Power of the Term Structure during Recent Monetary Regimes," *Journal of Finance* (June 1988): 339–356.

Exhibit 7.4 **TERM STRUCTURE OF INTEREST RATES AT THREE POINTS IN TIME**

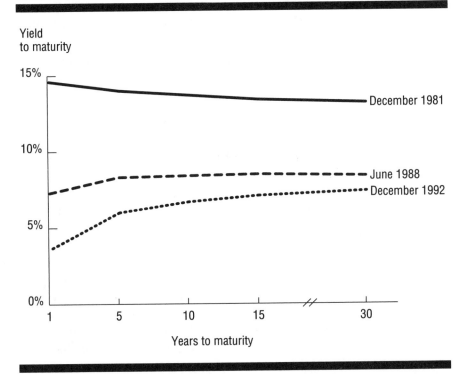

The expected inflation rate over a given period can be derived from the term structure of interest rates as follows:

1. Determine the nominal risk-free rate of interest for the time period over which you want to estimate inflation (use the same interval that will be used to calculate the weighted average cost of capital, usually ten or more years).

2. Estimate the real rate of interest. This is a controversial issue and different sources provide different estimates. Ibbotson Associates estimate the real rate as the difference between the annualized rate of return on U.S. Treasury bills and the Consumer Price Index (for all urban consumers, not seasonally adjusted). For the interval 1926 to 1991, their real rate is 0.5 percent per year. However, this rate fluctuates wildly. Looking at individual decades, real rates have ranged from −5.4 percent in the 1940s to 4.1 percent in the 1980s. Given

this volatility and the sense that investors are less likely to be surprised by inflation going forward as they were in the 1940s and 1970s, we recommend using a real rate estimate of 2–3 percent, which is in the range of the long-term growth in GDP.

3. Calculate the expected inflation rate from the nominal and real rates using the following formula:

$$\text{Expected inflation} = \frac{(1 + \text{Nominal rate})}{(1 + \text{Real rate})} - 1$$

Suppose the 10 year rate on government bonds is 7.0 percent and the real rate of interest is expected to be 3.0 percent. Then, the expected general inflation rate over the next ten years would be 3.9 percent. Note that the expected inflation rate is not the same for all time periods. For example, if the one year rate on government securities is 5.0 percent and if we expect the short term real rate to be 3.0 percent then the expected inflation for the next year would be 1.9 percent. If the expected inflation for the next year is 1.9 percent and the ten-year expected inflation is 3.9 percent then the rate over the last nine years must be higher than 3.9 percent so that the 10-year average will be 3.9 percent. In fact, you could estimate the expected inflation rate for each year of the forecast using the term structure of interest rates and use it for your forecast.

Length of Forecast

For practical purposes, most forecasts should be divided into two periods: an explicit forecast period (say, ten years) and the remaining life of the company (Year 11 on). A detailed forecast is done for the first period. Cash flow from the second, more distant, period is valued using a continuing-value formula as described in detail in Chapter 9.

The explicit forecast period should be long enough so that the company reaches a steady state by the end of the period. The steady state can be described as follows:

- The company earns a constant rate of return on all new capital invested during the continuing-value period.
- The company earns a constant rate of return on its base level of invested capital.

- The company invests a constant proportion of its earnings back into the business each year.

The most common approach is to make the forecast period as long as you expect the company to have sustainable rates of return on new investment above the company's cost of capital. Micro-economic analysis suggests that over time, competition will drive the returns in many industries to the level of the cost of capital. Once the company's returns have converged on its cost of capital, it is relatively simple to estimate the company's continuing value. Therefore, forecasting until convergence simplifies the continuing-value problem. If this is your approach, the forecast periods should be for as long as returns above the weighted average cost of capital are sustainable.

When in doubt, make a longer rather than shorter forecast. We would rarely use a forecast period of less than seven years. The forecast period should never be determined by the company's own internal planning period. Just because the company forecasts out only three years does not justify using three years for the valuation. A rough forecast beyond three years is certainly better than no forecast.

If a company is in a cyclical industry, it is important that your forecast capture a complete cycle. Failure to do so may result in wildly unrealistic continuing-value assumptions, because the up or down phase of the cycle may be projected to last forever. It is best to put long-run forecasts (averaging out cyclical effects) into your continuing-value assumptions.

CHECK OVERALL FORECAST FOR REASONABLENESS

The final step in the forecasting process is to construct the free cash flow and value drivers from the income statements and balance sheets and to evaluate the forecast. The forecast should be evaluated the same way the company's historical performance was analyzed. To understand how the key value drivers are expected to behave, ask:

- Is the company's performance on the key value drivers consistent with the company's economics and the industry competitive dynamics?

- Is revenue growth consistent with industry growth? If the company's revenue is growing faster than the industry's, which competitors are losing share? Will they retaliate? Does the company have the resources to manage that rate of growth?

- Is the return on capital consistent with the industry's competitive structure? If entry barriers are coming down, shouldn't expected returns decline? If customers are becoming more powerful, will margins decline? Conversely, if the company's position in the industry is becoming much stronger, should you expect increasing returns? How will returns and growth look relative to the competition?

- How will technology changes affect returns? Will they affect risk?

- Can the company manage all the investment it is undertaking?

Finally, you must understand the financing implications of the forecast. Will the company have to raise large amounts of capital? If so, can it obtain the financing? Should it be debt or equity? If the company is generating excess cash, what options does it have for investing the cash or returning it to shareholders?

PRESTON CORPORATION

In Chapter 6, we presented a historical analysis of Preston Corporation. In this section, we will develop a forecast of Preston's financial performance. Recall from Chapter 6 that Preston's return on capital has been consistently lower than its WACC and also lower than its major competitors.

EVALUATE STRATEGIC POSITION

Preston's strategic position is fundamentally unattractive. While average returns on invested capital in the industry will probably improve somewhat, these returns are unlikely to exceed the industry's cost of capital by much. Furthermore, Preston does not appear to have any significant competitive advantage that will help it to beat the rest of the industry.

We developed the following insights after conducting analyses of customer segmentation, competitive business systems, and industry structure.

- The customers that Preston has targeted are a broad range of small-to-medium shippers with fairly similar needs. They are mainly concerned with price and on-time delivery. Most customers currently believe that almost all truckers provide comparable on-time delivery and therefore focus mostly on price. Preston has done nothing to carve out a niche for itself by providing a differentiating service to any group of customers.
- A business system analysis provided similarly discouraging information.
  - Preston and many of its competitors have unionized labor. The non-unionized truckers have significant cost advantages.
  - Other than labor costs, all competitors have access to the same equipment and technology.
  - The larger competitors appear to enjoy significant economies of scale in their ability to efficiently consolidate their shipments from many customers and to ensure that their trucks are always full.
  - Several smaller competitors have carved out niches that they dominate through superior service and knowledge of the customers shipping needs.
  - Unfortunately, Preston does not have the scale economies of the larger players nor has it taken control of any customer segment.
- An industry structure analysis demonstrated that the primary factors affecting the industry are entry/exit barriers. Substitutes, supplier bargaining, and customer bargaining power are not critical factors in the industry. On the negative side, entry barriers are low. Just about anyone can buy a truck and set up a trucking business. On the positive side, exit barriers are also low and many competitors were leaving the market as they realized they could not compete profitably.

In summary, while the overall outlook for the industry is improving (as evidenced by firming prices), the fundamental outlook is unattractive, except perhaps for the largest carriers who may be able achieve cost advantages through larger scale and for the niche players who dominate certain market segments. Preston appears to be attempting to achieve the size necessary in selected markets to realize the scale economies of the largest players in those markets. It is not clear whether Preston will succeed. Overlying all this, however, is the uncertainty about competitive behavior. Since competition is primarily on price, future price wars are always possible.

DEVELOP PERFORMANCE SCENARIOS

We developed three performance scenarios for Preston.

1. *Moderate Performance.* Under this scenario, the industry avoids major price wars so overall industry returns on capital improve to approximately the cost of capital. Preston's performance also improves as management moves to emphasize several geographic regions where it is better positioned to achieve some scale economies, and as management completes several initiatives to improve productivity. However, Preston never really achieves the scale or segment dominance to earn outstanding returns.

2. *Downside.* Under this scenario, the industry price wars continue, keeping industry returns below the cost of capital. Preston's performance continues to be weak.

3. *Upside.* Like the first scenario, the industry avoids price wars and industry returns approach the cost of capital. In this scenario, however, Preston finds several geographic niches and is able to gradually achieve returns somewhat above the industry.

FORECAST INDIVIDUAL LINE ITEMS

We present the line item forecast for the moderate performance scenario. The detailed projections are laid out in Exhibits 7.5 and 7.6. We forecasted Preston's performance for ten years because we believe that was a sufficient period for the industry to shake out and for Preston's long-term performance level to be established.

The Preston forecast is a demand-driven forecast. Most items are driven by the sales forecast. Our approach to forecasting each item is certainly not the only appropriate technique. It would be impossible to enumerate all the possibilities. Therefore, we have chosen to present one method to indicate the types of issues that should be addressed.

Revenues

Revenue growth is determined by the growth in the quantity of carrier services provided (tonnage) and prices (rates). Tonnage is largely determined by the level of industrial production and by the ability of the company to capture increased market share as the industry continues to undergo consolidation. Through the first half of 1988, Preston's tonnage was 18.7 percent higher than it was during the same period of 1987. After taking into account

Exhibit 7.5 PRESTON CORPORATION, MODERATE CASE, FORECAST OPERATING ASSUMPTIONS

	1988	1989	1990	1991	1992	1993	1994	1995	1996	1997	Perp
Operations											
Revenue growth	20.8%	14.8%	12.6%	10.8%	9.3%	9.5%	9.4%	9.6%	9.7%	9.9%	9.4%
Operating expense/ revenues	91.5%	90.7%	90.0%	89.5%	89.0%	89.0%	89.0%	89.0%	89.0%	89.0%	89.0%
Other expense/revenues	0.0%	0.0%	0.0%	0.0%	0.0%	0.0%	0.0%	0.0%	0.0%	0.0%	0.0%
EBDIT Margin	8.5%	9.3%	10.0%	10.5%	11.0%	11.0%	11.0%	11.0%	11.0%	11.0%	11.0%
Operating lease adjustments/revenues	-0.2%	-0.2%	-0.2%	-0.2%	-0.2%	-0.2%	-0.2%	-0.2%	-0.2%	-0.2%	-0.2%
Depreciation/revenues	4.6%	4.7%	4.8%	4.8%	4.9%	5.0%	5.0%	5.0%	5.1%	5.1%	5.1%
Operating margin	4.1%	4.9%	5.5%	5.9%	6.3%	6.3%	6.2%	6.2%	6.2%	6.2%	6.1%
Working capital/revenues											
Operating cash	1.9%	1.9%	1.9%	1.9%	1.9%	1.9%	1.9%	1.9%	1.9%	1.9%	1.9%
Accounts receivable	13.3%	13.3%	13.3%	13.3%	13.3%	13.3%	13.3%	13.3%	13.3%	13.3%	13.3%
Inventories	2.5%	2.5%	2.5%	2.5%	2.5%	2.5%	2.5%	2.5%	2.5%	2.5%	2.5%
Other current assets	0.9%	0.9%	0.9%	0.9%	0.9%	0.9%	0.9%	0.9%	0.9%	0.9%	0.9%
Accounts payable	3.9%	3.9%	3.9%	3.9%	3.9%	3.9%	3.9%	3.9%	3.9%	3.9%	3.9%
Other current liabilities	6.1%	6.1%	6.1%	6.1%	6.1%	6.1%	6.1%	6.1%	6.1%	6.1%	6.1%
Net working capital	8.6%	8.6%	8.6%	8.6%	8.6%	8.6%	8.6%	8.6%	8.6%	8.6%	8.6%
Property, Plant, and Equipment Input Values:											
CapX/revs (Input, Mode 1)	6.9%	9.8%	9.0%	8.3%	7.8%	7.4%	7.5%	7.5%	7.5%	7.5%	7.5%
NPPE/Revs (Input, Mode 2)	37.0%	36.5%	36.0%	35.5%	35.0%	34.5%	34.0%	33.5%	33.0%	32.5%	32.0%
Depr/Last year's GPPE	9.5%	9.5%	9.5%	9.5%	9.5%	9.5%	9.5%	9.5%	9.5%	9.5%	9.5%
Retirements/last year's GPPE	4.0%	4.0%	4.0%	4.0%	4.0%	4.0%	4.0%	4.0%	4.0%	4.0%	4.0%

Exhibit 7.6 **PRESTON CORPORATION, MODERATE CASE, OTHER FORECAST ASSUMPTIONS,** $ MILLIONS

	1988	1989	1990	1991	1992	1993	1994	1995	1996	1997	Perp
Taxes											
EBIT tax rate	39.0%	39.0%	39.0%	39.0%	39.0%	39.0%	39.0%	39.0%	39.0%	39.0%	39.0%
Marginal tax rate	39.0%	39.0%	39.0%	39.0%	39.0%	39.0%	39.0%	39.0%	39.0%	39.0%	39.0%
Incr def tax/tax on EBIT	10.0%	10.0%	10.0%	10.0%	10.0%	10.0%	10.0%	10.0%	10.0%	10.0%	10.0%
Financing											
Int rate on excess marketable securities	8.0%	8.0%	8.0%	8.0%	8.0%	8.0%	8.0%	8.0%	8.0%	8.0%	8.0%
Int rate on short-term debt	8.1%	8.1%	8.1%	8.1%	8.1%	8.1%	8.1%	8.1%	8.1%	8.1%	8.1%
Int rate on long-term debt	8.1%	8.1%	8.1%	8.1%	8.1%	8.1%	8.1%	8.1%	8.1%	8.1%	8.1%
Int rate on new long-term debt	10.8%	10.8%	10.8%	10.8%	10.8%	10.8%	10.8%	10.8%	10.8%	10.8%	10.8%
Dividend payout ratio	45.0%	45.0%	45.0%	45.0%	45.0%	45.0%	45.0%	45.0%	45.0%	45.0%	45.0%
Rate on operating leases	10.8%	10.8%	10.8%	10.8%	10.8%	10.8%	10.8%	10.8%	10.8%	10.8%	10.8%
Minority interest											
Min Int(IS)/income after-tax	0.0%	0.0%	0.0%	0.0%	0.0%	0.0%	0.0%	0.0%	0.0%	0.0%	0.0%
Minority Int payout ratio	0.0%	0.0%	0.0%	0.0%	0.0%	0.0%	0.0%	0.0%	0.0%	0.0%	0.0%
Minority interest (BS)	0.0	0.0	0.0	0.0	0.0	0.0	0.0	0.0	0.0	0.0	0.0

Exhibit 7.6 Continued

	1988	1989	1990	1991	1992	1993	1994	1995	1996	1997	Perp
Other ratios											
Nonoperating income growth	0.0%	0.0%	0.0%	0.0%	0.0%	0.0%	0.0%	0.0%	0.0%	0.0%	0.0%
Other assets/revenues	1.6%	1.6%	1.6%	1.6%	1.6%	1.6%	1.6%	1.6%	1.6%	1.6%	1.6%
Nonoperating assets growth rate	0.0%	0.0%	0.0%	0.0%	0.0%	0.0%	0.0%	0.0%	0.0%	0.0%	0.0%
Other liabs/revenues	0.0%	0.0%	0.0%	0.0%	0.0%	0.0%	0.0%	0.0%	0.0%	0.0%	0.0%
Cap operating leases/ revenues	2.2%	2.2%	2.2%	2.2%	2.2%	2.2%	2.2%	2.2%	2.2%	2.2%	2.2%
Other values ($)											
Amortization of goodwill ($)	0.6	0.6	0.6	0.6	0.6	0.6	0.6	0.6	0.6	0.6	0.6
Special items ($)	0.0	0.0	0.0	0.0	0.0	0.0	0.0	0.0	0.0	0.0	0.0
Extraordinary items ($)	0.0	0.0	0.0	0.0	0.0	0.0	0.0	0.0	0.0	0.0	0.0
Effects of accounting change ($)	0.0	0.0	0.0	0.0	0.0	0.0	0.0	0.0	0.0	0.0	0.0
Short-term debt ($)	0.0	0.0	0.0	0.0	0.0	0.0	0.0	0.0	0.0	0.0	0.0
Long-term debt ($)	118.1	115.5	51.4	49.7	48.7	32.1	31.2	30.5	30.0	29.5	29.5
Preferred stock ($)	0.0	0.0	0.0	0.0	0.0	0.0	0.0	0.0	0.0	0.0	0.0
Preferred dividends ($)	0.0	0.0	0.0	0.0	0.0	0.0	0.0	0.0	0.0	0.0	0.0
Capitalized operating leases ($)	13.4	15.4	17.4	19.2	21.0	23.0	25.2	27.6	30.3	33.3	36.4

a seasonal drop in tonnage during the fourth quarter, we project total tonnage growth to be 16.2 percent in 1988.

The industry is currently facing a large upswing in demand, and as a result, many companies are operating at levels near their short-term capacity. For these reasons, we forecast a large increase in Preston's tonnage, slowing over the next several years to a permanent real growth level of 3 percent, which is our forecast of the long-term rate of real industrial production growth.

As discussed earlier, rates in the industry are firming. The industry enacted a 3.3 percent rate increase in October 1987 and additional 3.5 percent rate increases in April and late June 1988. This growth is in contrast to the recent rate stagnation faced by the industry due to increased competition since deregulation, and it is allowing the industry to move closer to achieving normal returns on its invested capital. However, rate increases are implemented slowly because approximately half of the industry's demand is locked in at defined rates in contracts. Thus, full rate increases cannot be achieved until these contracts expire.

We are therefore forecasting the recent and future rate increases to be gradually phased in, and thus we expect an increase of 4 percent during 1988 and a slow growth in rates over the next several years. We forecast the rate growth to eventually level off to the rate of expected inflation. Our revenue growth forecast is as follows (the total revenue growth is the product rather than the sum of the component growth rates):

	Tonnage growth	Rate growth	Revenue growth
1988	16.2%	4.0%	20.8%
1989	9.5	4.8	14.8
1990	7.0	5.2	12.6
1991	4.8	5.7	10.8
1992	3.0	6.1	9.3
1993	3.0	6.3	9.5
1994	3.0	6.2	9.4
1995	3.0	6.4	9.6
1996	3.0	6.5	9.7
1997	3.0	6.7	9.9

Operating Expenses

Preston's operating expenses as a percentage of revenues have fluctuated between 91.6 percent and 93.6 percent during the last five years. Over the past several years a few trends are apparent in specific components of this category. Claims and insurance costs as a percentage of revenues have risen by almost 40 percent since 1985. Much of this increase has been due to the occurrence of an unusually high number of severe accidents; therefore, we believe this trend will stop. Over the same period, salaries, wages, and fringes as a percentage of revenues, and purchased transportation as a percentage of revenues, have experienced small yet steady increases and declines, respectively.

We forecast operating expenses to decline as a percentage of revenues during the next several years. A primary reason for this forecast is our expectation of continued rising rates. We believe the recent rate increases enacted by Preston will more than offset the effects of the new three-year labor contract that took effect April 1, 1988, between the Teamsters and the trucking industry. (The contract calls for a 7 percent wage-cost increase in the first year, and a 2.5 percent to 3 percent increase in each of the following years.) In addition, because of its relatively slow growth, Preston's labor costs as a percentage of revenues will be less affected by the new contract than those of faster-growing firms. This is because newly and recently hired employees will receive the largest pay increases, and these employees are most prevalent at quickly growing firms. Overall, rates should rise more quickly than costs in the near future, and thus Preston's gross margin should also rise.

Depreciation Expense

Depreciation as a percentage of gross property, plant, and equipment has remained in the 9 to 10 percent range over the past six years. This should not change, so we have forecasted depreciation to equal 9.5 percent of the prior period's gross property, plant, and equipment.

Working Capital

For valuation purposes, operating working capital is defined as the sum of the operating cash, accounts receivable, inventories, and prepaid expenses less accounts payable and other current liabilities. We did not discern any clear trends in Preston's working capital as a percentage of revenues. Over the last three years, net operating working capital has remained in the range of 8.2 percent to 9.1 percent of revenues. None of the individual components has shown significant change, either. We will forecast Preston's working capital to remain about where it has been relative to revenues.

Consider the following when forecasting working capital:

- How does the company's inventory accounting method (LIFO versus FIFO) affect its reported inventories?
- Does the company's changing mix of business affect its need for working capital?

- Is the company planning any action to reduce its working capital (for example, just-in-time inventory system)?
- If a trend in working capital is discernible, will the improvement/deterioration continue or will it stabilize?

Year-end working capital can be fairly volatile simply because it is measured only on the last day of the year. Average measures are probably more stable, yet not generally available. Therefore, do not give too much weight to minor, random, year-to-year fluctuations. Focus instead on major trends.

Fixed Assets

Preston owns a variety of fixed assets, including trailers, tractors, trucks, freight terminals, retail outlets for the sale of salvaged freight, and tire-recapping facilities. Fixed assets are probably the trickiest part of the forecast. Most of the company's revenues, costs, and working capital are affected somewhat equally by inflation. Since fixed assets are not replaced each year, however, it is difficult to forecast the cost of replacing old assets that wear out.

For Preston, we have made some fairly simple assumptions. We assume it takes a stable amount of fixed assets to generate each dollar of sales. We expect that the relatively low levels of inflation experienced over the past several years will persist in the near future and will not materially alter this assumption. Therefore, we predict that over the forecast period, the ratio of revenue to property, plant, and equipment will gradually move closer to its historical average. Note that these assumptions would not work well with fast-growing companies or in an unstable inflationary environment.

Accumulated depreciation is the prior period's accumulated depreciation, plus the current period's depreciation expense, minus the book value of assets retired in the current period.

We will assume that fixed assets are used until they are fully depreciated and that they have no material scrap value. Therefore, the amount of assets retired from gross property, plant, and equipment will equal the amount of the reduction in accumulated depreciation. We have set the level of retirements at 4 percent of gross property, plant, and equipment, near recent historical levels.

Income Taxes

We estimated Preston's historical marginal income tax rate to be about 49 percent. This was a 46 percent federal rate, plus an effective 3 percent state and local rate. The 1986 Tax Reform Act reduced Preston's marginal federal rate to 40 percent in 1987 and to 34 percent beginning in 1988.

Adding a provision for state and local taxes (net of the federal tax benefit derived from them), we estimate Preston's marginal income tax rate will be 45 percent in 1987 and 39 percent beginning in 1988.

Preston's EBIT tax rate has historically been below its marginal rate, as shown in Exhibit 6.18. This was primarily due to investment tax credits that have been eliminated by the 1986 Tax Reform Act. Therefore, we have forecasted Preston's EBIT tax rate to equal its marginal income tax rate.

The total income tax provision on the income statement is the sum of two elements: Preston's EBIT multiplied by the EBIT tax rate, and the marginal tax rate multiplied by Preston's net interest income and nonoperating income less interest expense.

The increase in accumulated deferred income taxes as a percentage of the income tax provision has fluctuated widely. Deferred taxes can have a significant effect on the timing of free cash flow, because they represent the delay of a cash outflow—taxes. They arise because, in calculating its taxes, a company uses a depreciation schedule that is different from the schedule it uses to produce its financial statements. We are forecasting the increase in accumulated deferred taxes to be 10 percent of Preston's taxes on EBIT.

Financing

The amortization schedule for Preston's existing debt is provided in the annual report. New debt or marketable securities are created automatically in our forecast to balance the sources and uses of cash.

The interest rate on existing debt is forecast to equal the effective rate in 1987, 8.1 percent. The rate on new debt and operating leases is equal to Preston's current marginal borrowing rate of 11 percent. This rate is derived in Chapter 8, on estimating the cost of capital.

We also expect Preston to have a $0.53 per share dividend payout in 1988. For the remainder of the forecast period, we expect dividends to average approximately 45 percent of net income.

Other

Goodwill amortization should remain constant at $0.6 million per year since we are not forecasting any acquisitions. The amount of goodwill on the balance sheet will decline each year by the amount of the amortization.

We expect nonoperating income to be zero. It is impossible to generalize about the treatment of nonoperating items; just be careful and remember to take them into consideration in your valuation.

Other assets on the balance sheet are forecast to remain at the same percentage of revenues as they were in 1987. Since we possess no information regarding what this category contains, we are assuming that a certain level of these assets is necessary to generate each dollar of revenue.

CHECK OVERALL FORECAST FOR REASONABLENESS

Exhibits 7.7 to 7.14 show the resulting forecast of Preston's financial performance for the moderate performance scenario. The following table summarizes Preston's performance in this scenario.

	1983–87	Forecast 1988–1992	Forecast 1993–1997
Revenue growth	13.1*	13.6%	9.6%
EBIT growth	12.6	36.3	9.1
Pretax ROIC	9.4	12.3	14.7
After-tax ROIC	7.6	8.0	9.5
WACC	11.1	9.7	9.7

* Excludes acquisition

As anticipated, Preston's performance in this scenario is substantially improved over recent years, but its ROIC does not beat its WACC, even in the long run. Therefore, Preston's marginal ROIC is less than its WACC. As a result, the strong growth will not create any value. Overall, the results are consistent with the scenario we outlined.

As for the financing implications of this scenario, Preston's coverage ratio remains between 2 and 3 times EBIT. This is because Preston's relatively high growth rate coupled with moderate return on capital means that its investment rate averages near 100 percent. As a result, Preston must borrow to pay dividends and interest expense. This level of coverage probably does not provide enough cushion in this volatile environment. Preston should probably consider reducing its dividends to conserve financial flexibility if performance does not improve substantially.

Exhibit 7.7 **PRESTON CORPORATION, MODERATE CASE, FORECASTED INCOME STATEMENT,** $ MILLIONS

	1988	1989	1990	1991	1992	1993	1994	1995	1996	1997	Perp
Revenues	610.5	700.9	789.2	874.4	955.7	1,046.5	1,144.9	1,254.8	1,376.5	1,512.8	1,655.0
Operating expenses	(588.6)	(635.7)	(710.3)	(782.6)	(850.6)	(931.4)	(1,019.0)	(1,116.8)	(1,225.1)	(1,346.4)	(1,473.0)
Other expenses	0.0	0.0	0.0	0.0	0.0	0.0	0.0	0.0	0.0	0.0	0.0
Depreciation expense	(28.3)	(32.8)	(37.5)	(42.2)	(47.1)	(51.9)	(57.3)	(63.1)	(69.6)	(76.6)	(84.4)
Operating income	23.6	32.3	41.4	49.6	58.1	63.2	68.6	74.9	81.8	89.8	97.7
Amortization of goodwill	(0.6)	(0.6)	(0.6)	(0.6)	(0.6)	(0.6)	(0.6)	(0.6)	(0.6)	(0.6)	(0.6)
Nonoperating income	0.0	0.0	0.0	0.0	0.0	0.0	0.0	0.0	0.0	0.0	0.0
Interest income	0.3	0.0	(0.0)	0.0	0.0	(0.0)	(0.0)	0.0	0.0	(0.0)	(0.0)
Interest expense	(11.6)	(16.0)	(19.5)	(24.3)	(26.9)	(29.0)	(31.8)	(34.3)	(37.1)	(40.1)	(43.4)
Special items	0.0	0.0	0.0	0.0	0.0	0.0	0.0	0.0	0.0	0.0	0.0
Earnings before taxes	11.7	15.8	21.3	24.7	30.6	33.6	36.2	40.0	44.2	49.1	53.7
Income taxes	(4.8)	(6.4)	(8.6)	(9.9)	(12.1)	(13.3)	(14.4)	(15.8)	(17.5)	(19.4)	(21.2)
Minority interest	0.0	0.0	0.0	0.0	0.0	0.0	0.0	0.0	0.0	0.0	0.0
Income before extra items	6.9	9.4	12.8	14.8	18.4	20.2	21.9	24.2	26.7	29.7	32.5
Extraordinary items	0.0	0.0	0.0	0.0	0.0	0.0	0.0	0.0	0.0	0.0	0.0
Effect of accounting change	0.0	0.0	0.0	0.0	0.0	0.0	0.0	0.0	0.0	0.0	0.0
Net income	6.9	9.4	12.8	14.8	18.4	20.2	21.9	24.2	26.7	29.7	32.5

Exhibit 7.7 Continued

	1988	1989	1990	1991	1992	1993	1994	1995	1996	1997	Perp
Statement of retained earnings											
Beginning retained earnings	85.8	89.6	94.8	101.8	109.9	120.1	131.2	143.2	156.5	171.2	187.6
Net income	6.9	9.4	12.8	14.8	18.4	20.2	21.9	24.2	26.7	29.7	32.5
Common dividends	(3.1)	(4.2)	(5.7)	(6.7)	(8.3)	(9.1)	(9.8)	(10.9)	(12.0)	(13.4)	(14.6)
Preferred dividends	0.0	0.0	0.0	0.0	0.0	0.0	0.0	0.0	0.0	0.0	0.0
Adjustments to retained earnings	0.0	0.0	0.0	0.0	0.0	0.0	0.0	0.0	0.0	0.0	0.0
Ending retained earnings	89.6	94.8	101.8	109.9	120.1	131.2	143.2	156.5	171.2	187.6	205.4

Exhibit 7.8 **PRESTON CORPORATION, MODERATE CASE, FORECASTED BALANCE SHEET,** $ MILLIONS

	1988	1989	1990	1991	1992	1993	1994	1995	1996	1997	Perp
Operating cash	11.6	13.4	15.0	16.7	18.2	19.9	21.8	23.9	26.2	28.8	31.5
Excess marketable securities	0.0	0.0	0.0	0.0	0.0	0.0	0.0	0.0	0.0	0.0	0.0
Accounts receivable	81.2	93.3	105.0	116.3	127.2	139.2	152.3	167.0	183.2	201.3	220.2
Inventories	15.3	17.6	19.8	21.9	24.0	26.3	28.7	31.5	34.5	38.0	41.5
Other current assets	5.5	6.4	7.2	7.9	8.7	9.5	10.4	11.4	12.5	13.7	15.0
Total current assets	113.7	130.6	147.0	162.9	178.0	195.0	213.3	233.8	256.4	281.8	308.3
Gross property plant and equipment	345.7	394.6	444.6	495.4	546.7	603.3	664.7	732.4	806.5	888.3	975.1
Accum. depreciation	(119.8)	(138.8)	(160.5)	(184.9)	(212.2)	(242.2)	(275.4)	(312.0)	(352.3)	(396.6)	(445.5)
Net property plant and equipment	225.9	255.8	284.1	310.4	334.5	361.1	389.3	420.4	454.3	491.7	529.6
Goodwill	23.8	23.2	22.6	22.0	21.4	20.8	20.2	19.6	19.0	18.4	17.8
Other operating assets	9.8	11.2	12.6	14.0	15.3	16.7	18.3	20.1	22.0	24.2	26.5
Investments and advances	0.0	0.0	0.0	0.0	0.0	0.0	0.0	0.0	0.0	0.0	0.0
Total assets	373.2	420.8	466.4	509.3	549.3	593.6	641.1	693.8	751.7	816.1	882.2

Exhibit 7.8 Continued

	1988	1989	1990	1991	1992	1993	1994	1995	1996	1997	Perp
Short-term debt	0.0	0.0	0.0	0.0	0.0	0.0	0.0	0.0	0.0	0.0	0.0
Accounts payable	23.7	27.3	30.7	34.0	37.2	40.7	44.5	48.8	53.5	58.8	64.3
Other current liabilities	37.5	43.1	48.5	53.8	58.8	64.4	70.4	77.2	84.7	93.0	101.8
Total current liabilities	61.3	70.4	79.2	87.8	95.9	105.0	114.9	126.0	138.2	151.9	166.1
Long-term debt	118.1	115.5	51.4	49.7	48.7	32.1	31.2	30.5	30.0	29.5	29.5
New long-term debt	59.3	94.0	186.1	212.0	232.3	270.4	294.1	320.2	348.4	379.6	409.6
Deferred income taxes	21.3	22.6	24.3	26.3	28.7	31.2	34.0	37.0	40.4	44.0	48.0
Other non-interest liabilities	0.0	0.0	0.0	0.0	0.0	0.0	0.0	0.0	0.0	0.0	0.0
Minority interest	0.0	0.0	0.0	0.0	0.0	0.0	0.0	0.0	0.0	0.0	0.0
Preferred stock	0.0	0.0	0.0	0.0	0.0	0.0	0.0	0.0	0.0	0.0	0.0
Common stock and paid-in capital	23.6	23.6	23.6	23.6	23.6	23.6	23.6	23.6	23.6	23.6	23.6
Retained earnings	89.6	94.8	101.8	109.9	120.1	131.2	143.2	156.5	171.2	187.6	205.4
Treasury stock	0.0	0.0	0.0	0.0	0.0	0.0	0.0	0.0	0.0	0.0	0.0
Cummulative translation and other adjustments	0.0	0.0	0.0	0.0	0.0	0.0	0.0	0.0	0.0	0.0	0.0
Total common equity	113.2	118.4	125.4	133.5	143.7	154.8	166.8	180.1	194.8	211.2	229.0
Total liabilities and equity	373.2	420.8	466.4	509.3	549.3	593.6	641.1	693.8	751.7	816.1	882.2

Exhibit 7.9 **PRESTON CORPORATION, MODERATE CASE, FORECASTED NOPLAT**, $ MILLIONS

	1988	1989	1990	1991	1992	1993	1994	1995	1996	1997	Perp
NOPLAT											
Net Sales	610.5	700.9	789.2	874.4	955.7	1,046.5	1,144.9	1,254.8	1,376.5	1,512.8	1,655.0
Operating expenses	(558.6)	(635.7)	(710.3)	(782.6)	(850.6)	(931.4)	(1,019.0)	(1,116.8)	(1,225.1)	(1,346.4)	(1,473.0)
Other expenses	0.0	0.0	0.0	0.0	0.0	0.0	0.0	0.0	0.0	0.0	0.0
Depreciation expense	(28.3)	(32.8)	(37.5)	(42.2)	(47.1)	(51.9)	(57.3)	(63.1)	(69.6)	(76.6)	(84.4)
Adj for operating leases	1.5	1.7	1.9	2.1	2.3	2.5	2.7	3.0	3.3	3.6	3.9
EBIT	25.1	34.0	43.3	51.7	60.3	65.7	71.3	77.9	85.1	93.4	101.6
Taxes on EBIT	(9.8)	(13.3)	(16.9)	(20.1)	(23.5)	(25.6)	(27.8)	(30.4)	(33.2)	(36.4)	(39.6)
Change in deferred taxes	1.0	1.3	1.7	2.0	2.4	2.6	2.8	3.0	3.3	3.6	4.0
Deferred taxes accounting change	0.0	0.0	0.0	0.0	0.0	0.0	0.0	0.0	0.0	0.0	0.0
NOPLAT	16.3	22.1	28.1	33.5	39.2	42.6	46.3	50.5	55.2	60.6	65.9
Taxes on EBIT											
Provision for income taxes	4.8	6.4	8.6	9.9	12.1	13.3	14.4	15.8	17.5	19.4	21.2
Tax shield on interest expense	4.5	6.2	7.6	9.5	10.5	11.3	12.4	13.4	14.5	15.6	16.9
Tax shield on operating lease interest	0.6	0.6	0.7	0.8	0.9	1.0	1.1	1.2	1.3	1.4	1.5
Tax on interest income	(0.1)	0.0	0.0	0.0	0.0	0.0	0.0	0.0	0.0	0.0	0.0
Tax on nonoperating income	0.0	0.0	0.0	0.0	0.0	0.0	0.0	0.0	0.0	0.0	0.0
Taxes on EBIT	9.8	13.3	16.9	20.1	23.5	25.6	27.8	30.4	33.2	36.4	39.6

Exhibit 7.9 Continued

	1988	1989	1990	1991	1992	1993	1994	1995	1996	1997	Perp
Reconciliation to net income											
Net income	6.9	9.4	12.8	14.8	18.4	20.2	21.9	24.2	26.7	29.7	32.5
Add: increase in deferred taxes	1.0	1.3	1.7	2.0	2.4	2.6	2.8	3.0	3.3	3.6	4.0
Add: Goodwill amortization	0.6	0.6	0.6	0.6	0.6	0.6	0.6	0.6	0.6	0.6	0.6
Add: Extraordinary items	0.0	0.0	0.0	0.0	0.0	0.0	0.0	0.0	0.0	0.0	0.0
Add: Special items after tax	0.0	0.0	0.0	0.0	0.0	0.0	0.0	0.0	0.0	0.0	0.0
Add: Minority interest	0.0	0.0	0.0	0.0	0.0	0.0	0.0	0.0	0.0	0.0	0.0
Adjusted net income	8.5	11.3	15.1	17.5	21.4	23.4	25.2	27.8	30.6	34.0	37.1
Add: Interest expense after tax	7.1	9.7	11.9	14.8	16.4	17.7	19.4	20.9	22.6	24.4	26.5
Add: Interest expense on operating leases	0.9	1.0	1.1	1.3	1.4	1.5	1.7	1.8	2.0	2.2	2.4
Total income available to investors	16.4	22.1	28.1	33.5	39.2	42.6	46.3	50.5	55.2	60.6	65.9
Less: Interest income after tax	(0.2)	0.0	0.0	0.0	0.0	0.0	0.0	0.0	0.0	0.0	0.0
Less: Nonoperating income after tax	0.0	0.0	0.0	0.0	0.0	0.0	0.0	0.0	0.0	0.0	0.0
NOPLAT	16.3	22.1	28.1	33.5	39.2	42.6	46.3	50.5	55.2	60.6	65.9

Exhibit 7.10 **PRESTON CORPORATION, MODERATE CASE, FORECASTED INVESTED CAPITAL,** $ MILLIONS

	1988	1989	1990	1991	1992	1993	1994	1995	1996	1997	Perp
Operating current assets	113.7	130.6	147.0	162.9	178.0	195.0	213.3	233.8	256.4	281.8	308.3
Noninterest bearing liabilities	(61.3)	(70.4)	(79.2)	(87.8)	(95.9)	(105.0)	(114.9)	(126.0)	(138.2)	(151.9)	(166.1)
Operating working capital	52.5	60.2	67.8	75.1	82.1	89.9	98.4	107.8	118.3	130.0	142.2
Net property plant and equipment	225.9	255.8	284.1	310.4	334.5	361.1	389.3	420.4	454.3	491.7	529.6
Other assets net of other liabilities	9.8	11.2	12.6	14.0	15.3	16.7	18.3	20.1	22.0	24.2	26.5
Value of operating leases	13.4	15.4	17.4	19.2	21.0	23.0	25.2	27.6	30.3	33.3	36.4
Operating invested capital	301.5	342.7	381.9	418.8	452.9	490.7	531.1	575.9	624.8	679.1	734.7
Excess marketable securities	0.0	0.0	0.0	0.0	0.0	0.0	0.0	0.0	0.0	0.0	0.0
Goodwill	23.8	23.2	22.6	22.0	21.4	20.8	20.2	19.6	19.0	18.4	17.8
Nonoperating investments	0.0	0.0	0.0	0.0	0.0	0.0	0.0	0.0	0.0	0.0	0.0
Total investor funds	325.3	365.9	404.5	440.8	474.3	511.5	551.3	595.5	643.8	697.5	752.5
Equity	113.2	118.4	125.4	133.5	143.7	154.8	166.8	180.1	194.8	211.2	229.0
Deferred income taxes	21.3	22.6	24.3	26.3	28.7	31.2	34.0	37.0	40.4	44.0	48.0
Adjusted equity	134.5	141.0	149.7	159.9	172.3	188.0	200.8	217.1	235.2	255.2	277.0
Interest bearing debt	177.4	209.5	237.5	261.7	281.0	302.5	325.3	350.7	378.4	409.1	439.1
Value of operating leases	13.4	15.4	17.4	19.2	21.0	23.0	25.2	27.6	30.3	33.3	36.4
Total investor funds	325.3	365.9	404.5	440.8	474.3	511.5	551.3	595.5	643.8	697.5	752.5

Exhibit 7.11 PRESTON CORPORATION, MODERATE CASE, FORECASTED FREE CASH FLOW, $ MILLIONS

	1988	1989	1990	1991	1992	1993	1994	1995	1996	1997	Perp
EBIT	25.1	34.0	43.3	51.7	60.3	65.7	71.3	77.9	85.1	93.4	101.6
Taxes on EBIT	(9.8)	(13.3)	(16.9)	(20.1)	(23.5)	(25.6)	(27.8)	(30.4)	(33.2)	(36.4)	(39.6)
Change in deferred taxes	1.0	1.3	1.7	2.0	2.4	2.6	2.8	3.0	3.3	3.6	4.0
NOPLAT	16.3	22.1	28.1	33.5	39.2	42.6	46.3	50.5	55.2	60.6	65.9
Depreciation	28.3	32.8	37.5	42.2	47.1	51.9	57.3	63.1	69.6	76.6	84.4
Gross cash flow	44.5	54.9	65.6	75.8	86.2	94.6	103.6	113.7	124.8	137.2	150.3
Increase in working capital	9.8	7.8	7.6	7.3	7.0	7.8	8.5	9.4	10.5	11.7	12.2
Capital expenditures	60.0	62.8	65.8	68.5	71.1	78.5	85.5	94.2	103.5	114.0	122.3
Increase in other assets	1.5	1.4	1.4	1.4	1.3	1.5	1.6	1.8	1.9	2.2	2.3
Inv in operating leases	2.4	2.0	1.9	1.9	1.8	2.0	2.2	2.4	2.7	3.0	3.1
Gross investment	73.6	74.0	76.7	79.1	81.2	89.7	97.7	107.9	118.5	130.9	140.0
Free cash flow before goodwill	(29.1)	(19.1)	(11.1)	(3.3)	5.0	4.8	5.9	5.8	6.3	6.3	10.4
Investment in goodwill	0.0	0.0	0.0	0.0	0.0	0.0	0.0	0.0	0.0	0.0	0.0
Free cash flow	(29.1)	(19.1)	(11.1)	(3.3)	5.0	4.8	5.9	5.8	6.3	6.3	10.4
Nonoperating cash flow	0.0	0.0	0.0	0.0	0.0	0.0	0.0	0.0	0.0	0.0	0.0
Foreign currency translation effect	0.0	0.0	0.0	0.0	0.0	0.0	0.0	0.0	0.0	0.0	0.0
Cash flow available to investors	(29.1)	(19.1)	(11.1)	(3.3)	5.0	4.8	5.9	5.8	6.3	6.3	10.4

Exhibit 7.11 Continued

	1988	1989	1990	1991	1992	1993	1994	1995	1996	1997	Perp
Financing flow											
AT interest income	(0.2)	0.0	0.0	0.0	0.0	0.0	0.0	0.0	0.0	0.0	0.0
Incr/(Decr) excess marketable securities	(3.2)	0.0	0.0	0.0	0.0	0.0	0.0	0.0	0.0	0.0	0.0
AT interest expense	7.1	9.7	11.9	14.8	16.4	17.7	19.4	20.9	22.6	24.4	26.5
Interest on operating leases	0.9	1.0	1.1	1.3	1.4	1.5	1.7	1.8	2.0	2.2	2.4
Decr/(Incr) in debt	(34.3)	(32.0)	(28.0)	(24.2)	(19.3)	(21.5)	(22.8)	(25.4)	(27.7)	(30.7)	(30.0)
Decr/(Incr) in operating leases	(2.4)	(2.0)	(1.9)	(1.9)	(1.8)	(2.0)	(2.2)	(2.4)	(2.7)	(3.0)	(3.1)
Minority interest (IS and BS)	0.0	0.0	0.0	0.0	0.0	0.0	0.0	0.0	0.0	0.0	0.0
Common dividends	3.1	4.2	5.7	6.7	8.3	9.1	9.8	10.9	12.0	13.4	14.6
Share repurchases	0.0	0.0	0.0	0.0	0.0	0.0	0.0	0.0	0.0	0.0	0.0
Preferred dividends	0.0	0.0	0.0	0.0	0.0	0.0	0.0	0.0	0.0	0.0	0.0
Incr/(Decr) in treasury stock	0.0	0.0	0.0	0.0	0.0	0.0	0.0	0.0	0.0	0.0	0.0
Decr/(Incr) in preferred	0.0	0.0	0.0	0.0	0.0	0.0	0.0	0.0	0.0	0.0	0.0
Decr/(Incr) in common	0.0	0.0	0.0	0.0	0.0	0.0	0.0	0.0	0.0	0.0	0.0
Total financing flow	(29.1)	(19.1)	(11.1)	(3.3)	5.0	4.8	5.9	5.8	6.3	6.3	10.4

Exhibit 7.12 **PRESTON CORPORATION, MODERATE CASE, KEY PERFORMANCE RATIOS**

	1988	1989	1990	1991	1992	1993	1994	1995	1996	1997	Perp
Return on invested capital (Beg. of year)											
All operating exp/revenues	91.3%	90.5%	89.8%	89.3%	88.8%	88.8%	88.8%	88.8%	88.8%	88.8%	88.8%
Depreciation/revenues	4.6%	4.7%	4.8%	4.8%	4.9%	5.0%	5.0%	5.0%	5.1%	5.1%	5.1%
EBIT/revenues	4.1%	4.9%	5.5%	5.9%	6.3%	6.3%	6.2%	6.2%	6.2%	6.2%	6.1%
Net PPE/revenues	31.8%	32.2%	32.4%	32.5%	32.5%	32.0%	31.5%	31.0%	30.5%	30.0%	29.7%
Working capital/revenues	7.0%	7.5%	7.6%	7.8%	7.9%	7.8%	7.9%	7.8%	7.8%	7.8%	7.9%
Net other assets/revenues	3.2%	3.3%	3.4%	3.4%	3.5%	3.5%	3.5%	3.5%	3.5%	3.5%	3.5%
Revenues/invested capital	2.4	2.3	2.3	2.3	2.3	2.3	2.3	2.4	2.4	2.4	2.4
Pretax ROIC	9.8%	11.3%	12.6%	13.5%	14.4%	14.5%	14.5%	14.7%	14.8%	14.9%	15.0%
Cash tax rate	35.1%	35.1%	35.1%	35.1%	35.1%	35.1%	35.1%	35.1%	35.1%	35.1%	35.1%
After-tax ROIC	6.4%	7.3%	8.2%	8.8%	9.4%	9.4%	9.4%	9.5%	9.6%	9.7%	9.7%
After-tax ROIC (including goodwill)	5.8%	6.8%	7.7%	8.3%	8.9%	9.0%	9.1%	9.2%	9.3%	9.4%	9.5%
Return on invested capital (avg.)											
Net PPE/revenues	34.4%	34.4%	34.2%	34.0%	33.7%	33.2%	32.8%	32.3%	31.8%	31.3%	30.9%
Working capital/revenues	7.8%	8.0%	8.1%	8.2%	8.2%	8.2%	8.2%	8.2%	8.2%	8.2%	8.2%
Net other assets/revenues	3.6%	3.6%	3.6%	3.6%	3.6%	3.6%	3.6%	3.6%	3.6%	3.6%	3.6%
Revenues/invested capital	2.2	2.2	2.2	2.2	2.2	2.2	2.2	2.3	2.3	2.3	2.3
Pretax ROIC	9.0%	10.6%	12.0%	12.9%	13.8%	13.9%	14.0%	14.1%	14.2%	14.3%	14.4%
After-tax ROIC	5.8%	6.9%	7.8%	8.4%	9.0%	9.0%	9.1%	9.1%	9.2%	9.3%	9.3%
After-tax ROIC (including goodwill)	5.4%	6.4%	7.3%	7.9%	8.6%	8.6%	8.7%	8.8%	8.9%	9.0%	9.1%

Exhibit 7.12 Continued

	1988	1989	1990	1991	1992	1993	1994	1995	1996	1997	Perp
Growth rates											
Revenue growth rate	20.8%	14.8%	12.6%	10.8%	9.3%	9.5%	9.4%	9.6%	9.7%	9.9%	9.4%
EBIT growth rate	95.9%	35.6%	27.3%	19.3%	16.8%	8.8%	8.6%	9.1%	9.3%	9.7%	8.8%
NOPLAT growth rate	101.9%	35.6%	27.3%	19.3%	16.8%	8.8%	8.6%	9.1%	9.3%	9.7%	8.8%
Invested capital growth rate	17.7%	13.6%	11.4%	9.7%	8.2%	8.3%	8.2%	8.4%	8.5%	8.7%	8.2%
Investment rates											
Gross investment rate	165.3%	134.7%	117.0%	104.4%	94.2%	94.9%	94.3%	94.9%	95.0%	95.4%	93.1%
Net investment rate	278.7%	186.3%	139.6%	110.0%	87.2%	88.7%	87.3%	88.5%	88.7%	89.6%	84.3%
Financing											
Coverage (EBIT/interest)	2.2	2.1	2.2	2.1	2.2	2.3	2.2	2.3	2.3	2.3	2.3
Debt/total capital (book)	62.8%	65.5%	67.0%	67.8%	67.8%	67.8%	67.8%	67.7%	67.7%	67.7%	67.5%
Average ROE	6.2%	8.1%	10.5%	11.5%	13.3%	13.6%	13.6%	13.9%	14.3%	14.7%	14.8%

Exhibit 7.13 **PRESTON CORPORATION, MODERATE CASE, FORECASTED ECONOMIC PROFIT**, $ MILLIONS

	1988	1989	1990	1991	1992	1993	1994	1995	1996	1997	Perp
Return on invested capital	6.4%	7.3%	8.2%	8.8%	9.4%	9.4%	9.4%	9.5%	9.6%	9.7%	9.7%
WACC	9.7%	9.7%	9.7%	9.7%	9.7%	9.7%	9.7%	9.7%	9.7%	9.7%	9.7%
Spread	−3.3%	−2.4%	−1.5%	−0.9%	−0.3%	−0.3%	−0.3%	−0.2%	−0.1%	0.0%	0.0%
Invested capital (beg of year)	256.2	301.5	342.7	381.9	418.8	452.9	490.7	531.1	575.9	624.8	679.1
Economic profit (before goodwill)	(8.6)	(7.2)	(5.1)	(3.5)	(1.5)	(1.3)	(1.3)	(1.0)	(0.6)	0.0	0.1
NOPLAT	16.3	22.1	28.1	33.5	39.2	42.6	46.3	50.5	55.2	60.6	65.9
Capital charge	(24.9)	(29.3)	(33.2)	(37.0)	(40.6)	(43.9)	(47.6)	(51.5)	(55.9)	(60.6)	(65.9)
Economic profit	(8.6)	(7.2)	(5.1)	(3.5)	(1.5)	(1.3)	(1.3)	(1.0)	(0.6)	0.0	0.1

Exhibit 7.14 PRESTON CORPORATION, MODERATE CASE, SUPPORTING CALCULATIONS, $ MILLIONS

	1988	1989	1990	1991	1992	1993	1994	1995	1996	1997	Perp
Change in working capital											
Incr in operating cash	1.5	1.7	1.7	1.6	1.5	1.7	1.9	2.1	2.3	2.6	2.7
Incr in accts receivable	17.8	12.0	11.8	11.3	10.8	12.1	13.1	14.6	16.2	18.1	18.9
Incr in inventories	3.4	2.3	2.2	2.1	2.0	2.3	2.5	2.8	3.1	3.4	3.6
Incr other current assets	0.5	0.8	0.8	0.8	0.7	0.8	0.9	1.0	1.1	1.2	1.3
(Incr) in accts payable	(4.8)	(3.5)	(3.4)	(3.3)	(3.2)	(3.5)	(3.8)	(4.3)	(4.7)	(5.3)	(5.5)
(Incr) other current liabilities	(8.7)	(5.6)	(5.4)	(5.2)	(5.0)	(5.6)	(6.0)	(6.8)	(7.5)	(8.4)	(8.7)
Net change in working capital	9.8	7.8	7.6	7.3	7.0	7.8	8.5	9.4	10.5	11.7	12.2
Capital expenditures											
Increase in net PPE	31.7	29.9	28.3	26.3	24.1	26.5	28.2	31.1	33.9	37.4	37.9
Depreciation	28.3	32.8	37.5	42.2	47.1	51.9	57.3	63.1	69.6	76.6	84.4
Capital expenditures (net of disposals)	60.0	62.8	65.8	68.5	71.1	78.5	85.5	94.2	103.5	114.0	122.3
Investment in goodwill											
Inc/(dec) bal sheet goodwill	(0.6)	(0.6)	(0.6)	(0.6)	(0.6)	(0.6)	(0.6)	(0.6)	(0.6)	(0.6)	(0.6)
Amortization of goodwill	0.6	0.6	0.6	0.6	0.6	0.6	0.6	0.6	0.6	0.6	0.6
Investment in goodwill	0.0	0.0	0.0	0.0	0.0	0.0	0.0	0.0	0.0	0.0	0.0
Nonoperating cash flow											
Extraordinary items	0.0	0.0	0.0	0.0	0.0	0.0	0.0	0.0	0.0	0.0	0.0
AT nonoperating income	0.0	0.0	0.0	0.0	0.0	0.0	0.0	0.0	0.0	0.0	0.0
Change in investments and advances	0.0	0.0	0.0	0.0	0.0	0.0	0.0	0.0	0.0	0.0	0.0
Nonoperating cash flow	0.0	0.0	0.0	0.0	0.0	0.0	0.0	0.0	0.0	0.0	0.0

REVIEW QUESTIONS

1. Outline the basic steps in producing a firm's financial forecast.

2. It has been said repeatedly that adding value translates into an ROIC greater than WACC. How does this result from competitive advantages in an evaluation of strategic position?

3. Discuss how customer segmentation, business system, and industry structure analysis contribute to an analysis of value added for the firm.

The table following question 5 presents data for Cincinnati Milacron, a member of the machine tools industry universe. Cincinnati Milacron (CMZ) is traded on the New York Stock Exchange. It produces machine tools and products and services for the metal cutting industry. Use the data provided on CMZ to formulate your answers to questions 4 and 5.

4. Given the historical data, construct three scenarios for CMZ value.

5. Using the three scenarios, produce and comment on the forecasts for CMZ.

Cincinnati Milacron, Inc.

	1989	1990	1991	1992	1993
Current Assets	499	489	443	429	484
Current Liabilities	240	236	255	237	369
Debt in Current Liabilities	25	12	7	21	78
Long Term Debt	218	200	244	207	236
Total Assets	686	693	598	579	730
Capital Expenditures	34	34	16	18	23
Change in Deferred Taxes	4	(5)	3	2	2
Sales	851	838	754	789	1,029
Operating Expenses	626	624	579	592	765
General Expenses	151	157	132	134	191
Depreciation	23	24	24	21	26
Investment Income	4	2	2	3	2
Interest Expense	22	20	19	19	16
Miscellaneous Income, Net	3	(33)	(75)	–	(70)
Income Taxes	18	4	10	11	8

8

Estimating the
Cost of Capital

Both creditors and shareholders expect to be compensated for the opportunity cost of investing their funds in one particular business instead of others with equivalent risk. The weighted average cost of capital is the discount rate, or time value of money, used to convert expected future cash flow into present value for all investors.

The most important general principle to recognize when developing a WACC is that it must be consistent with the overall valuation approach and with the definition of the cash flow to be discounted. To be consistent with the entity free cash flow approach we are using, the estimate of the cost of capital must:

- Comprise a weighted average of the marginal costs of all sources of capital—debt, equity, and so on—since the free cash flow represents cash available to all providers of capital.

- Be computed after corporate taxes, since the free cash flow is stated after taxes.

- Use nominal rates of return built up from real rates and expected inflation, because the expected free cash flow is expressed in nominal terms (recall that in Chapter 7 we suggested an approach to developing an estimate of expected inflation using the term structure of interest rates).

- Adjust for the systematic risk borne by each provider of capital, since each expects a return that compensates for the risk taken.

- Employ market value weights for each financing element, because market values reflect the true economic claim of each type of financing outstanding, whereas book values usually do not.
- Be subject to change across the cash flow forecast period, because of expected changes in inflation, systematic risk, or capital structure.

FORMULA FOR ESTIMATING THE WACC

The general formula we recommend for estimating the after-tax WACC is as follows:

$$\text{WACC} = k_b(1-T_c)\frac{B}{V} + k_p\frac{P}{V} + k_s\frac{S}{V},$$

where

k_b = the pretax market expected yield to maturity on non-callable, nonconvertible debt,

T_c = the marginal tax rate for the entity being valued,[1]

B = the market value of interest-bearing debt,

V = the market value of the entity being valued $(V = B+P+S)$,

k_p = the after-tax cost of capital for noncallable, nonconvertible preferred stock (which equals the pretax cost of preferred stock when no deduction is made from corporate taxes for preferred dividends),

P = the market value of the preferred stock,

k_s = the market-determined opportunity cost of equity capital,

S = the market value of equity.

We have included only three types of capital (nonconvertible, noncallable debt; nonconvertible, noncallable preferred stock; and

---

[1] The marginal tax rate is the rate applied to a marginal dollar of interest expense. Usually it is the statutory rate. However, if the company has substantial tax loss carry-forwards or carry-backs, or faces possible bankruptcy so that its tax shields may never be used, the marginal tax rate can be lower than the statutory rate—even zero.

equity) in this formula. The actual weighting scheme may be more complex, because a separate market value weight is required for each source of capital that involves cash payments, now or in the future. Other possible items include leases (operating and capital), subsidized debt (for example, industrial revenue bonds), convertible or callable debt, convertible or callable preferred stock, minority interests, and/or warrants and executive stock options. A wide variety of unusual securities—for example, income bonds, bonds with payments tied to commodity indexes, and bonds that are extendable, puttable, or retractable—may also be included.

Noninterest-bearing liabilities, such as accounts payable, are excluded from the calculation of WACC to avoid inconsistencies and simplify the valuation. Noninterest-bearing liabilities have a cost of capital, just like other forms of debt, but this cost is implicit in the price paid for the goods generating the liability, and therefore shows up in the company's operating costs and free cash flow. Separating the implied financing costs of these liabilities from operating costs and free cash flow would be complex and time-consuming without improving the valuation.

The balance of this chapter describes the three related steps involved in developing the discount rate, or WACC:

1. Establishing target market value weights for the capital structure.
2. Estimating the opportunity cost of nonequity financing.
3. Estimating the opportunity cost of equity financing.

As a practical matter, the three are performed simultaneously.

STEP 1: DEVELOP TARGET MARKET VALUE WEIGHTS

The first step in developing an estimate of the WACC is to determine a capital structure for the company you are valuing. This provides the market value weights for the WACC formula.

To accomplish this step, it is helpful to think in terms of a target capital structure, for two reasons. First, at any point a company's capital structure may not reflect the capital structure that is expected to prevail over the life of the business. For example, capital structure might be affected by recent changes in the market value of the securities outstanding and the lumpiness of financing activities, particularly those involving securities offerings. Moreover, management may have plans to change the capital mix as an active policy decision. All of these factors mean that future financing levels could be different from current or past levels.

The second reason for using a target capital structure is that it solves the problem of circularity involved in estimating the WACC. This circularity arises because we need to know market value weights to determine the WACC, but we cannot know the market value weights without knowing what the market value is in the first place—especially the market value of equity. And to determine the value of equity, which is the objective of the valuation process itself, we must discount the expected free cash flow at the WACC. In essence, we cannot know the WACC without knowing the market value of equity, and we cannot know the market value of equity without knowing the WACC.

One way out of the circularity problem is to simply iterate between the weights used in the WACC and the resulting value of equity. The second approach is to work with the idea of a target capital structure, which will not be affected by changes in the value of the company and which also avoids potentially incorrect conclusions about the impact of capital structure on value.

To develop a target capital structure for a company, we suggest using a combination of three approaches:

1. Estimate, to the extent possible, the current market value-based capital structure of the company.
2. Review the capital structure of comparable companies.
3. Review management's explicit or implicit approach to financing the business and its implications for the target capital structure.

Estimating Current Capital Structure

Where possible, you should estimate market values of the elements of the current capital structure and review how they have changed over time. The best approach for estimating the market value-based capital structure is to identify the values of the capital structure elements directly from their prices in the marketplace. Thus, if a company's common stock is publicly traded, and its only other source of financing is corporate bonds that are also traded, the best way to develop a market value-based capital structure estimate is to simply multiply the number of each type of outstanding security by its respective price in the marketplace. Most of the difficulty arises because sources of funds often are not traded in a market-place where we can observe their prices directly.

You need to be prepared to deal with four broad categories of financing: debt-type financing; equity-linked/hybrid financing; minority interests; and common equity financing. In the paragraphs that follow, we provide guidance on how to estimate market values when market prices for the specific financing sources of the company are not available. Remember, should you be fortunate enough to have access to an actual market price, using it is always preferable to using a book value or other approximation.

Debt-type financing   Financing forms in this category normally obligate the company to make a series of payments to the holders of the outstanding instruments, according to a payment schedule stipulated in the financing documents. Interest, coupon, or dividend payments may be fixed or variable. In this category fall short-term and long-term debt, leases, and some preferred stock. Their value depends on three factors: the agreed-upon payment schedule, the likelihood the borrower will make the payments as promised, and the market interest rates for securities with a similar pattern of expected payments.

Generally, their market value can be approximated without difficulty. The process is as follows:

1. Identify the contractually promised payments. For example, is the financing instrument a variable-rate note with interest determined each six months at a fixed spread over the prime rate, or a twenty-year zero-coupon bond?

2. Determine the credit quality of the instrument to be valued. Credit ratings are often available for even illiquid issues, or can be estimated from ratings on other company borrowings (adjusting for the security of the specific instrument in bankruptcy) or from bond rating models that attempt to mimic the behavior of the rating agencies. (The Alcar Group, Inc., markets a software package and database service called APT! that estimates bond ratings using standard

financial ratios. Alcar's address is 5215 Old Orchard Road, Skokie, IL 60077.)

3. Estimate the yield to maturity for which the instrument would trade, were it publicly traded, by reference to market yields on securities with equivalent coupons, maturities, and ratings.

4. Calculate the present value of the stream of financing payments, using the yield to maturity on an equivalent issue as your discount rate. The resulting present value should approximate the market value. (This is equivalent to discounting expected payments at the expected market equilibrium rate of return.)

This approach will work well in most cases, but a few special situations might call for a different approach.

- *Interest rate option features,* such as "caps," "floors," and call provisions, have an effect on future payments, depending on the level of interest rates. They therefore affect the value of the security that contains them. Two approaches can be taken to adjust for these features. The first is to find a comparable security with a similar feature and use it as a proxy. The second is to use an option-pricing approach to estimate the value of the option feature separately. (See Chapter 15.)

- *Swaps.* Many companies enter into interest-rate and currency swap agreements that change the duration and/or currency profile of their financing. Swaps are off-balance-sheet transactions and are disclosed in the footnotes to the financial statements. They are also sometimes used by corporations to speculate on interest rates, and a company could have a debt swap outstanding even though it is financed entirely with common equity.

  For valuation purposes, swaps should be treated in the same way as any other financing instruments, with the promised cash flow in the agreement valued at the prevailing market rate. Practically speaking, this can be a complicated exercise and nearly impossible to do without specific information about the swap instruments themselves.

  When possible, if you can associate a swap with a specific outstanding instrument, you should estimate the value of the synthetic security that the combination of the security plus swap creates. For example, a company may have issued floating-rate debt and entered into an interest-rate swap that converts it to a five-year fixed-rate instrument. In this case, you would estimate the value of the five-year instrument using the standard procedure noted earlier.

- *Foreign currency obligations.* If a company has financing outstanding in a currency other than its home currency, the value of this financing will need to be stated in terms of the company's home currency. This involves a two-step process. First, value the debt in foreign currency terms according to the standard procedure. Second, translate the resulting foreign currency market value into the home currency by using the *spot* foreign exchange rate. For example, if a U.S. company has issued ten-year Swiss franc bonds, it would first determine the market value of the bonds in Swiss francs, using Swiss interest rates for equivalent issues (if necessary), and then translate the result into current U.S. dollars.

- *Leases.* Leases substitute for other forms of debt and can therefore be treated like debt. Standard accounting principles divide leases into two classes: capital leases and operating leases. Capital leases, as defined by the Financial Accounting Standards Board, are essentially those that transfer most of the ownership risk of the asset to the lessee. All other leases are considered operating leases.

  Capital leases are accounted for as if the lessee had purchased the asset and borrowed the funds. The present value of the lease payments is added to the company's assets with other fixed assets and to the liability side of the balance sheet alongside other debt. Operating leases do not appear on the balance sheet, and the lease payments are included with other operating costs. While the accounting treatment of capital and operating leases differs, the economics of the two types of leases is similar. Some companies carefully structure leases to keep them off the balance sheet, but the accounting treatment should not drive your valuation analysis.

  Since capital leases are already shown as debt on the balance sheet, their market value can be estimated just like other debt. Operating leases should also be treated like other forms of debt. The market value of an operating lease is the present value of the required future lease payments (excluding the portion of the lease payment for maintenance) discounted at a rate that reflects the riskiness to the lessee of the particular lease. (Required future lease payments on both capital and operating leases are disclosed in the financial statement footnotes if they are significant.)

As a practical matter, if operating leases are not significant, you should not bother to treat them as debt. Leave them out of the capital structure and keep the lease payments as an operating cost.

- *Callable debt.* The call feature gives the debt issuer the right to call in outstanding debt for a fixed premium above the face value. When interest rates fall, the call feature becomes valuable. Consequently, purchasers of fixed-rate debt that is callable (but not convertible) demand higher coupon rates to compensate them for the risk that their capital gain will be limited, if interest rates fall. Callable debt is equivalent to straight debt, less a put option; consequently, the coupon rate and yield to maturity may not be good estimates of the opportunity cost of capital. Instead, the option-pricing model should be used to estimate the opportunity cost of callable debt. (See Chapter 15.)

Equity-linked/hybrid financing   Companies commonly have, in addition to fixed-income obligations, financing that has all or part of its return linked to the value of all or part of the business. These financing forms include warrants and convertible securities (convertible debt and convertible preferred stock). When these securities are traded, their market value should be determined from their current market prices. When they are not traded, estimating their market value is more difficult than is the case with fixed-income obligations.

- *Warrants.* Usually warrants represent the right to buy a set number of shares of the company's equity at a predetermined price. They can also be warrants to purchase other types of securities, such as preferred stock or additional debt. Warrants are essentially long-term options having an original issue exercise period of five to ten years, with a "strike price" equal to the price the holder would pay, on exercise, to acquire the underlying security. Since they are options, warrants should be valued using option-pricing approaches. If the company you are valuing has a large number of warrants outstanding, their cost should be included in the company's WACC. (See Copeland and Weston 1988, 472-80.)[2]

- *Convertible securities.* Convertibles securities represent a combination of straight, nonconvertible financing and a specified number of warrants that comprise the conversion feature. Their value and their true opportunity cost cannot be determined properly without recognizing the value of the conversion feature (warrant). The stated interest rate on these issues is lower than on straight-debt equivalents because the conversion feature has value. Investors are willing to pay for this value by foregoing the higher yield available on nonconvertible securities. As with warrants, the extent of the yield they will forgo depends on how far in or out of the money the conversion feature is. The deeper in the money it is, the lower the traded yield, and vice versa. Since each convertible bond is a portfolio of straight debt and warrants, the true opportunity cost is higher than for straight debt but lower than for equity.

  To deal with the existence of convertible securities in a company's capital structure, follow an approach similar to the one used for warrants.

In summary, hybrid securities are more difficult to value than straight nonequity financing. If they are very important in a particular situation, use the guidelines just set out and employ an option-pricing approach.

Minority interests   As discussed in Chapter 6, minority interests represent claims by outside shareholders on a portion of a company's business. Minority interests usually arise after an acquisition when the acquiring company does not purchase all of the target company's shares outstanding. They can also arise if the company sells a minority stake in one of its subsidiaries to a third party.

---

[2] T.E. Copeland and J.F. Weston, *Financial Theory and Corporate Policy,* 3rd edition (Reading Mass: Addison Wesley, 1988).

Consolidated cash flows of a company usually include the cash due to minority interests, therefore the value of the minority interest will be subtracted from the entity value to obtain the equity value. Furthermore, if the minority interest has the same risk as the company, the value of the minority interest is added to the value of equity in the WACC calculation. (If the risk is different, then the minority interest will have a separate opportunity cost and weight in the WACC formula.)

The treatment of minority interests depends on the information available. If the minority shares are publicly traded, then their approximate value can be determined directly from the market prices for the shares. If, as is more often the case, the shares are not traded, then theoretically we should value the *subsidiary* separately, using the discounted free cash flow valuation approach and compute the value of the minority stake according to the percentage of the subsidiary's shares the minority shareholders own.

If information about the subsidiary's free cash flow cannot be developed, then the value of the minority stake could be approximated by applying price-to-earnings or market-to-book ratios for similar companies to the minority's share of income or net assets. Both of these items are disclosed in the financial statements—sometimes separately for each subsidiary in which a minority interest exists.

Common equity   In addition to estimating the market values of the pure nonequity and equity-linked financing, we also need to determine the value of equity before we can determine the total market value capitalization of the company and hence the target market value weights for the WACC formula.

If a traded market for the company's common shares exists, follow the familiar approach of using current market price multiplied by the number of shares outstanding. The current market price is the best available estimate of the market value of the equity and is superior to book values or averages of past market prices. It reflects investors' views about expected returns from holding the shares relative to alternative investments at the time of the valuation.

If a traded market does not exist for the shares, the situation is more difficult. This is one of the reasons why we might need to use comparables and discussions with management to estimate an implied target for the percentage of equity in the company's capital structure. These are discussed in the next section. Before proceeding to these approaches, though, we should note that we can develop an implied equity value by testing alternative values for the equity and their implications for the market value weights in the WACC computation. These alternative weights can be used to develop first estimates of the cost of capital and can be refined through a couple of iterations. Essentially, when the value of equity used in the WACC formula is approximately equal to the discounted cash flow value of equity produced by applying the discount rate to the free cash flows and the continuing value, then we have produced an implied economic capital structure for the business. (To follow this approach you will have had to estimate the market values of all the other financing components and an opportunity cost for each—discussed in the next section—as well as have in hand the free cash flow forecast and inputs to the continuing-value estimate. When described as part of a sequential process, this iterative approach sounds more complicated than it really is in practice, especially since the use of a PC-based valuation model makes the process of iterating relatively quick and easy.)

Review the Structures of Comparable Companies

In addition to estimating the market value-based capital structure of the company currently and over time, you should also review the capital structures of comparable companies. There are two reasons.

First, comparing the capital structure of the company you are valuing with those of similar companies will help you understand whether your current estimate of capital structure is unusual. For the company's capital structure to be different is perfectly acceptable, but you should understand the reasons why it is or is not. For instance, is the company by philosophy more aggressive or innovative in the use of nonequity financing, or is the current capital structure only a temporary deviation from a more conservative target? Often, companies finance acquisitions with debt they plan to pay down rapidly or refinance with a stock offering in the next year. Alternatively, is there anything different about the company's cash flow or asset intensity that, despite its being in a seemingly comparable situation, means its target capital structure can or should be fundamentally different from those of comparable companies? Answers to questions such as these can help you decide on the company's future target capital structure relative to its current one.

The second reason for reviewing comparable companies is a more practical one: in some cases you cannot directly estimate the current financing mix for the company. For privately held or thinly traded companies, or for divisions of a publicly traded company, a market-based estimate of the current value of equity may not be available. In these situations, you can use comparables to help assess the reasonableness of the estimate of the target proportion of equity developed through the iterative process described in the previous section.

Also, in the case of divisions of multibusiness companies, you may not even be able to determine the nonequity financing portion of the division's capital structure. One approach to this problem is to use the corporatewide capital structure. But this should be supplemented with a review of the approximate market value capital structures of similar companies. Chapter 11 provides more detailed guidance on handling the practical and conceptual problems of valuation for multibusiness companies, including how to develop relevant capital structures for each business.

Review Management's Financing Philosophy

When possible, you should discuss the company's capital structure policy with management to determine their explicit or implicit target market capital structure for the company and its businesses. In some cases, they will have in hand a very clear perspective on the capital structure they intend to employ on a division-by-division basis.

Even if management's approach is not well developed or is largely judgmental, you can still learn a lot from discussions with them about sensible targets for use in your valuation work. At some level, they will have targets for the types of financing they plan to employ. The targets may be expressed in terms of book values, but these can be converted into market values. Furthermore, management can provide insights into the factors that underlie their choice of financing and about comparable companies.

If you do not have direct access to management, you can glean similar information from the annual review sections of annual reports/10-Ks and from reports by security analysts.

In the next two sections we describe the approach to estimating the relevant opportunity costs for each type of financing commonly encountered, organized around fixed-income financing and common equity financing. In each case, we are seeking to estimate nominal, required rates of return, since our free cash flow estimates are expressed in nominal terms.

STEP 2: ESTIMATE THE COST OF NONEQUITY FINANCING

In this section we discuss approaches to estimating market opportunity costs for financing forms that do not have explicit equity features. These include the following:

- Straight investment-grade debt (fixed and variable rate).
- Below-investment-grade debt (for example, "junk" bonds).
- Subsidized debt (for example, industrial revenue bonds).
- Foreign-currency-denominated debt.
- Leases (capital leases, operating leases).
- Straight preferred stock.

Straight Investment-Grade Debt

If the company has straight debt that is not convertible into other securities—like common stock—and that is not callable, then we can use discounted cash flow analysis to estimate the market rate of return and the market value of the debt. For investment-grade debt, the risk of bankruptcy is low. Therefore, yield to maturity is usually a reasonable estimate of the opportunity cost.

The coupon rate—that is, the historical (or imbedded) cost of debt—is irrelevant for determining the current cost of capital. Always use the most current market rate on debt of equivalent risk. A reasonable proxy for the risk of debt is Moody's or Standard & Poor's bond rating. If the bond rating is not available, you will need to calculate traditional financial ratios—times-interest-earned, debt-to-equity, working capital, and so on—in order to compare the entity you are valuing with known firms, as a means of estimating the bond rating. (The APT! software package and database service by Alcar estimates bond ratings by using standard financial ratios.)

Most companies have variable-rate debt, either acquired through swaps, as an original security issue, or in the form of revolving bank loans. If the variable-rate loan has no cap or floor, then use the long-term rate, because the short-term rate will be rolled over and the geometric average of the expected short-term rates is equal to the long-term rate. If the variable-rate debt has a cap or floor, or if the interest payment is determined as a moving average of past rates, then an option is involved and the problem becomes much more complicated. For example, if market rates have risen and a variable rate loan is "capped out," then it becomes a "subsidized" form of financing that adds value to the company.

Below-Investment-Grade Debt

When dealing with debt that is less than investment grade, you must be aware of the difference between the expected yield to maturity and the promised yield to maturity. The promised yield to maturity assumes that all payments (coupons and principal) will be made as promised by the issuer. Consider the following simple example: A three-year bond promises to pay a 10 percent coupon at the end of each year, plus a face value of $1,000 at the end of the third year. The current market value of the bond is $951.96. What is the yield to maturity? If we use y to designate the promised yield to maturity, it can be computed by solving the following formula:

$$B_0 = \sum_{t=1}^{3} \frac{Coupon_t}{(1+y)^t} + \frac{Face}{(1+y)^3},$$

where

B_0 = the current market value of noncallable, nonconvertible debt.

$Coupon$ = the promised coupon paid at the end of time period t.

$Face$ = the face value of the bond, promised at maturity.

y = the promised yield to maturity.

The solution is $y = 12$ percent. However, this promised yield to maturity assumes that the debt is default-free. Suppose that we expect a 5 percent chance that the bond will default and pay only $400.

If we were to rewrite the formula, putting the bond's expected payments rather than its promised payments in the numerator, we could calculate the market's *expected* rate of return as opposed to the promised rate of return implicit in the yield to maturity. As recomputed, the market expected rate of return on the risky debt would be 11.09 percent. Thus, the rate of return that the market expects to earn is 91 basis points lower than the promised yield to maturity. The promised yields on junk bonds are very different (frequently much higher) from the expected yields that the market anticipates on these risky securities. Thus, yields are not always what they seem.

Our problem, then, is that we need to compute the expected yield to maturity, not the quoted, promised yield. We can do this if we have the current market price of the low-grade bond and estimates of its expected default rate and value in default, or if we can estimate its systematic risk (beta). Unfortunately, the necessary data are usually unavailable. Default rates on original issue corporate bonds in the United States as calculated by Altman (1989) are given in Exhibit 8.1. As you can see, orignal issue junk bonds (those with the lowest rating) have very large default rates after a period of time (31 percent after 5 years).

If the necessary data is not available, as a reasonable fallback position, *use the yield to maturity on BBB-rated debt*, which reduces most of the effects of the difference between promised and expected yields.

Although the promised yield to maturity is not equivalent to the opportunity cost of capital for debt with high default risk, it can serve as a useful proxy for the market's estimate of default risk.

Exhibit 8.1 **THE CUMULATIVE PROBABILITY OF DEFAULT FOR BONDS ISSUED BETWEEN 1971 AND 1987,** PERCENT

Original S&P rating	1	2	Years since maturity 3	4	5
AAA	0.00	0.00	0.00	0.00	0.00
AA	0.00	0.00	1.81	2.20	2.33
A	0.00	0.31	.71	.71	.71
BBB	0.04	0.29	.46	.46	.91
BB	0.00	0.62	1.25	1.56	1.84
B	1.98	2.88	3.60	7.69	11.53
CCC	2.99	5.78	9.52	30.22	31.17

Source: Data from E. Altman, "Measuring Corporate Bond Mortality and Performance," *Journal of Finance* (September 1989): 915.

Exhibit 8.2 **PROMISED YIELDS VERSUS BOND RATINGS,
APRIL 1993,** PERCENT

Term	Risk-free	AAA	AA	A	BBB	BB	B
1 month	2.27%	2.83%	3.29%	3.90%	4.56%	5.10%	6.48%
3 months	2.86	3.42	3.88	4.49	5.15	5.69	7.07
6 months	2.96	3.52	3.98	4.59	5.25	5.79	7.17
1 year	3.23	3.79	4.25	4.86	5.52	6.06	7.44
2 years	3.73	4.29	4.75	5.36	6.02	6.56	7.94
5 years	5.11	5.67	6.13	6.74	7.40	7.94	9.32
10 years	6.06	6.62	7.08	7.69	8.35	8.89	10.27
15 years	6.61	7.17	7.63	8.24	8.90	9.44	10.82
20 years	6.61	7.17	7.63	8.24	8.90	9.44	10.82
25 years	6.96	7.52	7.98	8.59	9.25	9.79	11.17
30 years	6.98	7.54	8.00	8.61	9.27	9.81	11.19

Source: Alcar APT!

Exhibit 8.2 shows the relationship between promised yields to maturity and maturity periods for portfolios of bonds varying in risk from default-free U.S. government obligations to B-rated corporate debentures. The table was plotted in the Autumn of 1993. Exhibit 8.3 graphs the relationship between the promised yield to maturity and the bond rating for bonds with ten years to maturity.

Subsidized Debt

The coupon rate on industrial revenue bonds is below the market rate for taxable bonds of equivalent risk because they are tax-free to investors. They should enter into the WACC at their current market yield to maturity, where known. If the bonds are not traded, their yield can be estimated by reference to similarly rated tax-free issues that are actively traded (or from similar new issues of tax-exempt debt).

Foreign-Currency-Denominated Debt

When an obligation is denominated in a foreign currency, the local currency nominal rate of return is usually an inappropriate measure

Exhibit 8.3 **PROMISED YIELDS VERSUS BOND RATINGS ON
TEN YEAR DEBT, APRIL 1993**

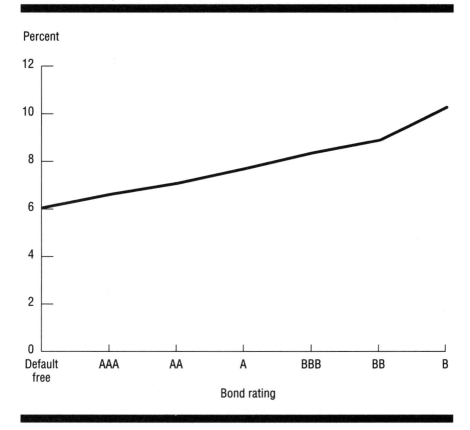

Source: Alcar APT!

of the actual cost of capital to the issuer in its home currency. This is
due to the foreign exchange exposure inherent in the financing.

When a company issues foreign-currency-denominated debt,
its effective cost equals the after-tax cost of repaying the principal
and interest *in terms of the company's own currency.* Usually the all-in
cost of borrowing in foreign currency will be close to the cost of
borrowing in domestic markets due to the interest-rate parity relationship enforced by the active arbitrage engaged in by issuers,
investors, and intermediaries in the cash, forward exchange, and
currency swap markets.

The interest-rate parity relationship (leaving minor transaction costs and temporary, small arbitrage opportunities aside) generally guarantees the following relationship (further explained in Chapter 12):

$$1+k_b = \frac{X_o}{X_f}(1+r_o),$$

where

k_b = the domestic pretax cost of N-year debt.

X_o = the spot foreign exchange rate (units of foreign currency per dollar).

X_f = the N-year forward foreign exchange rate (units of foreign currency per dollar).

r_o = the foreign interest rate on an N-year bond.

To illustrate, suppose that your domestic borrowing rate is 7.25 percent and that the rate on a one-year loan denominated in Swiss francs is 4 percent. How would these rates compare? If the spot exchange rate is 1.543 francs per dollar, and the one-year forward rate is 1.4977 francs per dollar, then the equivalent *domestic* one-year borrowing rate is 7.15 percent for the Swiss franc loan.

$$1+k_b = \left[\frac{1.543}{1.4977}\right](1+0.04),$$
$$= 1.0715 \text{ or } k_b = 7.15\%.$$

Usually, the equivalent domestic borrowing rate on foreign-currency-denominated debt will be very close to the domestic borrowing rate. Arbitrage virtually guarantees this result.

Although we can use forward rate contracts to estimate equivalent domestic rates for relatively short-term debt (less than 18 months), no easily referenced forward markets exist farther out. For longer-term borrowing, we recommend you assume the domestic equivalent rate is roughly equal to the actual domestic rate.

Leases

Leases, both capital and operating, are substitutes for other types of debt. Therefore, it is reasonable in most cases to assume that their opportunity cost is the same as for the company's other long-term debt.

Straight Preferred Stock

The cost of preferred stock that is perpetual, noncallable, and non-convertible can be calculated as follows:

$$k_p = \frac{\text{div}}{P},$$

where

k_p = the cost of preferred stock.
div = the promised dividend on the preferred stock.
P = the market price of the preferred stock.

If the current market price is not available, use yields on similar-quality issues as an estimate. For a fixed-life or callable preferred stock issue, estimate the opportunity cost by using the same approach as for a comparable debt instrument. In other words, estimate the yield that equates the expected stream of payments with the market value. For convertible preferred issues, option-pricing approaches are necessary.

STEP 3: ESTIMATE THE COST OF EQUITY FINANCING

To estimate the opportunity cost of equity capital, we currently recommend using the capital asset pricing model (CAPM) or the arbitrage pricing model (APM). Both approaches have problems associated with their application. For example, they are subject to measurement problems. But they are theoretically correct; they are risk-adjusted and account for expected inflation. In contrast, many other approaches to computing the cost of equity are conceptually flawed. For example, the dividend yield model, the earnings-to-price ratio model, and the dividend yield model with a growth term (sometimes called the Gordon growth model) give incorrect results.

The Capital Asset Pricing Model

The CAPM is discussed at length in all modern finance texts.[3] These detailed discussions will not be reproduced here. (In this section, we assume you are generally familiar with the principles that underlie the approach.) In essence, the CAPM postulates that the opportunity cost of equity is equal to the return on risk-free securities, plus the company's systematic risk (beta), multiplied by the market price of risk (market risk premium). The equation for the cost of equity (k_s) is as follows:

$$k_s = r_f + \left[E(r_m) - r_f \right](\text{beta}),$$

where

r_f	= the risk-free rate of return.
$E(r_m)$	= the expected rate of return on the overall market portfolio.
$E(r_m) - r_f$	= the market risk premium.
beta	= the systematic risk of the equity.

The CAPM is illustrated in Exhibit 8.4. The cost of equity, k_s, increases linearly as a function of the measured undiversifiable risk, beta. The beta for the entire market portfolio is 1.0. This means that the average company's equity beta will also be about 1.0. In our experience it is very unusual to observe a beta greater than 2.0 or less than 0.1. The market risk premium (the price of risk), which varies from country to country, is measured as the slope of the CAPM line in Exhibit 8.4—that is, the slope is $E(r_m) - r_f$.

To implement the CAPM approach, we need to estimate the three factors that determine the CAPM line: the risk-free rate, the market risk premium, and the systematic risk (beta). The balance of this section describes a recommended approach for estimating each.

Determining the risk-free rate   Hypothetically, the risk-free rate is the return on a security or portfolio of securities that has no default risk whatsoever, and is completely uncorrelated with returns on

---

[3] J. F. Weston and T. E. Copeland, *Managerial Finance*, 9th edition (Fort Worth: The Dryden Press, 1992).

Exhibit 8.4 **THE CAPITAL ASSET PRICING MODEL**

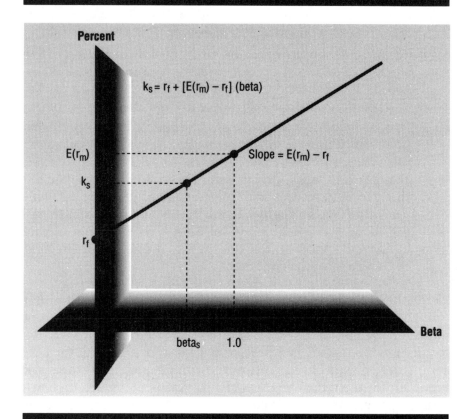

anything else in the economy. Theoretically, the best estimate of the risk-free rate would be the return on a zero-beta portfolio. Due to the cost and complexity of constructing zero-beta portfolios, they are not available for use in estimating the risk-free rate.

We have three reasonable alternatives that use government securities: (1) the rate for Treasury bills, (2) the rate for ten-year Treasury bonds, and (3) the rate for thirty-year Treasury bonds. We recommend using a ten-year Treasury-bond rate, for several reasons.

- First, it is a long-term rate that usually comes close to matching the duration of the cash flow of the company being valued. Since the current Treasury-bill rate is a short-term rate, it does not match duration properly. If we were to use short-term rates, the appropriate choice would be the short-term rates that are expected to apply in each future period, not today's short-term interest rate. In essence, the ten-year rate is a geometric weighted average estimate of the *expected* short-term Treasury-bill rates over the evaluation horizon.

- Second, the ten-year rate approximates the duration of the stock market index portfolio—for example, the S&P 500—and its use is therefore consistent with the betas and market risk premiums estimated relative to these market portfolios.

- Finally, the ten-year rate is less susceptible to two problems involved in using a longer-term rate, such as the thirty-year Treasury-bond rate. Its price is less sensitive to unexpected changes in inflation, and therefore has a smaller beta than the thirty-year rate; and the liquidity premium built into ten-year rates *may* be slightly lower than that which is in thirty-year bonds. These are technical details, with a minor impact in normal circumstances. But they do argue in the direction of using a ten-year bond rate.

Determining the market risk premium   The market risk premium (the price of risk) is the difference between the expected rate of return on the market portfolio and the risk-free rate, $E(r_m) - r_f$. We recommend using a 5 to 6 percent market risk premium for U.S. companies. This is based on the long-run geometric average risk premium for the return on the S&P 500 versus the return on long-term government bonds from 1926 to 1992.[4] Since this is a contentious area that can have a significant impact on valuations, we elaborate our reasoning in detail here.

- We use a very long time frame to measure the premium rather than a short time frame to eliminate the effects of short-term anomalies in the measurement. The 1926–1992 time frame reflects wars, depressions, and booms. Shorter time periods do not reflect as diverse a set of economic circumstances.

- We use a geometric average of rates of return because arithmetic averages are biased by the measurement period. An arithmetic average estimates the rates of return by taking a

[4] Ibbotson Associates, *Stocks, Bonds, Bills and Inflation 1993 Yearbook* (Chicago, 1993).

simple average of the single period rates of return. Suppose you buy a share of a nondividend-paying stock for $50. After one year the stock is worth $100. After two years the stock falls to $50 once again. The first period return is 100 percent; the second period return is −50 percent. The arithmetic average return is 25 percent [(100 percent−50 percent)/2]. The geometric average is zero. (The geometric average is the compound rate of return that equates the beginning and ending value.) We believe that the geometric average represents a better estimate of investors' expected returns over long periods of time.

- Finally, we calculate the premium over *long-term* government bond returns to be consistent with the risk-free rate we use to calculate the cost of equity.

Some analysts recommend using the arithmetic average rate of return. Depending on the time frame chosen and the type of average, the market risk premium can vary significantly, as shown in the following table.

	1926–93	1962–93
Risk premium based on:		
Arithmetic average returns	6.9%	4.2%
Geometric average returns	5.0	3.6

Source: Ibbotson Associates 1994 Yearbook.

Clearly, your valuation can change substantially if you switch from 6.9 to 3.6 percent. Three issues must be resolved. Should you use a more recent, but shorter, time frame? Should you choose the arithmetic or the geometric average? Should the forecasted risk premium be based on historical estimates or analysts' forecasts? Since we believe that the market risk premium is essentially a random walk, better estimates are provided by the longer time frame. Sure, things have changed, but they have not changed in a predictable fashion. Thus, the risk premium is best described as a random walk, and the longer time frame (which encompasses a stock market crash, expansions, recessions, two wars, and stagflation) is the best estimate of the future.

To contrast the geometric and average rates of return, we can go back to the earlier example where we observed two periods of

Exhibit 8.5 **RATE OF RETURN DATA FOR FOUR LIKELY PATHS**

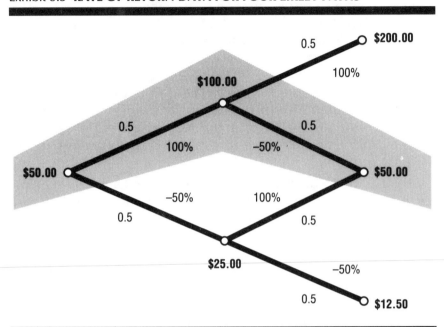

return, the first with a rate of 100 percent and the second with −50 percent. What can we infer from these data? If we are willing to make the strong assumption that each return is an independent observation from a stationary underlying probability distribution, then we can infer that four equally likely return paths actually exist: 100 percent followed by 100 percent, 100 percent followed by −50 percent, −50 percent followed by 100 percent, and −50 percent followed by 50 percent. These possibilities are illustrated in Exhibit 8.5. The shaded area represents what we have actually observed, and the remainder of the binomial tree is what we have inferred by assuming independence.

The difference between the arithmetic and geometric averages is that the former infers expected returns by assuming independence, and the latter treats the observed historical path as the single best estimate of the future. If you believe it is proper to apply equal weighting to all branches in the binomial tree, then your expected wealth is as follows:

$$\tfrac{1}{4}(\$200) + \tfrac{1}{2}(\$50) + \tfrac{1}{4}(\$12.50) = \$78.125.$$

Exactly the same value can be obtained by computing the arithmetic average return:

$$\tfrac{1}{4}(100\%) + \tfrac{1}{2}(25\%) + \tfrac{1}{4}(-50\%) = 25\%,$$

and applying it to the starting wealth as follows:

$$\$50 \ (1.25) \ (1.25) = \$78.125.$$

If you believe, as we do, that the best estimate of future wealth is the single geometric average return—that is, 0 percent—then the expected wealth after two periods is $50.

Note that the arithmetic return is always higher than the geometric return and that the difference between them becomes greater as a function of the variance of returns. Also, the arithmetic average depends on the interval chosen. For example, an average of monthly returns will be higher than an average of annual returns. The geometric average, being a single estimate for the entire time interval, is invariant to the choice of interval. Finally, empirical research by Fama and French (1988), Lo and MacKinlay (1988), and Poterba and Summers (1988) indicates that a significant long-term negative autocorrelation exists in stock returns.[5] Hence, historical observations are not independent draws from a stationary distribution.

A recent example of the problematic nature of choosing a short time interval to estimate arithmetic average returns occurred during the summer of 1987. Many analysts were using the relatively low 2.5 to 3.5 percent risk premium taken from the 1962–85 time period. This low estimate helped to justify the extraordinarily high prices observed in the stock market at that time. After all, the argument went, it does not make sense to use long-term rates, because extraordinary events like a stock market crash cannot happen again. Our opinion is that the best *forecast* of the risk premium is its long-run geometric average.

Although we recommend using the long-term historical geometric average risk premium, a frequently mentioned alternative is based on analysts' forecasts. The expected rate of return on the

[5] A. Lo and C. MacKinlay, "Stock Market Prices Do Not Follow Random Walks: Evidence from a Simple Specification Test," *Review of Financial Studies* (Spring 1988): 41–66; E. Fama and K. French, "Dividend Yields and Expected Stock Returns," *Journal of Financial Economics* (October 1988): 3–25; J. Poterba and L. Summers, "Mean Reversion in Stock Prices: Evidence and Implications," *Journal of Financial Economics* (October 1988): 27–59.

market portfolio, $E(r_m)$, is estimated by adding the analysts' consensus estimate of growth in the dividend of the S&P 500 index, g, to the dividend yield for the index, Div/S:

$$E(r_m) = \frac{Div}{S} + g.$$

The risk-free rate is then subtracted from the expected return on the market to obtain the forecast of the market risk premium. We have little faith in this method, for two reasons. First, analysts have shown limited skill in forecasting price changes (growth) for the S&P 500. And second, the formula that provides the basis for this approach implicitly assumes perpetual growth at a constant rate, g. This is a particularly stringent assumption.

Estimating the systematic risk (beta)   The approach to use in developing the estimate of beta depends on whether the company's equity is traded or not.

If the company is publicly traded, you are indeed fortunate and can use published estimates. We recommend you use betas published by BARRA (formerly Rosenberg Associates). BARRA predicted betas are updated quarterly for approximately seven thousand companies listed on the New York Stock Exchange, the American Stock Exchange, and NASDAQ. These estimates of systematic risk are based on the financial ratios of each company. They change as the financial ratios do, and more accurately reflect the market's most recent estimate of equity risk.

To find that estimates of betas from different services vary is not completely unusual. We have three rules of thumb:

1. If one of the services produces higher-quality betas, throw out the others.
2. If two high-quality services provide betas that differ by no more than 0.2, take the average and use it.
3. If the betas are farther apart than 0.2, construct an equally weighted industry average beta.

Because measurement errors tend to cancel out, industry averages are more stable than company betas. When constructing the industry average, be sure to unlever the company betas and then apply the leverage of the company you are valuing, using the methodology described in Chapter 11 of this book.

If you can only find one estimate of beta, but it does not seem to make sense (for example, it is negative, greater then 2, or differs radically from betas for other similarly leveraged companies in the same industry), then use the approaches suggested in Chapter 11 for estimating betas for untraded companies.

The problem of estimating betas for business units within a company is discussed in Chapter 11, and betas for foreign companies are discussed in Chapter 12.

Is Beta Dead?

In June of 1992 Eugene Fama and Ken French of the University of Chicago published a paper in *The Journal of Finance* that received a great deal of attention because they concluded:

> In short, our tests do not support the most basic prediction of the SLB model [The Capital Asset Pricing Model] that average stock returns are positively related to market betas.[6]

Theirs was the most recent in a long line of empirical studies that questioned the usefulness of measured betas in explaining the risk premium (above the riskless rate) on equities. For example Banz (1981) and Reinganum (1981) found a prominent size effect that added to the explanation of cross-sectional returns, in addition to beta. Basu (1983) found a seasonal (January) effect. Bhandari (1988) demonstrated that the degree of financial leverage was important. And Stattman (1980) as well as Rosenberg, Reid, and Lanstein (1985) found that average returns are positively related to the firm's equity book to market ratio.[7]

---

[6] E. Fama and K. French, "The Cross-Section of Expected Stock Returns" *The Journal of Finance* 47, no. 2 (June 1992): 427–465.
[7] R. Banz, "The Relationship between Return and the Market Value of Common Stocks," *Journal of Financial Economics* 9 (1981): 3–18; M. Reinganum, "A New Empirical Perspective on the CAPM," *Journal of Financial and Quantitative Analysis* 16 (1981): 439–462; S. Basu, "The Relationship between Earnings Yield, Market Value, and the Return for NYSE Common Stocks: Further Evidence," *Journal of Financial Economics* 12 (1983): 129–156; L. Bhandari, "Debt/Equity Ratio and Expected Common Stock Returns: Empirical Evidence," *The Journal of Finance* 43 (1988): 507–528; D. Stattman, "Book Values and Stock Returns," *The Chicago MBA: A Journal of Selected Papers* 4 (1980): 25–45; B. Rosenberg, K. Reid, and R. Langstein, "Pervasive Evidence of Market Inefficiency," *Journal of Portfolio Management* II (1985): 9–17.

If beta is not dead, then surely it's wounded. Fama and French found that equity returns are inversely related to the size of a company measured by the value of its equity capitalization, and positively related to the ratio of the book value of the company's equity to its market value. When these variables were taken into account, beta added nothing to their ability to explain the returns on equity.

One practical implication is that one might estimate the required return on the equity of a company by looking up its size and market-to-book ratio in a table of average risk premia over the risk-free rate. This might give better results than using estimates of beta and the CAPM. Another possible implication, and one that Fama and French hint at, is the need to use a multifactor approach like the Arbitrage Pricing Model.

The Arbitrage Pricing Model

The APM can be thought of as a multifactor analogue to the CAPM. The CAPM explains security returns as a function of one factor, which is called the market index, and is usually measured as the rate of return on a well-diversified portfolio such as an equally weighted New York Stock Exchange index. The APM cost of equity is defined as follows:

$$k_s = r_f + \left[E(F_1) - r_f\right]beta_1 + \left[E(F_2) - r_f\right]beta_2 + \ldots + \left[E(F_k) - r_f\right]beta,$$

where

$E(F_k)$ = the expected rate of return on a portfolio that mimics the kth factor and is independent of all others.

$beta_k$ = the sensitivity of the stock return to the kth factor.

Instead of one measure of systematic risk, the APM includes many. Each beta measures the sensitivity of a company's stock return to a separate underlying factor in the economy. Empirical work suggests that five important and fundamental factors are changes in

1. The industrial production index—a measure of how well the economy is doing in terms of actual physical output.

2. The short-term real rate, measured by the difference between the yield on T-bills and the Consumer Price Index.

3. Short-term inflation, measured by unexpected changes in the Consumer Price Index.

4. Long-term inflation, measured as the difference between the yield to maturity on long- and short-term U.S. government bonds.

5. Default risk, measured by the difference between the yield to maturity on Aaa- and Baa-rated long-term corporate bonds.

Empirical evidence also confirms that the APM explains expected returns better than the single-factor CAPM.[8] In addition, the APM can add insight into the type of risk that is relevant. This is illustrated in Exhibit 8.6. The axes are two of the fundamental factors, the industrial production index and short-term inflation. The diagonal dotted lines represent constant returns with different combinations of risk. Any portfolio at the origin (point F) has no exposure to either factor, and therefore earns the riskless rate, r_f.

For a portfolio at point G, exposure to the systematic risk of unexpected inflation has increased but is offset by decreased risk relative to the industrial production index. The net result is that point G earns the riskless rate, just like point F, but is exposed to a different bundle of risks. A similar story can be told about points A, M, and B. All earn the same expected return as the CAPM market portfolio, $E(r_m)$, but have varying exposures to the risk of unexpected inflation and changes in the industrial production index.

Exhibit 8.7 shows the difference in risk premiums as calculated by the APM and the CAPM for five industries. Oil, savings and loans, and money center banks are riskier in every dimension. Forest products are less risky, and electric utilities have much less default risk. A larger risk premium means that the industry is more sensitive to a given type of risk than would be predicted by the CAPM. For example, savings and loans are more sensitive to unex-

---

[8] For example, see N.F. Chen, "Some Empirical Tests of the Theory of Arbitrage Pricing," *Journal of Finance* (December 1983): 1393–1414; N.F. Chen, S. Ross, and R. Roll, "Economic Forces and the Stock Market," *Journal of Business* (July 1986): 383–403; M. Berry, E. Burmeister, and M. McElroy, "Sorting out Risks Using Known APT Factors," *Financial Analysts Journal* (March/April 1988): 29–42.

Exhibit 8.6 **THE ARBITRAGE PRICING MODEL**

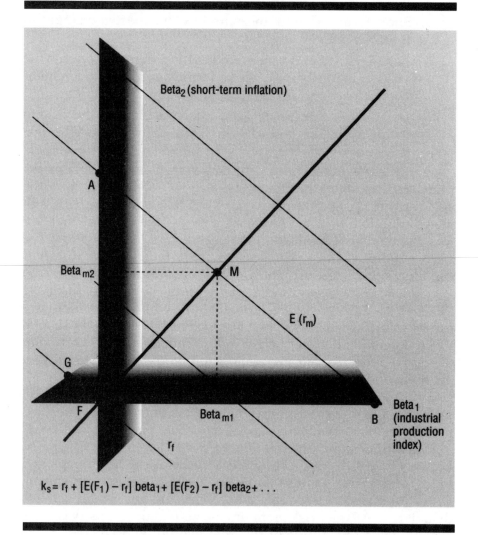

$$k_s = r_f + [E(F_1) - r_f]\,beta_1 + [E(F_2) - r_f]\,beta_2 + \ldots$$

pected changes in long-term inflation, and the market charges a risk premium—that is, it requires a higher cost of equity.

Exhibit 8.8, produced using Alcar's APT! program, shows the net effect of using the CAPM versus the APM to estimate the cost of equity for nine industries. The importance of these differences for valuation of an all-equity perpetual stream of cash flows is reflected in the last column. For example, the 4.7 percent higher APM

Exhibit 8.7 **DIFFERENCES IN RISK PREMIUMS BETWEEN APM AND CAPM, BY INDUSTRY,** 1988

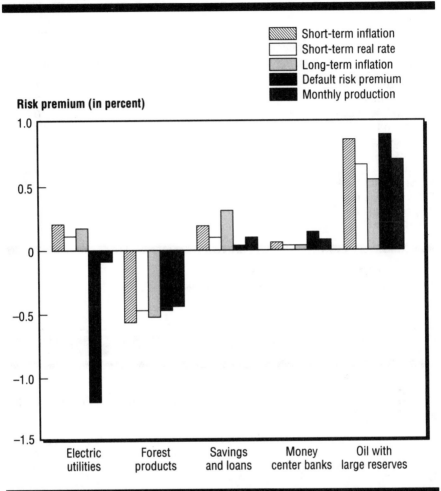

Source: Alcar's APT!, McKinsey analysis.

cost-of-equity estimate in the oil industry means that equity cash flows discounted using the CAPM would be overvalued by 25 percent. Cost-of-equity estimates using the APM are significantly lower for forest products and electric utilities, and significantly higher for money center banks, large S&Ls, and for oil companies with more than 50 percent of their assets in oil reserves.

Exhibit 8.8 **COMPARISON OF CAPM AND APM COST-OF-EQUITY ESTIMATES,** 1988

Industry	Number of companies	Cost-of-equity estimate			Percentage change in value
		CAPM	APM	Difference	
Brokerage	10	17.1%	17.4%	−.3%	−1.7%
Electric utilities	39	12.7	11.8	.9	7.6
Food and beverage	11	14.4	14.3	.1	0.7
Forest products	7	16.8	15.0	1.8*	12.0
Large savings and loans	18	15.8	19.6	−3.8*	−17.7
Mining	15	14.7	14.2	.5	3.5
Money center banks	12	15.9	16.9	−1.0*	−5.9
Oil with large reserves	12	14.4	19.1	−4.7*	−24.6
Property and casualty insurance	13	14.6	13.7	.9	6.6

Source: Alcar's APT!, McKinsey analysis.

* Statistically significant at the 5 percent confidence level.

PRESTON CORPORATION

We estimated Preston's WACC to be 9.7 percent on July 1, 1988, calculated as follows:

	Target weight	Pretax cost	After-tax cost	Contribution to WACC
Debt				
•Short-term debt	7.2%	11.0%	6.7%	0.5%
•Industrial revenue bonds	6.2	7.8	4.8	0.3
•Convertible debt	7.6	11.0	8.3	0.7
•Other long-term debt	33.0	11.0	6.7	2.2
• Capital leases	0.9	11.0	6.7	0.1
•Operating leases	4.5	11.0	6.7	0.2
	59.4%			4.0
Common equity	38.7	13.9	13.9	5.4
$5.58 options	0.5	24.6	24.6	0.1
$10.26 options	1.4	17.0	17.0	0.2
	100.0%			9.7%

We assumed that Preston would maintain its capital structure at current levels, so the target weights are based on the market values of its capital on July 1, 1988, summarized as follows:

	Book value ($ millions)	Estimated market value ($ millions)	Percentage of total market value
Short-term debt*	$17.6	$17.6	7.2%
Industrial revenue bonds	15.2	15.2	6.2
Convertible debt	27.7	18.6	7.6
Other long-term debt	80.3	80.3	33.0
Capital leases	2.3	2.3	0.9
Operating leases	–	11.0	4.5
Total debt	$143.1	145.0	59.4%
Common equity**	129.7	94.3	38.7
$5.58 options	–	1.2	0.5
$10.26 options	–	3.3	1.4
Total capitalization	$272.8	$243.8	100.0%

 * Current portion of long-term debt has been classified with long-term debt.
** Includes deferred income taxes of $20.3 million in the book value.

ESTIMATING COST AND MARKET VALUE

The following sections describe how we estimated the cost of each capital source and its market value.

Short-Term Debt

Short-term debt matures within one year, so in most cases its book value approximates its market value. The cost of Preston's short-term debt was assumed to equal the cost of its long-term debt, 11 percent (this calculation is described later), since the short-term debt will probably be continuously rolled over. Applying Preston's marginal tax rate of 39 percent resulted in an after-tax cost of 6.7 percent.

Industrial Revenue Bonds

We assumed that Preston's industrial revenue bonds had a pretax cost roughly 30 percent less than its other long-term debt. This resulted in a pretax cost of 7.8 percent and an after-tax cost of 4.8 percent. We also assumed that the book value of these bonds approximated their market value.

Convertible Debt

At the time of our estimate, Preston had $27.8 million of subordinated convertible debentures outstanding, with a coupon rate of 7 percent. These were convertible into Preston's common stock at $26 per share. Because the current share price was $16.25, these bonds were so far out of the money that we believed they behaved as straight debt and had the same pretax cost as Preston's other long-term debt (11 percent). Because of their conversion feature, convertible bonds have lower coupon rates than straight debt. As a result of these lower interest payments, Preston's convertible debt had a lower interest tax shield and thus a higher after-tax cost than its other debt. We calculated the market value of the convertible bonds, approximately $18.5 million, by discounting their coupon payments and principal repayment at Preston's pretax cost of long-term debt, 11 percent.

The after-tax cost of Preston's convertible debt was estimated as follows:

$$\frac{\text{After-tax cost of}}{\text{convertible debt}} = \text{Pretax cost}\left(1 - \frac{\text{Coupon rate}}{\text{Opportunity cost}} \times \text{Tax rate}\right),$$

$$= 11\%\left(1 - \frac{7\%}{11\%} \times 39\%\right),$$

$$= 8.3\%.$$

Other Long-Term Debt

Most of Preston's long-term debt was not publicly traded, so market quotes were not available. Some of Preston's debt was, however, rated by Moody's at Ba. We assumed that Preston's cost of long-term debt was equal to the cost for other similarly rated companies, or 11 percent. In addition, since much of Preston's long-term debt had floating rates, we assumed that its book value approximated its market value.

Capital Leases

We estimated the cost of Preston's capital leases to equal the cost of long-term debt, 11 percent. We also assumed that their market value was equal to their book value, $2.3 million.

Operating Leases

We estimated the cost of Preston's operating leases to equal the cost of long-term debt, 11 percent. Our estimate of the principal amount of the operating leases, $11 million was derived by discounting Preston's minimum future lease payments at the 11 percent cost of debt.

Common Equity

Using the CAPM, we estimated Preston's cost of equity to be 13.9 percent, as follows:

$$k_s = r_f + [E(r_m) - r_f](\text{beta})$$
$$k_s = 8.8\% + (5.5\% \times 0.93) = 13.9\%$$

The following assumptions were used:

- A risk-free rate of 8.8 percent, the yield to maturity of ten-year Treasury bonds.
- A market risk premium of 5.5 percent.
- A predicted beta of 0.93 from BARRA's equity beta book.

On July 1, 1988, the market value of Preston's equity was $94.3 million, based on a share price of $16.25 and a total of 5.8 million shares outstanding.

Options

Roughly 2 percent of Preston's current capital structure was executive stock options. Although option pricing is beyond the scope of this chapter, we used the Black-Scholes European call option formula as a method of approximating the market values of the two classes of stock options outstanding.[9] Our calculations indicated that the $5.58 options (which could not be exercised until the stock price reached $21.25) had an opportunity cost of approximately 24.6 percent and a market value of $1.2 million; and the $10.26 options had an approximate opportunity cost of 17 percent and a market value of $3.3 million. The before-tax and after-tax cost was the same.

[9] For details, see T. E. Copeland and J. F. Weston, *Financial Theory and Corporate Policy*, 3rd Edition, Reading, Mass.: Addison Wesley: 268–276.

REVIEW QUESTIONS

1. Does the existence of a sinking fund on a debt issue necessarily reduce the cost of debt capital? Assume you are trying to cost two bonds. Each has coupon of 10 percent per year payable at the end of each of two years, with principal to be repaid at the end of the second year. Let one bond have a sinking fund provision that stipulates the deposit of half of face value at the end of one year, the other half at the end of the second year.

2. Consolidated Freightways (ticker symbol *CNF*) issued series B 8.5 percent cumulative, convertible preferred stock in 1989 as part of the Thrift and Stock Trust Plan (TASP) for employee participation. Find the cost of the straight portion of this layer of capital. How would this cost be affected by the cumulative and convertibility features of the issue?

3. How would you formulate the U.S. equivalent to German currency denominated yield on 90-day German notes payable? The spot Deutsche Mark rate is 0.68 USD/DM and the 90 day forward rate is 0.71 USD/DM. The 90-day rate on EuroDM deposits is 5 percent per annum.

4. Derive the Arbitrage Pricing Model for a two-factor model.

5. Show how the Capital Asset Pricing Model is a special case of the APT.

6. As the financial analyst in charge of portfolios primarily in energy stocks, you determine that there are two factors that affect energy holdings: the inflation rate and the energy stock growth rate in relation to the growth rate for oil and gas stocks. The market price of the two factors are 0.08 and 0.06, respectively. There is a zero covariance between the two factors. The zero beta portfolio's rate of return is 9 percent. The beta for the energy portfolio is 1.5 with respect to both factors. What should the rate of return on the portfolio be? Interpret how changes in factors affects your expectations.

The table following question 9 contains the relevant data for questions 7 through 9.

7. Compare and contrast the risk characteristics of the three firms, their industry, and the market, as represented by the S&P 500 Composite Index.

8. Describe a process for measuring the expected return on CMZ, GIDL, and PH stocks if the returns generating process is specified by one factor, the S&P 500.

9. Using the table, measure and comment on the expected risk-return relationship between CMZ, GIDL, and PH stock prices and the market.

Below is end-of-month stock market data for three forms in the machine tools industry (SIC 3540). The tickers symbols are CMZ for Cincinnati Milacron, GIDL for Giddings and Lewis, and PH for Parker-Hannifin. Use this data to answer questions 7 through 9.

CMZ, GIDL, and PH

Date	S&P 500 Comp	Machine Tools	CMZ	GIDL	PH
Aug-90	324.19	75.83	14.13	7.63	23.38
Sep-90	305.06	69.18	12.63	6.88	22.75
Oct-90	304.00	52.84	9.50	6.75	19.88
Nov-90	317.95	51.20	9.13	8.63	22.38
Dec-90	330.85	58.10	11.00	8.88	23.88
Jan-91	340.91	69.30	13.00	9.56	26.75
Feb-91	367.74	73.98	13.63	9.94	26.38
Mar-91	375.35	68.13	13.00	10.94	25.25
Apr-91	382.76	61.54	11.13	11.00	26.25
May-91	382.79	72.39	13.75	11.69	29.25
Jun-91	371.59	68.34	12.50	11.31	26.88
Jul-91	387.81	70.43	13.00	12.00	26.63
Aug-91	396.64	67.75	12.25	12.50	26.38
Sep-91	386.88	61.70	10.50	14.19	25.50
Oct-91	392.96	57.08	9.25	13.13	30.13
Nov-91	376.55	49.38	7.75	12.88	29.38
Dec-91	417.01	70.31	11.75	15.13	30.63
Jan-92	410.34	84.31	14.38	19.38	32.13
Feb-92	415.35	90.21	15.63	22.13	34.75
Mar-92	407.52	96.71	17.00	19.88	33.63
Apr-92	412.02	94.57	17.00	19.94	34.88
May-92	412.17	80.05	14.38	22.56	32.88
Jun-92	403.83	77.34	14.50	22.50	29.13
Jul-92	422.23	77.12	13.50	23.75	30.00

CMZ, GIDL, and PH (Continued)

Date	S&P 500 Comp	Machine Tools	CMZ	GIDL	PH
Aug-92	413.51	71.64	14.25	20.50	29.50
Sep-92	417.80	70.72	14.88	19.50	30.50
Oct-92	420.13	72.72	15.63	19.75	28.13
Nov-92	429.19	82.49	16.25	23.75	28.38
Dec-92	438.82	86.72	16.50	25.50	29.63
Jan-93	438.11	96.27	19.75	27.00	32.63
Feb-93	440.87	99.04	20.63	27.50	32.38
Mar-93	451.67	97.29	20.00	27.25	32.50
Apr-93	438.02	98.74	25.50	22.88	29.75
May-93	453.44	104.24	27.88	23.25	32.13
Jun-93	450.53	93.42	24.38	21.38	33.13
Jul-93	447.19	83.23	21.25	19.50	31.13
Aug-93	460.13	96.05	23.00	24.00	34.00
Sep-93	460.11	100.35	25.00	24.00	34.13
Oct-93	464.61	98.58	24.00	24.25	34.25
Nov-93	462.36	90.47	20.00	24.25	36.00
Dec-93	470.58	97.62	22.00	25.75	37.75
Jan-94	473.20	108.06	25.38	27.50	38.25
Feb-94	470.69	100.90	23.88	25.50	35.38
Mar-94	445.55	99.89	23.38	25.50	35.38
Apr-94	451.87	94.06	20.75	25.25	43.38
May-94	456.34	86.85	20.50	22.00	43.13
Jun-94	447.63	74.20	20.88	15.50	42.63
Jul-94	452.57	77.78	21.63	16.50	43.13
Aug-94	475.49	86.22	23.50	18.75	42.00

9

Estimating
Continuing Value

Chapter 5 introduced the continuing value concept as a device for simplifying company valuations. This chapter describes several approaches to estimating continuing value and how they can be applied.

As we stated earlier, a company's expected cash flow can be separated into two time periods and the company's value defined as follows:

| Value | = | Present value of cash flow *during* explicit forecast period | + | Present value of cash flow *after* explicit forecast period |

The second term in this equation is the *continuing value*. It is the value of the company's expected cash flow beyond the explicit forecast period. Using simplifying assumptions about the company's performance during this period—for example, assuming a constant rate of growth—permits us to estimate continuing value with one of several formulas. Using a continuing-value formula eliminates the need to forecast in detail the company's cash flow over an extended period.

A high-quality estimate of continuing value is essential to any valuation, because continuing value often accounts for a large percentage of the total value of the company. Exhibit 9.1 shows continuing value as a percentage of total value for companies in four industries. In these examples, continuing value accounts for anywhere from 56 percent to 125 percent of total value. Although these

Exhibit 9.1 **CONTINUING VALUE AS A PERCENTAGE OF TOTAL VALUE, EIGHT-YEAR FORECAST PERIOD**

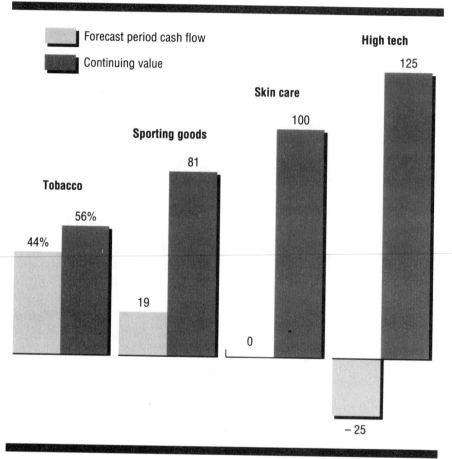

continuing values are large, this does not mean that most of a company's value will be realized in the continuing-value period. It often just means that the cash inflow in the early years is offset by outflow for capital spending and working capital investment—investments that should generate higher cash flow in later years. The proper interpretation of continuing value will be discussed in more detail later in this chapter.

The continuing-value approaches outlined in the following pages are all consistent with the overall discounted cash flow and economic profit frameworks. This is important, because we often see continuing value treated as though it is somehow different from the DCF valuation of the explicit forecast period. For example, in acquisitions, we see analysts estimating continuing value by applying a price earnings multiple five years down the road equal to the multiple they are currently considering paying for the company. In other words, they are assuming that the target company is, in effect, worth what they are willing to pay for it (adjusted for growth during the intervening five years), regardless of its economics, and that someone else would be willing to pay the same price. This type of circular reasoning clearly leads to inaccurate valuations. The approaches we recommend not only provide consistency with the company's economic performance, they provide insight into the underlying forces driving the value of the company.

Estimating continuing value involves four steps:

1. Select an appropriate technique.
2. Decide on a forecast horizon.
3. Estimate the valuation parameters and calculate the continuing value.
4. Discount the continuing value to the present.

STEP 1: SELECT AN APPROPRIATE TECHNIQUE

We recommend using one of three DCF techniques and one economic profit technique for estimating continuing value.

Three DCF Techniques

The three recommended DCF techniques are the long explicit forecast, the growing free cash flow perpetuity formula, and the value-driver formula. They all provide the same continuing value estimate when the underlying economic assumptions are consistent.

Long explicit forecast   One approach to continuing value is to avoid it altogether by carrying out the explicit forecast for a very long period of time (75 or more years) so that any value beyond the explicit forecast would be insignificantly small. Since such a forecast is unlikely to be very detailed, the two formulas below often work just as well with less effort.

Growing free cash flow perpetuity formula   The growing free cash flow perpetuity formula assumes that the company's free cash flow will grow at a constant rate during the continuing value period using the following formula:

$$\text{Continuing value} = \frac{FCF_{T+1}}{WACC - g},$$

where

FCF_{T+1} = the normalized level of free cash flow in the first year after the explicit forecast period.

WACC = the weighted average cost of capital.

g = the expected growth rate in free cash flow in perpetuity.

This technique provides the same result as a long explicit forecast when the company's free cash flow is forecast to grow at the same rate. The formula is the algebraic simplification of a growing perpetuity. (See Copeland and Weston 1988, Appendix A, for the derivation of the formula.[1] This formula is only valid if g is less than WACC.)

Caution! This formula is easily misused. It is particularly important to correctly estimate the normalized level of free cash flow that is consistent with the growth rate you are forecasting. For example, if growth in the continuing value period is forecast to be less than the growth in the explicit forecast period (as is normally the case) then the proportion of NOPLAT that needs to be invested to achieve growth is likely to be less as well. Hence in the continuing value period more of each dollar of NOPLAT becomes free cash flow available for the investors. If this transition is not taken into consideration, the continuing value could be significantly understated. Later in this chapter we give an example that illustrates what can go wrong when using this formula.

Value-driver formula   The third technique expresses the growing free cash flow perpetuity formula in terms of the value drivers: ROIC and growth, as follows:

[1] Thomas E. Copeland and J. Fred Weston, *Financial Theory and Corporate Policy*, 3rd ed. (Reading, MA: Addison Wesley, 1988).

$$\text{Continuing value} = \frac{\text{NOPLAT}_{T+1}\,(1 - g/\text{ROIC})}{\text{WACC} - g},$$

where

NOPLAT_{T+1} = the normalized level of NOPLAT in the first year after the explicit forecast period

g = the expected growth rate in NOPLAT in perpetuity

ROIC = the expected rate of return on net new investment

This value-driver formula produces the same result as the growing cash flow perpetuity formula because the denominators are identical and the numerator is a way of expressing free cash flow in terms of the key value drivers. The expression g/ROIC represents the proportion of NOPLAT invested in additional capital or the investment rate (see Chapter 5). So the overall expression represents NOPLAT times one minus the investment rate, or free cash flow. Appendix A proves the equivalence of the two formulas.

A variation of the value-driver formula is the two-stage value-driver formula. This formula allows you to break up the continuing value period into two periods with different growth and ROIC assumptions. For example, you might assume that during the first eight years after the explicit forecast period the company would grow at 8 percent per year and earn an incremental ROIC of 15 percent. After those eight years, the company's growth would slow to 5 percent and incremental ROIC would drop to 11 percent.

$$\text{CV} = \left[\frac{\text{NOPLAT}_{T+1}(1 - g_A/\text{ROIC}_A)}{\text{WACC} - g_A}\right]\left[1 - \left(\frac{1 + g_A}{1 + \text{WACC}}\right)^{N-1}\right]$$
$$+ \left[\frac{\text{NOPLAT}_{T+1}(1 + g_A)^{N-1}(1 - g_B/\text{ROIC}_B)}{(\text{WACC} - g_B)(1 + \text{WACC})^{N-1}}\right],$$

where

CV = continuing value.

N = the number of years in the first stage of the continuing value period.

g_A = the expected growth rate in the first stage of the CV period.

g_B = the expected growth in the second stage of the CV period.[2]

$ROIC_A$ = the expected ROIC during the first stage of the CV period.

$ROIC_B$ = the expected ROIC during the second stage of the CV period.

Same results   A simple example demonstrates that all three techniques produce the same continuing-value estimate when the same underlying assumptions are used. We begin with the following cash flow projections:

	Year 1	2	3	4	5
NOPLAT	100	106	112	120	126
Net investment	50	53	56	60	63
Free cash flow	50	53	56	60	63

The above pattern continues after the first five years presented. In this example, the growth rate in NOPLAT and free cash flow each period is 6 percent. The rate of return on net new investment is 12 percent, calculated as the increase in NOPLAT from one year to the next, divided by the net investment in the prior year. The WACC is assumed to be 11 percent. First, use a long forecast, say 150 years:

$$CV = \frac{50}{1.11} + \frac{53}{(1.11)^2} + \frac{56}{(1.11)^3} + \frac{50(1.06)^{149}}{(1.11)^{150}}.$$

$$CV = 999.$$

Next, use the growing free cash flow perpetuity formula:

$$CV = \frac{50}{11\% - 6\%}.$$

[2] Note that g_B must be less than WACC for this formula to be valid.

$$CV = 1,000.$$

Finally, use the value-driver formula:

$$CV = \frac{100\ (1 - 6\%/12\%)}{11\% - 6\%}.$$

$$CV = 1,000.$$

All three approaches yield the same result (though the long forecast approach is slightly off because it ignores the cash flow beyond 150 years).

Which of the approaches should you use? We generally use the value-driver formula, because it is easier than developing a 75-year projection and is not as easy to misuse as the growing FCF perpetuity. In addition, it forces you to think about the value drivers explicitly in estimating the continuing value.

Economic Profit Technique

With the economic profit approach, the continuing value does not represent the value of the company after the explicit forecast period, instead it represents the incremental value over the company's invested capital at the end of the explicit forecast period.

The total value of the company is as follows:

$$
\text{Value} =
\begin{array}{c}
\text{Invested capital} \\
\text{at beginning of} \\
\text{forecast}
\end{array}
+
\begin{array}{c}
\text{Present value} \\
\text{of forecasted} \\
\text{economic profit} \\
\textit{during} \text{ explicit} \\
\text{forecast period}
\end{array}
+
\begin{array}{c}
\text{Present value} \\
\text{forecasted} \\
\text{economic profit} \\
\textit{after} \text{ explicit} \\
\text{forecast period}
\end{array}
$$

While the economic profit continuing value (the last term in the preceding equation) is different from the DCF continuing value, the value of the company will be the same given the same projected financial performance.

The recommended economic profit formula is as follows:

$$CV = \frac{\text{Economic Profit}_{T+1}}{\text{WACC}} + \frac{(\text{NOPLAT}_{T+1})(g/\text{ROIC})(\text{ROIC}-\text{WACC})}{\text{WACC}(\text{WACC}-g)},$$

where

$$\text{Economic Profit}_{T+1} = \text{the normalized economic profit in the first year after the explicit forecast period.}$$

$$\text{NOPLAT}_{T+1} = \text{the normalized NOPLAT in the first year after the explicit forecast period.}$$

$$g = \text{the expected growth rate in NOPLAT in perpetuity.}$$

$$\text{ROIC} = \text{the expected rate of return on net new investment.}$$

$$\text{WACC} = \text{the weighted average cost of capital.}$$

This formula says that the value of economic profit after the explicit forecast equals the present value of economic profit in the first year after the explicit forecast in perpetuity, plus any incremental economic profit after that year created by additional growth at returns exceeding the cost of capital. If expected ROIC = WACC, the second half of the equation equals zero, and the continuing economic profit value is the value of the first year's economic profit in perpetuity.

As a side note, the continuing value using a discounted cash flow approach will equal the sum of the economic profit continuing value plus the amount of invested capital in place at the end of the explicit forecast period.

Comparison with Other Continuing-Value Approaches

A number of other continuing-value approaches are used in practice, often with misleading results. Some of these are acceptable if used carefully. However, we prefer the approaches just recommended because they explicitly rely on the underlying economic assumptions embodied in the company analysis. The other approaches tend to hide the underlying economic assumptions. Exhibit 9.2 illustrates, for a sporting goods company, the wide dispersion of continuing-value estimates arrived at by different techniques. This section explains why we prefer the recommended approaches.

Exhibit 9.2 **CONTINUING-VALUE ESTIMATES FOR A SPORTING GOODS COMPANY, ARRIVED AT BY DIFFERENT TECHNIQUES**

Technique	Assumptions	Continuing value, $ millions
Book value	Per accounting records	$268
Liquidation value	80% of working capital	186
	70% of net fixed assets	
Price-to-earnings ratio	Industry average of 15×	624
Market-to-book ratio	Industry average of 1.4×	375
Replacement cost	Book value adjusted for inflation	275
Perpetuity based on final year's cash flow	Normalized FCF growing at inflation rate	428

We classify the most common techniques into two categories: (1) DCF approaches, and (2) non-cash flow approaches.

Other DCF approaches   The recommended DCF formulas can be modified to derive additional continuing-value formulas with more restrictive (and sometimes unreasonable) assumptions.

The first variation is the *convergence* formula. For many companies in competitive industries, the return on net new investment can be expected to eventually converge to the cost of capital as all the excess profits are competed away. This assumption allows a simpler version of the value-driver formula, as follows:

$$CV = \frac{NOPLAT}{WACC}.$$

The derivation begins with the value-driver formula:

$$CV = \frac{NOPLAT\left(1 - \frac{g}{ROIC}\right)}{WACC - g}.$$

Assume that ROIC = WACC. In other words, the return on incremental invested capital equals the cost of capital.

$$CV = \frac{NOPLAT\left(1 - \frac{g}{WACC}\right)}{WACC - g},$$

$$CV = \frac{NOPLAT\left(\frac{WACC - g}{WACC}\right)}{WACC - g}.$$

Canceling the term WACC − g leaves a simple formula:

$$CV = \frac{NOPLAT}{WACC}.$$

The growth term has disappeared from the equation. This does not mean that the nominal growth in NOPLAT will be zero. It means that growth will add nothing to value, because the return associated with growth just equals the cost of capital. This formula is sometimes interpreted as implying zero growth (not even with inflation), even though this is clearly not the case.

Misinterpretation of the convergence formula has led to another variant: the *aggressive* formula. This formula assumes that earnings in the continuing-value period will grow at some rate, most often the inflation rate. The conclusion is then drawn that earnings should be discounted at the real WACC, rather than the nominal WACC. The resulting formula is as follows:

$$CV = \frac{NOPLAT}{WACC - g}.$$

Here, g is the inflation rate. This formula can substantially overstate continuing value because it assumes that NOPLAT can grow without any incremental capital investment. This is very unlikely (or impossible), because any growth will probably require additional working capital and fixed assets.

To show how this formula relates to the value-driver formula, let us assume that the return on incremental capital investment (ROIC) approaches infinity.

$$CV = \frac{NOPLAT\left(1 - \frac{g}{ROIC}\right)}{WACC - g}.$$

$$\text{ROIC} \to \infty, \text{ therefore } \frac{g}{\text{ROIC}} \to 0.$$

$$CV = \frac{\text{NOPLAT} (1 - 0)}{\text{WACC} - g}.$$

$$CV = \frac{\text{NOPLAT}}{\text{WACC} - g}.$$

Exhibit 9.3 compares the two new DCF formulas. This exhibit shows how the average return on invested capital (both existing and new investment) behaves under the two assumptions. In the aggressive case, NOPLAT grows without any new investment, so the return on invested capital eventually approaches infinity. In the convergence case, the average return on invested capital moves toward the weighted average cost of capital (WACC) as new capital becomes a larger portion of the total capital base.

Non-cash flow approaches   In addition to the DCF techniques, non-cash flow approaches to continuing value are sometimes used. Four commonly used approaches are liquidation value, replacement cost, price-to-earnings ratio, and market-to-book ratio.

The *liquidation-value approach* sets the continuing value equal to an estimate of the proceeds from the sale of the assets of the business, after paying off liabilities at the end of the explicit forecast period. Liquidation value is often far different from the value of the company as a going concern. In a growing, profitable industry, a company's liquidation value is probably far below the going-concern value. In a dying industry, liquidation value may exceed going-concern value. Do not use this approach unless liquidation is likely at the end of the forecast period.

The *replacement-cost approach* sets the continuing value equal to the expected cost to replace the company's assets. This approach has a number of drawbacks. Most important are the following:

- Only tangible assets are replaceable. The company's "organizational capital" can be valued only on the basis of the cash flow the company generates. The replacement cost of the

Exhibit 9.3 **RATES OF RETURN IMPLIED BY ALTERNATIVE CONTINUING-VALUE FORMULAS**

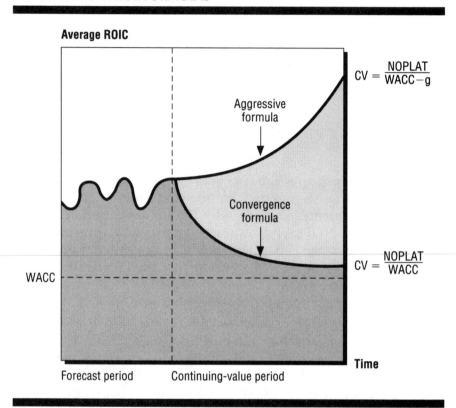

company's tangible assets may greatly understate the value of the company.

- Not all the company's assets will ever be replaced. Consider a machine used only by this particular industry. The replacement cost of the asset may be so high that it is not economical to replace it. Yet, as long as it generates a positive cash flow, the asset is valuable to the ongoing business of the company. Here, the replacement cost may exceed the value of the business as an ongoing entity.

The *price-to-earnings (P/E) ratio approach* assumes the company will be worth some multiple of its future earnings in the continuing period. Of course, this will be true; the difficulty arises in trying to estimate an appropriate P/E ratio.

Suppose today's current industry average P/E ratio is chosen. Today's P/E ratio reflects the economic prospects of the industry during the explicit forecast period as well as the continuing-value period. However, prospects at the end of the explicit forecast period are likely to be very different from today's. Therefore, we need a different P/E ratio that reflects the company's prospects at the end of the forecast period. What factors will determine that ratio? As we discussed in Chapter 5, the company's expected growth, the rate of return on new capital, and the cost of capital are the primary determinants of its P/E ratio. These are the same factors that are in the value-driver formula. So unless you are comfortable using an arbitrary P/E ratio, you are much better off with the value-driver formula.

We should note here that one trap analysts fall into in acquisition situations is the circular reasoning that the P/E ratio for the continuing value will equal the P/E ratio paid for the acquisition. In other words, if I pay 18 times earnings, I should be able to sell the business for 18 times earnings. However, in most cases, the reason a company is willing to pay a high P/E for an acquisition is that it believes it can take actions to greatly improve earnings. So the effective P/E it is paying on the improved level of earnings will be much less than 18. Once the improvements are in place and earnings are higher, buyers will not be willing to pay the same P/E unless they can make additional improvements.

The *market-to-book ratio approach* assumes the company will be worth some multiple of its book value, often the same as its current multiple or the multiples of comparable companies. This approach is conceptually similar to the P/E approach and therefore faces the same problems. In addition to the complexity of deriving an appropriate multiple, the book value itself is distorted by inflation and key accounting assumptions. Once again, the DCF approaches are easier to use.

STEP 2: SELECT THE FORECAST HORIZON

After selecting a continuing-value method, the next step is to decide how long to make the explicit forecast period. If a very long forecast period is used (75 or more years), then continuing value is largely irrelevant; this step and the next can be skipped.

While the length of the explicit forecast period you choose is important, it does not affect the value of the company but only the distribution of value of the company between the explicit forecast period and the years that follow. Exhibits 9.4 and 9.5 illustrate this. In this example, no matter what the length of the forecast period, the company value is $893. With a forecast horizon of five years, the present value of the continuing value accounts for 79 percent of total value, while with a ten-year horizon, the present value of continuing value accounts for only 60 percent of total value.

The choice of forecast horizon can have an indirect impact on value if it is associated with changes in the economic assumptions underlying the continuing-value estimate. Analysts may unknowingly change their performance forecasts when they change their

Exhibit 9.4 **COMPARISON OF TOTAL VALUE ESTIMATES BASED ON DIFFERENT FORECAST HORIZONS**

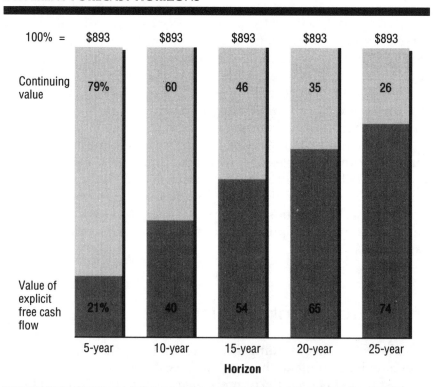

Exhibit 9.5 **COMPARISON OF TOTAL VALUE CALCULATIONS FOR FIVE-YEAR AND TEN-YEAR HORIZONS,** $ MILLIONS

Overall assumptions	Years 1–5	Years 6+
Return on new investment (ROIC)	16%	12%
Growth rate (g)	9	6
WACC	12	12

5-year horizon	1	2	3	4	5	Base for CV
NOPLAT	$100.0	109.0	118.8	129.5	141.2	$149.6
Depreciation	20.0	21.8	23.8	25.9	28.2	
Gross cash flow	$120.0	130.8	146.6	155.4	169.4	
Gross investment	76.3	83.1	90.6	98.7	107.6	
FCF	$43.8	47.7	52.0	56.7	61.8	
Discount factor	0.893	0.797	0.712	0.636	0.567	
Present value of cash flow	39.1	38.0	37.0	36.0	35.0	

$$\text{Present value of continuing value} = \frac{\text{NOPLAT}(1 - g/\text{ROIC})}{\text{WACC} - g}[1/(1 + \text{WACC})]^5 = \frac{\$149.6(1 - 6\%/12\%)}{12\% - 6\%}(0.5674) = \$707.5$$

Present value of
FCF 1-5 $185.1
Continuing value   707.5
Total value $892.6

Exhibit 9.5 Continued

10-year horizon	1	2	3	4	5	6	7	8	9	10	Base for CV
NOPLAT	$100.0	109.0	118.8	129.5	141.2	149.6	158.6	168.1	178.2	188.9	200.2
Depreciation	20.0	21.8	23.8	25.9	28.2	29.9	31.7	33.6	35.6	37.8	
Gross cash flow	$120.0	130.8	142.6	155.4	169.4	179.6	190.3	201.7	213.9	226.7	
Gross investment	76.3	83.1	90.6	98.7	107.6	104.7	111.0	117.7	124.7	132.2	
FCF	$43.8	47.7	52.0	56.7	61.8	74.8	79.3	84.1	89.1	94.5	
Discount factor	0.893	0.797	0.712	0.636	0.567	0.507	0.452	0.404	0.361	0.322	
Present value of cash flow	39.1	38.0	37.0	36.0	35.0	37.9	35.9	34.0	32.1	30.4	

$$\text{Present value of continuing value} = \frac{\text{NOPLAT}(1 - g/\text{ROIC})}{\text{WACC} - g}[1/(1 + \text{WACC})]^{10} = \frac{\$200.21(1 - 6\%/12\%)}{12\% - 6\%}(0.3220) = \$537.2$$

Present value of
FCF 1-10	$355.4
Continuing value	537.2
Total value	$892.6

forecast horizon. For example, many forecasters assume that the rate of return on new invested capital equals the cost of capital in the continuing-value period, but that the company will earn returns exceeding the cost of capital during the explicit forecast period. When they extend the explicit forecast period, they also extend the time period during which returns on new capital are expected to exceed the cost of capital. Therefore, extending the forecast period leads to an increase in value, attributable to the increase in the rate-of-return assumptions.

The explicit forecast period should be long enough so that the business will have reached a steady state of operations by the end of the period. This is because any continuing-value approach relies on the following key assumptions:

- The company earns constant margins, maintains a constant capital turnover, and, therefore, earns a constant return on existing invested capital.
- The company grows at a constant rate and invests the same proportion of its gross cash flow in its business each year.
- The company earns a constant return on all new investments.

For example, suppose you expect the company's margins to decline over time as its customers become more powerful. Margins are currently 12 percent and you forecast they will fall to 9 percent over the next seven years. The explicit forecast period in this case must be at least seven years, because continuing-value approaches cannot account for the declining margin (at least not without much computational complexity). The business must be operating at an equilibrium level for the continuing value approaches to be useful.

Exhibit 9.6 illustrates for Innovation, Inc., how a company's cash flow patterns can also affect the choice of the forecast period. The company is making value creating investments in the early years of the forecast, but free cash flow is negative due to these large up-front investments. After the early years, free cash flow increases significantly as the projects begin to pay off and additional investment declines. Finally, free cash flow levels off and begins to grow at a steady rate. In this example, the forecast should be extended until the free cash flow growth becomes constant.

The cash flow pattern for Innovation, Inc., raises the important issue of interpretation of continuing-value estimates. It appears from Exhibit 9.6 that 85 percent of Innovation's value comes from

Exhibit 9.6 **INNOVATION, INC., FREE CASH FLOW FORECAST AND VALUATION**

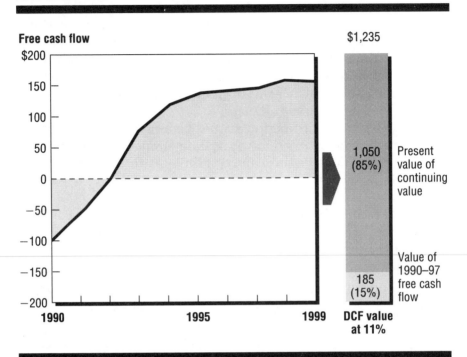

the continuing value. Exhibit 9.7 suggests an alternative interpretation of where value is coming from (a business components approach). Innovation has a base business that earns a steady 12 percent return on capital and is growing at 4 percent per year. It also has developed a new product line, which will require several years of negative cash flow due to the construction of a new plant. Exhibit 9.7 shows that the base business has a value of $877 or 71 percent of Innovation's total value. So 71 percent of the company's value comes from operations that are currently generating strong cash flow. But the company has decided to reinvest this cash flow in a profitable new product line. This does not mean that 85 percent of the value is more than eight years out. It just means that the cash flow pattern mechanically results in the appearance that most of the value is a long way off.

We can also use the economic profit model for another interpretation on continuing value. Exhibit 9.8 compares the components of value for Innovation, Inc., for the two interpretations discussed

Exhibit 9.7 **INNOVATION, INC., VALUATION BY COMPONENTS**

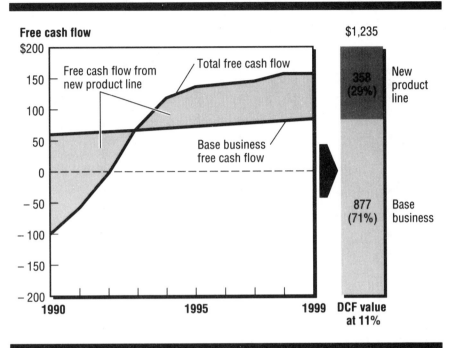

above, as well as the economic profit model. Under the economic profit model 62 percent of Innovation's value is simply its invested capital. The rest of the value is the present value of projected economic profit (8 percent for economic profit before 1998 and 30 percent for economic profit after 1998).

To summarize, choose a longer rather than shorter forecast period. We rarely use a forecast period shorter than seven years. Furthermore, the forecast period should not be determined by the company's internal planning period. Just because the company forecasts out only three years does not justify a three-year forecast period for purposes of valuation. A rough forecast beyond three years is better than no forecast.

STEP 3: ESTIMATE THE PARAMETERS

The parameters that must be defined in order to estimate continuing value are net operating profits less adjusted taxes (NOPLAT),

---

Exhibit 9.8 **INNOVATION, INC., COMPARISON OF CONTINUING VALUES**

$1,235		$1,235		$1,235	
1,050 (85%)	Present value of continuing value	358 (29%)	New product line	364 (30%)	Economic profit continuing value
				104 (8%)	PV of 1991–98 economic profit
		877 (71%)	Base business	767 (62%)	Invested capital at beginning of 1990
185 (15%)	Value of 1990–97 free cash flow				
Free cash flow approach		Business components approach		Economic profit approach	

free cash flow (FCF), rate of return on new investment (ROIC), rate of growth in NOPLAT (g), and weighted average cost of capital (WACC). Careful estimation is critical because continuing value is highly sensitive to the value of these parameters, particularly the growth assumption. Exhibit 9.9 shows how continuing value (calculated using the value-driver formula) is affected by various combinations of growth rate and rate of return on new investment. The example assumes a $100 base level of NOPLAT and a 10 percent WACC. Notice that at a 14 percent expected rate of return on new capital, changing the growth rate from 6 percent to 8 percent increases the continuing value by 50 percent, from about $1,400 to about $2,100.

Fundamentally, estimating the continuing-value parameters should be an integral part of the whole forecasting process. The

Exhibit 9.9 **IMPACT OF CONTINUING-VALUE ASSUMPTIONS**
(WACC = 10%; NOPLAT = $100)

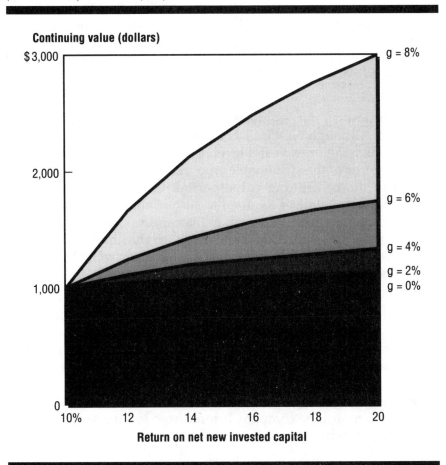

continuing-value parameters should reflect a coherent forecast for the long-term economic situation of the company and its industry. Specifically, the continuing-value parameters should be based on the expected steady state condition that the company will migrate toward in the particular scenario you are valuing.

General Guidelines

Following are some general suggestions regarding continuing-value parameters for the value-driver and the free cash flow perpetuity formulas.

NOPLAT   The base level of NOPLAT should reflect a normalized level of earnings for the company at the midpoint of its business cycle. For example, revenues should generally reflect the continuation of the trends in the last forecast year adjusted to the midpoint of the business cycle. Operating costs should be based on sustainable margin levels, and taxes should be based on long-term expected rates.

Free cash flow   First, estimate the base level of NOPLAT as just described. Although NOPLAT is usually based on the last forecast year's results, the prior year's level of investment is probably not a good indicator of the sustainable amount of investment needed for growth in the continuing-value period. Carefully analyze how much investment will be required to sustain the forecasted growth rate. Often the forecasted growth in the continuing-value period is lower than in the explicit forecast period, so the amount of investment should be a proportionately smaller amount of NOPLAT. An exhibit later in this chapter demonstrates this principle.

ROIC   The expected rate of return on new investment should be consistent with expected competitive conditions. Economic theory suggests that competition will eventually eliminate abnormal returns, so for many companies, set ROIC = WACC. If you expect the company will be able to continue its growth and to maintain its competitive advantage, then you might consider setting ROIC equal to the return the company is forecasted to earn during the explicit forecast period.

Growth rate   Few companies can be expected to grow faster than the economy for long periods of time. The best estimate is probably the expected long-term rate of consumption growth for the industry's products plus inflation. We also suggest that sensitivities be analyzed to understand how the growth rate affects value estimates.

WACC   The weighted average cost of capital should incorporate a sustainable capital structure and an underlying estimate of business risk consistent with expected industry conditions.

Exhibit 9.10 shows the likely relative positions of various industries along different continuing-value parameters.

Exhibit 9.10 **LIKELY RELATIVE POSITIONS OF SELECTED INDUSTRIES ALONG CONTINUING-VALUE PARAMETERS**

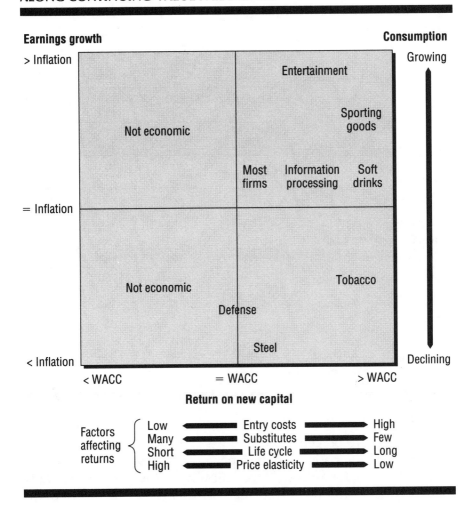

Potential Pitfalls

Some of the common mistakes made in estimating continuing values include naive base-year extrapolation, naive overconservatism, and purposeful overconservatism.

Naive base-year extrapolation   Exhibit 9.11 illustrates a common error in forecasting the base level of free cash flow. From Year 9 to Year 10 (the last forecast year), the company's earnings and cash

Exhibit 9.11 **RIGHT AND WRONG WAYS TO FORECAST THE BASE FREE CASH FLOW**

	Year 9	Year 10	Year 11 (5% growth)	
			Incorrect	Correct
Sales	$1,000	$1,100	$1,155	$1,155
Operating expenses	(850)	(935)	(982)	(982)
EBIT	150	165	173	173
Cash taxes	(60)	(66)	(69)	(69)
NOPLAT	90	99	104	104
Depreciation	27	30	32	32
Gross cash flow	$117	$129	$136	$136
Capital expenditures	30	33	35	35
Increase in working capital	27	30	32	17
Gross Investment	$57	$63	$67	$52
Free cash flow	$ 60	$ 66	$69	$84
Memo: Year-end working capital	$ 300	$ 330	$362	$ 347
Working capital/sales	30%	30%	31%	30%
Increase in working capital/ sales	2.7%	2.7%	2.7%	1.5%

flow grew by 10 percent. The forecast suggests that growth in the continuing-value period will be 5 percent per year. A naive, and incorrect, forecast for Year 11 (the continuing-value base year) simply increases every cash flow from Year 10 by 5 percent, as shown in the third column. This forecast is wrong because the increase in working capital is far too large for the increase in sales. Since sales is growing more slowly, the proportion of gross cash flow devoted to increasing working capital should decline significantly, as shown in the last column. In the last column, the increase in working capital is the amount necessary to maintain the year-end working capital at a constant percentage of sales. The naive approach results in a continual increase in working capital as a percentage of sales and will significantly understate the value of the company. Note that in the third column, free cash flow is 18 percent lower than it should be.

Naive overconservatism   Many analysts always assume the incremental return on capital in the continuing-value period will equal the cost of capital. This also relieves them of having to forecast a growth rate, since growth in this case neither adds nor destroys value. For some businesses, this is obviously wrong. For example, both Coca-Cola's and PepsiCo's soft drink businesses earn very high returns on invested capital, and their returns are unlikely to fall substantially as they continue to grow. Assuming that ROIC = WACC for these businesses would substantially understate their values. This applies equally to just about any business that sells something proprietary that is unlikely ever to be duplicated.

Purposeful overconservatism   Analysts sometimes are overly conservative because of the uncertainty and size of the continuing value. If continuing value is estimated properly, the uncertainty cuts both ways: the results are just as likely to be higher than the estimate as they are to be lower. So conservatism overcompensates for the uncertainty. This is not to say, however, that you should not be concerned about the uncertainty. That is why careful development of scenarios is a critical element of any valuation.

STEP 4: DISCOUNT THE CONTINUING VALUE TO THE PRESENT

The continuing value you have estimated is the value at the end of the explicit forecast period. This estimate must be discounted back to the present at the WACC before it can be added to the present value of the explicit free cash flow.

PRESTON CORPORATION

We will use the value-driver approach to estimate Preston's DCF continuing value. The values of the parameters for the Moderate Performance scenario are estimated as follows:

- The NOPLAT at the beginning of the continuing-value period (one year after the last forecast year) is 1997's NOPLAT, increased by a rate of growth reflecting our forecast for 1998. In Chapter 7, we forecast Preston's 1998 NOPLAT to be $65.9 million.

- Preston's WACC is forecasted to remain at 9.7 percent. We do not foresee any significant change in Preston's capital structure or business risk.

- Preston's return on net new invested capital beyond 1997 is forecasted to equal its WACC, 9.7 percent. This is consistent with the forecast performance in the years leading up to 1997 in this scenario.

- We expect that Preston's NOPLAT will grow at slightly above the rate of inflation. This forecast is based on the assumption that the nominal growth in its level of business is tied to nominal industrial production growth. Therefore, we forecast a nominal growth rate of 9 percent (3 percent real growth plus 6 percent inflation).

Using these parameters in the recommended continuing-value formula results in an estimated continuing value of $680 million in 1997.

$$ CV = \frac{NOPLAT_{1988}\left(1 - \frac{g}{ROIC}\right)}{WACC - g} . $$

$$ CV = \frac{\$65.9\left(1 - \frac{9.0\%}{9.7\%}\right)}{9.7\% - 9.0\%} . $$

$$ CV = \$680. $$

Using the economic profit approach and the same parameters, results in a continuing value of economic profit after 1997 equal to $0.6 million calculated as follows:

$$ CV\ of\ Economic\ Profit = \frac{Economic\ Profit_{1998}}{WACC} + $$

$$ \frac{NOPLAT_{1988}\left(\frac{g}{ROIC}\right)(ROIC - WACC)}{WACC\left(WACC - g\right)} . $$

$$ = \frac{0.06}{9.7\%} + \frac{65.9\left(\frac{9.0\%}{9.7\%}\right)(9.7\% - 9.7\%)}{9.7\%\left(9.7\% - 9.0\%\right)} . $$

$$ CV\ of\ Economic\ Profit = 0.6 + 0 = 0.6 . $$

The continuing value is so small because Preston is just earning its WACC during the forecast. Adding the amount of invested capital at the end of 1997 to the continuing value of economic profit gives a total continuing value of $680 million, the same as the DCF approach.

$$CV = \text{Invested capital}_{1997} + \text{CV of Economic Profit.}$$
$$= 679.1 + 0.6.$$
$$= 679.7.$$

REVIEW QUESTIONS

1. Describe the differences between continuing-value cash flow period and the explicit forecast period that precedes the continuing-value period.

2. Outline the steps needed to produce an estimate of continuing value.

3. Describe several non-cash approaches to continuing value. Why might DCF approaches to continuing value be superior to non-cash approaches?

4. A client explains that her firm's value must be affected by the choice of explicit forecast horizon. Build a model to contest her claim. Assume a short horizon of three years, a longer horizon of six years, with explicit forecast growth rate of 11 percent, return on new investment of 18 percent, continuing value growth of 5 percent, and return on new investment of 14 percent, with weighted average cost of capital over both periods of 14 percent. Offer an explanation of the results.

5. Your client remains skeptical. Why use two different representations of value, free cash flow, and economic profit? Demonstrate that the present value of economic profit plus beginning invested capital equals the present value of free cash flows.

6. Demonstrate for your client the equivalence between free cash flow and economic profit representations of value with a model similar to the three-year horizon model in question 4. Discuss the similarities, differences, and usefulness of each representation.

7. Value Cincinnati Milacron using data from the previous several chapters.

10

Calculating and Interpreting Results

The final phase of the valuation process involves calculating and testing the company's value, then interpreting the results in terms of the decision context involved.

STEP 1: CALCULATE AND TEST RESULTS

Once the preceding valuation steps have been completed for each scenario being examined, calculating the company's equity value is a straightforward process. It involves the following:

1. Discounting the forecasted free cash flow and continuing value at the company's weighted average cost of capital to determine the total value of the company's operations. For the economic profit approach, discount the forecasted economic profit and the economic profit continuing value at the WACC and add the invested capital at the beginning of the explicit forecast period.

2. Adding the value of any nonoperating assets whose cash flows were *excluded* from free cash flow and economic profit to estimate the value of the total entity. Such items might include excess marketable securities and investments in unrelated subsidiaries. The value of these assets should be estimated on the basis of their respective expected cash flows

and appropriate discount rates, or by reference to their market values. For example, because excess marketable securities are zero-net-present-value investments, the present value of all future cash flow related to marketable securities equals their current market value (which for most money market instruments also equals their book value).

3. Subtracting the market value of all debt, hybrid securities, minority interest, or other claims superior to the residual equity. The estimation of market values of these financings was explained in Chapter 8.

Exhibit 10.1 illustrates what this typical calculation of equity value might look like.

After estimating the equity value for each scenario, you should perform several checks to test the logic of the results, minimize the possibility of errors, and ensure you have a good understanding of the forces driving the valuation. These checks involve asking such questions about the results as the following:

- Is the resulting value consistent with the value drivers implied by the forecast? For example, a company that has been projected to earn rates of return on invested capital far above its WACC should have a value far above such benchmarks as

Exhibit 10.1 **SAMPLE VALUATION SUMMARY**

Value of operations	$5,000
Excess marketable securities	300
Investments in unconsolidated subsidiaries	50
Other nonoperating assets	100
Company value	5,450
Short-term interest bearing debt	(200)
Long-term interest bearing debt	(1,200)
Capital leases	(300)
Capitalized value of operating leases	(100)
Minority interest	(20)
Preferred stock	(100)
Warrants	(50)
Equity value	3,480

its book value. If the resulting value is low, a computational error has probably been made.

- How does the resulting value compare to the company's market value? If your estimate of value is far from the market value, try to identify the causes of the difference as concretely as possible. Do you expect higher revenue growth? Higher margins? Lower capital spending?

- Do any of the results require special explanation? Are there obvious issues, such as significant deviations from historical trends, that should be explained? Are the results as expected? If not, can you explain why not? What factors caused the results to be different from expected?

- Are the financial aspects of the forecast (amounts of debt and marketable securities) achievable and desirable? If debt or excess marketable securities are excessive relative to the company's targets, how should the company resolve the imbalance? Should it raise equity if too much debt is projected? Should the company be willing to raise equity at its current market price?

As you begin to synthesize the results of your valuation, we suggest that you lay out the value of each scenario against its value drivers and any critical operating assumptions (like gross margins or capital spending), including nonquantified assumptions like new product development and the expected competitive response. This should help provide an overall perspective on each scenario and the relationships among them.

The final step is to estimate a most likely value, based on the probability of each scenario. Assign probabilities to each scenario, multiply the probabilities times the value of each scenario, and add the resulting values to find the most likely value. This last step may not be necessary; just having the scenario values may provide enough information to make whatever decisions are necessary.

STEP 2: INTERPRET THE RESULTS WITHIN THE DECISION CONTEXT

The purpose of valuing a company is always to help guide some management or investment decision, be it acquisition, divestiture, or adoption of internal strategic initiatives. The results must be analyzed from the perspective of the decision at hand. And since uncertainty and risk are involved in most business decision, *you should always think of value in terms of scenarios and ranges of value that reflect this uncertainty.*

The decision based on any one scenario will generally be obvious, given its estimated impact on shareholder value. But interpreting multiple scenarios, developing the level of confidence you should have in your results, and determining how they should be presented (all relative to the decision at hand) are considerably more complex. At a minimum, we would suggest you do the following:

1. Clearly identify the primary value drivers in each scenario tested and differences in value among scenarios, as well as the key assumptions underlying those drivers.

2. Understand how much the key variables underlying the results of each scenario could change without altering the decision. This provides a sense of the margin for error in the decision. Obviously, a large margin gives greater comfort in the decision. But too large an error margin is suspicious. Reconsider your assumptions by asking the following questions:

   • If the decision is clearly affirmative (to go ahead with the contemplated action), what would have to go wrong to invalidate the decision? How likely is that to occur?

   • If the decision is negative, what are the upside possibilities that are being passed up?

3. Assess the likelihood of change in the key assumptions underlying each scenario (assigning each a probability of occurrence). For example, consider the following:

   • The impact and likelihood of change in the broad environmental assumptions underlying the scenario. How critical are they to the results? Some industries are more dependent on basic environmental conditions than others. Home building, for example, is highly correlated with the overall health of the economy. Branded food processing, on the other hand, is less affected by broad economic trends.

- Assumptions about the competitive structure of the industry. A scenario that assumes substantial market share increases is probably less likely in a highly competitive and concentrated market than in an industry with fragmented and inefficient competition.
- Assumptions about the company's internal capabilities to achieve the results predicted in the scenario. For example, can the company develop the products on time and manufacture them within the expected range of costs?

4. Develop alternative scenarios suggested by the preceding analyses. The process of examining initial results may well uncover unanticipated questions that are best resolved through evaluating additional scenarios. This implies that the valuation process is inherently circular. Doing the valuation itself often provides insights that lead to additional scenarios and analyses.

A FEW LAST THOUGHTS

Valuation depends mainly on understanding the business, its industry, and the general economic environment, and then doing a careful job of forecasting. Careful thought and hard work leads to foresight. Correct methodology is only a small, but necessary, part of the valuation process. Over the years we have seen many pitfalls that can easily be avoided. What follows are a few words of wisdom about common problems.

Avoid Shortcuts

Invest the time upfront to build an appropriate valuation model instead of trying to draw conclusions from an incomplete or inadequate model. The upfront investment in a complete model always pays off.

- Avoid short cuts in the model; they almost always cost you time and aggravation in the long run. Include complete income statements and balance sheets, as well as cash flow statements and key performance ratios, such as return on invested capital, operating margins, capital turnover, etc. Just a cash flow statement with no balance sheet is not sufficient.

- Ground the model in historical financial statements. Include five to ten years of historical financial data, so the forecast can be analyzed in light of historical performance and to ensure that the forecast is anchored in fact.

- Understand the accounting and tax complications of the company's financial statements. Understanding the accounting is often critical to understanding the economics of the business.

Avoid Hockey Sticks

The obvious example of a hockey stick is the forecast that predicts a remarkable turnaround for an underperforming company in a declining industry. A good preventive for forecasts that are wildly optimistic is to require specification of the exact actions necessary to cause the turnaround and why current management is likely to implement them. A more subtle, but no less relevant, pitfall can trip up those who forecast in cyclical industries. Continuing-value estimates are particularly sensitive to the phase of the cycle on which the estimates are based. As illustrated in Exhibit 10.2, problems can occur if the end of the forecast period falls anywhere other than on an average year. In Exhibit 10.2, the end of the forecast period falls near the peak of the earnings cycle. Consequently, the company will be overvalued because the peak earnings are used in the continuing-value assumption. The solution to this problem, is to forecast far enough out to capture a complete cycle, and to use an average year as the NOPLAT input to the continuing-value formula.

Use Longer Forecast Horizons

Longer forecast horizons are better than shorter horizons, for two reasons. First, a long forecast horizon forces you to be explicit about your forecast assumptions over a longer period of time. Second, analysts feel a strong tendency to use the convergence continuing-value model, and it may be entirely inappropriate for the case at hand. For example, the perpetuity model assumes that the return on new investment equals the weighted average cost of

Exhibit 10.2 **A FORECAST PERIOD THAT WILL RESULT IN A POOR
VALUATION OF A CYCLICAL BUSINESS**

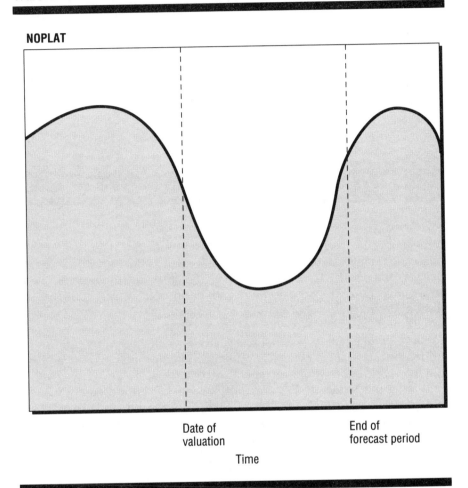

NOPLAT

Date of
valuation

End of
forecast period

Time

capital. For companies like PepsiCo, which have returns well
above their WACC and established brand names, it is unreasonable
to assume that their returns fall to WACC after a ten-year forecast
horizon. Either the forecast horizon should be much longer or the
convergence model should not be used. If you use the convergence
model in your valuation, test its validity by doubling your forecast
period to see how sensitive your valuation is to the convergence assumption.

Don't Double-Count Undervalued Assets

An almost irresistible temptation is to double-count undervalued assets on the balance sheet. For example, Cannon Mills owned hundreds of houses in the town of Cannonapolis, and they were carried on the books at 1920 prices. Assuming that rents were properly forecasted in the company's cash flows, the value of the houses is already included in its present value. Adding in the current market value of the houses would be double-counting.

PRESTON CORPORATION

We will now complete and analyze the Preston valuation. First, we will calculate the equity value of Preston for the Moderate Performance scenario. Exhibits 10.3 and 10.4 show the calculation of the value of Preston's operations using the DCF and economic profit approaches, respectively. The value of Preston's operations equals $244.3 million. Both approaches yield exactly the same value. Note that we adjusted both results by a mid-year adjustment factor equal to one-half of a year's value at Preston's WACC to adjust for the fact that we conservatively discounted economic profit and FCF as if they were entirely realized at the end of each year.

Under the Moderate Performance scenario, Preston's equity value is $84.5 million or $14.57 per share as shown on Exhibit 10.5. To calculate the equity value we added Preston's excess marketable securities to the value of its operations and subtracted the value of debt, operating leases, stock options and its after-tax unfunded pension liability. Note that since its unfunded pension liability was relatively small, we did not adjust Preston's free cash flow and invested capital as recommended in Chapter 6.

The value of Preston's operations is slightly less than the amount of its invested capital ($244.3 million versus $256.2 million) in this scenario. This is consistent with our forecast of Preston's performance for this scenario in which ROIC gradually increases to close to Preston's WACC. So it does not appear that we have made any calculation errors.

We also valued the other two scenarios for Preston. The results are summarized in Exhibit 10.6. Note that the value of the downside scenario is zero. Technically, the value based on the forecast was negative, because the value of debt and other claims exceeded the value of operations. However, we know that equity values cannot drop below zero, so we set it at zero for this scenario.

Exhibit 10.3 **VALUE OF PRESTON'S OPERATIONS USING DCF APPROACH,**
$ MILLIONS

Year	Free cash flow	Discount factor	Present value of FCF
1988	(29.1)	0.9116	(26.5)
1989	(19.1)	0.8310	(15.8)
1990	(11.1)	0.7575	(8.4)
1991	(3.3)	0.6905	(2.3)
1992	5.0	0.6295	3.1
1993	4.8	0.5738	2.8
1994	5.9	0.5231	3.1
1995	5.8	0.4768	2.8
1996	6.3	0.4347	2.7
1997	6.3	0.3962	2.5
Continuing value	679.8	0.3962	269.3
Value of operations before adjustment			233.3
Mid-year adjustment factor			1.0474
Value of operations			244.3

We assigned a much higher probability to the downside scenario than the upside scenario, because of the difficulty Preston will have differentiating its services in order to beat its cost of capital and the likelihood of continued price wars in the industry. When we weight the scenario values by their probabilities, we arrive at an equity value of $13.32 per share, or about 18 percent less than Preston's market value. Overall, we are more pessimistic than the market about Preston's outlook, but not by much. As potential investors, we would not buy shares of Preston at the current time. This is consistent with some of the stock analysts' views on Preston, which held that it was slightly overpriced based on their skepticism about the industry's ability to avoid price wars.

As you can see from Exhibit 10.6, Preston's value is highly sensitive to changes in forecasted performance. This is partly due to Preston's relatively high debt levels. Small changes in the value of operations are magnified by Preston's debt when translated into equity values. Second, in the Moderate Performance case, Preston earns just less than its WACC (a negative 1 percent spread). This spread becomes a positive 1 percent in the Upside case. Even though the ROIC is changing by only 2 points, the operating value increases substantially, because the spread of the ROIC versus the WACC shifts from negative to positive.

Exhibit 10.4 **VALUE OF PRESTON'S OPERATIONS USING ECONOMIC PROFIT APPROACH,** $ MILLIONS

Year	Economic profit	Discount factor	Present value of economic profit
1988	(8.6)	0.9116	(7.8)
1989	(7.2)	0.8310	(6.0)
1990	(5.1)	0.7575	(3.9)
1991	(3.5)	0.6905	(2.4)
1992	(1.5)	0.6295	(0.9)
1993	(1.3)	0.5738	(0.8)
1994	(1.3)	0.5231	(0.7)
1995	(1.0)	0.4768	(0.5)
1996	(0.6)	0.4347	(0.3)
1997	0.0	0.3962	0.0
Continuing value	0.6	0.3962	0.2

Present value of economic profit	(22.9)
Invested capital (end of 1987)	256.2
Value of operations before adjustment	233.3
Mid-year adjustment factor	1.0474
Value of operations	244.3

Exhibit 10.5 **VALUE OF PRESTON'S EQUITY,** $ MILLIONS

Value of operations	244.3
Excess marketable securities	3.2
Company value	247.5
Debt	(143.1)
Capitalized value of operating leases	(11.0)
After-tax unfunded pension liability	(4.4)
Stock options	(4.5)
Equity value	$84.5
Equity value per share	$14.57

Exhibit 10.6 **SUMMARY OF PRESTON SCENARIO VALUES**

| | Scenario | | |
	Downside	Moderate	Upside
Average revenue growth 1988 to 1997	9.2%	11.6%	11.6%
Average ROIC 1988 to 1997	6.0%	8.8%	10.7%
Company value ($ millions)	$84.3	$247.5	$368.1
Equity value ($ millions)	$0.0	$84.5	$205.1
Equity value per share	$0.00	$14.57	$35.37
Probability	30%	55%	15%
Expected value per share		$13.32	

REVIEW QUESTIONS

1. Detail the final steps needed to produce a company's value.

2. Produce a preliminary analysis of the value of Cincinnati Milacron using the following three scenarios: a conservative scenario with 3 percent continuing base growth; a medium performance scenario with 4 percent growth; an aggressive scenario with 6 percent growth. The purpose of the analysis is to determine the resilience of CMZ's equity market position among its competitors in the long run. This is the first of many steps in the process of determining this position. Keep all other value drivers constant.

3. Discuss the pitfalls of valuation analysis in the context of the CMZ analysis you just performed.

Applying Valuation

11

Multibusiness Valuation

Many valuations involve multibusiness companies whose futures depend on successful management of the portfolio of business units under their control. Multibusiness valuation is useful for several purposes, not the least of which is simply *understanding the business*. Strategic decisions for most multibusiness companies take place at the business-unit level. Thorough understanding of the company requires careful analysis of the threats and opportunities faced by each business unit. Hence, a company valuation built from separate valuations of business units provides much deeper insight than a company valuation that looks at the organization as a whole. The separate valuation of business units is at the heart of value-based planning at such companies as AT&T, PepsiCo, Hillenbrand, Heinz, Marriott, and Union Carbide. More arcane planning targets, such as return on equity or return on assets, fail to link directly to value and are easier for division managers to manipulate.

Multibusiness valuation is also useful for determining break-up value and for assessing acquisition candidates. It can help to create a clearer picture of headquarters costs and benefits, since headquarters can be valued as if it were a separate cost center. The central question is usually whether benefits of headquarters are commensurate with costs or if some of the extra layers of overhead can be trimmed.

Perhaps the most important use of multibusiness valuation is assessing opportunities for *restructuring* a company by taking advantage of all conceivable value enhancements, either internal or external. The focus of this chapter is using multibusiness valuation to assess restructuring opportunities. We begin by reviewing the pentagon model introduced in Chapter 2.

THE RESTRUCTURING PENTAGON

Exhibit 11.1 provides a pentagon framework for thinking about value creation in a multibusiness company using internally avail-

Exhibit 11.1 **PENTAGON FRAMEWORK FOR ASSESSING RESTRUCTURING OPPORTUNITIES**

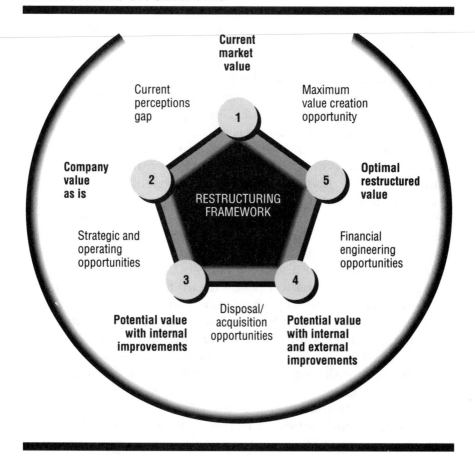

able information. Recall that this is the pentagon used by Ralph Demsky in our example in Chapter 2.

First, the *"as is" discounted cash flow* valuation is compared with the *current market value* of the company. Any difference between these values is a *perceptions gap*. If the market-determined shareholder value is less than the "as is" value, then management needs to do a better job of communicating with the market so that the market value increases. A share repurchase program is also a possibility. In the opposite case, a negative perceptions gap may mean the company is a potential takeover target and needs to close the gap by managing assets better.

One way to close a negative perceptions gap is to undertake *internal improvements* (for example, increasing operating margins and sales growth, and decreasing working-capital requirements). By taking advantage of strategic and operating opportunities, the company can realize its potential value as a portfolio of assets. These are the myriad fine-tuning opportunities that arise from understanding the relationship between operating parameters of each business unit and value creation. These key value drivers were a main focus of Chapter 4.

The next step is determining the value-enhancement potential that arises from *external opportunities*—shrinking the company via sell-offs, expanding it through acquisitions, or both. Unrelated businesses are particularly good candidates for sell-offs. For example, an electric utility that owns a drugstore chain may discover that it knows nothing about retail sales and that it is better off selling the chain to another owner. Divestiture can enhance value to the seller, which can then redeploy the cash received to improve its core business. The flip side of the coin, and something to be cautiously considered, is acquisition. Although profiting from acquisition is difficult, the right business combination can bring great rewards.

The maximum value of the company, including internal and external improvements and benefits from financial engineering, is its *optimal restructured value.* A thorough multibusiness valuation can provide sound advice on how to implement internal improvements and restructure to do the best possible job for shareholders.

We now turn our attention to the economics of restructuring. We discuss, in turn

- Looking at the market-determined value.

- Doing an "as is" valuation.
- Considering internal and external improvements.
- Putting it all together to achieve maximum value.

DETERMINING THE MARKET VALUE OF A COMPANY

The first step toward restructuring is simple. Just look at the current market value of the company—its equity and its debt. This value tells you the market's expectation for the future of the company. Usually, the market-determined value will agree with a discounted cash flow valuation of the company as it is currently operated, because very little gap typically exists between publicly available information as reflected in the market price and inside information known to management. Differences between the two values are caused by asymmetric information. For example, management may have had good news that has not yet been released, so that the DCF value is higher than the market value, or the market is anticipating a takeover and the premium to be received if an offer is made.

The perceptions gap can also be used as a reality test for management. Sometimes management's perception of the future of the company is unrealistic. For example, executives in the steel industry have been known to follow a policy of investing heavily in capital that returned more than the cost of debt but less than the weighted average cost of capital. Since earnings grew, they thought they were doing well, but the market had a different opinion and share prices fell. The market requires that the return on invested capital exceed the cost of capital in order for value to be created.

VALUING THE MULTIBUSINESS COMPANY "AS IS"

Valuing a multibusiness company "as is" is fundamentally the same as valuing a single-business company. The discounted cash flow process that was detailed in Chapter 6 comprises the basic knowledge needed in order to do a multibusiness valuation. What makes multibusiness valuation more complex is that each business unit has its own capital structure and cost of capital, business units often share cash flows, and headquarters costs and benefits are hard to estimate.

Exhibit 11.2 shows the steps in valuing a multibusiness company "as is." The outcome is separate valuations of each business unit and of corporate headquarters. These values provide the basis for the restructuring pentagon. The business units can be thought of as building blocks that can be fine-tuned via operating improvements, sold to owners who are willing to pay a premium to put them to a better alternative use or manage them better, or

---

Exhibit 11.2 **STEPS IN VALUING A MULTIBUSINESS COMPANY "AS IS"**

1. Define business units

- Separate into lines of business
- Keep headquarters separate

2. Collect business-unit data

- Identify comparables and collect data
- Use unconsolidated financials

3. Perform business-unit valuations

- Identify business-unit
  cash flows
  tax rates
  capital structures
  discount rates
- Identify headquarters
  cost
  benefits
  discount rates
- Discount business-unit and headquarters cash flows

4. Aggregate business-unit values

- Add corporate headquarters costs and benefits to unit values
- Double-check debt, risk, and overhead cost allocations
- Triangulate against total company DCF value

combined with business units of another company in an acquisition.

Each step in the process of multibusiness valuation is described in detail in the following pages.

Step 1: Define Business Units

Business units are defined as separable entities that have no significant synergies with any other part of the company. In principle, they could be split off as stand-alone businesses or sold to another company. Corporate headquarters costs that can be attributed to business units should be treated as business-unit costs. The remaining headquarters costs should be kept with headquarters as a cost center.

A good rule of thumb is to define business units at the smallest practical level of aggregation. For example, a company may have a consumer products division, but consumer products can be broken down into soap, toiletries, and detergents. These are logically separable business units as long as they do not have interdependent means of production, distribution, or marketing.

Identifying business units and allocating cash flows among them is not always easy. Exhibit 11.3 illustrates a hypothetical company that markets three products: plastics, fuels, and bicycles. Plastics and fuels are joint products from a single chemical plant. This same plant produces synthetic rubber as a by-product, which is used for the manufacture of bicycle tires. How shall business units be defined? How shall we handle the joint product and by-product problems?

As Exhibit 11.3 suggests, the easiest solution is to create two business units. The first combines the joint product—plastics and fuels—under a single roof. This is advisable because they are produced in a single facility, and because their production is interdependent. Management of the business unit must maximize value by choosing the best output mix of plastics and fuels given market demand, production constraints for the two products, and the cost of their inputs. The general principle is to combine joint products (interdependent or contingent products) into a single business unit whenever possible.

Business Unit 2 produces bicycles. It is clearly independent of business Unit 1, except for the fact that a by-product of business Unit 1, synthetic rubber, is an input for the bicycle division. This

Exhibit 11.3 **DEFINITION OF BUSINESS UNITS FOR A HYPOTHETICAL COMPANY**

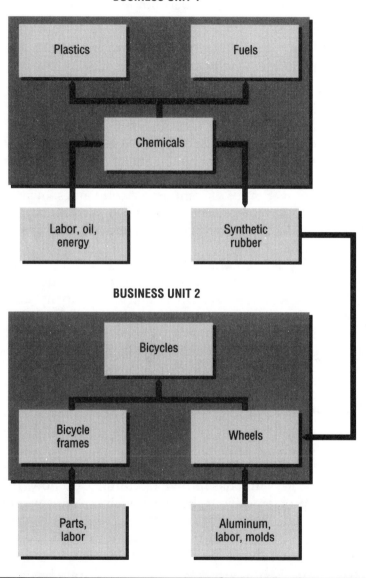

product could be acquired elsewhere from another supplier. Hence, the bicycle division is logically separable as a business unit. Synthetic rubber can be "sold," at a market-determined transfer price, by business Unit 1 to business Unit 2. If the transfer price is not acceptable to business Unit 2, it should be allowed to purchase synthetic rubber from a third party.

Step 2: Collect Business-Unit Data

If you are analyzing a company from the outside (for example, in a merger and acquisition review), you will not have detailed business-unit accounting data to use. At best, you will have data on revenues, operating margins, and identifiable assets by line of business from the segment information in annual reports. For example, if you do not have data on capital employed, it can be estimated using asset turnover ratios of comparable companies. In any event, you will want to carefully select as many comparable companies as possible and collect data on them. (Appendix B contains a list of useful data sources.)

If your analysis is conducted from inside a company, you can use the company's accounting system to provide business-unit data. Often you will need to request that the company's information be reclassified to conform to the business-unit definitions relevant to your study. Once the internally generated data is ready, you will need to compare it with publicly available data on comparable businesses.

Step 3: Perform Business-Unit Valuations

As the how-to-do-it-section, this is the longest and most detailed. The following general principles apply:

- Each business unit has its own operating cash flow. Transfer-pricing problems, if any, between business units will need to be resolved. The cost of corporate services (for example, accounting services) that the business unit would use were it self-sufficient should be allocated to it.

- Corporate headquarters is kept as a separate business unit with identifiable costs and benefits. The tradeoff between these costs and benefits determines the optimal size of headquarters.

- The effective tax rate for each business unit, when viewed as a separate entity, is different from when the unit is viewed as part of the multibusiness corporation.
- Each business unit has a unique capital structure, which can be determined from its cash flow, from the assets that are attributed to it, and from studying comparable companies. A unique WACC corresponds to the business risk and financial structure of each business unit.
- Headquarters should be valued by discounting its cash flow at the relevant risk-adjusted cost of capital.

Keeping these principles in mind, we turn to a detailed discussion of the issues involved in valuing business units. From this point forward, we assume that the valuation is from an insider's point of view, that is, all internal data is readily accessible.

Identify business-unit cash flows   The guiding principle is to estimate business-unit cash flows assuming each unit is stand-alone, separate from the remainder of the company. This approach will help later in determining whether the business unit should remain under the corporate umbrella or be split off. Additionally, it will provide a good perspective for analyzing the costs and benefits of corporate headquarters. To identify business-unit cash flows, we need to deal with two typical problems: transfer pricing and corporate overhead.

Transfer pricing is the problem that arises when the output of one business unit is the input of another. A high price will increase profits of the supplier at the expense of the user, and vice versa. The recommended solution is to establish a transfer price as close as possible to the market price of close substitutes. Unfortunately, this can be a difficult task if substitutes are hard to find. The main idea, however, is to approximate market prices so that profit is appropriately allocated to the supplier or to the user of the good or service.

Taxation often complicates transfer pricing. One of the benefits of the corporate umbrella (that is, of headquarters) is that it can establish a transfer-pricing system that keeps profits in the jurisdiction that has the lowest tax burden. As a result, one set of (artificial) transfer prices may be used for tax purposes and another set of (market-determined) prices for determining business unit-cash flows. This topic is covered in greater depth in Chapter 12, in which we discuss the issues involved in valuing foreign subsidiaries.

Allocating corporate overhead is a problem closely related to transfer pricing. The central issue is whether business units would use corporate services if they were spun off to become separate entities. Many services *would* be used, for example, accounting, legal, computer, and internal consulting services. Whenever possible, the cost of these services should be allocated to business units on a usage basis or, failing that, on the basis of a reasonable proxy for usage, such as operating income, revenues, capital employed, or numbers of employees.

In theory, market prices should be used for allocation purposes. For example, one hour of a headquarters accountant's time should be billed to a division based on the market price of accountants' time in general—that is, at the opportunity cost to the division. Any difference between the market price and the actual salary paid to the accountant by headquarters is a benefit, or cost to, headquarters. Clearly, record keeping for this kind of system can get out of hand with too much detail, and few companies will implement it. However, the general principle remains—headquarters costs that would not be borne by business units were they separate (for example, the headquarters jet) should not be allocated.

Determine the cash flow costs and benefits of corporate headquarters   Attributable to headquarters are the costs and benefits that arise from combining business units under a single corporate umbrella rather than running them as separate entities. Determining these costs and benefits is a difficult exercise that requires a great deal of judgment, but it can be an important aspect of the corporate restructuring question. At one extreme, headquarters is merely an extra level of fat, and great value can be obtained by breaking up the business units, selling them, and demolishing corporate headquarters. At the opposite extreme, headquarters can be too lean for its optimal role in risk management, tax planning, and strategic planning.

Headquarters costs are all costs that should not be allocated to business units. They include the *nonallocatable portions of*

- Headquarters executive salaries, wages, bonuses, and benefits;

- Directors' insurance and fees;
- Office space (buildings and land) and equipment;
- Headquarters support staff (accounting, legal, planning, personnel, and administrative);
- Corporate-level advertising;
- Corporate-level research and development;
- Corporate-level charitable contributions;
- Transportation and communications; and
- Corporate-level consulting.

The portion of each cost item to be retained at headquarters is somewhat subjective. For example, consider the remuneration of headquarters executives. If the remuneration of business-unit presidents is lower than it otherwise might be were they at stand-alone companies, then it may be reasonable to allocate a portion of headquarters executive costs to the business units. As always, the relevant consideration is: What would business-unit costs be were the companies separate?

To illustrate headquarters costs from an outsider's point of view, we took a look at the 25 largest companies in the *Fortune* 500 industrial list using fiscal 1986 publicly available data. Exhibit 11.4 shows the results.

To compute corporate headquarters expenses, we used the business segment exhibit in the annual report and looked up the corporate expense number located there. No guarantee exists that this number is defined in the same way from company to company, because of differences in the way headquarters expenses are (or are not) allocated to business units. We used the corporate expense number as reported if taxes and financing costs were not included. When they were, and when we knew the tax and financing figures, we made adjustments to estimate the pretax, prefinancing corporate expense. Occasionally, the pretax corporate expense number had to be estimated, when tax and financing expenses were unknown, by assuming interest income of 7 percent on marketable securities, a 10 percent interest expense rate on debt, and a 46 percent corporate income tax rate. After-tax corporate expenses were capitalized by dividing them by the company's real unlevered cost of equity, because we assumed no inflationary growth.

Headquarters costs averaged 1.9 percent of the 1986 year-end market value of their equity (or if you like, 1.3 percent of the

Exhibit 11.4 **1986 HEADQUARTERS COST FOR 22 OF THE 25 LARGEST INDUSTRIALS***

Company	HQ cost $ Millions	HQ cost as percentage of market equity	Capitalized HQ cost as percentage of total equity value	HQ cost as a percentage of sales
Texaco	$ 736	8.5%	185%	2.3%
General Motors	1,015	4.8	58	1.0
Allied Signal	249	3.6	34	2.1
Mobil	456	2.8	35	1.0
Chrysler	121	2.3	15	0.5
Atlantic Richfield	213	2.0	31	1.5
Procter & Gamble	257	2.0	15	1.7
Chevron	306	2.0	23	1.3
Occidental Petroleum	82	1.8	155	0.5
Tennaco	92	1.6	130	0.6
DuPont	304	1.5	11	1.1
Shell Oil	334	1.3	16	2.0
Boeing	100	1.3	6	0.6
RJR Nabisco	139	1.1	11	0.8
General Electric	389	1.0	5	1.1
USX	54	1.0	22	0.4
Rockwell International	58	0.9	4	0.5
Exxon	406	0.8	8	0.6
Philip Morris	126	0.7	6	0.6
Amoco Corporation	113	0.7	7	0.6
United Technology	25	0.4	3	0.2
McDonnell Douglas	11	0.4	3	0.1
Average		1.9%	36%	1.0%

* The corporate expense line in the business segment section of the annual report may be defined inconsistently across companies; therefore, our average results for the entire group have greater validity than those for individual companies.

market value of their assets). By comparison, managers of mutual funds usually receive an average of about 0.5 percent of assets under management. As a percentage of sales, HQ costs averaged 1.0% in 1986. In 1989, the top ten companies averaged 1.3 percent.

To compare the present value of headquarters costs with the market value of equity, we capitalized the after-tax cost stream by assuming it would grow at a real rate of 2.5 percent per year and that it had the same risk as the business as a whole. (We used the unlevered beta in the capital asset pricing model, and discounted at the real unlevered cost of equity.) The results, shown in column 3 of Exhibit 11.4, are amazing. For example, if Texaco had cut its headquarters costs to 0.9 percent of its revenues (the average for 21 companies excluding Texaco), it would have saved $448 million per year, pretax. Its 1986 operating profit, which was $1.882 billion, would have increased 24 percent. If these savings were viewed as permanent, the value created for shareholders would have been astronomical. (Since 1986, Texaco has made a concerted effort to cut corporate center costs. In 1987, reported corporate expenses dropped to $378 million, a decline of 49 percent.)

Companies with above-average headquarters costs need to take a careful look to identify ways of trimming excess fat or to be sure that headquarters benefits exceed costs. When headquarters costs exceed benefits by a wide margin, the company, regardless of its size, will have a large gap between its potential value and its value as is.

Headquarters benefits are usually more difficult to identify than costs. We have divided them into two broad categories: those that are quantifiable; and others that, while important, are extremely difficult to measure.

Benefits that can be quantified (with difficulty) are tax advantages and greater debt capacity. Tax advantages attributable to headquarters arise primarily from the lack of an adequate secondary market for tax shields. A group of business units with highly variable year-to-year taxable earnings can share tax shields by operating under a corporate umbrella. The losses of Unit A can be used immediately to shelter the gains of Unit B, so the business unit does not have to wait for tax carry-forwards or carry-backs. Conglomerates constructed from business units with low taxable-income variability are likely to benefit less from a corporate tax umbrella than conglomerates built from diverse business units with highly variable income.

Headquarters also provides the benefit of the present value of tax shelters that arise from corporate-level tax planning. In addition to the ability to use tax losses immediately, corporate headquarters is often able to undertake international tax planning (for example, transfer pricing) that might not be available were the business units operating separately.

Finally, greater debt capacity is created because business-unit cash flows are not perfectly correlated. Once the capital structure for each business unit has been developed and business-unit debt has been totaled, a portion attributable to headquarters might yet remain. (See the discussion of determining business-unit capital structure and cost of capital, later in this step, for more on how to allocate debt to business units.) The present value of the tax shield arising from this debt is a benefit of headquarters. Of course, if the company owes no corporate-level taxes, this benefit evaporates.

Benefits that are not easily measured include prospective synergies and information advantages. Operating synergies are an obvious benefit of combining business units. If, for example, the company makes an acquisition that allows the existing sales force to assume the duties of the target's sales force, the present value of the realized savings is a benefit due, at least initially, to headquarters, because it resulted from the decision to acquire and combine two businesses. The "vision" of headquarters is not part of continuing operations and, although very valuable, is impossible to forecast as part of cash flows.

Information and communications advantages complete the list of headquarters benefits. Although difficult to quantify, they can be important. Nobel laureate Kenneth Arrow contends that informational advantages of vertical integration can be valuable because they reduce uncertainty. For example, a manufacturer may decide it is optimal to own production facilities to eliminate variability in supplies that might disrupt production.

Determine business-unit tax rates The relevant tax rate for valuing a business unit depends on the taxes it would be paying were it not under a corporate umbrella. As mentioned earlier, when a business unit is separated from the parent it loses its ability to shelter taxable income with losses elsewhere in the parent and must resort to tax carry-forward and tax carry-back provisions of the tax code. This consideration is also relevant when deciding whether to spin off a unit or to sell it to another company. A simple spin-off may increase the unit's tax rate, whereas sale to another company that can shelter the unit's earnings may be more advisable. Effective tax rates may change for less-obvious reasons as well. For example, tax advantages of transfer pricing or multinational taxation may be different if a business unit is separated from the parent.

To determine the business unit's tax rate, first determine its taxable income as a stand-alone entity over the foreseeable future. Then use the tax code to determine its adjusted tax rate, as described in Chapter 6.

Since we are treating corporate headquarters as a separate business unit for valuation purposes, its effect on taxes must also be estimated. In most cases, headquarters (the corporate umbrella) is a means for generating tax shelters; hence, its implied tax rate is negative. The present value of headquarters tax shelters is a benefit to the company. (The appropriate discount rate is discussed in the following paragraphs.)

Determine business-unit capital structure and cost of capital The *capital structure* of each business unit should be consistent with that of comparable companies in its industry and with the overall philosophy of its parent. For example, if the parent is aggressive and chooses a Baa bond rating, then business units will normally have capital structures that bring them to a Baa rating within their industry. (Of course, exceptions to every rule exist. If one business unit— a finance company, for example—requires a higher bond rating to do business, then its debt capacity is lower. It might carry an Aa bond rating, while other business units carry a Baa rating or lower.)

The debt capacity of business units may vary considerably. An insurance subsidiary, for example, may be able to carry an 80 percent debt-to-capital ratio, while a manufacturing subsidiary might only have a 25 percent debt-to-capital ratio. The basis for determining business-unit capital structure will usually depend on cash flow or capital employed at the business unit. Debt-to-capital ratios or interest-coverage ratios for comparables provide a basis for estimating industry norms.

The difference between the sum of all business-unit debt and total companywide debt should be attributed to corporate headquarters. A portion of it may represent tied financing—for example, a real estate mortgage on the wholly owned corporate headquarters building. Any remaining debt results from the fact that the debt capacity of a portfolio of business-unit cash flows that are not perfectly correlated has less variance than the sum of the separate cash flows. Consequently, the combination of separate business units under a corporate umbrella provides greater debt capacity. The present value of the interest tax shield is a benefit of headquarters.

Having determined the target capital structure and tax rate of each business unit, you still need to estimate the cost of equity in order to establish its weighted average cost of capital. In the case of a division of a company or a nonpublic company, no betas are published. To estimate them you have to rely on wit and guile. We recommend using one of four approaches: (1) management comparisons, (2) comparison companies, (3) a multiple regression approach, or (4) earnings before interest and taxes (EBIT) regressed against a market index.

1. *Management comparisons.* A crude but often effective way of estimating betas is to elicit the help of management. Have three to five managers sit down and position the division or project being analyzed relative to the list of industries shown in Exhibit 11.5. You do not need to show managers the actual betas, or even to explain the concept. Just have a few of them circle the industry with risk closest to their division. If they closely agree (and they usually do), you will have a reasonable estimate of the levered beta of the division.

Exhibit 11.5 **INDUSTRY BETAS**

Levered Beta	Industry	Levered Beta	Industry
1.55	Brokerage	1.14	Real estate
1.41	Restaurants	1.09	Chemicals
1.36	Hotels	1.04	Food and kindred products
1.32	Building and construction	1.01	Banks
1.26	Electric machinery	0.98	Paper and allied products
1.25	Scientific instruments	0.96	Food stores
1.24	Airline	0.88	Metal mining
1.18	Machinery (excluding electric)	0.86	Petroleum refining
1.16	Motion pictures	0.73	Electric and gas utilities
1.16	Retail stores	0.71	Railroads
1.14	Textile mill products		

Source: Wilshire Associates, Inc. (1981). *Capital Market Equilibrium Statistics,* Santa Monica, California.

2. *Comparison companies.* A second approach is to ask management to identify the publicly traded competitors most similar to the division. Having this list is useful, because you can then look up the betas for these companies, which are presumed to have similar risk. But there is a catch. Beta is a measure of the systematic risk of the levered equity of the comparison companies, and these companies will usually employ leverage different from that used by the division you are attempting to value. To get around this problem, you have to "unlever" the betas of the comparison companies to obtain their business risk, then relever using the target capital structure of the division you are analyzing.

   The unlevered beta measures the business risk of a company by removing the effect of financial leverage. The observed equity beta computed from market return data presents a picture of the risk of equity given the company's existing leverage. To unlever the beta, you need data on the company's levered beta, its target capital structure, and its marginal tax rate.

   For example, suppose that the levered beta of Comparison Corporation is 1.2 and that it has a debt-to-equity ratio of 1.3. The division you are valuing has a target debt-to-equity ratio of 0.8. To estimate the unlevered equity beta of the division, the following formula will prove useful. (We should note that levering and relevering betas is a conceptually tricky business, especially for extreme leverage situations. For example, the following formula assumes that debt is risk free. In addition, the corporate marginal tax rate may change as a function of leverage, and the formula assumes that it does not.)

$$\text{beta}_L = \left[1 + \left(1 - T_c\right)B/S\right]\left(\text{beta}_u\right),$$

where

beta_L = the levered equity beta.
T_c = the corporate marginal tax rate.
B/S = the debt-to-equity ratio for the division, estimated in terms of market value.
beta_u = the unlevered equity beta (a measure of the business risk of the division).

To use this formula, you also need to know the marginal tax rate of both Comparison Corporation and of the division you are studying. Suppose the tax rate of Comparison Corporation is 25 percent and that your tax rate will be 34 percent. The unlevered beta (the operating risk) of Comparison Corporation is as follows:

$$\text{beta}_u = \frac{\text{beta}_L}{1 + (1 - T_c)B/S}.$$

$$= \frac{1.2}{1 + (1 - 0.25)1.3} = 0.61.$$

Relying on the assumption that Comparison Corporation has the same business risk as your division, you can now estimate the levered beta of your division as follows:

$$\text{beta}_L = \left[1 + (1 - 0.34)0.61\right] = 0.93$$

Knowledge of the levered beta allows you to estimate the cost of equity for your division using the capital asset pricing model, as discussed in Chapter 8.

3. *Multiple regression approach.* One of the most difficult problems with estimating the cost of equity for business units is that good comparables can rarely be found, because most companies have multiple lines of business and different percentages of their assets in each. A way around this problem is to recognize that the business risk (that is, the unlevered beta) of a multidivision company is a weighted average of the risks of each line of business, as illustrated in Exhibit 11.6. Note also that business risk, on the assets side of the balance sheet, equals the weighted average of all risks on the liabilities side. This is a demonstration of the principle of the conservation of risk.

In the United States, at least, it is possible to use line-of-business data to estimate the percentages of assets that companies have tied up in their separate lines of business. If you have data on two companies, each with two lines of business, and know the company unlevered betas as well as the

Exhibit 11.6 **COMPANY RISK AS A WEIGHTED AVERAGE OF ITS BUSINESS-UNIT RISKS**

ASSETS

Business unit	Market value weight	Unlevered beta	Contribution to asset risk
A	W_A	β_A	$W_A\beta_A$
B	W_B	β_B	$W_B\beta_B$
•	•	•	•
•	•	•	•
•	•	•	•
Z	W_Z	β_Z	$W_Z\beta_Z$
		Asset risk* $=$	$\Sigma W_i\beta_i$

LIABILITIES

Source of capital	Market value weight	Beta	Contribution to liability risk
Debt	W_D	β_D	$W_D\beta_D$
Preferred	W_P	β_P	$W_P\beta_P$
Common	W_C	β_C	$W_C\beta_C$
		Liability risk* $=$	$\Sigma W_j\beta_j$

* Asset risk = liability risk.

asset weights, then you can construct two equations with two unknowns:

$$beta_{u1} = W_{A1}beta_{UA} + W_{B1}\,beta_{UB}$$
$$beta_{u2} = W_{A2}beta_{UA} + W_{B2}\,beta_{UB}$$

It is then easy to solve for the unlevered line-of business betas, $beta_{UA}$ and $beta_{UB}$.

If there are more companies than lines of business, the unlevered business-unit betas can be estimated by running a linear regression of the unlevered company betas against the weights for the lines of business, being careful to suppress the constant term. The coefficients from the regression are unbiased estimates of the business-unit betas.

Exhibit 11.7 illustrates data for forest products companies. Our regression results based on these data indicated
the following:

Unlevered beta for building products $= 1.08$
Unlevered beta for paper products $= 0.88$

The unlevered beta represents an estimate of the operating
risk of the business unit. Next, the actual tax rate and leverage of the business unit, along with the estimated unlevered
beta, can be used to compute an estimate of its levered beta.
Given the levered beta of a business unit, the capital asset
pricing model, as discussed in Chapter 8, can be used to
compute the cost of equity, k_s.

4. *Covariance of earnings before interest and taxes.* The least practical of the four recommended methods for estimating the
beta of a division is to collect a history of annual or quarterly EBIT for the entity being valued, and regress EBIT
against the rate of return on a market index collected for
similar intervals.

$$EBIT_t = a + b \, (\text{market return}_t)$$

The slope (b) of this regression is an estimate of the unlevered beta of the stock; however, it needs to be scaled because
it will be expressed in dollars, not a percentage.

Exhibit 11.7 **FOREST PRODUCTS COMPANIES DATA**

Company	Levered beta	Unlevered beta	Market debt/ equity	Asset weights Building	Paper
Champion Int'l	1.23	0.86	70.4%	0.15	0.85
Chesapeake Corp.	0.88	0.59	82.5	0.06	0.94
Great Northern Nek.	1.21	1.10	16.9	0.04	0.96
Louisiana-Pacific	1.32	0.98	57.9	0.79	0.21
Pope and Talbot	1.18	1.06	18.9	0.51	0.49
Longview Fibre	1.16	1.01	24.6	0.26	0.74
Temple Inland	1.16	0.99	28.4	0.19	0.81

Therefore, it needs to be divided by an estimate of the market value of the assets in the division. This would be a good measure of beta, except for two additional problems. First, when valuing a division, historic data for EBIT is often either nonexistent, or it has too few observations to be useful. Second, measurement errors in the data can lead to badly biased estimates of beta. Use this method only as a last resort.

A final note about betas. When changes in risk are expected across time, you have to be prepared to estimate a changing equity beta. Sometimes a company's strategic plan implies that risk is expected to change. Usually this is the risk of the company's portfolio of assets, but it could also pertain to the portfolio of liabilities. For example, a young company, recently gone public, is risky now (high beta), but is expected to have declining risk across time. Although we cannot suggest foolproof steps for estimating the changing risk, it will change. This implies that the weighted average cost of capital may also change (decline) as the company matures. Consequently, it becomes necessary to discount Year-N cash flows at a risk-adjusted rate approximate for the risk in Year N, not other years when the risk might be higher or lower.

After you have estimated the cost of equity, you can compute the weighted average cost of capital for each business unit. This will be used as a discount rate for the business-unit after-tax cash flows.

$$\text{WACC} = k_b(1-T)\frac{B}{B+S} + k_s\frac{S}{B+S}.$$

The cost of debt, k_b, is the same as the long-term bond rate, given the bond rating of the business unit. The tax rate is the business-unit effective tax rate. The percentage of debt in the capital structure, $B/(B+S)$, is based on target market value capital structures for comparables and adjusted for the policy (conservative or aggressive) of headquarters. The cost of equity, k_s, uses the relevered beta of comparables, and the percentage of equity is 1 minus the percentage of debt.

Determine discount rate for headquarters costs   You can determine the discount rate of the headquarters by breaking down headquarters cash flows into three categories, each to be discounted at a rate appropriate for its risk: tax shields provided by debt, noninterest tax shields, and headquarters costs.

Tax shields provided by debt have the same risk as corporate debt and should be discounted at the pretax cost of debt, k_b. The present value of these tax shields (assuming they will be available perpetually) is the marginal tax rate, T_c, times the market value of debt, B.

Noninterest tax shields (due to transfer pricing or the fact that losses of one division can shelter gains at another) depend on the probability of realizing them. Thus, cash flows must be defined as *expected* cash flows from noninterest tax shields. The appropriate discount rate for transfer-pricing tax shields depends on the business risk of the company. Financial leverage is irrelevant because transfer-pricing schemes are expenses before interest. For these reasons, expected transfer-pricing tax shields should be discounted at the unlevered cost of equity for the company as a whole. Tax shields based on the fact that losses in one business unit can shelter gains in another should be discounted at the levered cost of equity, because they can be realized only on income after interest expenses.

Headquarters costs (for example, executive and staff compensation, or legal expenses) should be discounted at a rate somewhere between the risk-free rate and the unlevered cost of equity, depending on their covariance with general business conditions (with the market portfolio). Choice of the actual rate is difficult and subjective. Companies whose headquarters costs do not fluctuate with the economy should discount them at the risk-free rate. For most companies, however, headquarters costs tend to rise in good business conditions (as executives and staff receive higher compensation) and fall during recessions. If the changes correlate well with operating profits, then the discount rate could be as high as the unlevered cost of equity. Note that changes in headquarters costs that are not correlated with business conditions (for example, one-time "fat-trimming" efforts) do not affect the discount rate.

Step 4: Aggregate Business-Unit Values

The final step in multibusiness valuation is to aggregate headquarters costs and benefits with business-unit values. In addition to simply adding these up, you should also double-check your valuation by adding up the separate debt components to be sure that they equal total corporate debt. Also, you should add business-unit and headquarters cash flows to see that they come close to corporate cash flows during the historical period. (It is difficult, if not impossible, to ensure that, during the forecast period, the sum of individual business-unit cash flows equals the separately estimated corporate-level forecast in a year-by-year comparison, because the average of business-unit growth rates is unlikely to equal the corporate growth rate.) This is a good way of checking your assumptions for consistency.

Exhibit 11.8 shows how the values of two hypothetical divisions can be added. From these, one subtracts headquarters costs and adds headquarters benefits and the value of excess marketable securities. The result is the aggregated value of the company. When the market value of corporate debt has been subtracted, the result should be the value of equity for the company as it currently is. If your results triangulate fairly well with the present value of the discounted cash flow of the company as a whole, you have a good valuation. If not, you need to locate and deal with the discrepancy.

An important by-product of your analysis is a careful look at the costs and benefits of headquarters. If costs exceed benefits by a wide margin, then headquarters may contain too much fat and cost reduction may be in order; in extreme cases, benefits may be negligible and shareholders may be better off if the company is broken up.

A few special situations need to be discussed along with the process of aggregation. For example, how should unconsolidated subsidiaries be handled? How can double-counting be avoided? And what should be done with excess debt and marketable securities?

Unconsolidated subsidiaries are often an important part of a company. They are clearly separable business units, but how should we think about the cash flows they provide to the parent? Assuming they are not foreign subsidiaries, the best approach is to value them separately, then multiply their equity value by the fraction that the parent owns, and add their result to your estimate of the parent's equity value. An alternative approach is to discount expected dividends paid from the subsidiary to the parent at a cost of equity appropriate for the riskiness of the dividend stream. This method is

Exhibit 11.8 **"AS IS" MULTIBUSINESS VALUATION**

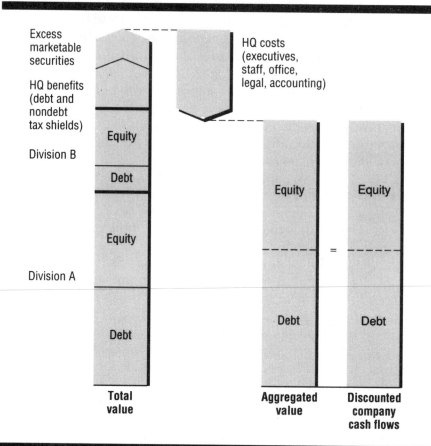

difficult to use because dividends are discretionary and, therefore, difficult to forecast.

Double-counting can occur when an undervalued asset is carried on the books of a business unit. For example, Weyerhaeuser owns thousands of acres of timberland that is carried on the books at low value. An almost irresistible temptation exists to estimate the market value of the forest and add it to the present value of cash flow. To do so, however, would be double-counting, because expected cash flow already assumes that harvested trees will be used to produce lumber. They are, in every sense, an inventory. As with inventory, their value is not added, because it is already included in future cash flow as an input to production.

Another common example of double-counting is corporate headquarters or other real estate carried at low book value. The rental opportunity cost of the buildings is already reflected in a cash flow that is higher than it might otherwise be if the company were to sell its headquarters, then lease the office space. You cannot have it both ways. Either discount the cash flow as it is, or subtract the expected rental cost from the cash flow and add the market value of the headquarters building.

Excess marketable securities build up in the projected balance sheet of a business unit if it is doing well or, alternately, if extra debt is borrowed. This effect is a normal part of the forecasting process and, as discussed in Chapter 7, it has no effect on the present value of a business unit. Excess cash held by the company at the start of the valuation period is a different matter. It should not be allocated to business units. Its value should simply be kept separate and added to the other values during the aggregation stage, as shown in Exhibit 11.8.

ESTIMATING POTENTIAL VALUE WITH INTERNAL IMPROVEMENTS

After completing the valuation of the company by aggregating the separate values of all business units, the next step in restructuring is to define and implement, wherever possible, internal operating improvements. Even business units that will be sold should be fixed up as long as the cost of improvements is less than the extra sales premium that the improvements will bring. It is a little like fixing up your car or your house in an effort to attain the best possible profit from the sale.

Chapter 4 provided details on the key value drivers that affect the discounted cash flow value of companies. Exactly the same principles apply to business units. Consequently, we will not reiterate them here. Every business unit should be fine-tuned as much as possible. Furthermore, corporate headquarters costs should be carefully studied and cut back when burdensome. It is helpful to determine the present value of headquarters costs as a percentage of the value of total assets, and then compare across companies within the same industry.

ESTIMATING POTENTIAL VALUE WITH EXTERNAL IMPROVEMENTS

Once every business unit has been fine-tuned by implementing all possible internal improvements, you are ready to consider external possibilities. Some business units, even though fine-tuned, can be more valuable in alternative uses, and should be sold. In other instances they cannot be made profitable (by anyone) and should be shut down. The flip side of the coin is acquisition. Business-unit combinations that provide real synergies can do much to enhance value.

Analyze Value Creation from Breakups

Breakup is a generic term referring to several different methods of restructuring a company via the disposition of assets. This can imply the sale of individual assets, for example real estate, or the sale of entire business units.

The most common method is *divestiture* or *sell-off*, where a business unit is sold for cash to another company. The motivation is usually straightforward: the assets can be better managed by another company. Consequently, the buyer is willing to pay a higher price than the current value of the business unit to its parent (even after paying capital gains taxes on the sale). Two thousand divisions and subsidiaries were divested from parent companies in the United States in 1984 and 1985 alone. Academic studies generally indicate increases in share price for divesting companies and for companies acquiring related businesses, but not for companies that acquire unrelated businesses.[1]

Spin-offs involve dividending shares of a business unit to existing shareholders of the parent company in a nontaxable event. The "Dividend News" section of *The Wall Street Journal* listed 160 spin-offs between 1962 and 1981. Several reasons for spin-offs have been given. They include avoiding regulatory constraints, renegotiation

---

[1] For effects on selling companies, see P.C. Jain "The Effect of Voluntary Sell-Off Announcements on Shareholder Wealth," *Journal of Finance* (March 1985): 209–224. For effects on acquiring companies, see N. W. Sicherman and R. H. Pettway, "Acquisition of Divested Assets and Shareholders' Wealth," *Journal of Finance* (December 1987): 1261–1273.

of labor contracts, tax avoidance (particularly when creating oil royalty or real estate trusts), and capitalizing on situations where the value of the parts is greater than the value of the whole—the anergy effect. Academic studies indicate an average 5.02 percent positive abnormal return to shareholders of completed spin-offs.[2]

Leveraged buyouts (LBOs) involve the sale of a business unit to its managers, who finance the purchase with high financial leverage. Often the parent retains partial equity ownership and/or lends to the LBO. Since the company formed from an LBO is usually privately held, we have little systematic evidence on how LBO owners fare. On the other hand, ample evidence exists that the sellers benefit. [3]

Equity carve-outs are the least-common means for selling assets. Between 1963 and 1983, approximately 76 carve-outs were announced by publicly held companies. In a carve-out, new shares are issued to the public that represent ownership in the business unit to be carved out. Depending on who issues the shares either the parent or the subsidiary keeps the cash. The average effect on shareholders' wealth upon announcement of the carve-out is an increase of 1.8 percent.[4]

As illustrated in Exhibit 11.9, the analysis of asset disposition starts from a base-case market valuation of the company "as is." To this value is added the gain from disposition of the business unit—the difference between the market value of the business unit as a stand-alone entity as operated by its current parent and the market price when disposed of. From this value we must subtract tax liabilities created by sale of the business unit, expected losses of benefits provided by the current corporate umbrella (for example, tax

[2] See T. E. Copeland, E. F. Lemgruber, and D. Mayers, "Corporate Spinoffs: Multiple Announcement and Ex-Date Abnormal Performance," chap. 7 in *Modern Finance and Industrial Economics*, ed. T. E. Copeland (New York: Basil Blackwell, 1987); also see K. Schipper and A. Smith, "Effects of Recontracting on Shareholder Wealth," *Journal of Financial Economics* (April 1983): 437–467.

[3] See H. DeAngelo, L. DeAngelo, and E. Rice, "Going Private: The Effects of a Change in Corporate Ownership Structure," *Midland Corporate Finance Journal* (Summer 1984): 35–43.

[4] See K. Schipper and A. Smith, "A Comparison of Equity Carve-Outs and Seasoned Equity Offerings," *Journal of Financial Economics* (January/February 1986): 153–186.

Exhibit 11.9 **VALUING THE EFFECTS OF ASSET DISPOSITION (SELL-OFF),** $ MILLIONS

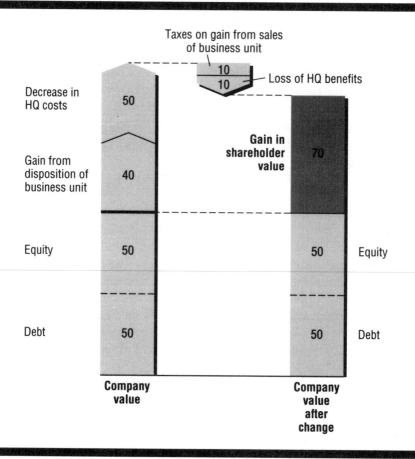

shelters), and anticipated decreases in unallocated headquarters costs. For instance, as business units are disposed of, cuts should be made at headquarters (fewer administrators, less office space, and so on).

The value created from disposing of a business unit must come from cash flow benefits. It is important to search for benefits that are not related to headquarters per se. Here are a few relevant questions to ask:

- Are projected business-unit labor contract costs higher, lower, or unchanged following the disposition?

- Do any regulatory constraints change? If so, how will they affect cash flow?

- How do taxes change?

- How does the cost of accessing capital markets change? Will the cost of capital be affected?

- Would any operating changes result in higher cash flow if the business unit were owned by another company?

- Is the disposition a taxable transaction? If so, can it be structured differently to reduce taxes?

- Will disposition of the business unit result in better management incentives to create value? Why?

In each case, it is essential to consider whether breakup is really necessary. Could the company achieve the same benefits by continuing to own the business and by improving it?

Analyze Asset Acquisition

On the flip side of the restructuring coin is the search for acquisitions. Finding an acquisition candidate is only the beginning. You must also pick a strategy for enhancing the value of the company once it has been acquired, for figuring out an acquisition price that is high enough to deter competitive bids yet low enough to allow a profit, and for choosing the right approach to implement the acquisition. Since mergers and acquisitions are the main topic of Chapter 14, we only survey some broad issues here. Acquisitions are risky business. Academic studies largely agree that bidding firms, on average, do not benefit from acquisitions.

Exhibit 11.10 illustrates the economics of an acquisition. The acquiring company must identify real (not imaginary) synergies and/or operating improvements whose present value exceeds the takeover premium necessary to gain control. Additional value can be created be selling some of the acquired assets for an economic gain—that is, the difference between the "as is" economic value of the assets and their sale price less taxes.

One of the most common errors in acquisition analysis is that synergies are not properly evaluated and often amount to no more than wishful thinking. To identify and value synergies is no simple task. Often economies of scale are cited as a way of cutting costs or achieving higher market share. But you should pin down exactly

Exhibit 11.10 **VALUE CHANGES IN AN ACQUISITION,** $ MILLIONS

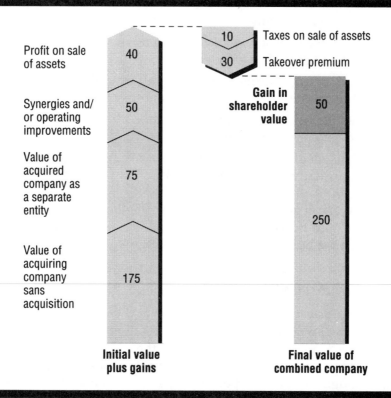

Profit on sale of assets	40
	10 Taxes on sale of assets
	30 Takeover premium
Synergies and/ or operating improvements	50
	Gain in shareholder value 50
Value of acquired company as a separate entity	75
	250
Value of acquiring company sans acquisition	175

Initial value plus gains   **Final value of combined company**

how the gains can be attained. For example, will quantity discounts be gained in ordering materials; will working capital be reduced; or will plant and equipment be utilized more efficiently? When two business units are combined, often savings are realized from sales force reductions. In another case, in a shrinking industry, an acquisition allowed a company to shut down one of its competitors and thereby retard further price reductions and cut transportation costs. Another possibility is that, to the extent the cash flows of the two companies are not highly correlated, their combination may reduce costs associated with cash flow variability. For example, it may be possible to carry more debt, to realize the tax shelters immediately instead of having to carry them forward or back, or to avoid costly layoffs and retraining.

The proper economic perspective for acquisitions is to value the acquiring company without the acquisition and then with it. If the value does not increase after deducting the takeover premium and taxes, the merger should not be pursued. Too often a myopic perspective results in valuing the cash flow of the takeover candidate alone without putting equal weight on how the cash flow of the acquiring firm might change. For example, a well-established, mature company may wish to acquire a portfolio of small, new technology companies (even though many will fail) because if one of them succeeded on its own, the cash flow of the mature company would be significantly and adversely affected. This strategy is particularly relevant in industries where changing technology is important.

DETERMINING THE OPTIMAL RESTRUCTURED VALUE OF A MULTIBUSINESS COMPANY

The final stage of the restructuring pentagon is to determine the optimal value of the company—the sum of all internal and external improvements. The difference between this and the market-determined value of the company represents value that can be attained by current management if it has the will and foresight to implement changes in a timely manner. As we illustrated in Chapter 2, the best management will make sure that the value gap between existing and restructured values is as small as possible in order to benefit all of the company's stakeholders in the face of global competition.

SUMMARY

Large multibusiness companies can benefit tremendously from a self-evaluation that values each business unit as well as the corporate center. Business units that would be more valuable if operated by someone else should be divested; other units that are earning less than their cost of capital and cannot be sold, should be liquidated. Viable core businesses should be improved and growth should be enhanced either through internal investment or via merger and acquisition. In a competitive environment, management must continually obtain the maximum return from its portfolio of businesses. Failure to do so means pressure from activist shareholders, or a takeover attempt, or loss of employment to global competition.

REVIEW QUESTIONS

1. What is the relationship between the weighted average cost of capital and the return required by pure business risk?

2. The cost of equity capital changes with debt structures. Show how and why this is so.

3. Discuss the relationship between business risk and equity risk. What is the relationship between the unlevered beta and the levered beta?

4. In projected cash flows for Hershey you notice that the market beta is 1.009, nearly the same as the index for the average asset in the economy. The debt to equity ratio is 1:3. If Hershey decides to expand its operations by issuing more debt, what will happen to the cost of equity?

5. A diversified mining and chemical firm has an opportunity to establish a basic chemicals operation in Southeast Asia. Project financing partners are willing to stake debt at 20 percent of the total estimated project outlay. Use the data in the following table to determine what return the company should expect to earn on its 80 percent equity stake.

	Dow	Dupont	Olin	United
Beta	1.25	1.15	1.3	1.25
Long-Term Debt ($,000)	3,338,000	3,232,000	474,000	1,408,000
Average Stock Price	57	28	50	83
Shares Outstanding (,000)	275,300	718,450	20,500	68,830
Bond Rate	9.75%	9.20%	10.45%	9.75%

12

Valuing Foreign
Subsidiaries

Valuing foreign subsidiaries of multinational companies follows
the same basic approach and employs the same principles as valuing business units of domestic companies. However, several new
wrinkles need to be considered:

- Foreign currency translation.
- Differences in foreign tax and accounting regulations.
- The interrelationship between transfer pricing and foreign
  taxes.
- The lack of good data (Appendix B at the end of the book in-
  cludes a list of currently available public sources for non-U.S.
  company data).
- The need to evaluate political risk.
- The effect of foreign exchange (FX) hedging on value.
- Determining the appropriate cost of capital.

We shall discuss these issues in the context of reviewing the steps
in the process of valuing a foreign subsidiary.

A PREVIEW OF THE PROCESS

Exhibit 12.1 illustrates the cash flow pattern for a hypothetical parent company domiciled in the United States with a wholly owned

---

Exhibit 12.1 **CASH FLOW FOR A U.S. COMPANY'S FOREIGN SUBSIDIARY**

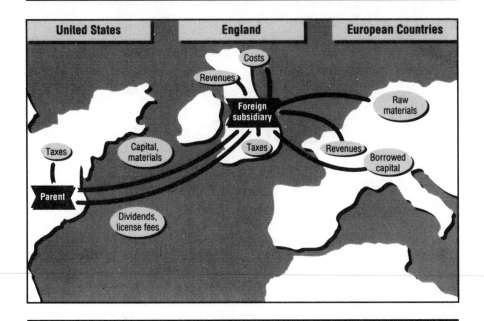

subsidiary domiciled in England, which receives revenues from France (as well as from England), pays for raw materials supplied from Denmark (in addition to labor and raw material costs in England), and borrows in Switzerland (as well as in England). The English subsidiary receives capital and materials from its U.S. parent and returns cash flow in the form of dividends and license fees. Taxes are paid by the parent in the United States and by the subsidiary in England. This example is sufficiently rich to illustrate most of the complexities of valuing a foreign subsidiary, and we will follow it throughout this chapter. We will assume that this valuation is from inside the parent company—that is, that we have full access to internal financial and planning data for the multinational parent.

Exhibit 12. 2 shows the steps in valuing a foreign subsidiary. These steps constitute the major portion of this chapter. The starting point is to forecast free cash flow in each foreign currency. For our example company, we will forecast English revenues in pounds sterling and French revenues in francs. Next, we will con-

Exhibit 12.2 **STEPS IN VALUING A FOREIGN SUBSIDIARY**

1. Forecast free cash flow in the foreign currency

- Use nominal foreign currency cash flow
- Make accounting adjustments for FX translation, foreign accounting standards, and for "hidden assets"
- Use foreign inflation predictions
- Estimate the effective tax rate
- Use appropriate transfer prices

2. Use forward FX rates to convert cash flow to subsidiary's domestic currency

- Predict forward FX rates
- Translate foreign-denominated cash flow to subsidiary's domestic currency

3. Estimate the subsidiary's cost of capital

- Estimate subsidiary's capital structure
- Estimate cost of equity
- Estimate after-tax cost of debt
- Use the after-tax weighted average cost of capital to discount cash flows

4. Estimate the subsidiary value in your domestic currency

- Discount the foreign currency free cash flow at the subsidiary's cost of capital
- Translate the subsidiary value to your currency using the spot FX rate

vert nonsterling cash flow into pounds sterling by using forward FX rates. Once we have converted all expected cash flow to pounds, we will discount it at the English cost of capital. We will then convert the resulting sterling value to dollars, the home currency, by using the spot FX rate.

The last part of this chapter focuses on two valuation issues that relate to most situations, although they are not discussed as steps: evaluation of political risk and the effect of FX hedging on value.

STEP 1: FORECAST FREE CASH FLOW IN THE FOREIGN CURRENCY

In the first step, our objective is to accurately forecast foreign currency cash flow, not to translate it into the domestic currency of our foreign subsidiary. Regardless of the currency involved, it is important to carefully attend to differences in accounting standards, inflation rates, and tax rates. Transfer pricing is also important and can be tricky. For example, when tax considerations are relevant, the best transfer price may not be the market price, but rather the price that minimizes the multicountry tax burden of the parent company.

Use Nominal Foreign Currency Cash Flow

Since most business executives think in terms of future cash flow forecasts that include inflationary expectations, and since market discount rates also reflect expected inflation, we recommend that foreign currency cash flow forecasts be stated in nominal rather than real terms.

Make Accounting Adjustments

To forecast expected cash flow to the foreign subsidiary in foreign currency units, certain accounting adjustments must be made. As long as foreign subsidiary cash flow is forecasted in the foreign currency, no problems arise when doing a valuation. Often, however, financial statements of the foreign subsidiary have already been converted by the parent company using U.S. accounting standards, and it may be necessary to adjust them back to the foreign currency to avoid distorting cash flow forecasts. The following paragraphs discuss three issues: (1) how to deal with foreign exchange translation; (2) the need to understand foreign accounting standards; and (3) the need to search for "hidden assets" that can lead to understating the value.

Dealing with foreign exchange translation   When historical financials based on U.S. accounting standards are supplied by the parent, they should be restated in their original foreign currency units before an attempt is made to forecast foreign currency cash flow. This will help you avoid occasional distortions created by U.S. accounting conventions. It is especially important to focus on cash flow in high-inflation economies, because cash accounting accurately reflects the timing of cash flow while accrual accounting does not. If you cannot obtain subsidiary historical financials stated in the foreign currency from the parent, you should reverse-engineer the U.S. financial statements.

To reverse-engineer the U.S. statements, you must understand the accounting principles involved. In 1981, the U.S. Financial Accounting Standards Board issued FASB No. 52 on Foreign Currency Translation. For "normal inflation" economies (where prices *less* than double in a three-year period), translation gains and losses on the balance sheet are carried directly to the equity account under the *current method* of accounting and do not affect net income. The current exchange rate is applied to all balance sheet items except equity, and the average exchange rate for the period is used for translating the income statement. For "high inflation" economies (where prices *more* than double in three years), the *temporal method* is used (FASB No. 8). Historical exchange rates are applied to assets carried at historical costs, and current rates to monetary current assets.

Both methods are illustrated in the example set out in Exhibit 12.3. The foreign subsidiary is assumed to have acquired fixed assets at the beginning of the year when the foreign currency was at $0.95 per unit. By year's end the exchange rate was $0.85, and the average during the year was $0.90. The subsidiary used last-in-first-out (LIFO) inventory accounting with an applicable historical exchange rate of $0.91.

The temporal method begins by estimating the dollar equivalent for all assets and liabilities and computing retained earnings, $85, as a residual. Since no dividends are paid, retained earnings (or the change in retained earnings) must equal net income. Once all income statement items have been determined, the foreign exchange gain of $70 is computed as a plug figure. Note that since no cash flow (past, present, or future) is associated with the foreign exchange gain, it is irrelevant for valuation.

The current method, under FASB 52, starts with the income statement, converting all items at the average exchange rate during the year. Net income is transferred as retained earnings to the

Exhibit 12.3 **EXAMPLE OF TRANSLATING FOREIGN SUBSIDIARY FINANCIAL STATEMENTS**

Balance sheet	Foreign currency	Temporal method Rates used	Temporal method U.S. dollars	Current method Rates used	Current method U.S. dollars
Cash and receivables, net	100	.85	$ 85	.85	$ 85
Inventory	300	.91	273	.85	255
Fixed assets, net	600	.95	570	.85	510
	1,000		$928		$850
Current liabilities	180	.85	153	.85	153
Long-term debt	700	.85	595	.85	595
Equity					
Common stock	100	.95	95	.95	95
Retained earnings	20		85		18
Equity adjustment from foreign currency translation	—		—		(11)
	1,000		$928		$850
Income statement					
Revenue	130	.90	$117	.90	$117
Cost of goods sold	(60)	.93*	(56)	.90	(54)
Depreciation	(20)	.95*	(19)	.90	(18)
Other expenses, net	(10)	.90	(9)	.90	(9)
Foreign exchange gain/(loss)	—		70		—
Income before taxes	40		103		36
Income taxes	(20)	.90	(18)	.90	(18)
Net income	20		$ 85		$ 18

Source: Peat, Marwick, Mitchell and Company, Statement of Financial Accounting Standards, No. 52, Foreign Currency Translation (1981), p. 52.

* Historical rates for cost of goods sold and depreciation of fixed assets.

balance sheet; all assets and liabilities are translated at the current spot exchange rate; common stock is translated at the historical rate; and the equity adjustment from foreign currency translation is a plug figure.

Understanding foreign accounting standards   This book cannot cover every accounting system in the world and the many changes that occur every year. The best that we can do is to describe a few key problems and hope that these examples will help you discover the rest. As always, the objective is to identify all cash flow to the subsidiary as a first step. More information about how to do this is provided in Chapter 13.

Conventions for restating balance sheets often cause problems. Many countries allow assets to be restated periodically at market or replacement value. This can make measuring the gross investment component of cash flow difficult. For the purpose of calculating free cash flow, gross investment must be a cash outlay equal to cash changes in working capital, capital expenditures, cash investment in goodwill, and cash increases in net other assets. These figures can always be determined on U.S. accounting statements because balance sheet figures are stated as book values. Any changes, therefore, are cash flow. This relationship breaks down if assets are periodically restated to market value. The solution is usually to reverse market value figures by figuring out the changes in equity that are not attributable to retained earnings.

Consolidation standards are another frequently encountered problem. For example, part of the reason that the price-to-earnings ratios of Japanese companies are high (often in hundreds) relative to U.S. standards is that Japanese parent firms do not consolidate the earnings of their minority ownership in a large number of sub-sidiaries (and dividends paid by subsidiaries are extremely low). The numerator of the price-to-earnings ratio, the market value of the parent, reflects ownership of subsidiaries, but the denominator, earnings, does not—hence the high ratio. Whenever the appropri-ate information is attainable, all cash flow attributable to a business unit from ownership of subsidiary assets and liabilities should be consolidated for the purpose of valuing the business unit.

Searching for "hidden assets"   In some countries, the difference between the market and book values of assets can be substantial. For instance, Japanese companies customarily own minority inter-ests in the common stock of their business partners (customers and suppliers). These securities are rarely traded and remain on the books at their historical purchase price, often a small fraction of the current worth. Their current market value should be captured in your valuation.

Real estate is another example of a hidden asset whose book value is often far below the market value you should attribute to it in your valuation. Be careful, however, because market value of real estate reflects its rental value. Only the value of underutilized land should be included. If the company is using land that it owns and if it sells the land, then it has to pay tax on the sale and it must pay rent on the property where it relocates. These costs should also be reflected in your valuation.

Use Foreign Inflation Predictions

In addition to understanding the accounting conventions of the countries in question, you should take their economic climates into account by using foreign inflation predictions to forecast nominal cash flow. Even if you are estimating cash flow for an English subsidiary, growth rates for revenues denominated in pesetas should be consistent with forecasted Spanish inflation rates, not English inflation rates. In Chapter 7, we discussed how to calculate expected inflation given the term structure of interest rates and an estimate of the real rate of return.

Estimate the Effective Tax Rate

The taxation of multinational corporations is complex. Furthermore, tax codes are constantly changing. Any valuation requires understanding at least two perspectives: the domestic code applicable to the parent and the code of the foreign country where the subsidiary is located. And, in most cases, it also requires understanding tax codes (and their enforcement) in every country where the parent company and its subsidiaries do business. If taxes are material to your valuation, consult a qualified tax expert.

One technical issue relevant to valuing subsidiaries of multinational companies is the treatment of foreign tax credits. Exhibit 12.4 provides examples of current U.S. tax treatment of foreign tax credits. In this example, the local tax rates are 34 percent on U.S. income, 20 percent on income in Country E, and 60 percent on Country M income. U.S. taxes are computed as 34 percent of consolidated pretax income less foreign tax credits, which may not exceed 34 percent of foreign income. Therefore, whenever foreign tax credits reach the maximum allowable under U.S. law, as in the first example in Exhibit 12.4, consolidated taxes paid equal the total of local taxes, and no corporate tax penalty is levied. However, when tax credits are below the maximum allowable, as in the second example in Exhibit 12.4, consolidated taxes exceed the total of local taxes, and a U.S. corporate tax penalty is levied. In effect, the U.S.

Exhibit 12.4 **TAX CALCULATIONS FOR A U.S. COMPANY WITH AND WITHOUT EXCESS FOREIGN TAX CREDITS**

1. With excess foreign tax credits

	U.S.	Country E ops.	Country M ops.	Consolidated
Pretax income	$1,000	$200*	$300*	$1,500
Local tax rate	× 34%	×20%	×60%	
Local taxes	340	40	180	
U.S. tax rate				× 34%
Preliminary U.S. taxes				510
Less: foreign tax credits				−170**
Net U.S. taxes				340
Foreign taxes				+220
Consolidated income taxes				560
Less: total local taxes				−560
Corporate tax penalty				0

2. Without excess foreign tax credits

	U.S.	Country E ops.	Country M ops.	U.S., E, and M consolidated	U.S. and M consolidated
Pretax income	$1,000	$400*	$100*	$1,500	$1,100
Local tax rate	× 34%	× 20%	× 60%		
Local taxes	340	80	60		
U.S. tax rate				× 34%	× 34%
Preliminary U.S. taxes				510	374
Less: foreign tax credits				−140**	−34
Net U.S. taxes				370	340
Foreign taxes				+140	+60
Consolidated income taxes				510	400
Less: total local taxes				−480	−400
Corporate tax penalty				30	0

* Includes only income subject to U.S. tax rates.
** Foreign tax credit is the foreign taxes paid or the foreign income times U.S. tax rate ($500 × 34% = $170), whichever is lower.

tax code may raise the effective tax rate for subsidiaries located in lower-tax countries.

For the second example in Exhibit 12.4, the U.S. tax code has raised the average effective tax rate to the parent company on income in Country E from 20 percent to $(30 + 80)/400 = 27.5$ percent. The marginal effective tax rate on Country E income is 34 percent, the U.S. tax rate. Hence, the effective tax rate in a foreign country may not be its domestic statutory rate, because given the specific circumstances, it may depend on the parent company's tax rate. For the second example in Exhibit 12.4, if this situation were expected to persist for the long run, it might be advisable for the parent to sell Company E to an owner from Country E. The reason, of course, is that the after-tax cash flow would be higher from the perspective of a Country E owner.

Use Appropriate Transfer Prices

Many tactics exist for reducing profits in high-tax jurisdictions. For example, you can charge out as many headquarters functions as possible; charge subsidiaries for research and development expenses; borrow at the subsidiary level; consolidate same-country profitable subsidiaries with unprofitable subsidiaries to take advantage of tax-loss carry-forwards; bill back employee stock options to other countries; use cost-plus accounting to reduce foreign profit; increase royalty charges to a foreign subsidiary; establish management-fee arrangements; consider leaving high-tax jurisdictions; and take advantage of transfer pricing. All of these maneuvers are subject to scrutiny by tax authorities. Nevertheless, tax planning obviously can have a major impact on the value of multinational corporations.

Transfer pricing between business units of a multinational company is one of the most important tax minimization methods and determines where profits are reported.[1] The interrelationship between transfer pricing and effective tax rates is complex. For instance, let us go back to Exhibit 12.4, and suppose that the profits

---

[1] Actually, foreign income is separated into ten "income baskets" by the 1986 U.S. Tax Reform Act. Baskets are categorized by type of income—for example, passive interest, DISC dividends, foreign-trade income of foreign sales corporations, and foreign oil and gas extraction income. Income that generates high foreign tax credits can be combined with low-foreign-tax-credit income within but not across baskets.

reflected in the first example are based on market prices. The economics textbooks usually recommend that, tax considerations aside, all decision making should be based on market prices. In this example, however, tax considerations cannot be ignored. Suppose transfer pricing enables the parent company to shift $200 of pretax income from its subsidiary in Country M, the high-domestic-tax country, to Country E, the low-tax environment. The results are shown in the next-to-last column of the second example. Consolidated income taxes have declined from $560 to $510, but a corporate tax penalty of $30 emerges.

The $30 corporate tax penalty under the transfer-pricing scheme makes it tempting to consider selling Subsidiary E to a foreign company also domiciled in Country E. But from the perspective of the buyer, the subsidiary can earn only $200 of pretax profits, calculated using market prices, not the parent's artificial transfer prices. Therefore, the value of business-unit E depends on one's point of view. From the parent's point of view, using artificial transfer prices, it is worth $3,200, given the assumptions in Exhibit 12.5.

$$(\$400 - \$80) \div 10\% = \$3,200.$$

But from the point of view of an owner domiciled in Country E and using market prices, it is worth only

$$(\$200 - \$40) \div 10\% = \$1,600.$$

Exhibit 12.5 **VALUE OF VARIOUS BUSINESS COMBINATIONS TO THE PARENT***

Business combination	Using example 1 in Exhibit 10.4, which assumes market pricing	Using example 2 in Exhibit 10.4, which assumes transfer pricing
Combined U.S. + M + E	$9,400	$9,900
Sell E, keep U.S. and M	9,400	8,600
Sell M, keep U.S. and E	9,120	9,640
All three separate	9,400	8,600

* Values are estimated by assuming the businesses have no debt, that cash flows are perpetuities, and that the cost of capital is 10 percent.

After considering the interaction of transfer pricing and the U.S. tax code for multinationals, the optimum decision for the U.S. parent is to employ transfer pricing to minimize taxes and to retain both of its foreign subsidiaries. As shown in Exhibit 12.5, the value of this combination is the pretax profit, $1,500, less consolidated taxes of $510, capitalized at 10 percent, for a total of $9,900. If Subsidiary E were sold for $1,600 (after taxes), the total value (including the value of the U.S. operation and the subsidiary in M) would be only $8,600.

The answer would change if the situation in example 2 of Exhibit 12.4 were to reflect market prices. Then, it would be best to sell Subsidiary E. The resulting value (not shown in Exhibit 12.5) would be $3,200 from selling Subsidiary E, plus $7,000 for the remaining U.S. plus M operation. The alternative of keeping all three operations would be worth only $9,900.

Some companies build simulation models to deal with the complexities of tax minimization and ownership. An "as is" valuation of a foreign subsidiary should assume the actual pricing mechanism employed by the parent, whether it is an artificial transfer-pricing or a market-pricing mechanism. An assessment of restructured values, however, should look at all alternatives and all points of view to discover how the greatest value can be created by changing pricing mechanisms or changing ownership.

STEP 2: CONVERT ALL CASH FLOW TO THE SUBSIDIARY'S DOMESTIC CURRENCY

Once all cash flow has been forecasted in terms of the currency where it originates, it should be converted into the currency of the subsidiary prior to discounting. We call this the *forward-rate method* for evaluating foreign cash flow. If all of the subsidiary's cash flow is already denominated in local currency, step 2 is unnecessary and you can skip to step 3.

The forward-rate method is useful when separate components of cash flow must be valued—for example, French sales revenues received by the English subsidiary but denominated in francs. This method uses the forward foreign exchange rate to convert forecasted French franc flow to sterling cash flow on a year-by-year basis. Then it combines this with other sterling-equivalent cash flow received by the English subsidiary, and discounts it at the

English weighted average cost of capital. As a practical matter, for most currencies forward exchange rates are not available farther out than 18 months. Therefore, using this method means forecasting long-term foreign exchange rates, a task that will be explained shortly.

A mathematically equivalent alternative to the forward-rate method is the *spot-rate method*. We will employ it in step 3 to discount all of the subsidiary's cash flow, which has been restated in pounds sterling at the English subsidiary's cost of capital, to translate its present value to U.S. dollars at the spot exchange rate.

The spot-rate method is not generally used to convert partial cash flow such as a revenue stream denominated in French francs, because no practical way exists to estimate a risk-adjusted French discount rate for the revenue stream alone. Estimating the appropriate discount rate for total cash flow from operations is difficult enough.

To implement the forward-rate method, you must (1) use interest-rate parity to forecast future spot foreign exchange rates, and (2) use the future spot FX rates to convert future predicted foreign currency cash flow into the subsidiary's domestic currency. To illustrate, we will focus on a stream of revenue received from France by the English subsidiary. The forecasted French franc costs are illustrated in Exhibit 12.6.

Use Interest-Rate Parity to Forecast Forward FX Rates

Forecasting foreign exchange rates depends on using the interest-rate parity theory, which is founded on the idea that changes in foreign exchange rates are based on the ratio of expected inflation rates between two countries. Exhibit 12.7 plots the relationship between domestic inflation and domestic interest rates for 47 countries over the period 1977 to 1981. Indeed, inflation does explain most of the difference in nominal interest rates within each country.

Across countries, the interest-rate parity theory is expressed as follows: the expected spot foreign exchange rate in year t, X_{ft}, is equal to the current spot FX rate, X_0, multiplied by the ratio of nominal rates of return in the two countries over the forecast interval, t.[2]

---

[2] For a derivation, see T.E. Copeland and J.F. Weston, *Financial Theory and Corporate Policy*, 3rd edition (Reading, Mass.: Addison Wesley, 1988), 790–803.

Exhibit 12.6 **ENGLISH SUBSIDIARY'S FORECASTED FRENCH REVENUES,**
FRENCH FRANCS, MILLIONS

Year	French franc revenue	Forecasted future spot FX rate, £/franc	£ equivalent cash revenue
1	106 fr.	.0969 £/fr. next year	£10.27
2	114	.0976 £/fr. 2 yrs. ahead	11.13
3	123	.0984 £/fr. 3 yrs. ahead	12.10
4	119	.0987 £/fr. 4 yrs. ahead	11.75
5	125	.0992 £/fr. 5 yrs. ahead	12.40

$$X_{ft} = X_0 \left[\frac{1+N_f}{1+N_d} \right]^t,$$

where

f = the foreign currency.
d = the domestic currency.

To illustrate the theory for a single year, suppose that our English subsidiary can borrow one-year money in Switzerland at a 4 percent nominal interest rate, N_f, while the borrowing rate in England is 7.1 percent. Suppose the spot exchange rate, X_0, is 2.673 Swiss francs per pound sterling, and the one-year forward rate, X_f, is 2.5944 Swiss francs per pound. We can use interest-rate parity to estimate what English borrowing rate a 4 percent Swiss borrowing rate is equivalent to.

$$1 + N_d = (1+N_f)(X_0/X_{ft}).$$
$$= (1.04)(2.673 \text{ Fr.}/£ \div 2.594 \text{ Fr.}/£).$$
$$= 7.15\%.$$

In this example, no practical difference exists between borrowing in England at 7.1 percent or in Switzerland at 4 percent, because the Swiss rate is equivalent to 7.15 percent in England. In our experi-

Exhibit 12.7 **THE RELATIONSHIP BETWEEN INFLATION AND INTEREST RATES IN 47 COUNTRIES**

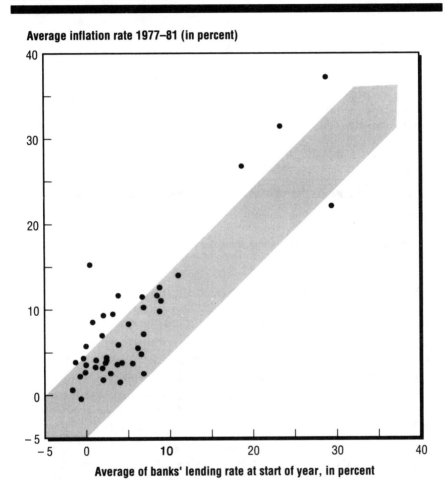

Average inflation rate 1977–81 (in percent)

Average of banks' lending rate at start of year, in percent

Source: Morgan Guaranty Bank World Financial Markets.

ence, the foreign borrowing rate, when converted to a domestic equivalent rate, is usually very close to the domestic rate (unless there are tax implications).

Next, let's show how to use interest-rate parity to forecast future spot FX rates and use that information to convert the French franc revenues in Exhibit 12.6 to English pounds. Exhibit 12.8 uses UK and French data to illustrate. The first two rows are the term

Exhibit 12.8 **EXAMPLE OF FORECASTING FORWARD EXCHANGE RATES***

	1-year	2-year	3-year	4-year	5-year
1. British gilts, N_d	8.71%	8.88	9.03	9.11	9.18
2. French francs, N_f	7.49%	7.86	8.06	8.30	8.43
3. $[(1 + N_d)/(1 + N_f)]^t$	1.0113	1.0195	1.0272	1.0303	1.0351
4. Spot rate £/fr., X_o	.0958	.0958	.0958	.0958	.0958
5. Forecasted forward exchange rate, £/fr., X_f	.0969	.0976	.0984	.0987	.0992
6. Revenues in francs	106.00	114.00	123.00	119.00	125.00
7. Revenues in £	10.27	11.13	12.10	11.74	12.39

Source: Robert LeFevre, SA Supplement, Trimesterial (June 1988); *Financial Times* of London (June 1988); McKinsey analysis.

* N_f and N_d are, respectively, the foreign and domestic nominal interest rates; X_{ft} and X_0 are, respectively, the one-year forward rate in year t and the current spot rate.

structures of interest rates on government debt for England and France in June 1988. The third row is the ratio of nominal rates. We know from the interest-rate parity theory that the ratio of nominal rates multiplied by the current spot rate (pounds/francs) provides an estimate of the forward exchange rate. Remember that the "domestic" currency is francs when converting francs to pounds.

As indicated in the fifth row, the market is forecasting that the pound will weaken versus the franc. If the government bond market is extremely thin or even nonexistent, you will not be able to use the ratio of actual term structures (as in Exhibit 12.8) to help forecast forward exchange rates. In this situation, your best fallback position is to use interest-rate parity directly by supplying your own estimates of the expected real rates and expected inflation rates in both countries.

Convert Forecasted Foreign Cash Flow to the Subsidiary's Domestic Currency

The French franc revenues in line 6 of Exhibit 12.8 are converted to pound sterling revenues (line 7) by using the interest-rate parity relationship. Once all revenues and costs of the English subsidiary have been converted to pounds sterling, the result is a complete forecast of the subsidiary income statement and balance sheet in pounds sterling. The next step is to discount this cash flow at the English weighted average cost of capital.

STEP 3: ESTIMATE FOREIGN CURRENCY DISCOUNT RATE

To estimate the foreign currency discount rate, the general principle is to discount foreign cash flow at foreign risk-adjusted rates. The same assumptions about expected inflation should form the basis for both expected cash flow and the discount rate.

The fact that a subsidiary is located in a foreign country does not change the definition of the weighted average cost of capital. As before,

$$WACC = k_b(1 - T)\frac{B}{B + S} + k_s\frac{S}{B + S},$$

where

k_b = the before-tax cost of debt.
T = the marginal effective tax rate.
B = the market value of debt.
S = the market value of equity.
k_s = the opportunity cost of equity.

The two most common errors in setting the WACC are (1) making ad hoc adjustments for risk; and (2) using the parent country WACC to discount foreign currency cash flow. Regarding the first point, ad hoc adjustments to the discount rate to reflect political risk, foreign investment risk, or foreign currency risk are entirely inappropriate. As we shall explain later on, political risk is best handled by adjusting expected cash flow, weighting it by the probability of various scenarios. Foreign currency or foreign investment risk is handled by the spot exchange rate, and is perfectly symmetrical. An equal chance of a gain or a loss of purchasing power exists. Regarding the second point, it should be clear that if cash flow is predicted in units of the foreign currency, then it should be discounted at the foreign country discount rate, because this rate reflects the opportunity cost of capital in the foreign country, including expected inflation and the market risk premium.

Estimate the Subsidiary Target Capital Structure

The target capital structure for a subsidiary is the mix of financing, stated in market values, that it would maintain in the long run on a stand-alone basis. The actual capital structure imposed on the subsidiary by its parent may depart widely from the subsidiary's target. For tax reasons, the subsidiary may be loaded up with debt, for example. The tax effect of this type of transfer-pricing arrangement is captured when expected cash flow is estimated and should not be double-counted when estimating the discount rate.

If the accounting statements of the subsidiary do not reflect its long-run target capital structure, then it may be possible to locate comparables from the same country, or even to use comparables from other countries. Be cautioned, however, that differing accounting policies regarding the treatment of the book value of assets and of equity, and regarding consolidation, can distort comparables based on book values. Another approach is to use coverage ratios. Given domestic interest rates, determine how much debt could be carried so that the ratio of pretax operating cash flow to interest and other fixed financing charges is reasonable, given industry standards.

Estimate the Cost of Equity

No evidence exists that the capital asset pricing model (CAPM) or the arbitrage pricing model (APM) are not valid within every economy. Although they have already been described earlier in the book, they are rewritten here for convenience.

The CAPM is as follows:

$$E(R_i) = R_f + \left[E(R_m) - R_f\right] \text{beta}_i,$$

where

$E(R_i)$	= the market expected rate of return on the ith security.
R_f	= the risk-free rate.
$E(R_m)$	= the expected rate of return on the market portfolio (usually proxied by an equally weighted equity index).

$E(R_m) - R_f$ = the market risk premium.

beta$_i$ = the undiversifiable risk of the ith security.

The CAPM has been used to explain the market's expected rate of return on all securities. If you have an estimate of the beta for equity, then $E(R_i) = k_s$ and the cost of equity can be estimated directly from the CAPM. The APM is as follows:

$$E(R_i) = R_f + \left[E(f_1) - R_f\right]\text{beta}_{i1} + \ldots + \left[E(f_N) - R_f\right]\text{beta}_{iN},$$

where

$E(f_1)$ = the expected return on factor 1.

$E(f_N)$ = the expected return on factor N.

beta$_{i1}$ = undiversifiable risk of security i relative to factor 1.

$E(f_1) - R_f$ = the risk premium for factor 1.

Regardless of which model is used, the major problem outside of the United States is lack of good data. Appendix B lists sources for betas for companies in most developed countries. They can be used to find comparables for business-unit betas using the methods recommended in Chapter 11. Government bond rates from the country where the subsidiary is located can be used as estimates of the risk-free rate (unless serious default risk exists). If government debt is not reasonably risk-free, then the interest rate parity theory can be used to convert U.S. government rates to foreign country equivalents.

Almost no information is readily available on market risk premiums—that is, $E(R_m) - R_f$—for non-U.S. economies. In many cases, however, it can easily be estimated from publicly available data sources. For example, an estimate for Germany was obtained by using monthly data for the difference between short-term government debt and the monthly rate of return for the Frankfurt stock index from 1970 to 1985. The average geometric difference, 3.8 percent, is an estimate of the market risk premium over this time period.[3] Over the same time interval, the (geometric) risk premium in the United States was 2 percent. To estimate the long-term geometric risk premium for Germany, we add the differential over the 1970

---

[3] Our thanks to Professor Hermann Göppl at Karlsruhe Universität for providing this estimate.

to 1985 interval—that is, 3.8 percent −2 percent = 1.8 percent—to the long-term U.S. market risk premium, 5.0 percent, to obtain 6.8 percent. Similar logic for Japan produces a result of approximately 4.2 percent. Because of the globalization of capital markets, it is reasonable to assume that market risk premiums are approximately equal across developed nations.[4]

The debate about the relative costs of capital among countries continues. The overarching principle, however, is that in the absence of effective government controls to block the flow of capital, the required return on investments of equivalent risk must be the same across all national borders *after adjusting for expected inflation.* If this were not a valid principle, then enormous flows of capital would quickly bring markets into equilibrium. Understanding inflation and risk differentials is key. As we saw earlier, a 4 percent borrowing rate in Switzerland is not necessarily cheaper than a 7 percent rate in England, because Switzerland has lower expected inflation. Furthermore, a 4.2 percent risk premium in Japan is not necessarily cheaper than a 5.0 percent premium in the United States, because the risk of the Nikkei is less than that of the S&P 500, for two reasons: (1) the Nikkei is more of a blue chip index, and (2) the Japanese bonus system of worker compensation provides a better buffer to protect shareholders in bad times. When a company is successful, Japanese workers receive very large bonuses (by U.S. standards) but when revenues are less than expected, workers may receive little or nor bonus. The effect is to provide a cushion that reduces the variability of free cash flow to shareholders.

Estimate the After-Tax Cost of Debt

As with equity, the objective regarding debt is to use the foreign country opportunity cost to discount cash flow estimated in terms of the foreign currency.

The cost of nonconvertible, noncallable debt is its expected yield to maturity. If debt is callable or convertible, you can refer to Chapter 15 of this book.

The relevant tax rate is the statutory marginal tax rate in the country where the subsidiary resides. It is the tax shield that would

---

[4] For evidence to support this point of view, see S. Wheatley, "Some Tests of International Equity Integration," *Journal of Financial Economics* (September 1988): 177–212.

prevail if one more unit of debt were added, or zero if no debt tax shield is available (either because other tax shields completely exhaust taxable profits or because interest on debt is not tax-deductible).

Use the After-Tax Weighted Average Cost of Capital

If the subsidiary's target capital structure is assumed to remain constant, then the WACC can also be kept constant over the relevant discount period. An exception to this rule would arise if government controls were expected to change market rates in a predictable fashion.

STEP 4: DISCOUNT FREE CASH FLOW AND TRANSLATE TO THE DOMESTIC CURRENCY

Having determined the subsidiary's weighted average cost of capital, you are ready to discount the free cash flow forecasted in step 1 and convert it to your domestic currency. Exhibit 12.9 shows expected free cash flow to our example subsidiary in England. It is discounted to the present at the subsidiary's WACC, assumed to be 11.8 percent, and then converted to dollars by multiplying the present value in pounds sterling by the spot exchange rate, 0.560 pounds/dollar.

One caveat is in order here: Because we have discounted cash flow to the subsidiary, its present value in the domestic currency (dollars in our example) to the parent may be different if a country has restrictions that limit the expatriation of free cash flow back to the parent. Although ways around these constraints can sometimes be found—for example, barter or transfer pricing—the thing to keep in mind is that the value to the parent depends on the quantity and timing of free cash flow (or cash equivalents) that can actually be paid out.

VALUING POLITICAL RISK AND THE EFFECT OF HEDGING

Two topics remain to be discussed: how to evaluate political risk and the effect of FX hedging on value. Both topics are thorny. Effective evaluation of political risk, even if handled in the techni-

Exhibit 12.9 **ENGLISH SUBSIDIARY FREE CASH FLOW, DISCOUNTED AT THE ENGLISH RATE AND CONVERTED TO DOLLARS**

	Free cash flow	Present value factor at 11.8% foreign rate	Present value
1989	£100	0.8945	£89.45
1990	115	0.8000	92.01
1991	130	0.7156	93.03
1992	142	0.6401	90.89
1993	160	0.5725	91.60
1994	180	0.5121	92.18
1995	196	0.4580	89.78
1996	225	0.4097	92.18
1997	252	0.3665	92.35
1998	280	0.3278	91.78
Continu-ing value	2,653	0.3278	869.61
		PV in £	£1,784.86
		÷ Spot rate £/$	÷ 0.56
		= PV in $	$3187.25

cally appropriate fashion (as discussed in this section) depends largely on obtaining good information. Otherwise, analysis merely amounts to garbage-in-garbage out. Hedging is a conceptually difficult topic mainly because it is hard to justify on theoretical grounds as beneficial to shareholders.

Evaluating Political Risk

Political risks take many forms. Exhibit 12.10 shows the results of interviews of 80 managers of multinational firms who ranked various risk categories from highest risk (1) to lowest risk (10).[5] Often overlooked are the major political risks in industrialized countries (such as price controls), which can be equally as devastating as risks in less-developed countries.

[5] S. J. Kobrin, *Managing Political Risk Assessment: Strategic Response to Political Change* (Berkeley: University of California Press, 1982).

Exhibit 12.10 **RELATIVE IMPORTANCE OF POLITICAL RISKS, ACCORDING TO MANAGERS OF MULTINATIONALS**

Less-developed countries		Industrialized countries	
Mean/ rank	Risk	Mean/ rank	Risk
1.8	Civil disorder	3.2	Price controls
2.4	Expropriation	3.7	Labor disruptions
3.6	War	4.4	Remittance restrictions
5.3	Remittance restrictions	5.5	Civil disorder
5.5	Labor disruptions	5.5	Fiscal changes
5.7	Partial expropriation	6.0	Expropriation
6.0	Price controls	6.9	Partial expropriation
7.3	Fiscal changes	7.2	Contract cancellation
7.6	Contract cancellation	8.4	War

Source: S. J. Kobrin (1982).

The scenario approach to risk analysis used to forecast expected cash flow domestically can be applied equally well to foreign political risk. Exhibit 12.11 provides a simplified example suggested by Robert Stobaugh, Jr.[6] In this example, the economic outcomes can be regrouped into four mutually exclusive scenarios. Either the plant is not nationalized, or it is nationalized with adequate compensation, inadequate compensation, or no compensation. When these scenarios are matched with cash flow estimates, expected cash flow can be estimated year by year and discounted back to the present. The values obtained in this way can then be multiplied by the probabilities of each outcome, to obtain an expected value. Although assigning probabilities to scenarios is difficult, we recommend this approach over the alternative—arbitrarily raising the hurdle rate—because cash flow scenarios require careful thought, and as a result can provide better insights into the problem. Remember, though, that the expected (or average) outcome will never occur. It is only a probability-weighted average of all the things that might happen.

[6] R. Stobaugh, Jr., "How to Analyze Foreign Investment Climates," *Harvard Business Review* (September/October 1969): 108.

Exhibit 12.11 **HYPOTHETICAL CASH FLOW SCENARIOS FOR POLITICAL RISK EVALUATION**

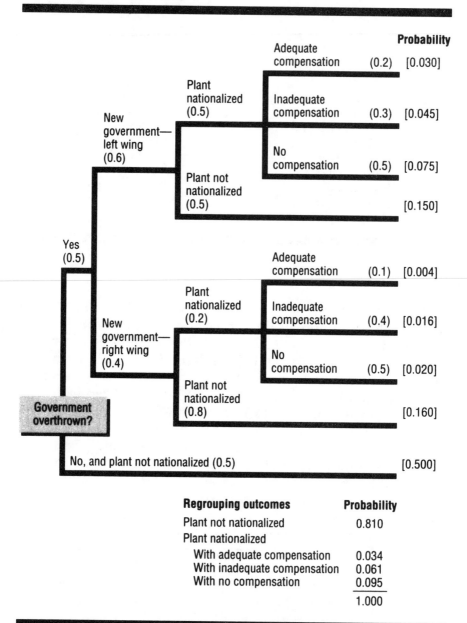

Source: R. Stobaugh, Jr. (1969).

If the country where the subsidiary is domiciled imposes restrictions on the amount of capital that can be repatriated, the parent can discount only that portion of cash flow that is available for repatriation. In some cases, this may imply that the subsidiary is worth more if sold to a buyer from the country where the subsidiary resides. In other situations, it may mean that the subsidiary should be closed down entirely.

Valuing the Effect of Hedging

It is not unusual for multinational companies to take large positions in foreign exchange forward contracts to hedge against unexpected changes in floating exchange rates. Though designed to reduce currency risk, this practice is risky in itself. It has resulted in many well-publicized disasters. For example, Volkswagen lost $200 million, and Spectra Physics had an entire year's profits wiped out by inappropriate foreign exchange trading positions. Mettalgeselschaft lost a reported $1.2 billion in 1993. Also, other ways of hedging exist. For example, if the local currency might decline in value, a company can reduce holding of local currency cash and marketable securities; delay accounts payable; invoice exports in the foreign currency and imports in the domestic currency; tighten trade credit in the foreign currency; and borrow more in the foreign currency.

Hedging programs can affect the expected cash flow of a company, its opportunity cost of capital, both, or neither. Exhibit 12.12 shows the trade-off between risk and return from two perspectives: total and undiversifiable risk. All successful hedges decrease total risk, but not necessarily undiversifiable risk.[7] Hedging programs that do not change expected cash flow or expected returns do not change the undiversifiable risk (the beta) of the company. They are merely diversifying; they have no effect on value because neither expected cash flow nor the discount rate changes. The company starts at point A and stays there. Other hedging programs affect ex-

---

[7] Total risk may be partitioned into diversifiable risk, which is uncorrelated with the economy (usually company-specific events), and undiversifiable risk. Diversifiable risk has no opportunity cost because it can be eliminated at little or no cost. Therefore, diversifiable risk is unrelated to expected rates of return. Undiverisifiable risk (beta) is positively related to expected return, according to the capital asset pricing model.

Exhibit 12.12 **RISK/RETURN TRADE-OFFS OF HEDGING PROGRAMS**

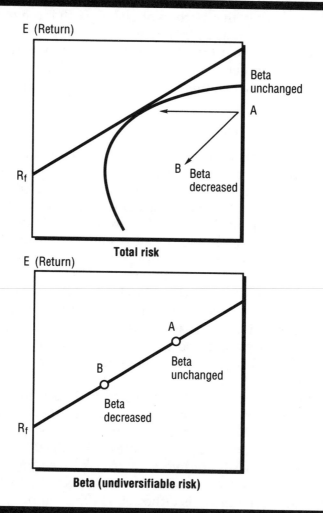

pected cash flow and expected returns. Usually, expected returns decline and so do both diversifiable and undiversifiable risk (beta). The company moves from point A to point B in such a way that the decline in undiversifiable risk is offset by the decline in expected return. Although the risk-return profile of the company has been altered, no change in value necessarily results, because the risk reduction is offset by decreases in expected return. However, both the change in expected cash flow and the change in the discount rate (due to changed undiversifiable risk) should be estimated and included in your valuation if the hedging program has a material effect on the company.

Apart from secondary effects, hedging programs often have little or no effect on value, whether they are static hedges (for example, forward contracts) or dynamic hedges (for example, portfolio insurance).

Although the primary effects of hedging programs are of little concern to us, secondary effect can *sometimes* have a significant impact on value. The most significant secondary effects of hedging are costs associated with variability. Although they do not necessarily affect the opportunity cost of capital, they do affect expected free cash flow and, therefore, the value of the company. Bankruptcy costs are the most obvious example of costs associated with variability. Others are cost of business disruption, for example, loss of skilled labor, cuts in research and development, and loss of customer confidence. Altman (1984) estimates that the expected costs of bankruptcy range from 8.1 percent to 17.5 percent of the value of the company.[8] Hedging programs that can reduce the probability of bankruptcy have their primary effect on expected cash flow. Whenever hedging programs have significant effects on expected cash flow, their impact should be captured in the valuation.

Hedging can also affect the company's effective tax rate. By smoothing cash flow, hedging makes use of carry-forward or carry-back provisions of the tax code unnecessary because tax shields are used immediately. The result is to decrease the company's effective tax rate and thus to increase value. This secondary effect of hedging is usually small and can be ignored.

SUMMARY

This chapter has focused primarily on the example of valuing the English subsidiary of a U.S. parent multinational corporation. The first step was to forecast all cash flow, wherever it occurred, in the local currency. Next, this cash flow was translated year by year into pounds sterling, the subsidiary's currency, by using forecasts of the

---

[8] E. Altman, "A Further Empirical Investigation of the Bankruptcy Cost Question," *Journal of Finance* (September 1984): 1067–1089.

future spot foreign exchange rates. Once all free cash flow was stated in sterling, it was discounted at the weighted average cost of capital for the subsidiary. The resulting sterling value of the company was then converted to dollars at the spot exchange rate.

Along the way, we covered a number of difficult issues: the need to understand foreign (and U.S.) accounting standards, the transfer-pricing problem, forecasting forward FX rates, evaluating political risk, and understanding the effect of FX hedging on value.

REVIEW QUESTIONS

1. Outline the steps in the valuation of a foreign subsidiary. How does the process differ from the valuation of a domestic organization? What are the most important risks encountered in the valuation process?

2. Apply the valuation steps to the Montreal, PQ, Canada-based Quebecor, Inc. The firm's major products and services include advertising, books, daily newspapers, de-inked pulp, wood chips, and woodlands' management. The major subsidiaries of Quebecor include Tej Quebecor (India), Quebecor Printing (USA), Imprimeries Fecome-Quebecor SA (France), and Graficas Monte Alban SA de CV (Mexico), as well as three domestic subsidiaries.

3. The Southern Company, a U.S. electric utility, is about to translate it's Argentinean subsidiary's balance sheet and income statements into U.S. dollars. Argentina is well known for its relatively high inflation rate. Explain the method of foreign currency translation that would be appropriate for Southern Co. The following table presents hypothetical data from the Argentinean subsidiary. Consider both appreciating and depreciating exchange rates.

Argentinean Subsidiary

Cash & Rec Net of NIBCLs	50
Inventory	20
Working Capital	70
Net Fixed Assets	930
	1,000
Debt	720
Equity	280
FX Gain (Loss)	–
	1,000
Revenue	2,000
Operating Costs	(1,760)
SG&A	(100)
Depreciation	(28)
FX Gain	–
Operating Income	112
Taxes	(45)
NOPLAT	67

Argentinean Subsidiary (Continued)

ROIC	6.73%
Tax Rate	40.00%
Op Inc/Sales	5.61%
Sales/Capital	2.00
WC/Sales	3.50%
NFA/Sales	46.50%
Op Exp/Sales	88.00%
SG&A/Sales	5.00%
Dep/Sales	1.40%
Debt/Capital	72.00%
Equity/Capital	28.00%

4. The French subsidiary of Quebecor wants to value the following French franc cash flows:

	1	2	3	4	5	6
Cash Flow (francs)	300	320	410	380	420	450
Nff	6.9375%	7.9375%	9.1375%	10.4375%	11.6375%	12.7375%
Ncd	7.5625%	8.4625%	9.4625%	10.5625%	11.7625%	12.7625%

Provided are the forecasted nominal French franc (Nff) and Canadian dollar one (Ncd) year forward interest rates. The current Canadian dollar to French franc spot rate is 2.27 C$/Ff. The U.S. cost of capital is 14 percent over this forecast period. Your supervisor also needs an explanation of the process whereby you arrived at the present value.

5. A U.S. gas marketing company is bidding on the delivery of Dutch originated (North Sea) natural gas to a German chemical company in 90 days for US $1,000,000. The following rates are quoted by the German chemical company's London bank:

	DM	US$	Fl
90-day Eurocurrency rates in following currencies	0.0575	0.06125	0.050625
Spot Rates currency/US$	1.942		0.609

Should the German chemical firm contract directly with the Dutch producer or work with the U.S. gas marketer?

6. The U.S. subsidiary of Robert Bosch GMBH must purchase German parts to assemble antilock braking systems. Suppose that on April 10, 1995, the factory agrees to buy parts valued at DM 1,000,000 from German producers on June 23, 1995. The factory purchaser believes that the dollar will depreciate further before the sale date, making the DM it must buy more expensive. The currency prices facing the firm on April 10 are 0.7288 $/DM on 125,000 DM/contract June futures. How can the U.S. importer lock in the dollar costs regardless of whether the dollar depreciates or appreciates relative to the DM?

13

Valuation Outside of the United States

In the first chapter of the book we argued that valuation is the best metric for decision making and that the increasing drive for higher productivity, which is being forced by globalization of the world economy, will require managers to take actions that maximize shareholder value. Managers in Europe and to a lesser extent in Asia are reluctant to accept the maximization of shareholder value as the primary reason for using valuation and are therefore unlikely to embrace value-based management. However, they do need to make transactions across borders—joint ventures, divestitures, and acquisitions. In these situations, it is absolutely necessary to have the correct value estimates. Overpaying for acquisitions is a classic mistake. Very often valuation ratios such as price/earnings or market/book ratios are used to accomplish the task. However, as shown in Exhibit 13.1, they are largely useless. Illustrated there are valuation multiples for nine companies in the automobile industry in 1988, located in six different countries. The price-earnings multiples range from 50.5 to 4.8. It is not entirely obvious that Daimler Benz or BMW in Germany would want to pay 19.9 times earnings for Ford, Chrysler, or General Motors when their average P/E is only 4.8. Market-to-book ratios are also badly aligned across countries.

There are two problems with trying to use ratios for cross-border valuations. First, accounting standards across national borders are often quite different. Consequently, earnings of Daimler in

Exhibit 13.1 **INTERNATIONAL COMPARISONS OF VALUATION
MULTIPLES FOR NINE AUTOMOBILE COMPANIES, 1988**

Country	Number of companies	Price/ earnings	Market/ book	Dividend yield
USA	3	4.8	.74	6.5%
Japan	1	17.2	1.90	0.8
England*	1	50.5	5.19	1.8
Sweden	1	10.4	2.33	3.0
Italy	1	5.5	1.21	2.1
W. Germany	2	19.9	2.23	2.0

*Reflects takeover bid for Jaguar by Ford.

Germany, using German commonly accepted accounting princi-
pals, is not the same as earnings for Daimler using U.S. GAAP. For
example, for the first nine months of 1993 Daimler lost $105 million
according to German accounting standards, but according to U.S.
GAAP the company lost $1.19 billion. Either way, cash flow was
the same. Second, it is much better to understand the synergies in a
merger using a detailed discounted cash flow approach rather than
a valuation multiple approach, because the details often force
clearer thinking.

Exhibit 13.2 shows the DCF valuation of the nine automobile
companies. Each was valued using nominal cash flows denominated in the company's home currency (e.g. deutsch marks for
Daimler Benz). Discount rates were also taken from the home country. The market value of the company scaled by its book value was
then regressed against the DCF value also scaled by book. The results show a 93+ percent correlation. Clearly, DCF valuation works
well outside of the United States. In fact, in our collective experience, we have valued companies in over two dozen different countries for activities as diverse as privatization, merger, value-based
management, joint venture, and divestiture. The first edition of this
book was translated into Italian, French, Japanese, and German.
Discounted cash flow valuation is an important decision-making
tool that is being used more and more all around the world.

The remainder of this chapter illustrates many of the problems
of doing valuations around the world by organizing the material

Exhibit 13.2 **CORRELATION BETWEEN DCF AND MARKET VALUE FOR NINE AUTOMOBILE COMPANIES, DECEMBER 1988**

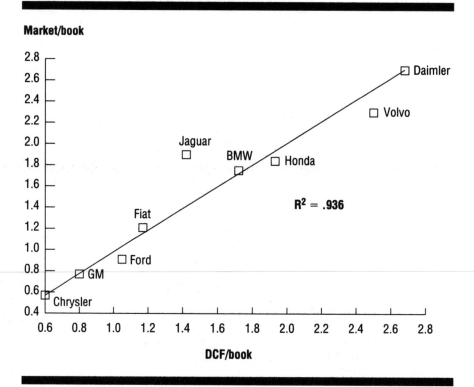

Source: Compustat; Value Line; McKinsey analysis.

into four nonmutually exclusive and certainly not exhaustive segments. The first covers differences in accounting standards that affect the estimation of cash flows. The second discusses the cultural differences that are relevant for valuations—especially in Japan. The third answers whether or not differences in the cost of capital across national borders is an impediment to business activities. And the fourth reviews some of the special problems of valuation in less developed countries.

DIFFERENCES IN ACCOUNTING STANDARDS

Exhibit 13.3 is a return on equity tree for a division of a Dutch insurance company, Aegon, shown two ways—using U.S. GAAP

Exhibit 13.3 **ROE IMPACT OF USING DUTCH ACCOUNTING PRACTICES RATHER THAN U.S. GAAP, 1988,** PERCENT; U.S. $ MILLIONS

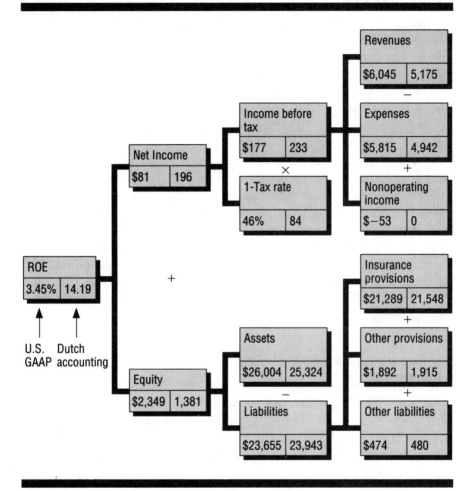

Source: McKinsey analysis.

accounting and using Dutch accounting practices. Aegon's shares are listed on multiple stock exchanges and the company has to report its results using a variety of accounting principles. Using Dutch accounting, its ROE was 14.2 percent in 1988 and using U.S. GAAP its ROE was only 3.5 percent.

There are three major differences that explain the results. First, the Dutch balance sheet does not show goodwill and capitalized expenses. In the Netherlands, goodwill created in an acquisition is usually written off immediately. These differences accounted for 4 percent out of the 11 percent difference. Next, the Dutch income statement does not show nonoperating losses. This accounted for 2 percent out of the difference. Finally, the effective tax rate under Dutch accounting is much lower. This accounted for 5 percent out of the 11 percent difference. This simple example shows the frailty of using accounting based measures of performance, for example the spread between ROE and the cost of equity. Even the economic profit metric would probably show value being created according to Dutch accounting standards and value being destroyed according to U.S. accounting standards.

With discounted cash flow valuation, free cash flows are the same regardless of the accounting standards of the country you are working in. Cash is cash, and any accounting system that has complete information made publicly available can be used to estimate the future cash flows of a company. For example, Exhibit 13.4 shows the correlation between discounted cash flows and market values of 15 Italian companies in 1990. Even though Italian accounting standards are different than those in the U.S., discounted cash flow methodology works very well. The correlation is 95.4 percent.

Six Major Accounting Difficulties

There are six primary areas of concern when comparing accounting systems. They are affected by local accounting standards. The European Economic Community (EEC) is working toward creating common standards within the continent. For example, the seventh directive, which requires consolidation of foreign subsidiaries, was implemented in 1992.

Failure to consolidate the earnings of partially owned or foreign subsidiaries can result in substantial underreporting of the parent company earnings. In some accounting systems the consolidation of foreign subsidiary earnings is voluntary even if the subsidiary is wholly owned. Although the EEC seventh directive has largely eliminated this problem, it remains an issue in other parts of the world.

Reserves are often used to create noncash write-offs of anticipated long-term expenses such as pensions, reorganization, maintenance, and other costs. On the other hand, sometimes deductions are taken from provisions on the balance sheet and taken onto the

Exhibit 13.4 **CORRELATION BETWEEN DCF AND MARKET VALUE FOR 15 ITALIAN COMPANIES, 1990**

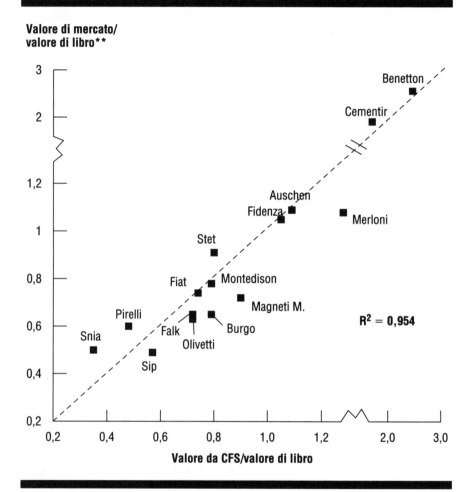

Source: McKinsey analysis.

* Utilizzando informazioni pubbliche.
** Capitalizzazione al 28 settembre 1990 (Borsa valori di Milano), valore di libro del patrimonio netto di competenza al 30/6/1990.

income statement as a reduction of costs. These movements can have the effect of smoothing earnings and result in hidden reserves through excess provisions. To obtain free cash flows, the change in nontax provisions on the balance sheet should be added back to EBIT after taxes.

Many countries allow assets to be written up to market value, assessed value, or replacement cost. This practice can increase and easily distort cross company estimates of the return on invested capital. Furthermore, capital expenditures cannot be calculated as the increase in *net* property and equipment on the balance sheet plus depreciation expense for the period. When fixed assets are revalued at replacement cost (for example), the change in net fixed assets will include a noncash amount for reevaluation. If assets are revalued, capital expenditures must be estimated as the increase in net property, plant, and equipment, minus the change in the revaluation reserve, plus depreciation expenses.

In some countries, for example, Germany, the annual report to the shareholders and the tax books use virtually identical accounting standards, and in other countries, the United States, for example, there are two different sets of books. Differences between earnings as reported on the public financial statements and earnings on the tax books can be created by differences in depreciation methods, deferred tax effects, and by reserve accounting.

Capital and operating leases are substitutes for senior secured debt in the capital structure of the firm. If they are treated as "off balance sheet financing" it becomes more difficult to compare the financial results of companies within the same industry if their mix of owned and leased assets is substantially different.

Goodwill is the difference between the book value of the assets of an acquired company and the price paid in acquisition. The treatment of goodwill varies widely among countries. Goodwill may or may not be a tax deductible expense. It may be written off immediately against reserves (or equity) or it may be written off over a period as long as 40 years. Comparison of ROIC across companies (even within national borders) can be significantly distorted by the treatment of goodwill.

Exhibits 13.5 and 13.6 summarize the accounting treatment of the aforementioned issues as of the beginning of 1993 for most European countries and the United States.

Converting to Cash Flow: A German Example

For all practical purposes German financial statements are identical for tax purposes and for reporting to the public. Since German managers have incentives to reduce their company's tax burden, many accounting practices are used to reduce reported earnings

Exhibit 13.5 **SUMMARY OF MAJOR ACCOUNTING DIFFICULTIES, 1993**

Country	Consolidation of parent and subsidiary accounts required?	Transfers to/from reserves are reasonably traceable?	Periodic asset revaluation allowed?	Reported financial statements may differ from tax accounts
Belgium	Only if ownership exceeds 50%.	Yes.	Only on an item-by-item basis.	Seldom, due to relatively minor timing differences.
Denmark	Yes.	Yes.	Assets may be written up to market value.	Yes, mainly due to book depreciation differing from tax depreciation.
France	Yes, when listed on the stock exchange.	Yes.	Write-up to appraised value is allowed.	Yes, deferred tax effects disclosed in footnotes.
Germany	Required as of December 31, 1989.	Varies, large contingent liabilities or reserves may be undisclosed.	No, fixed assets are carried at cost.	Seldom, due to relatively minor timing issues.
Italy	Only if required by the securities regulatory agency.	Varies, few disclosures and limited prior data restrict tracing.	Yes, according to an index and government decree.	Minor differences due to timing issues.
Netherlands	Mandatory only for group companies.	Yes.	Yes, up to replacement value.	Yes, due to major differences in depreciation and timing methods.

Exhibit 13.5 Continued

Country	Consolidation of parent and subsidiary accounts required?	Transfers to/from reserves are reasonably traceable?	Periodic asset revaluation allowed?	Reported financial statements may differ from tax accounts
Norway	Only if ownership exceeds 50%.	Varies, significant disclosures may be unavailable.	Only under special circumstances.	Extremely rare.
Portugal	No requirement.	No, prior period data and disclosures are usually unavailable.	Yes, according to an official index and government decree.	No.
Spain	No requirement.	Varies, significant disclosures may be unavailable.	Yes, according to an official index and government decree.	Seldom, book and tax accounts are normally the same.
Sweden	Only if ownership exceeds 50%.	Varies, significant disclosures may be unavailable.	Only under special circumstances.	Extremely rare.
Switzerland	No requirements.	No, significant reserves may be undisclosed.	No, historical cost method only.	Extremely rare.
United Kingdom	Yes.	Yes.	Fixed assets may be carried at market value.	Yes, mainly due to depreciation and timing differences.
United States	Yes, if ownership exceeds 50%.	Yes.	No.	Yes.

Exhibit 13.6 **ADDITIONAL MAJOR ACCOUNTING DIFFICULTIES, 1993**

Country	Capitalization of financial leases required?	Purchased goodwill amortization period	Independent third-party audit required for listed companies?
Belgium	Yes.	Immediately against reserves.* to a maximum of 5 years.**	Yes.
Denmark	No requirement.	Immediately against reserves.* to a maximum of 5 years.**	Yes.
France	Not permitted, rental commitments disclosed in notes.	Immediately against reserves.* to a maximum of 5 years.**	Yes.
Germany	No requirement in the civil code.	Amortized up to 15 years for taxes; 1 to 4 years in annual report.	Yes.
Italy	No requirement in the civil code.	Immediately against reserves.* to a maximum of 5 years.**	Yes.
Netherlands	Yes.	Immediately against reserves* to a maximum of 5 years.**	Yes.

Exhibit 13.6 Continued

Country	Capitalization of financial leases required?	Purchased goodwill amortization period	Independent third-party audit required for listed companies?
Norway	No requirement.	Amortized over a "reasonable" period.	Yes.
Portugal	No requirement.	Goodwill accounting not recognized in civil code.	No.
Spain	No requirement.	Amortized over a "reasonable" period.	No.
Sweden	No, unless lease transfers ownership.	Amortized over 10–20 years.	Yes.
Switzerland	No requirement.	Amortized over a "reasonable" period.	Yes.
United Kingdom	Yes.	Immediately against reserves* up to "useful" economic life.	Yes.
United States	Yes.	40 years.	Yes.

* No income statement impact.
** May be extended under certain circumstances.

and thereby tax payments, even thought the "true" economic situation may be different.

Exhibits 13.7 and 13.8 give the income statement and balance sheets for a hypothetical German company. Exhibit 13.9 calculates the free cash flows and the financial flows. To show how the German financial statements can be used to estimate the company's cash flows, we will go through an explanation of each item in Exhibit 13.9. Notice that the total free cash flows from operations equal the total financial flows. The principal of separating operating cash flows from the financial flows is maintained.

Earnings before interest and taxes (EBIT) is the pretax income that the company would have earned if it had no debt and is often equal to the line called "Operating Income" on the company's income statement. EBIT is calculated by subtracting all tax deductible expenses from revenue. Revenue will normally include increases (decreases) in inventory and "own work capitalized," which reflects inventory increases. In Germany, depreciation and goodwill amortization are both tax deductible expenses. One problem for forecasting is that "other income and expense" may contain both ordinary and extraordinary items, which may not be separable except through interviews with management.

For most German corporations, taxable income is determined by annual changes in net worth. Under the net worth comparison method, taxable income is computed with reference to the increase in the company's net worth during the year, excluding items such as contributions to capital, premiums on shares issued, and certain types of foreign source income that are exempt from German taxes under a tax treaty.

Beginning in 1990, the standard rate of corporate income tax for resident companies is 50 percent. This must be considered in conjunction with a dividend distribution rate of 36 percent. For example, suppose a company has profits of DM 100 after all other taxes except for corporate income taxes. A resident company pays corporate income taxes of DM 50 if it retains all profits, or DM 36 if it fully distributes them, giving a dividend of DM 64. Losses may be carried forward indefinitely and carried back two years. These losses may not be transferred via merger or acquisition. Foreign losses may be deducted only if they are sustained in connection with certain "productive" activities (such as the production or distribution of goods). Special rules apply to losses incurred in countries with which Germany has a tax treaty.

Exhibit 13.7 **INCOME STATEMENT, HYPOTHETICAL GERMAN COMPANY,** DM MILLIONS

Umsatz	Sales Revenue	15,000
– Erhöhung order Verninderung des Bestands an fertigen und unfertigen Erzeugnissen	– Increase in finished goods inventory	(100)
+ Andere aktivierte Eigenleistungen	+ Own work capitalized	0
+ Sonstiger betrieblicher Ertag	+ Other operating income	0
– Materialaufwand	– Cost of materials	(6,000)
– Personalaufarand	– Personnel expenses	(4,000)
– Gesamt-Abschreibungen	– Depreciation and amortization	(400)
– Sonstige betriebliche Aufwendungen	– Other expenses	(3,060)*
= Ergebnis der gewöhnlichen Geschäftstätigkeit	= Operating income	1,440
+ Erträge aus Beteiligungen	+ Income from participations	0
+ Erträge aus Werpapieren sowie Zins-und ähnliche Erträge	+ Other financial (interest) income	17
– Zins-und ähnlicher Aufwand	– Interest expense	(431)
= Ergebnis der gewöhnlichen Geschäftstätgkeit	= Results from ordinary activities	1,026
– Sonstige steuern	– Miscellaneous taxes	0
– Steuern vom Einkommen und Ertrag	– Income taxes	(463)
= Jähresüberschuss	= Net income	563
	Dividends	350

* Including change in other provisions of DM 60.

Exhibit 13.8 BALANCE SHEET, HYPOTHETICAL GERMAN COMPANY, DM MILLIONS

		Prior Year	Current Year
Gesamtvermögen =	Total Assets =	12,370	12,663
Netto Sachanlagevermögen =	Net property, plant, and equipment =	4,800	5,000
+ Brutto Sachanagevermögen	+ Gross property plant	7,500	8,000
– Kumulierte Abschreibungen	– Accumulated depreciation	(2,700)	(3,000)
Übriges Vermögen	Other assets	950	1,000
Umlaufveriögen =	Short-term assets =	6,620	6,663
Flüssige Mittel	Cash	90	100
+ Wertpapiere	+ Marketable securities	320	163
+ Forderungen	+ Accounts receivable	2,900	3,000
+ Vorräte	+ Inventories	3,310	3,400
Gesamtes Eigen-und Fremdkapital =	Total liabilities and shareholders equity =	12,370	12,663
Eigenkapital =	Total shareholders equity =	4,390	4,603
Gezeichnetes kapital	Common shares	1,000	1,000
+ Kapitalrücklage	+ Share premium account	150	150
+ Gewinnrücklagen	+ Reserves	3,240	3,453
Gesamte langfristige Verbindlichkeiten =	Total long-term liabilities =	4,000	4,060
Langfristige Verbindlichkeiten	Long-term debt	3,500	3,500
+ Rückstellungen	+ Provisions	500	560
Kurzfristige Verbindlichkeiten =	Short-term liabilities =	3,980	4,000
Kurzfristige Schuldpositionen	Short-term debt	1,030	1,000
+ Verbindlichkeiten aus Lieferungen und leistungen	+ Accounts payable	2,050	2,000
+ Sonstige (Kurzfristige) Rückstellungen	+ Accrued liabilities	900	1000

Exhibit 13.9 FREE CASH FLOW AND FINANCIAL FLOWS, HYPOTHETICAL GERMAN COMPANY, DM MILLIONS

Free cash flows		Current year
1.	Earnings before interest and taxes (EBIT)	1,440
2. −	Taxes on EBIT	(507)
3. +	Deferred taxes	0
4. +	Increase in provisions	60
5. =	Net operating profit less adjusted taxes (NOPLAT)	993
6. +	Depreciation	400
7. =	Gross cash flow	1,393
8.	Increase in working capital	150
9. +	Capital expenditures	600
10. +	Investment in goodwill	0
11. +	Increase in other assets	50
12. =	Gross investment	800
	Gross cash flow	1,393
12. −	Gross investment	(800)
=	Free cash flow from operations	593
13. +	Non operating cash flows	0
=	Total free cash flows	593

Financial flows		Current year
14.	Decrease in excess marketable securities	(157)
15. −	After-tax interest income*	(7)
16. +	Decrease in debt	30
17. +	After-tax interest expense*	180**
18. +	Dividends	350
19. +	Tax credit to shareholders on dividends	197
=	Total financial flows	593

* Marginal effective cash tax rate = 58.3% (i.e., 16.67% + 50% − 50%(16.67%)).
** Interest expense of 431 multiplied by 1 − T = 1 − 0.583.

Taxes on EBIT are the taxes the company would pay if it had no debt or excess marketable securities. Cash taxes on operating income equal the total income tax provision (not including other taxes, e.g., property tax, which are already deducted from revenue) adjusted for the income taxes attributable to interest expense, interest income, and nonoperating items. Using exhibit 13.7, the calculation is:

Total income tax provision	DM 463
− Tax credit to shareholders	(197)
+ Tax shield on interest expense	251
− Tax on interest income	(10)
− Tax on non-operating income	0
= Tax on EBIT	DM 507

To compute the tax credit to shareholders, note that since net dividends were DM 350, gross dividends must have been DM 350, divided by one minus the 36 percent dividend tax rate, i.e., DM 350 ÷ (1−.64) = DM 547. Therefore DM 547 − DM 350 = DM 197 was withheld as a dividend tax. The tax shield on interest expense is a marginal tax rate of 58.3 percent multiplied times the interest expense of DM 43.1. The marginal tax rate results from a deductible municipal tax rate of 16.67 percent and the corporate tax rate.

Municipal tax rate (16.67%)(1 − 0.5)	=	8.33%
Corporate tax rate 50.00%	=	50.00%
Marginal tax rate		58.33%

Unlike the United States, deferred taxes are rarely created for a German corporation because tax and reporting statements are usually the same. In our example, deferred taxes are zero.

Nontax provisions in Germany are frequently made for anticipated long-term expenses such as pensions, reorganization, maintenance, and other costs. These provisions are added to the liabilities side of the balance sheet. Deductions are also made from provisions on the balance sheet and taken into the income statement as a reduction of costs These movements can have the effect of smoothing earnings and can result in hidden reserves through excess provisions. Just as in provisions for deferred taxes, an increase in provisions on the balance sheet represents a noncash transfer. Adjustments to a cash basis can be calculated by adding back the change in nontax provisions on the balance sheet to EBIT after taxes. In our numerical example this amount is DM 60.

In Germany, depreciation is based on assets valued at historical cost. Depreciation expense on the income statement (DM 400) is added to NOPLAT in order to arrive at gross cash flow (DM 1,393).

As in the U.S., operating working capital includes cash necessary for operations, plus receivables and inventories, minus accounts payable and accruals. It does not include excess marketable securities or cash, or any interest-bearing liability. The change in operating working capital for our example is:

Current year operating current assets	DM 6,500
− Current year operating current liabilities	(3,000)
− Previous year operating current assets	(6,300)
+ Previous year operating current liabilities	2,950
	DM 150

German capital expenditures on new property, plant, and equipment can be calculated as the increase in *net* property, plant, and equipment on the balance sheet, plus depreciation expense for the period. Technically, this calculation results in capital expenditures, less the net book value of retired assets. For our example:

Increase in net property, plant, and equipment	DM 200
+ Depreciation expense	400
= Capital expenditures	DM 600

Goodwill, which used to be a nondepreciable asset in Germany, can now be amortized over a 15-year period (for taxable years beginning after 1987) as a tax deductible expense. This applies only if the goodwill is acquired from a third party. In an individual company's balance sheet, the goodwill element inherent in the cost of an investment may not be amortized. In consolidated accounts, goodwill arising from consolidation is capitalized and amortized. The investment in goodwill is best calculated as the change in the goodwill account plus the amortization of goodwill in that period.

The increase in net other assets equals the expenditure on all other operating assets, including capitalized intangibles (such as patents or trademarks) and prepaid expenses, but net of increases in concurrent noninterest-bearing liabilities. In Germany, most noninterest-bearing liabilities are provisions. Increases in net other assets can be calculated directly from the change in the balance sheet accounts plus any amortization included in the "depreciation and amortization" account. In our example, the increase in net other assets in DM 50.

Gross investment is DM 800. When subtracted from gross cash flow of DM 1,393 we see that free cash flow is DM 593. Since there are no nonoperating cash flows, total free cash flow is also DM 593.

Financial flows must equal total free cash flows. The first financial flow is the decrease in marketable securities, which is DM 157 from the balance sheet. Next is after-tax interest income, which is calculated as interest income, DM 17, times one minus the marginal tax rate of 58.83%. The result is DM 7. The decrease in the debt (short-term) is DM 30. After-tax interest expense is the interest expense of DM 431, multiplied by one minus the tax rate (i.e., 1 − .583), resulting in an amount of DM 180. Net dividends are DM 350. And finally, the tax credit to shareholders on dividends is DM 197. These add up to total financial flows of DM 593, equaling total free cash flows.

The calculation of free cash flows for the German company serves to illustrate that cash is cash regardless of the accounting conventions that are being used. As long as the financial statements contain complete information, then it is possible to estimate the actual free cash flows and financial flows of a company—regardless of where it is domiciled.

CULTURAL DIFFERENCES

In additional to accounting differences across borders, one must also be aware of cultural differences. Let's use Japan as an example.

It is not unusual to find that the lion's share of a Japanese company's stock value does not come from the present value of its operating free cash flows. There are several reasons for this. First of all, cross holding of shares is customary for maintaining good business relationships. It is not unusual for a large Japanese company to hold an enormous portfolio of marketable securities, composed of small positions in the equity of every supplier and customer company. This propensity is encouraged in part by the fact that share repurchase is prohibited in Japan and that dividend payout is customarily quite a low percentage of earnings. Consequently, companies with excess cash flow find themselves putting it into marketable securities. One can think of these securities portfolios as negative debt—a reminder that the book debt-to-equity ratio of Japanese companies often overstates the riskiness of their financial position if they are willing to liquidate their marketable securities position to repay debt when needed.

A second source of nonoperating value is excess real estate held by Japanese companies. Banks often require that land be put up as collateral for loans. Also, many Japanese managers still believe real estate is a good investment. When companies hold excess real estate, the value of so doing is not captured in operating cash flows.

Exhibit 13.10 shows the components of value for a Japanese electronics company. Only 41 percent of the corporate entity value comes from the present value of operating cash flows (0.70 trillion

Exhibit 13.10 **VALUATION OF A JAPANESE ELECTRONICS COMPANY, 1992,** ¥ TRILLIONS

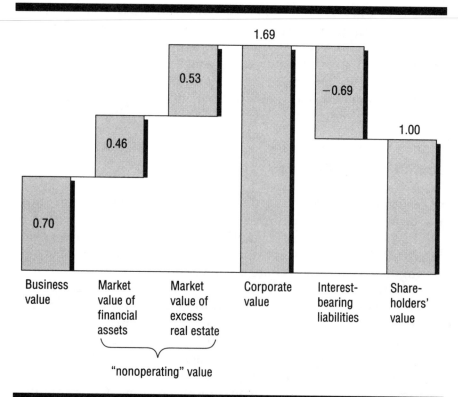

Source: 10K's; McKinsey analysis.

yen out of 1.69 trillion yen). Also note that although the market value debt to equity ratio is 0.69, if we net out the value of financial assets (excess marketable securities) from the value of debt the debt to equity ratio falls to 0.23, more than a 50 percent decrease.

The necessity of estimating the market value of nonoperating assets makes it difficult to value Japanese companies. In particular, one needs to track down the market value of excess real estate holdings. Once these difficulties are overcome there is a high correspondence between the market value and the discounted cash flow value of Japanese companies.

Exhibit 13.11 shows the results for the valuation of 28 companies in 1993, well after the end of the "bubble economy." When the market/book value is correlated with the DCF/book value based on Value Line forecasts, the correlation is 89 percent. Discounted cash flow valuation methodology works well in Japan also.

Exhibit 13.11 **HIGH CORRELATION BETWEEN MARKET VALUE AND DCF VALUES FOR 28 JAPANESE COMPANIES, 1993**

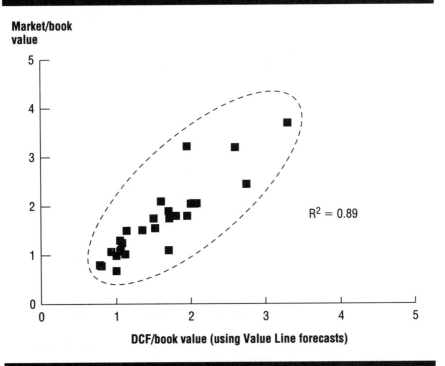

THE COST OF CAPITAL ACROSS BORDERS

One often hears the argument, especially in the popular press, that one country or another has a competitive advantage because the cost of capital is lower. For example the cost of capital in Japan might be lower because of the high Japanese savings rate.

Briefly stated, our point of view is that there is no difference in the costs of capital among developed countries after adjusting nominal costs of capital for differences in expected rates of inflation, risk, and taxation. If the cost of capital is really lower in Japan, for example, then the world would rush to borrow from Japanese lenders until supply and demand imbalance was eliminated and the cost of capital was the same across borders. Of course, government regulations or taxes could serve as barriers to the flow of capital and lead to differences.[1]

To compare the cost of capital in the U.S. versus Japan we studied differences in nominal default free rates on government debt, corporate debt rates, the cost of equity, and the debt-equity ratios. These are all components of a company's weighted average cost of capital. Apples-to-apples comparisons of cross border capital costs are not easy. For debt, one must be sure that the debt in both countries has (at least approximately) the same duration, credit risk, covenants, and special features (e.g., callability or convertibility). For equity, equivalent measures of risk must be used.

Government Debt

In both the U.S. and Japan, government bonds have little or no chance of default, therefore providing a relatively straightforward comparison as long as duration is held constant. Exhibit 13.12 shows nominal yields on 1 year government bonds in the U.S. and Japan. Nominal yields have been lower in Japan since 1977, but inflation rates have also been lower over the same time period as seen in Exhibit 13.13. The implication, of course, is that the

---

[1] We are not alone in our opinion, for example see J. Frankel, "The Japanese Cost of Finance: A Survey," *Financial Management,* Vol. 20, No. 1 (Spring 1991): 95–127; K. French and J. Poterba, "Are Japanese Stock Prices Too High?," CRSP Seminar on the Analysis of Securities Prices, University of Chicago, August 1989; and W. C. Kester, "Capital Ownership Structure Comparison of U.S. and Japanese Manufacturing Corporations," *Financial Management* (Spring 1986): 5–16.

Exhibit 13.12 **NOMINAL YIELDS ON GOVERNMENT BONDS,
U.S. AND JAPAN**

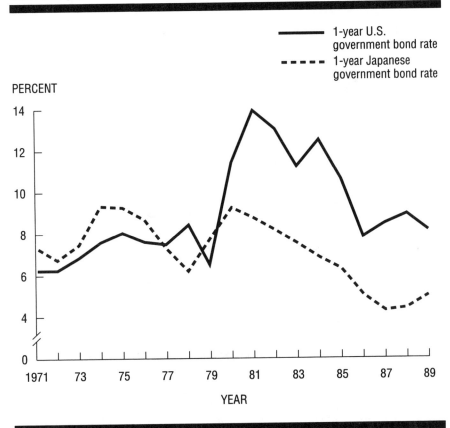

Source: International Financial Statistics; IMF.

dollar has depreciated against the yen. This is illustrated in Exhibit
13.14. Although differences in inflation are not the only explanation for devaluation of the dollar (differences in productivity and
the balance of trade matter too), they are a major factor.

To illustrate why it makes no difference whether one borrows in
yen or dollars, let's look at an example. In December of 1989, the
U.S. government could have issued one year notes at 5.77 percent
payable in yen or 8.24 percent payable in dollars. The FX rate at that
period of time was 145 yen to the dollar. The forward rate for exchange at the end of the year was 141.7 yen per dollar, anticipating

Exhibit 13.13 **RATE OF INCREASE IN CONSUMER PRICE INDEX, U.S. AND JAPAN**

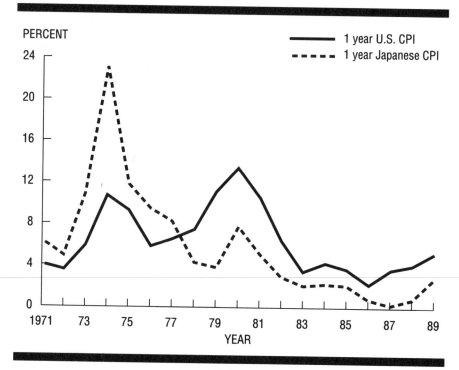

Source: International Financial Statistics; IMF.

that the higher rate of inflation in the U.S. would cause the dollar to devalue relative to the yen.

Tracing through the two alternatives, if the U.S. government borrows $1.00 today it expects to pay back $1.0824 at the end of the year. If it borrows 145 yen instead, it will pay back 1.0577 (145) = 153.4 yen at the end of the year. By that time the exchange rate is expected to be 141.7 yen per dollar, therefore 153.4 yen ÷ 141.7 yen/dollar equals $1.082. The cost is the same either way, and the U.S. government is not better off borrowing in yen. This implies that the cost of risk-free (default free) government debt is the same in both countries.

Corporate Debt

If the cost of government debt is the same in both countries, then similar forces serve to equilibrate the cost of capital for companies.

Exhibit 13.14 YEN/DOLLAR EXCHANGE RATE, AVERAGE OF BEGINNING AND END-OF-YEAR AVERAGE SPOT EXCHANGE RATES

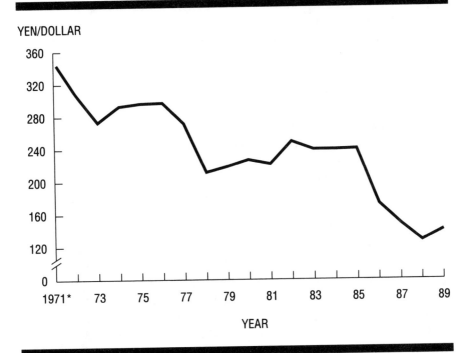

Source: International Financial Statistics; IMF.

* In August of 1971 the U.S. suspended gold convertiblity and de facto the dollar began to float relative to other major currencies.

However, corporate debt cost comparisons between the U.S. and Japan are much more difficult than government bond comparisons because:

1. The public market for corporate debt in Japan is thin to nonexistent and merely thin in the U.S.
2. Japanese corporate bonds often have warrants attached or conversion privileges that lower their stated yield to maturity.
3. Covenants on Japanese and U.S. corporate bonds are quite different.
4. Japanese banks often have inside information about their

borrowers because of interlocking equity ownership (an arrangement forbidden by the Glass-Stegal Act in the U.S.).

5. Prime rates are not directly comparable because one can borrow below prime in the U.S. and because the list of Japanese prime borrowers is more restrictive and therefore more "blue chip" than the list of U.S. prime borrowers.

To the best of our knowledge, no one has yet published a study that makes a good apples-to-apples comparison of U.S. and Japanese corporate lending rates.

To make a direct comparison between U.S. and Japanese corporate borrowing rates for your company you need to obtain quotes from U.S. and Japanese lenders on equivalent loan agreements (e.g. same duration, covenants, principal amount, fixed or variable rate, caps, etc.). You also need to get quotes on foreign exchange swaps to exchange a dollar-denominated loan for an equivalent yen-denominated loan and vice versa. To illustrate, we obtained actual quotes on a $200 million 5-year fixed-rate loan for a U.S.-based company. The loan was assumed to be collateralized for an AAA-rated company and to have no call or conversion features. The 5-year yen fixed rate of 7.00 percent was equivalent to a U.S. 5-year dollar fixed rate of 9.10 percent as shown in Exhibit 13.15. If the company borrows yen at a 5-year rate of 7 percent, it is possible to engage in a currency swap and an interest rate swap so that the company ends up paying a dollar denominated rate of 9.10 percent for the 5 year loan.

Equity

To study differences in the cost of equity between the U.S. and Japan we focused on eight Japanese companies that have American Depository Receipts (ADRs) traded on the New York Stock Exchange. Except for small differences caused by transaction costs, the rate of return for the same stock (e.g. Honda) is the same on the NYSE and the Nikkei. The risk is also the same and therefore the cost of equity is the same. In Exhibit 13.16 the eight Japanese ADRs are matched with U.S. comparables in the same industry. Note that the average betas of the Japanese companies are only slightly lower than their U.S. counterparts when their ADR returns are regressed against the equally weighted U.S. index, but are significantly lower when regressed against the Nikkei. This illustrates the problem of

Exhibit 13.15 **EQUIVALENCE OF CORPORATE BOND BORROWING RATES**

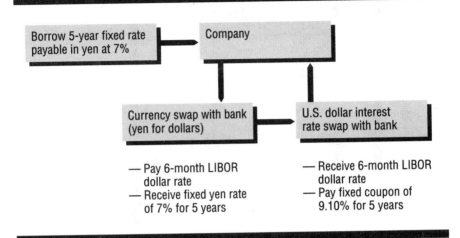

estimating betas for cross national comparisons. The same set of eight Japanese companies had half the measured risk (beta of 0.54 versus 1.05) when regressed against the Nikkei.

Since there is no profit obtainable from arbitrage between ADRs traded on the NYSE and the same securities in Tokyo, we know the cost of equity capital must be the same in both countries for this sample of companies. Therefore, we can conclude that if we use the CAPM (see Chapter 8 for an explanation) to estimate the cost of equity, as shown in Exhibit 13.17, a 14.38 percent cost of equity in the U.S. is equivalent to a 10.72 percent cost of equity in Japan. Note also, the small difference between the cost of equity for U.S. comparable companies and the eight Japanese ADRs.

Capital Structure

One often hears the argument that the cost of capital is lower in Japan because the Japanese use more debt. This does not seem to be true for our sample of eight ADRs as illustrated in Exhibit 13.18. The book value debt–to–total-capital ratios are roughly the same for the Japanese companies and their U.S. comparables, and their market value debt–to–total-capital ratios are actually lower. Based on a much larger sample, Carl Kester (1986) concludes that "... on a market value basis there is no significant country difference in leverage between U.S. and Japanese manufacturing after control-

Exhibit 13.16 **JAPANESE ADRs VERSUS U.S. COMPARABLES (BASED ON 1987 YEAR-END ACCOUNTING DATA),** PERCENT

Company	Number of U.S. comparables	Dividend yield		Return on invested capital		Beta		
		Japan	U.S.	Japan	U.S.	Japan*	Japan**	U.S.**
Hitachi	6	0.50	1.65	4.00	14.70	1.09	.61	1.23
Honda	3	0.80	3.53	11.20	22.80	1.08	.50	0.97
Kubota	3	0.60	1.97	4.20	14.40	0.74	1.00	0.99
Kyocera	5	0.80	0.50	12.40	2.90	1.11	.42	1.43
Matsushita	4	0.40	1.88	19.90	9.40	1.10	.95	1.12
Pioneer	5	0.80	0.00	9.60	1.60	0.98	.35	1.32
Sony	5	0.60	0.00	2.60	1.60	1.18	.30	1.32
TDK	4	0.80	1.78	8.30	9.50	1.09	.16	1.21
Average		0.60	1.41	9.02	9.61	1.05	.54	1.18

Source: McKinsey analysis, BARRA.

* Based on ADR stock returns regressed against an equally weighted U.S. index.
** Based on home country individual stock returns regressed against the home country index.

Exhibit 13.17 EQUITY COST USING HOME COUNTRY BETAS AND U.S. BETAS

HOME COUNTRY BETAS

Country	Cost of equity	=	Nominal risk-free rate*	+	Market price of risk**	×	Average beta		Risk premium component
U.S.	15.16%	=	8.08%	+	6.00%	×	1.18		7.08%
Japan	10.72%	=	6.40%	+	8.00%	×	0.54		4.32%
Difference	(4.44%)		(1.68%)						(2.76%)

U.S. BETAS

Country	Cost of equity	=	Nominal risk-free rate*	+	Market price of risk**	×	Average beta		Risk premium component
U.S.	15.16%	=	8.08%	+	6.00%	×	1.18		7.08%
Japan	14.38%	=	8.08%	+	6.00%	×	1.05		6.30%
Difference	(0.78%)		(0.00%)						(.78%)

* Rate on long-term government bonds, December 1989.
** Source: Ibbotson Associates, McKinsey analysis.

Exhibit 13.18 **COMPARABLE D/E RATIOS,** PERCENT

Company	Book value of debt/total capital		Market value of debt/total capital	
	Japan	U.S.	Japan	U.S.
Kubota	42.3	30.6	11.7	23.9
Hitachi	37.8	21.1	23.1	17.3
Matsushita	33.6	36.3	23.7	28.1
Pioneer	22.8	42.5	9.2	39.2
Sony	34.5	42.5	20.1	39.2
Kyocera	17.2	29.7	9.5	27.7
TDK	27.3	13.8	16.5	9.8
Honda	42.2	37.6	26.4	35.0
Average	32.2	31.7	17.5	27.5

ling for characteristics such as growth, profitability, risk, size, and industry classification."[2]

In sum, there are no differences in the cost of capital across national borders, at least for companies located in developed nations that have lowered their barriers to capital flows. The cost of government debt is the same after controlling for expected changes in FX rates. The cost of corporate debt is also the same after controlling for default as well as FX risk. And the cost of equity also appears to be the same after considering the difficulties of measuring beta. Last, but not least, the capital structures of companies in the same industry appear to be the same. It appears that the cost of capital is neither a source of advantage nor disadvantage across borders.

VALUATION IN DEVELOPING COUNTRIES

As globalization of the world economy brings mobile capital to more and more countries, valuation becomes more important—for privatization, for joint ventures, for mergers and acquisitions, and

[2] W.C. Kester, 1986.

for value-based management of subsidiaries in developing countries. Discounted cash flow methodology is certainly more difficult to use in these environments, and has greater error. Still, it is better than trying to use ratios based on comparables to do transactions. What do you do when a country has only 16 publicly traded companies and none of them are in the industry where you need to estimate a transaction price for an acquisition? You can't use price/earnings or market-to-book ratios from other countries, because the accounting standards and interest rates are different. Even if you do, these ratios provide little or no insight into how to value potential synergies or how to organize post merger integration of the businesses.

This brief section provides counsel on what to do with some of the thorny issues that have come to our attention:

- How to do valuations in high inflation environments.
- How to estimate the cost of capital when even the government has no debt being traded.
- What to do if there is government intervention.

Another issue, what to do about political risk, was discussed in Chapter 12.

Valuation in High Inflation Environments

Accounting numbers are quickly distorted by high inflation, making the historical perspective difficult to determine and forecasting a nightmare. If the government is not manipulating the foreign exchange market, one practical approach is to translate historical financial statements written in the domestic high inflation currency into a stable currency by using the historical spot FX rates. The restated financial statements usually show normal growth patterns for companies in the stable currency. It is also easier to forecast free cash flows in the stable currency. Having done so, they should be discounted at a weighted average cost of capital appropriate for companies of equivalent risk in the stable currency. For example, if the stable currency is U.S. dollars, then the discount rate would be a U.S.-based rate. The value of the company, obtained via this procedure, will be in U.S. dollars. It can be reconverted to the domestic currency of the developing country at the spot exchange rate.

There are two other approaches. Neither is without serious difficulties. You could try to forecast nominal cash flows and discount them at the nominal rate. However, developing countries with high inflation also tend to have highly variable inflation, making it very difficult to forecast nominal cash flows. Furthermore, uncertainty about inflation usually means there are no markets for long-term government debt instruments. Everything is short-term and indexed to the inflation rate. Consequently, it is difficult to figure out a long-term weighted average cost of capital. A second approach is to try to make all estimates in real terms. One tries to forecast the growth in revenues at the real rate appropriate for the products being marketed, costs at the real rate appropriate for them, and so on. The discount rate is the real risk-adjusted rate appropriate, given the riskiness of the free cash flows. This second approach is somewhat easier to apply because future rates of inflation need not be forecasted. However, it is not easy to estimate the real rates of growth that are appropriate for each portion of cash flows. Also, in developing economies the real rate is quite variable across time, and difficult to forecast.

Estimating the Cost of Capital

As mentioned above, financial markets in developing economies are often thin or nonexistent. If no long-term government bond yields are quoted, you need to come up with a substitute. Even if there is a quoted yield, it may not be default-free, as one would usually assume for the debt of developed nations.

Suppose you had to estimate the cost of capital for an equity position in a joint venture in an integrated oil company in China. Assuming that the venture will not use any debt, how would you estimate the required return on your equity? No one calculates CAPM betas for Chinese companies, the market risk premium is unknown, and there isn't any traded government debt that could be used to estimate the risk-free rate (even in the short term).

An approach that avoids the need to use sophisticated models like the CAPM or the APM (see Chapter 8) proceeds in two steps. First estimate the industrywide real required rate of return. Then either index your payments to inflation, or estimate the inflation premium you require and add it to the real rate.

The long-term rate of return on all equity securities investments in integrated oil companies can be estimated for the industry as a whole. Equity prices are continuously and rapidly adjusted to new information so that investors can expect to receive a return that compensates them for the risk they take when they invest in the stock. If bad news is received by the market, the stock price drops enough so that anticipated returns move back to their equilibrium level. Over a long period of time, actual ex post returns are good estimates of future required rates of return, if the underlying riskiness of the industry hasn't changed. Therefore, long-term average rates of return are often adequate proxies for the cost of equity.

The cost of equity for integrated oil companies, measured as a real rate, can be estimated as follows:

- For every comparison company in the industry, collect data on the nominal rate of return over a long period of time, for example, 20 years, the market value debt-to-equity ratio year by year, the tax rate year by year, and the company's cost of debt, year by year.
- Convert the observed equity return each year k_s, into an unlevered equivalent, k_u, by using the Modigliani Miller formula,

$$k_s = k_u + (k_u - k_b)(1 - T)\frac{B}{S},$$

  where k_u is the equity rate of return were the company 100 percent equity (i.e., the unlevered cost of equity); k_s is the observed levered equity return; k_b is the cost of debt; T is the statutory marginal tax rate; and B/S is the market value debt to equity ratio.
- Subtract the rate of inflation each year from the unlevered cost of equity, k_u, to obtain the real rate of return.
- Construct an industry index real rate of return by weighting each company k_u, by its market value of equity, divided by the market value of equity in the industry.
- Compute the geometric average real rate of return for the industry index.

The final result is an estimate of the real rate of return that is required on integrated oil investments in China.

China currently has double digit inflation, which is nearly impossible to forecast. If you can index your share of the joint venture payments to the inflation rate, you can avoid the need to compute a nominal required rate. If indexing is impractical or infeasible, then forecasted inflation needs to be factored in as follows:

$$1 + \text{nominal rate} = (1 + \text{real rate})(1 + \text{expected inflation}).$$

Last but not least is the fact that the mainland Chinese currency, the ren min bi "yuan," is officially exchanged into dollars at 5.8 yuan to the dollar (end of 1993), while the black market exchange rate is about 8 yuan to the dollar. A dollar buys roughly 33 percent more on the black market. The value of the joint venture to you and hence the rate of return on your investment will depend a great deal on whether the yuan can be converted at the official rate or the black market rate.

Government Intervention

Aside from intervening in the FX market, governments create other difficulties for valuation. For example, even though interest rates can be obtained, they may not be determined by free market forces, and may be inappropriate for use in valuations. In India, even though the government has deregulated the debt and equity markets, it still requires banks to buy government bonds at a rate unrelated to inflation, thereby distorting the real cost of borrowing in the country. The 90-day T-bill rate has been fixed at 4.6 percent per quarter (or 19.7 percent per annum) since 1974. Inflation has been running about 8 percent, averaged across the last decade, therefore the 90-day T-bill rate seems artificially high. On the other hand the 10-year T-bill rate has been around eleven percent, perhaps too low given that very recent inflation has been about 13 percent.

Clearly, the estimation of the cost of capital is not an exact science, even when yields are quoted on government securities.

SUMMARY

This chapter has covered a diverse set of issues involved in valuations outside of the U.S. You need to be aware that accounting standards differ quite a bit, but that cash is cash, and therefore it is almost always possible to estimate free cash flows. You should also be aware of cultural differences, such as interlocking ownership, that can catch the unaware analyst off guard. The bottom line is that discounted cash flow valuation works well in developed nations around the world. In less developed countries DCF values companies as well or better than other methods, but is more an art than a science due primarily to the lack of good market data.

A careful comparison of the cost of capital across borders indicates no differences after adjusting for inflation and risk. Of course, government imposed barriers to the free flow of capital can affect the cost of capital, but when the markets are allowed to work, the cost of capital is equal across borders.

REVIEW QUESTIONS

1. In what ways do accounting practices affect the calculation of an entity's value?
2. In the example of the hypothetical German company, show the correspondence of the statements to each of the accounting differences you outlined in question 1.
3. From where does the value of Japanese firms derive?
4. Is the cost of risk-free financing the same or different across international borders?
5. How is it possible that the cost of capital is the same in the United States and Japan?

14

Mergers, Acquisitions, and Joint Ventures

Chapter 11 discussed multibusiness valuation and restructuring. The fourth apex of the restructuring pentagon requires an examination of the potential value of a company with all possible external improvements. Obvious examples of such improvements are mergers, acquisitions, divestitures, and joint ventures. These are important enough to require a chapter in their own right.

Exhibits 14.1 and 14.2 demonstrate that merger and acquisitions (M&A) activity has grown rapidly in nominal dollar terms in the United States, and that two "merger waves" have occurred, the first in the mid-1960s and the second, 20 years later, in the late-1980s. Over the years, M&A activity has been highly correlated with plant and equipment expenditures, averaging between 16 and 20 percent of aggregate internal expenditures. This suggests that aside from regulatory influences, M&A activity can be viewed as an external investment alternative to internal growth. When internal growth builds up, external growth increases proportionately.

Exhibit 14.3 shows that cross-border M&A is active and growing with the EC being more active than the U.S. and Japan put together. The peak in activity was 1989, but the level of activity in 1991 was $41.4 billion and growing. We see, in Exhibit 14.4, that more than half of the M&A activity in the EC is cross-border, while only about 15 percent of the U.S. activity is cross-border.

Exhibit 14.5 provides data on the number of divestitures in the United States each year. Beginning in the early 1970s, corporate

Exhibit 14.1 **MERGER ACTIVITY IN THE UNITED STATES**

Year	Total dollar value paid* ($ Billions)	Total**	Number of transactions valued at		GNP deflator (1972=100)	1972 constant dollar consid- eration
			$100 million or more	$1,000 million or more		
1968	43.6	4462	46	—	82.5	52.8
1969	23.7	6107	24	—	86.8	27.3
1970	16.4	5152	10	1	91.4	17.9
1971	12.6	4608	7	—	96.0	13.1
1972	16.7	4801	15	—	100.0	16.7
1973	16.7	4040	28	—	105.7	15.8
1974	12.4	2861	15	—	115.1	10.8
1975	11.8	2297	14	1	125.8	9.4
1976	20.0	2276	39	1	132.1	15.1
1977	21.9	2224	41	—	140.1	15.6
1978	34.2	2106	80	1	150.4	22.7
1979	43.5	2128	83	3	163.4	26.6
1980	44.3	1889	94	4	178.6	24.8
1981	82.6	2395	113	12	195.5	42.2
1982	53.8	2346	116	6	207.2	26.0
1983	73.1	2533	138	11	215.3	34.0
1984	122.2	2543	200	18	223.4	54.7
1985	179.6	3001	270	36	231.4	77.6
1986	173.1	3336	346	27	249.7	69.3
1987	163.7	2302	301	36	257.7	63.5
1988	246.9	2258	369	45	267.8	92.2
1989	221.1	2366	328	35	279.6	79.1
1990	108.2	2074	181	21	291.8	37.1
1991	71.2	1877	150	13	303.6	23.5
1992	96.7	2574	200	18	311.6	31.0

Source: W. T. Grimm & Co. (1993); U.S. Department of Commerce.

* Based on the transactions that disclosed a purchase price.

** Total: net merger-acquisition announcements. The W.T. Grimm & Co. Research Department records publicly announced formal transfers of ownership of at least 10 percent of a company's assets or equity, where the purchase price is at least $500,000, and where one of the parties is a U.S. company. These transactions are recorded as they are completed; canceled transactions are deducted from total announcements in the period in which cancellation occurred, resulting in net merger-acquisition announcements for that period.

Exhibit 14.2 **PROFILE OF MERGER ACTIVITY, U.S.,** $ BILLIONS

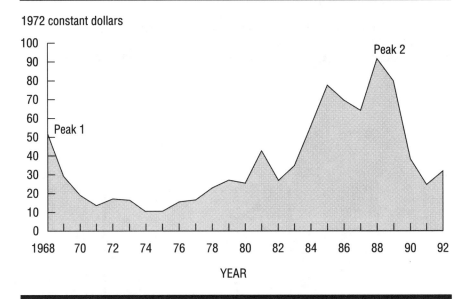

1972 constant dollars

Exhibit 14.3 **CROSS-BORDER M&A ACTIVITY IS GROWING RAPIDLY**

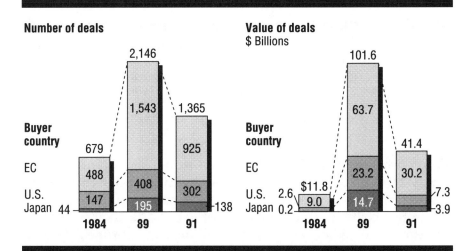

Source: KPMG Dealwatch; Daiwa; Yamaichi; Euromoney; EC; Mergerstat; Acquisition Monthly; McKinsey analysis; majority acquisitions for 1989–91; majority and minority acquisitions used for 1984 where majority data unavailable.

Note: Cross-border M&A peaked in 1989.

Exhibit 14.4 **CROSS-BORDER M&A AS A PERCENTAGE OF TOTAL MERGERS AND ACQUISITIONS**

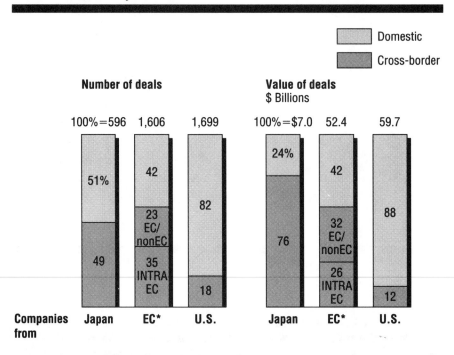

Source: KPMG Dealwatch; Yamaichi; EC; Mergerstat; McKinsey analysis; majority acquisitions for EC, U.S.; majority and minority acquisitions for Japan.

* Number and value of domestic deals for EC companies estimated based on 1991 data for number and value of corss-border deals and 1989/90 propertions of domestic and cross-border deals.

Note: Cross-border M&A as a percentage of total merger and acquisitions, 1991.

divestitures have represented between 40 and 50 percent of all corporate transactions. Combined M&A and divestiture activity plays a significant role in the reallocation of resources in the economy.

In this chapter, we do not attempt to provide an answer to the question of whether mergers, acquisitions, divestitures, and joint ventures are beneficial to the economy as a whole. A merger may be good for shareholders of both the acquiring and acquired companies, but bad for the economy. For example, if a monopoly position is created, it may be detrimental to consumers. On the other hand, real improvements in production efficiency can result in products of higher quality and lower cost. We can, however, say

Exhibit 14.5 **DIVESTITURE ACTIVITY IN THE UNITED STATES**

Year	Number of divestitures	Percentage of all transactions	Year	Number of divestitures	Percentage of all transactions
1966	264	11%	1980	666	35%
1967	328	11	1981	830	35
1968	557	12	1982	875	37
1969	801	13	1983	932	37
1970	1,401	27	1984	900	36
1971	1,920	42	1985	1,218	41
1972	1,770	37	1986	1,259	38
1973	1,557	39	1987	807	35
1974	1,331	47	1988	894	40
1975	1,236	54	1989	1,055	45
1976	1,204	53	1990	940	45
1977	1,002	45	1991	849	45
1978	820	39	1992	1,026	40
1979	752	35			

Source: W. T. Grimm & Co. (1993); *Mergerstat Review*, 1993.

something about the effect of M&A on owners of the bidding and target companies. The probability of success or failure is our first topic. Second, we discuss the major reasons for failure. Finally, we discuss the steps necessary for implementing a successful M&A program. The last part of the chapter contrasts joint ventures with mergers and discusses the reasons for success or failure.

MERGER PROGRAMS: THE PROBABILITY OF FAILURE

In the M&A arena, who wins, who loses, and why? Any company contemplating an acquisition must familiarize itself with the simple facts that external growth is extremely competitive and the probability of increasing its shareholders' wealth via such growth is low. Two broad types of research provide this warning. Academic studies have typically looked at the *ex ante* market reaction to the announcement of a merger, taking into account not only expected costs and benefits of the deal, but also the market's expectation that the deal will actually be consummated. The other approach is *ex post*, looking at the success or failure of merger programs after their completion. The bad news for potential acquirers is that neither approach provides grounds for an optimistic forecast. Therefore, M&A programs must be carefully conceived and executed.

Ex Ante Market Reactions

Exhibit 14.6 summarizes the results of dozens of academic studies. The lesson is that shareholders of acquired companies are the big winners, receiving on average a 20 percent premium in a friendly merger and a 35 percent premium in a hostile takeover. Shareholders of acquiring companies earn small returns, which are not even statistically different from zero, for friendly mergers.

To illustrate the usual methodology in academic studies, we have analyzed three banking mergers: Mellon/Girard, Bank of New York/Irving Trust, and Wells Fargo/Crocker. Exhibit 14.7 shows the market reaction to the initial merger announcement in terms of the effect on common share prices for both the acquiring and the acquired company.

Shareholder returns are plotted as the cumulative abnormal returns, CARs, around the announcement date, Day 0. The abnormal

Exhibit 14.6 **SUMMARY OF EMPIRICAL STUDIES OF SHARE PRICE CHANGES RESULTING FROM M&A ACTIVITIES**

Type of event	Average return to shareholders (Percent)
Merger	
Acquired company	20%
Acquiring company	2–3*
Tender offer for takeover	
Acquired company	35
Acquiring company	3–5
Sell-off	
Spin-off	2–5
Divestiture	
Seller	0.5–1.0
Buyer	0.34
Equity carve-out	2

Source: Copeland and Weston 1988, 754.
* Not statistically significant.

Exhibit 14.7 **CUMULATIVE ABNORMAL RETURNS AROUND
MERGER ANNOUNCEMENTS**

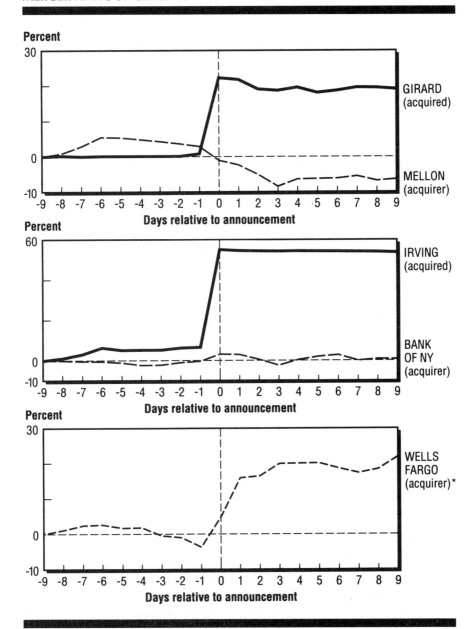

Source: McKinsey analysis.

* Crocker was not publicly traded at the time it was acquired by Wells Fargo, so no CAR data
are available.

return each day is the error or residual term, e_{jt}, in a regression of the security's return against that of a market index:

$$R_{jt} = \hat{a}_j + \hat{b}_j R_{mt} + e_{jt}$$

where

R_{jt} = the total return on the jth stock on day t

$\hat{a}_j, \hat{b}_j$ = the intercept and slope terms from a linear regression of R_{jt} and R_{mt} during a benchmark period (different from the period when CARs are estimated).

R_{mt} = the total return on an index representative of the entire market.

This procedure provides an estimate of company-specific information on a given day, after removing the effect of general market movements. The residual, e_{jt}, is also called the abnormal return, because without a company-specific event, the difference between the actual and predicted returns will average out to zero. The CARs plotted in Exhibit 14.7 can be interpreted as the excess shareholder returns attributable to news about the merger.

The CAR patterns in Exhibit 14.7 are typical. They wander around zero prior to the unexpected announcement of the merger, and then they jump (in a few days) to a new (permanent) level that reflects the market's *ex ante* expectation of the effect of the merger on shareholders of the acquiring and acquired companies. The Mellon/Girard deal is not unusual, with the acquirer's shareholders losing 4.97 percent in two days and the acquired company's shareholders gaining 20.98 percent. The Bank of New York/Irving Trust and Wells/Crocker deals are different because the acquiring shareholders earned positive returns, 3.29 percent and 19.61 percent respectively, in a few days. In the Bank of New York/Irving deal, the acquired company's shareholders gained an incredible 48.16 percent. Of course, a favorable initial market reaction does not mean that the merger will ultimately succeed.

Why did Wells Fargo do so well in its acquisition of Crocker? The main reason is that unique real synergies resulting from rationalization of overlapping branch banking systems were achieved quickly during postmerger integration. Furthermore, they could not be captured by a competing bidder, so Wells Fargo captured more of the benefit than would have been the case had there been strong competing bidders.

The academic evidence is primarily based on *ex ante* analysis. It reflects the market's expectation of the costs and benefits of the proposed merger and the probability that the deal will go through. On average, the market's estimate is correct. Shareholders of acquired companies receive most of the benefit, because competition among acquirers forces the target's price up to the point where little or no benefit to acquiring shareholders is left. Of course, this does not mean that acquirers never succeed. The market's initial reaction may be wrong. To learn more about why mergers succeed or fail, we must turn to *ex post* analysis.

Ex Post Analysis of Acquisitions

McKinsey & Company's Corporate Leadership Center studied 116 acquisition programs, usually involving multiple acquisitions in the U.S. and the U.K., between 1972 and 1983. We started with companies in either the *Fortune 200* largest U.S. industrials or the *Financial Times* top 150 U.K. industrials. We judged a program to be successful if it earned its cost of equity capital or better on funds invested in the acquisition program. In other words, income after taxes as a percentage of equity invested in the acquisition had to exceed the acquirer's opportunity cost of equity. Because it takes at least three years to determine whether an acquisition has been successful, our financial analysis looked at data available through the end of 1986. Programs usually involved multiple acquisitions. For example, General Mills made 47 acquisitions of small, high-growth, consumer-oriented companies as part of a single program.

In order to compare the market's *ex ante* reaction to our *ex post* judgment we studied the initial market reaction affecting the shareholder returns for nineteen acquisition announcements. Our *ex post* opinion is that the market was correct in ten out of the sixteen outcomes that we could judge; but only one of the five situations initially evaluated as a success by the market actually turned out that way. This does not mean the market is inefficient, only that full information on the eventual success or failure of a program is not available until well after the initial announcement.

Ex post analysis indicates that 61 percent of the programs we evaluated ended in failure, and only 23 percent in success; the results of the rest were indeterminate. Exhibit 14.8 shows the breakdown

Exhibit 14.8 **SUCCESS AND FAILURE RATES BY TYPE OF ACQUISITION**

100% = 116 ACQUISITION PROGRAMS

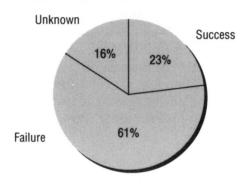

100% = 97 ACQUISITION PROGRAMS

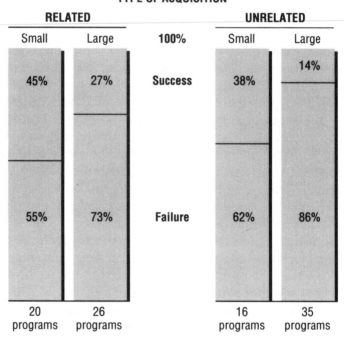

Source: McKinsey analysis.

for the 116 acquisition programs. Each program was categorized by the type of acquisitions it made. For the 97 programs that were either successes or failures, the greatest chance of success was only 45 percent for those programs in which acquiring companies bought smaller companies in related businesses. The acquired company was judged to be small if the purchase price was less than 10 percent of the acquiring company's market value. It was classified as related if the target's markets were similar to those of the acquiring company. If the target was large and in an unrelated line of business, the success rate fell to only 14 percent. This points to the conclusion that diversification is not a good motive for mergers.

Exhibit 14.9 uses the U.S. portion of the sample to show that the probability of success is also heavily influenced by the strength of the core business of the acquirer. Companies with strong core businesses prior to the start of their acquisition programs had a much better chance than those without strong core businesses. Of the 23 percent of the U.S. programs that were successful, fully 92 percent had strong core businesses.

In another study we screened 5,000 nonfinancial companies, requiring that their 1976 sales exceeded $250 million, that their average annual return to shareholders between 1977 and 1991 exceeded 15.85 percent, and that their growth in total capital was high (greater than 10.37 percent per year). This left a sample of 85 companies with high growth in total capital and high return to shareholders over a long period of time. We wanted to see whether these high growth companies achieved their results via internal organic growth or via acquisition. For these companies, acquisitions were a principle element in their growth strategy. As shown in Exhibit 14.10, 40 percent of them used acquisition as their main strategy and another 35 percent combined acquisitions with internal growth. Acquisition also seems to have maintained the vitality of acquirers, as illustrated in Exhibit 14.11. Most companies that grew via acquisition maintained high profitability (ROI greater than 9.8 percent) while the majority of companies using an internal growth strategy did not.

In sum, although the probability of success for the average buyer is only 50/50 at best, these odds can be improved by having a strong core business, buying companies in related businesses where the chance of achieving real economic synergies is highest, and buying smaller businesses that can easily be integrated during the post acquisition phase of the program.

Exhibit 14.9 **HOW CORE BUSINESSES PERFORMED PRIOR TO ACQUISITION PROGRAMS**

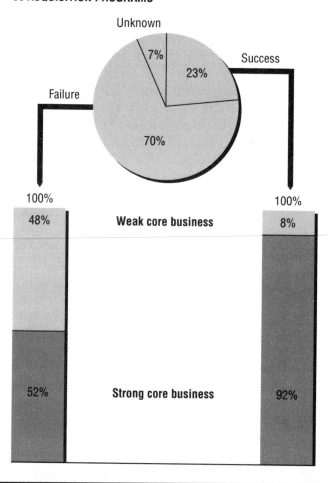

100% = 56 ACQUISITION PROGRAMS

Unknown

7%

23%

Success

Failure

70%

100%

48%   **Weak core business**   8%

100%

52%   **Strong core business**   92%

Source: McKinsey analysis.

MERGER PROGRAMS: REASONS FOR FAILURE

Why do so many acquisition programs fail? Many reasons can be given, including poor management and just plain bad luck. A pervasive reason, though, is that many acquirers pay too much. With

Exhibit 14.10 **PRINCIPLE ELEMENTS OF GROWTH STRATEGY,** PERCENT

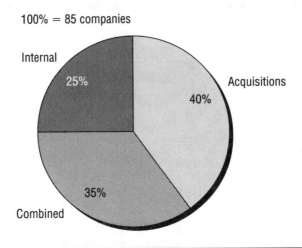

100% = 85 companies

Internal 25%

Acquisitions 40%

Combined 35%

Source: *Moody's*; annual reports; McKinsey analysis.

average takeover premiums in the 40 percent range, and with increasingly competitive markets for takeovers, it is all too easy to overpay. But why do companies overpay? The four primary reasons are overoptimistic appraisal of market potential, overestimation of synergies, overbidding, and poor post acquisition integration.

Overoptimistic Appraisal of Market Potential

Acquisition is a dangerous enterprise if based on the assumption that a market will rebound from a cyclical slump or that a company will turn around. No less problematic or uncommon is the assumption that rapid growth will continue indefinitely. Remember, if you pay a premium above market to acquire a company you will either need to capture synergies, improve the company's operations, or both. If you cannot do either, then you are betting against the market and the seller and both are likely to know more about the business than you do.

Overestimation of Synergies

Consider the following example. A large health services company paid several billion for a more profitable company in a related

Exhibit 14.11 **RETURN ON INVESTMENT (ROI) CHANGE BY PRINCIPAL ELEMENTS OF GROWTH STRATEGY,** PERCENT; NUMBER OF COMPANIES

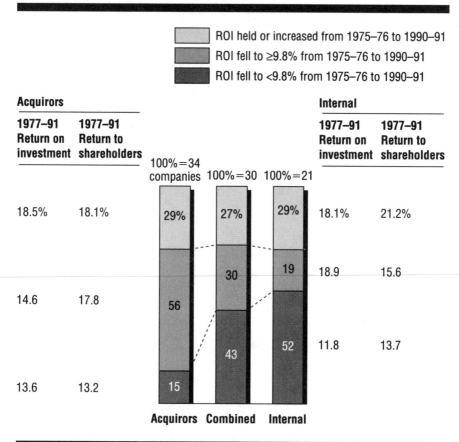

Source: *Compustat*; McKinsey analysis.

industry segment. Given its stepped-up investment base, the target's post acquisition after-tax earnings would have had to be around $500 million for the acquirer's return on its investment to approach its cost of capital, even after divesting over $600 million worth of the newly acquired company's businesses. In 1984, the year before the transaction was consummated, the target's earnings were about $225 million. After divestiture of units that had earned $45 million the previous year, it needed to close an earnings gap of over $275 million through "operating synergies." The acquirer's inability to make improvements of this magnitude resulted in destruction of significant shareholder value. From 1984 to 1986, overall market indices increased almost 18 percent in value, while the acquirer's returns to its shareholders fell 3.8 percent.

Overbidding

In the heat of a deal, the acquirer may find it all too easy to bid up the price beyond the limits of reasonable valuations. Remember the winner's curse. If you are the winner in a bidding war, why did your competitors drop out?

Poor Postacquisition Integration

It goes almost without saying that poor implementation can ruin even the best strategy. Unfortunately, in merger and acquisition situations the execution of a sound business strategy is made especially difficult by the complex task of integrating two different organizations. Relationships with customers, employers, and suppliers can easily be disrupted during the process, and this disruption may cause damage to the value of the business. Aggressive acquirers often believe they can improve the target's performance by injecting better management talent, but end up chasing much of the talent out. Yet it is this very integration that should yield the returns to make the acquisition pay off. Failure to integrate can be as costly as integrating poorly.

Exhibit 14.12 shows a typical losing pattern for unsuccessful merger programs. This death spiral, unfortunately, is all too common. The next section of this chapter talks about the steps in a disciplined acquisition program designed to maximize the probability of success.

STEPS IN A SUCCESSFUL MERGER AND ACQUISITION PROGRAM

We can break an acquisition program into the five distinct steps shown in Exhibit 14.13. Common sense is the rule of the day every step along the way. The process begins with a preacquisition phase that involves a careful self-examination of your company and the industry it is in. The process ends with a carefully planned post merger integration that is executed as quickly as possible to capture

Exhibit 14.12 **TYPICAL LOSING PATTERN FOR MERGERS**

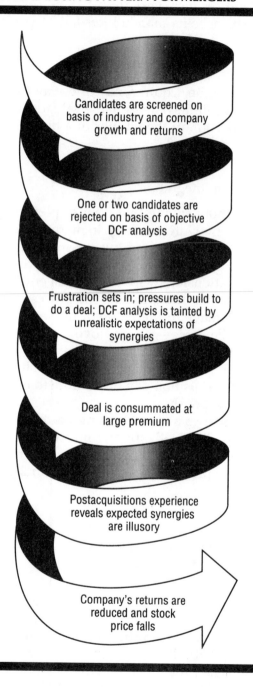

Candidates are screened on basis of industry and company growth and returns

One or two candidates are rejected on basis of objective DCF analysis

Frustration sets in; pressures build to do a deal; DCF analysis is tainted by unrealistic expectations of synergies

Deal is consummated at large premium

Postacquisitions experience reveals expected synergies are illusory

Company's returns are reduced and stock price falls

Exhibit 14.13 **STEPS IN A SUCCESSFUL MERGER AND ACQUISITION PROGRAM**

1. Manage preacquisition phase

- Instruct staff on secrecy requirements
- Evaluate your own company
- Identify value-adding approach
    - Understand industry structure, and strengthen core business
    - Capitalize on economies of scale
    - Exploit technology or skills transfer

2. Screen candidates

- Identify knockout criteria
- Decide how to use investment banks
- Prioritize opportunities
- Look at public companies, divisions of companies, and privately held companies

3. Value remaining candidates

- Know exactly how you will recoup the takeover premium
- Identify real synergies
- Decide on restructuring plan
- Decide on financial engineering opportunities

4. Negotiate

- Decide on maximum reservation price and stick to it
- Understand background and incentives of the other side
- Understand value that might be paid by a third party
- Establish negotiation strategy
- Conduct due diligence

5. Manage postmerger integration

- Move as quickly as possible
- Carefully manage the process

the premium that was paid for the acquisition. When the odds against successful external growth are so high, it pays to develop a careful program.

Step 1: Manage the Preacquisition Phase

Getting ready for an active acquisition campaign means taking a proactive stance. A crucial lesson is that secrecy must be maintained throughout the entire program. If the market gets wind of a rumored takeover attempt, the price of the target will go up, possibly enough to kill the deal. Staff must also be trained in doing valuations from an outsider's perspective using a library of publicly available data. A good starting point is to value your own company by valuing its business units and deciding what internal improvements might be feasible. In addition to training your staff, this exercise often provides valuable insights about how to obtain the maximum value out of your own business to keep from becoming an acquisition target yourself.

If you have valued your own company, if you understand its strengths and weaknesses, and if you understand the changing structure of your industry, then you are ready to have a brainstorming session to identify the value-adding approach that will work best for your company. Three possible approaches are as follows:

1. Strengthen or leverage your core business.
2. Capitalize on functional economies of scale.
3. Benefit from technology or skills transfer.

You can use the model of industry structure analysis illustrated in Exhibit 14.14 to think about ways of strengthening or leveraging your core business. Acquiring a foothold in a *substitute* business may be a critical defensive move to preserve the value of, for example, a strong sales/service capability. AT&T's purchases of NCR and McCaw were intended, at least in part, to protect AT&T's position in the long-distance telecommunications business. Monsanto's long-term efforts to enter the biotechnology industry have been predicated on exploiting new approaches to producing its existing product lines.

If the *customer* base is concentrating (as it is, for example, in trucking), or the company's value added to the customer's end

Exhibit 14.14 **MODEL OF INDUSTRY STRUCTURE ANALYSIS**

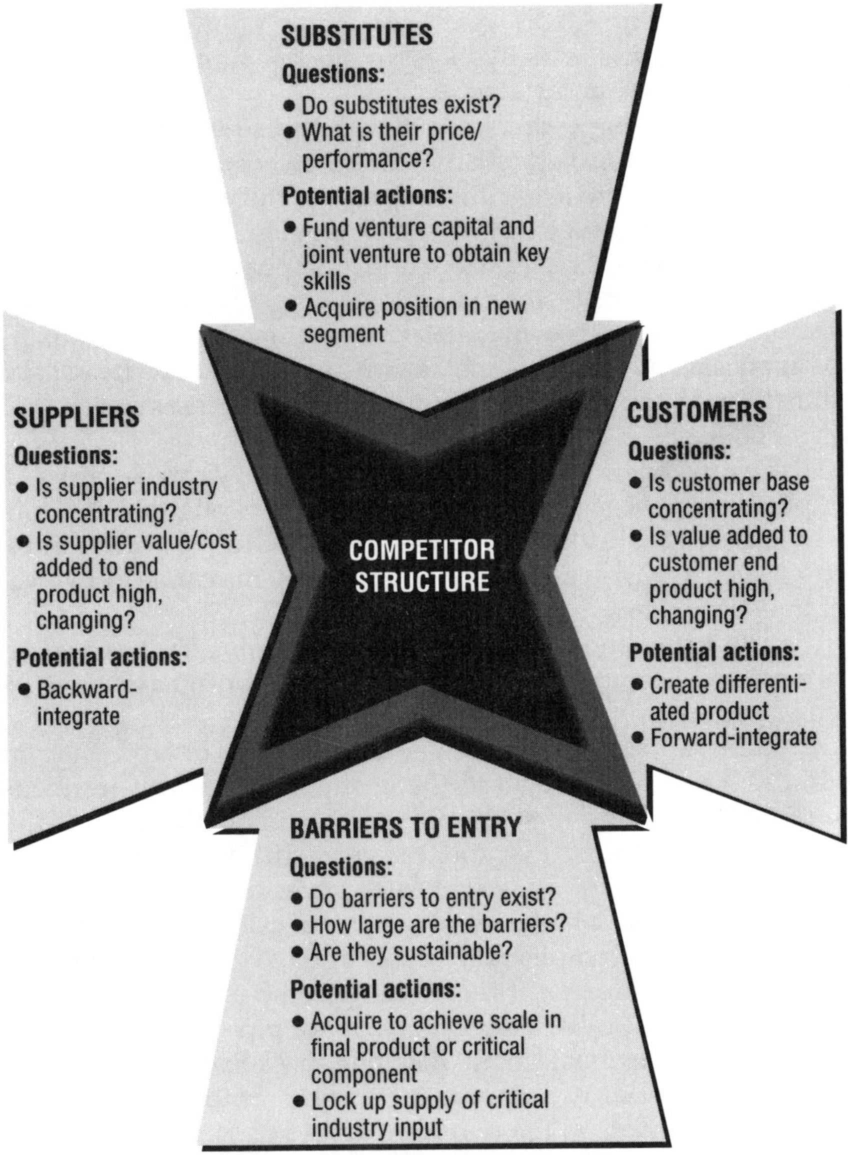

SUBSTITUTES

Questions:
- Do substitutes exist?
- What is their price/ performance?

Potential actions:
- Fund venture capital and joint venture to obtain key skills
- Acquire position in new segment

SUPPLIERS

Questions:
- Is supplier industry concentrating?
- Is supplier value/cost added to end product high, changing?

Potential actions:
- Backward-integrate

COMPETITOR STRUCTURE

CUSTOMERS

Questions:
- Is customer base concentrating?
- Is value added to customer end product high, changing?

Potential actions:
- Create differenti-ated product
- Forward-integrate

BARRIERS TO ENTRY

Questions:
- Do barriers to entry exist?
- How large are the barriers?
- Are they sustainable?

Potential actions:
- Acquire to achieve scale in final product or critical component
- Lock up supply of critical industry input

product is diminishing (as in general aviation assembly), acquisitions to forward-integrate and/or to create a clearly differentiated product may be needed to preserve existing margins. ConAgra's forward integration from grain and poultry into higher-value-added products has actually increased its operating margin in the face of a concentrating retail structure.

Acquisitions to preserve or create *barriers to entry* can have a major impact on industry profitability; however, antitrust regulations may restrict the feasibility of many of these deals. Achieving major scale advantages may create barriers to new entrants. Acquiring dominant positions in critical input factors can accomplish the same result—for example, (1) negotiating a long-term contract for a critical raw material; (2) acquiring the highest-quality raw materials in an area, such as gypsum deposits or fly ash for synthetic gypsum; and (3) acquiring regulated licenses such as cellular mobile or cable TV rights.

Backward integration into a *supplier* industry can be critical if suppliers are concentrating and/or pricing like oligopolies. Similarly, ensuring continuous access to periodically scarce input factors such as raw materials or key components can lead to competitive advantages.

Finally, acquisitions to concentrate *competitor structure* and reduce cutthroat competition due to over capacity can have a significant impact on profitability.

Exhibit 14.15 shows areas where economies of scale may be found. Our experience suggests that many companies overestimate functional economies of scale and underestimate the cost of running the matrix structure required to create the economies. For example, it is one thing to say that sales forces can be integrated to move more product via the same number of salespeople, but quite another thing to accomplish the vision. You have to get into the details. Do the sales forces of the merging companies make exactly the same customer calls? For example, it is a pipe dream to believe that two college textbook companies, one specializing in liberal arts books and the other in scientific texts, can profit from sales force savings. Salespeople in the two companies actually visit different parts of campus, with little redundancy. Another example is overlapping branch banking systems. It may not be possible to close down even branches across the street from each other if both are operating at full capacity.

Exhibit 14.15 **ANALYSIS OF POTENTIAL ECONOMIES OF SCALE**

1. Identify potential economies of scale

- Cut production costs due to greater volume or efficiency
- Increase sales force efficiency
- Combine R&D operations to increase efficiency
- Cut overhead costs

2. Analyze for effect

- What is the value created by the economies of scale?
- Is return on capital greater than WACC (though two high-cost producers create economies of scale by merging, has return increased enough to create value)?

3. Understand competitive position

- Will any government antitrust reaction occur?
- Will competitors be able to quickly replicate the same economies of scale?

Sometimes, but not often, value can be gained from skills or technology transfer via merger. But this approach, which is one we have seen often, is fraught with pitfalls. More often than not, managerial hubris creates overly optimistic self-assessments of leverageable skills.

One successful example of skills transfer, however, was when United Technologies acquired Otis Elevator in 1981. Improvements in general management skills resulted in working capital reductions and reduced corporate overhead. Improvements in functional capabilities enabled Otis to reengineer its product line and to introduce, six years ahead of schedule, a fully electronic elevator control system that (1) consumed 40 percent less energy than the existing product; (2) reduced passenger waiting time by 33 percent; and (3) required less maintenance while reducing the cost of maintenance.

Your approach to identifying the best value-adding approach should be to go for the low-hanging fruit first—to exploit your existing competitive advantage. Then, as refinements are needed, look for closely related opportunities.

Step 2: Screen Candidates

Successful acquirers undertake their own active screening process, independent of outside sources. Although you may explain your acquisition criteria to a broad spectrum of investment banks and business brokers, do not sit back and passively react to investment banking proposals for acquisition candidates. If someone approaches you with a company for sale, odds are that the company is being shopped around. In addition to establishing criteria for acquisition, it is also useful to develop a list of "knock-out criteria," as illustrated in Exhibit 14.16. Targets that are too large, too small, or in unrelated businesses can be quickly eliminated in order to focus on a short list of serious candidates. You should look at publicly held companies, divisions of companies, privately held companies, and foreign as well as domestic companies.

At this stage in the process, you should think carefully about the role of consulting firms, law firms, and investment banks. Each has its appropriate place, but the level of activity varies at each state of an acquisition. Legal and tax advice is necessary at all phases.

Once you have narrowed your list of candidates to a handful of realistic possibilities, you have to roll up your sleeves and get down to the detailed work of valuing each candidate and identifying an explicit strategy for earning back the merger premium you will have to pay.

Step 3: Value Remaining Candidates

The typical takeover premium in the 1980s has been close to 40 percent above the preacquisition market value of the target company.

When doing a detailed valuation of the few remaining candidates, remember the difference between the value to you and the price you pay. Your objective should be to pay only one dollar more than the value to the next highest bidder, and an amount that is less than the value to you. A framework for estimating the value to you is illustrated in Exhibit 14.17. You need to add to the value of your company the value of the target company operated "as is," without any takeover premium added in. Next you need to estimate the

Exhibit 14.16 **USE OF KNOCKOUT CRITERIA TO NARROW THE ACQUISITION CANDIDATE SAMPLE**

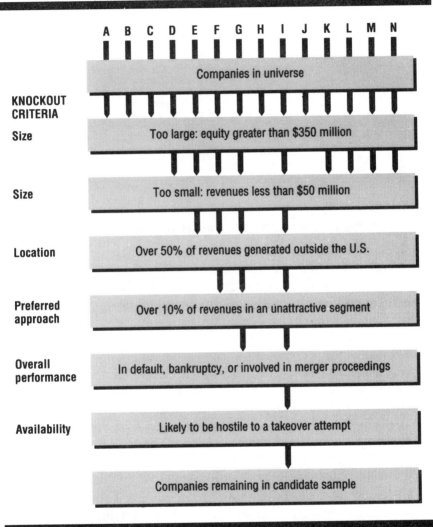

value of the synergies that are realistic. Part of this includes an assessment of how long it will take to capture them. After subtracting any transaction costs for doing the deal you are left with the value of the combined post merger company. Your value gain from the deal is the combined value less the value of your next best alternative—usually the stand alone value of your company and less the

Exhibit 14.17 **FRAMEWORK FOR EVALUATING THE VALUE OF AN ACQUISITION**

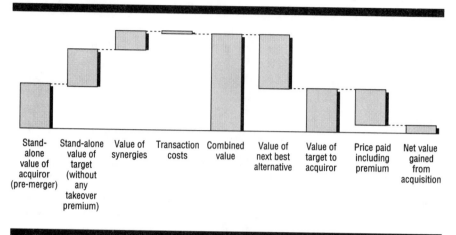

| Stand-alone value of acquiror (pre-merger) | Stand-alone value of target (without any takeover premium) | Value of synergies | Transaction costs | Combined value | Value of next best alternative | Value of target to acquiror | Price paid including premium | Net value gained from acquisition |

price you will be paying for the acquisition. Sometimes however, other factors need to be considered. For example, if the deal is not done, the next best alternative might be the value of your company in the face of stronger competition (because someone else acquired the target) and this value might be lower than the pre-merger stand alone value of your company.

When valuing synergies, you will need to identify not only the realistic synergies that you can obtain, but also those that may accrue to other potential acquirers. If the synergies that you can capture are less than those that can be captured by a competitor, you will lose in a bidding war. Synergies fall into one of three broad categories, as detailed by Bill Pursche (1988).[1]

1. *Universal.* Generally available to any logical acquirer with capable management and adequate resources. Examples are many economies of scale (such as leveraging the fixed cost of a management information system department) and some exploitable opportunities (for example, raising prices).

2. *Endemic.* Available to only a few acquirers, typically those in the same industry as the seller. These include economies of

[1] W. Pursche, "Building Better Bids: Synergies and Acquisition Prices," *Chief Financial Officer* USA (1988): 63–64.

scope (broadened geographic coverage) and most exploitable opportunities (redundant sales forces).
3. *Unique.* Opportunities that can be exploited only by a specific buyer (or seller).

The value to the buyer and seller depends on the type of synergy and who has it. If the synergy is unique and held by the seller, then the buyer has little hope of capturing any value in the bidding process. But if the buyer has the unique synergy, it can pay a low price (because there is no competing buyer) and keep most of the value. Endemic synergies fall in between, with the buyer and seller sharing the value created. And universal synergies must be paid for by the buyer (because anyone can compete). The ideal bid, after a careful analysis, is one that includes most or all of the universal synergies and perhaps some of the endemic synergies.

A variety of restructuring and financial engineering approaches can result in real value added for the acquiring company. Assets that are worth more to other owners can be profitably redeployed via liquidations, divestitures, spin-offs, or leveraged buyouts. The value of core businesses can be enhanced by reducing headquarters costs, implementing significant skills transfers, changing the industry structure, and capturing real synergies. Hidden asset values can be captured by exploiting overfunded pension plans, underutilized real estate, or other underutilized assets (such as timberlands, oil reserves, mineral deposits, or film libraries). Finally, alternative financing arrangements—including sale/leaseback arrangements, royalty trusts, master limited partnerships, partial equity offerings, letter stock, and contingency payment units—can also create value by better utilizing tax shelters, by reducing the capital base without cutting earnings, or by raising funds in an optimal way.

It is also important to understand the accounting and tax treatments of potential acquisitions. The two accepted accounting treatments for mergers in the United States are purchase and pooling. They are governed by Accounting Principles Board Opinions 16 and 17. Pooling of interests simply combines the financial statements of the merging companies. Purchase accounting requires that the difference between the price paid and the book value of the acquired assets be recorded as goodwill (an intangible asset) and written off as a nontax-deductible expense over a period not to exceed forty years.

The real danger in the accounting treatment of mergers is summarized in the following quotation from an FASB discussion memorandum (August 1976):

> Some have suggested that if many of the combinations (of businesses) accounted for by pooling of interests were required to be accounted for by the purchase method . . . they would not have been consummated, notwithstanding valid business reasons supporting their consummation.

Because purchase accounting requires the write off of goodwill and therefore lower earnings, most managers prefer pooling whenever possible. However, because the write off of goodwill most often does not affect taxes (in the United States), it has no impact whatsoever on cash flows or on the value of the company. (See the discussion of goodwill in Chapter 6.)

Which treatment creates the more value? We would say that (tax considerations aside) no difference exists between pooling and purchase. The accounting treatment has no effect on value created. Empirical support for this is provided in an article by Hong, Kaplan, and Mandelker. For a sample of 159 mergers, 122 used pooling and 37 used purchase. The researchers found no evidence whatsoever that shareholders of companies using the purchase treatment did worse than companies using pooling. Nevertheless, in a survey of the 122 companies that used pooling, 66 percent agreed with the aforementioned quotation that otherwise profitable acquisitions might not be consummated if the purchase treatment were required.[2]

The tax treatment of acquisitions is a constantly changing and extremely complex topic. Almost anything that we could commit to paper at this time would soon be outdated. Our recommendation, therefore, is that anyone working on a merger and acquisition should seek the counsel of a qualified tax expert.

Step 4: Negotiate

Merger fever can be a fatal disease complicated by managerial hubris at the negotiation phase. If you have done your homework carefully, you have assessed the value to you of the acquisition

---

[2] H. R. Hong, R. S. Kaplan, and G. Mandelker, "Pooling vs. Purchase: The Effects of Accounting for Merger on Stock Prices," *Accounting Review* 53 (1978): 31–47.

candidate. If you pay even one dollar more than this reservation price, you lose. An article by Mark Mitchell and Ken Lehn (1988) of the Securities and Exchange Commission indicates that bidders who fail in an acquisition because they overbid, or because they could not make the acquisition work, often become targets themselves. The cost of overpaying can be severe and will be suffered immediately.[3]

The keys to a successful negotiating strategy are as follows:

- Assess the value of the acquisition to you.
- Assess the value of the acquisition candidate to the existing owners and other potential buyers.
- Assess the financial condition of the existing owners and other potential acquirers.
- Assess the strategy and motivation of the existing owners and other potential acquirers.
- Determine whether the other parties are using or will use a negotiation intermediary, and examine the history of their approaches.
- Create a bid strategy, focusing on potential changes in value and on the initial offer, conditioned by the situation of the initial owners and of potential bidders.
- Understand the potential impact of anti-takeover provisions.

Not only should you know your own reservation price, but you should also know what the target is worth to other potential buyers, including the existing management in a leveraged buyout. If all goes well, you will not need to pay any more than one dollar more than the value to the next highest bidder. If you think you will be the second highest bidder, why enter the competition in the first place?

Just prior to negotiation, many acquirers achieve a toehold in the target company by purchasing up to 5 percent of its stock on the open market, and do so without causing a noticeable run-up in the price. Once the 5 percent limit has been exceeded, the Williams

[3] M.L. Mitchell and K. Lehn, "Do Bad Bidders Become Good Targets?" Working paper (Washington, D.C.: Office of Economic Analysis, Securities and Exchange Commission, 1985).

Act requires full disclosure. The purpose of a toehold, of course, is to reduce the cost of the acquisition by averaging the low cost of pre-announcement purchases with the high cost of shares purchased later at a premium.

Negotiation is an art. You should choose your negotiating team carefully. The best number-crunchers are usually not the best negotiators. Know the financial condition of the other side. Know the ownership structure of the target company. And develop your bidding strategies in advance. Should you start with a low bid, planning to give way later on, or should you go in with an exploding offer that is nonnegotiable and has a deadline? How much information about the target should you ask its management to supply? What will they be willing to give? What anti-takeover provisions do they have in place, and how resistant will they actually be? Exactly what are the backgrounds of their board of directors? What fairness opinions will be needed and who should supply them? What tax angles can be exploited in the deal?

Knowing the answers to these and other relevant questions, preplanning, and careful choice of your negotiating team will lead to the best possible outcome.

Step 5: Manage Postmerger Integration

Now you have bought a company and paid a hefty premium to do so. Postmerger integration is a fancy phrase for figuring out how to recoup your investment.

As shown in Exhibit 14.18, most acquirers destroy rather than create value after the acquisition. For 20 recent acquisitions, we looked at the acquired company's performance relative to its industry before and after acquisition. Performance was measured as return on sales rather than return on invested capital to avoid problems associated with a stepped-up asset basis. Prior to being acquired, 24 percent of the companies performed better than the industry average and another 53 percent performed better than 75 percent of their industry average. Postacquisition, these percentages dropped to 10 percent and 16 percent, respectively. Prior to being acquired, 78 percent of the target companies beat the 75 percent mark, but after acquisition only 26 percent did. Clearly, postmerger integration must be carefully planned and implemented to avoid destroying value.

Exhibit 14.18 **PRE- AND POSTACQUISITION PERFORMANCE OF
20 ACQUIRED COMPANIES RELATIVE TO INDUSTRY**

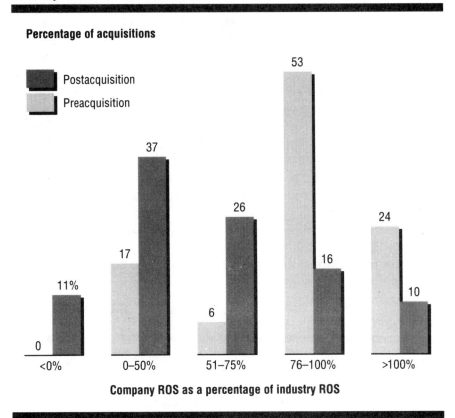

Percentage of acquisitions

Company ROS as a percentage of industry ROS

Source: McKinsey analysis.

One of the most important aspects of post merger integration, especially if the acquired company is relatively large, is to quickly decide on common management goals. It is unrealistic for one company to impose its will on another. Top-level management meetings need to hammer out a new direction that both companies can subscribe to.

The appropriate management action for recouping your investment will depend on your original philosophy of value creation. In many cases, it will be possible to reduce corporate center costs by combining functions. Remember, though, to keep the best people from both organizations and fire the worst. Nothing is worse for the morale of the target company than wholesale layoffs. In other situations, it will be advisable to sell off business units that are worth more to other parent companies. And in other cases, integration of management to facilitate skills transfers will be necessary.

The speed of action is crucial. The sooner cash flow improvements can be realized the better, both to increase value and reduce the amount of earnings dilution in the first year following acquisition. The incremental annual earnings needed to offset an acquisition premium climb precipitously as time passes. For example, as illustrated in Exhibit 14.19, if a $200-million company is purchased for a 30 percent premium at $260 million and the cost of the capital is 13 percent, then $60 million per year is needed in incremental cash flow to offset the premium if action is taken immediately. But if action is deferred three years, $87 million per year is needed to offset the premium.

Hanson Trust typifies the successful restructurer and financial engineer that implements quickly. Its success with this strategy led to average shareholder returns of about 38 percent per year

Exhibit 14.19 **COST TO A HYPOTHETICAL COMPANY OF DELAYING CASH FLOW IMPROVEMENTS,** $ MILLIONS

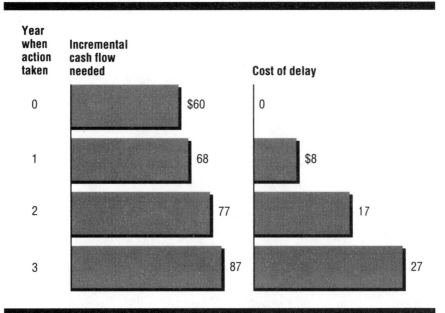

between 1975 and 1986—fifth best among the top 200 companies in the United Kingdom. Typical of its approach is the 1986 purchase of SCM Corporation for $930 million, following a seven-month tender/rebuttal battle. Hanson pursued two approaches to creating value after acquisition.

First, and most important, it sold individual business units to other owners who valued them more highly than the stock market had within SCM's portfolio. Hanson sold six major units (the paper operations, Glidden Paints, Durkee Foods, the kitchen subsidiary, a stamping machine unit, and Sylvachem) for approximately what it had paid for the entire corporation. Prospective buyers for several of these businesses had been lined up prior to the deal's closing. Hanson was left with the core SCM typewriter business (well into a major profit turnaround), some paper operations, and the titanium dioxide paint business. These businesses were projected to produce over $130 million in operating income on sales of $700 to $800 million.

Second, Hanson cut corporate staff and corporate/group executive layers by 90 percent. Of the 250 executives that SCM had employed in corporate or group line and staff positions prior to acquisition by Hanson, only 25 were required to run Hanson's new U.S. Operations.

As important as Hanson's approach was its timing. Within six months of the close of the acquisition, Hanson had recouped its total purchase price of $930 million on a pretax basis.

Exhibit 14.20 is a framework for postacquisition integration. Careful planning is required because of the large number of communications that need to be handled well. The extent of the integration ultimately planned has to be communicated to the top management team of the acquired company to insure that their expectations are properly managed so that key players can be locked in. A communications plan for *both* organizations must be developed to allay anxieties, and organizational structures and systems must be integrated to minimize operational disruptions and departures of talented people. Ultimately, the strategy of the combined entity must be clarified.

Postmerger integration is a difficult task that becomes monumental if the two organizations are nearly the same size. Perhaps this explains why successful mergers are more likely to consist of large companies acquiring small companies in the same industry.

Exhibit 14.20 **FRAMEWORK FOR POSTACQUISITION INTEGRATION**

1. Clarify purpose/set expectations

- Establish a transition mechanism
- Manage expectations of acquired management
- Reach agreement on top organizational issues
- Plan and schedule first postacquisition actions

2. Communicate, control, and plan integration

- Reassure key constituencies
- Agree on a "get-acquainted" stage
- Take the necessary control actions
- Plan integration process

3. Develop strategy/basic structure

- Organize fact-finding task forces
- Establish and test initial working hypotheses
- Build a fact-based understanding of the comparative business systems and market positions of the companies
- Identify opportunities for growth and enhancement of competitive advantage
- Rank priorities

4. Refine organization/strategy

- Review initial strategy, including test of anticipated operating synergies
- Review organizational similarities and differences
- Implement strategic and organizational change

JOINT VENTURES

Joint ventures are different from acquisitions in a variety of ways. First, they are partnerships and therefore involve no takeover premium. Second, to be successful they must be structured to allow effective control. As a form of cross-border alliance, JVs are particularly important. Of course, many alliance options are available as can be seen in Exhibit 14.21. Mergers and acquisitions tend to deal with the entire business system of a company and are more permanent in nature. Joint ventures can be targeted to focus on pieces of the business system (for example, sales, production, development) and can be dissolved after a period of time.

In their 1993 study of joint ventures, Bleeke and Ernst examined the partnerships of 150 companies ranked by market value—the 50 largest in each of the triad regions—the U.S., Europe and Japan.[4] Forty-nine alliances were uncovered. Their findings were:

1. Both cross-border acquisitions and cross-border alliances have roughly the same success rate (about 50 percent).
2. Acquisitions work well for core businesses and existing geographical areas. Alliances are more effective for edging into related businesses or new geographic areas.
3. Alliances between strong and weak rarely work.
4. Successful alliances must be able to evolve beyond their initial objectives. This requires autonomy and flexibility.
5. More than 75 percent of the alliances that are terminated end with an acquisition by one of the parents.

To be considered a success, an alliance had to pass two tests. First, both partners had to achieve their ongoing strategic objectives. Second, they both had to recover their financial cost of capital. For acquisitions exceeding 20 percent of the acquirer's market value, the deal was judged to be a financial success if the acquirer was able to maintain or improve its return on equity and return on assets. For smaller acquisition programs, interviews were conducted to assess their financial success. A comparison of cross-border mergers and acquisitions with cross-border alliances (Exhibit 14.22) shows approximately the same success rate—about 50 percent.

The motivation for cross-border M&A, however, seems to be different than for joint ventures. M&A seems to benefit from geographical overlap, perhaps because synergies such as consolidation of production facilities, integration of distribution networks, and reorganization of sales forces are more easily achieved with high

4 J. Bleeke and D. Ernst, eds., *Collaborating to Compete* (New York: John Wiley & Sons, Inc., 1993).

Exhibit 14.21 **A LIST OF ALLIANCE OPTIONS**

Alliances

	Develop new product markets	Share upstream risks	Share development costs	Leapfrog product technology	Increase capacity utilization	Exploit economies of scale	Fill product line gaps	Penetrate new geographic market
Acquisition				✓	✓	✓	✓	✓
Merger				✓	✓	✓	✓	
Core Business JV				✓	✓	✓	✓	✓
Sales JV				✓	✓		✓	✓
Production JV				✓	✓	✓		✓
Development JV			✓				✓	
Product swap			✓	✓		✓	✓	
Production license	✓		✓	✓	✓	✓		
Technology alliance	✓	✓						
Development license	✓	✓	✓					

Exhibit 14.22 **SUCCESS RATES FOR CROSS-BORDER DEALS**

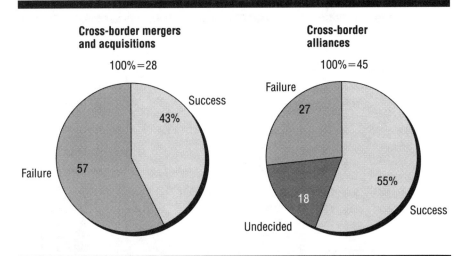

Source: Bleeke and Ernst, 1993.

geographical proximity (see Exhibit 14.23). Alliances, on the other hand are usually intended to expand the geographical reach of the partners. There are fewer alliances with high geographical overlap and they have a much lower success rate for both partners.

Ownership structure is also important for the success of joint ventures. When the ownership of the JV was evenly split between both parents the probability of success for both was 60 percent versus only 31 percent when the ownership split was uneven (see Exhibit 14.24). Alliances work best when both parents are strong. When one partner or the other is weak, the "weak link" becomes a drag on the venture's competitiveness that hinders successful management. When one parent has a majority stake, it tends to dominate decision making and put its own interests above those of its partner, or the joint venture itself.

Joint ventures work best when they have autonomy and flexibility. Flexibility is important because the relative power of the parents will inevitably change, as markets and customer needs shift over time, and because new technologies may arise. During their interviews with the top companies that have alliances, Bleeke and Ernst found that of those alliances that evolved, 79 percent were successful and 89 percent were still surviving at the end of their

Exhibit 14.23 **GEOGRAPHIC OVERLAP HELPS M&A BUT HURTS ALLIANCES,** PERCENT

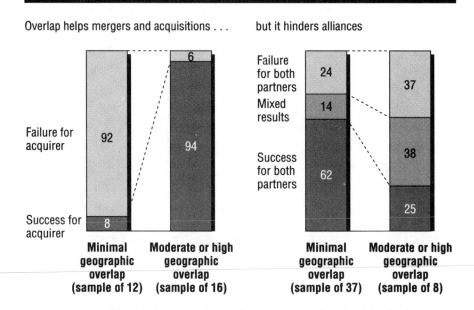

Overlap helps mergers and acquisitions . . .   but it hinders alliances

Source: Bleeke and Ernst, 1993.

sample period. Of those alliances whose scope had remained unchanged, only 33 percent were successful and more than half were terminated.

Flexibility and autonomy can be built by doing two things. First, give the joint venture a strong, independent president and a full business system of its own (R&D, sales, manufacturing, marketing, and distribution). Second, provide it with an independent, powerful board of directors.

One of the facts about joint ventures is that they have a limited life span. As shown in Exhibit 14.25, more than 75 percent of the terminated partnerships were acquired by one of the partners. This does not necessarily imply that the joint venture failed. Alliances often terminate after meeting the partners' goals. However, it does mean that it is useful to prepare for the eventual end of the alliance. If the eventual seller does not anticipate such an outcome, the sale can compromise its long-term strategic interests. Often the natural

Exhibit 14.24 SUCCESS RATE VS. OWNERSHIP STRUCTURE

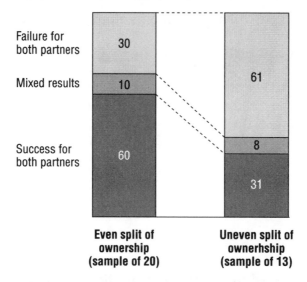

Failure for
both partners — 30

Mixed results — 10

Success for
both partners — 60

61

8

31

**Even split of
ownership
(sample of 20)**

**Uneven split of
ownerhship
(sample of 13)**

Source: Bleeke and Ernst, 1993.

Exhibit 14.25 ALLIANCES USUALLY ACQUIRED BY A MAJOR PARTNER

The way to win in cross-border alliances

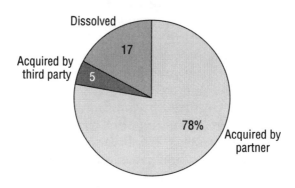

Dissolved 17

Acquired by
third party 5

78% Acquired by
partner

(Sample of 18 terminated partnerships)

Source: Bleeke and Ernst, 1993.

buyer is the company that is the most willing to invest to build the joint venture.

In a separate study by the McKinsey & Company Tokyo Office, including more than 700 alliances between Japanese and non-Japanese companies, it was learned that Japanese partners have been the acquirers in approximately 70 percent of the terminating alliances. Of course, the tendency of Japanese companies to be buyers can be good news to Western partners that want to improve a business in a joint venture setting prior to divestiture.

SUMMARY

Merger and acquisition activity (as well as divestiture) is a cyclical phenomenon correlated with the level of plant and equipment expenditures. External investment is a substitute for internal investment. It is also influenced by structural factors such as regulatory, technological, tax, and competitive changes.

An active market for corporate control dramatically reduces the chances of success for acquiring companies. Even in situations where the acquired company is in the same line of business as the acquirer and is small enough to allow easy postmerger integration, the likelihood of success is only about 50 percent.

A disciplined acquisition program is essential. You must have control of the process. Don't rely on the deals brought to you by third parties. Find your own targets, starting with a self-analysis that leads to a value-adding approach. Identify useful knockout criteria in the screening process. Before bidding on a candidate, understand exactly how you intend to recoup a takeover premium. Identify real synergies and try to find synergies that are unique—ones that cannot be captured by another bidder. Decide on your maximum reservation price and stick to it as part of a carefully planned negotiation strategy. Finally, move as quickly as possible during postmerger integration and carefully manage the process.

Joint ventures are a form of alliance that permits temporary relationships, which focus more specifically on parts of the business system. Although they are successful for both partners only about half of the time, their success rate is improved if there is a low geographical overlap, and if the alliance is provided with autonomy and flexibility between two strong parents with equal ownership.

REVIEW QUESTIONS

1. Summarize the key characteristics of worldwide M&A activity. What opportunities for growth and decline might there be for firms in this arena?

2. What are the principal lessons to be learned from the analysis of M&A activity upon the announcement of a change?

3. Outline the steps in a successful M&A plan.

4. Detail the components of a merger valuation. What synergies ought to be included in the analysis?

5. What are the methods of accounting treatment of mergers and how can they possibly affect value? Illustrate your answer by considering the merger of the Electric Car Manufacturer, Inc. with the Electric Car Marketer Corp. into ECMM Enterprises, Inc. The following chart contains the book value balance sheets (in $ million) of the two organizations with fair market value appraisals of property, plant, and equipment. Electric Car Manufacturer, Inc. purchases Electric Car Marketer Corp. for $145 million by issuing debt. "WC" is working capital (current assets net of noninterest-bearing current liabilities) and "NFA" is net fixed assets.

Electric Car Manufacturer					Electric Car Marketer			
WC	10	Equity	110		WC	20	Equity	25
NFA	100				NFA	5		
Total	110	Total	110		Total	25	Total	25
					Fair Market Value of NFA:			30

6. You have just completed a merger with the one firm that can possibly salvage your innovative R&D efforts at keeping competitive. Your consultants remind you that most firms do not realize their preacquisition expectations for value growth. Outline several steps to ensure postmerger integration.

7. What are the main reasons why you should consider a joint venture as opposed to a merger or acquisition?

15

Using Option Pricing Methods to Value Flexibility

Options give their owner the right (not the obligation) to buy or sell assets at a predetermined price (called the striking or exercise price) for a predetermined period of time (called the life of the option). *Call options* give the right to buy, and *put options* the right to sell. For valuations, it is important to remember that options can be found on both the assets and the liabilities sides of the balance sheet. Options on the assets side provide flexibility and create value when the cost of the option is lower than the benefits it provides. Options on the liabilities side affect the company's cost of capital.

Examples of *options on the assets side* of the balance sheet primarily have to do with flexibility. A company that has the option to shut down and restart operations, or to abandon them, is more flexible and therefore more valuable than the same company without these options. Asset options are important not only because they affect the values of companies that have them, but also because they provide explicit criteria for deciding when operations should be opened, closed, or abandoned. For example, an option to open and close a mining operation may add 30 to 40 percent to its ordinary present value based on expected cash flow. In addition, the option provides explicit decision rules; for example, "open the mine when the price of kryptonite exceeds $100 per ounce."

In practice, we have applied option pricing to a variety of asset option situations in which the value of flexibility was critical. In one case, the option value of a large mineral lease was 100 percent higher than its simple net present value. Although the mine was only marginally profitable at the time, the option to defer development until the mineral price rose made the value much higher than indicated by net present value analysis. In a large research and development effort, the option to abandon the project at critical decision nodes increased its value by 83 percent. These and other applications will be discussed in greater detail later on.

Options on the liabilities side of the balance sheet are easy to recognize. Convertible debt and preferred stock give their holder the right to exchange them for stock at a predetermined conversion ratio. Therefore, they contain call options. Warrants allow their owner to buy shares at a fixed price—again, a call option. Our standard approach to valuation requires that we subtract the market value of these liabilities from the entity value to estimate the value of equity. Furthermore, they have to be included in the weighted average cost of capital. This issue is far from trivial. For example, a recent random sample of one hundred companies listed on the New York Stock Exchange indicated that forty-three had convertible debt or preferred stock outstanding, and these securities contain imbedded call options. Another important liabilities-side application is leasing. Most operating leases give the leaseholder the right to cancel by paying a fee (that is, an American put option) or the right to purchase for a fixed price at the end of the lease (that is, a European call). An American option can be exercised at any time up to and including the maturity date. A European option can be exercised only on its maturity date.

The purpose of this chapter is not to turn you into an options rocket scientist. Rather, we show the relation between option pricing and familiar approaches like net present value and decision-tree analysis, provide examples of asset options and show how they have been used in practice, and show how liability options can significantly affect the cost of capital.

ASSET OPTIONS

Options on assets add flexibility to managerial decision making. In the broadest sense, we can think of flexibility as one way of managing risk, but not the only method. Two strategies can be used for dealing with uncertainty: (1) anticipation, and (2) resilience. If risks can be anticipated because they are predictable, then the most effective and least costly approach is often to construct a specialized but inflexible system that works best in the anticipated environment. Alternatively, if risks cannot be anticipated, a resilient system with a great deal of flexibility becomes the best approach. Take as an example the shock to the economic system created when OPEC dramatically raised crude oil prices in the early 1970s. Heavy energy consumers had not anticipated the change, and many were overspecialized because they could convert only oil. They quickly invested, to create flexibility for themselves, in multiple sources of energy (for example, natural gas, hydroelectric power, and coal, as well as oil). The motivation for investment was to create a valuable asset option for themselves—the ability to switch at low cost between sources of energy. This is a typical example of the worth of asset options in a changing environment.

Asset options give various types of flexibility, such as the option to defer an investment, to expand (or contract) the scale of an investment, to abandon a project, or to start up and shut down an ongoing operation (the switching option). Asset options are important in analyzing research and development programs, new product introduction, and in valuing businesses that develop and extract natural resources.

In this section we first compare standard net present value (NPV) methodology (naively applied) with decision-tree analysis (DTA) and the option-pricing model (OPM). In so doing, we illustrate that option pricing is a generic form of decision making that encompasses NPV and DTA as special cases. Second, we provide simple examples of various types of asset options—a taxonomy of asset options. And third, we briefly illustrate how McKinsey & Company has applied option pricing by describing a few case histories.

Comparing Decision-Making Approaches

Exhibit 15.1 illustrates an *event tree*. Good and bad outcomes (G, B) are at the event nodes, and probabilities (p_1, p_2, p_3) are along the branches. Traditional NPV techniques estimate the value of the project by estimating the expected payouts, and then estimating the appropriate risk-adjusted opportunity cost of capital based on a comparable security with equivalent risk. Everyone knows the

Exhibit 15.1 **EVENT TREE**

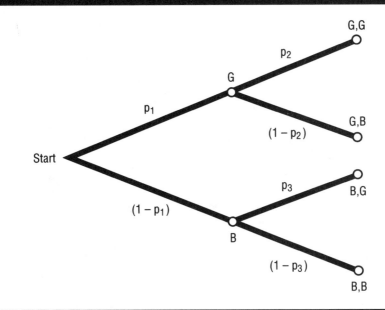

difficulties, both of estimating the payouts and of divining the discount rate; yet NPV is a widely accepted decision technique.

Exhibit 15.2 is a *decision tree*. The major difference from an event tree is that the nodes allow decisions to be made after information has been received and before proceeding to the next step. For example, if the bad (B) outcome turns up at the end of the first period, the decision maker may decide to stop the process, so that the lower outcomes in the second period can never occur. Clearly, DTA is superior to the NPV technique as naively applied in Exhibit 15.1. The problem with classic DTA is that it provides no recommendation about the appropriate risk-adjusted discount rate to use. That is where the option-pricing model makes an improvement.

The OPM allows decision nodes, like DTA, but it also searches for a comparable security with equivalent risk on which to base the discount rate. It combines the best features of NPV and DTA.

To further illustrate the differences among the three approaches, let us proceed with a numerical example, diagrammed in Exhibit 15.3. To keep things simple, suppose that two end-of-period states of nature (good and bad) are equally likely. We are

Exhibit 15.2 **DECISION TREE**

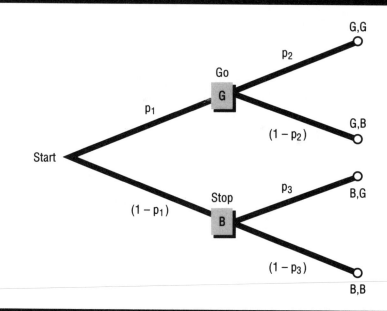

Exhibit 15.3 **PAYOUTS FOR A SIMPLE PROJECT**

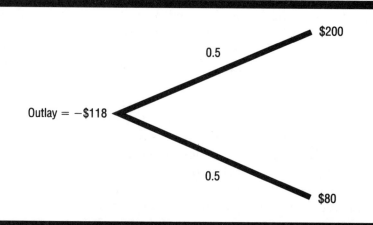

Exhibit 15.4 **DECISION TREE FOR A PERFECTLY CORRELATED SECURITY**

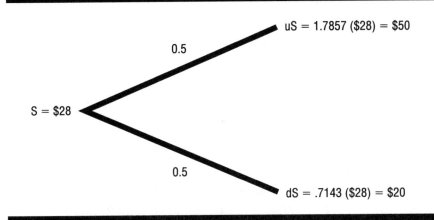

asked to evaluate a project that requires an investment outlay of $118. At the end of the year, it will return a stream of cash flows whose value at that time will be either $200 in the good state or $80 in the bad state. The states of nature are equally likely. What is the net present value of the project?

To determine the NPV, we need one more piece of information: the opportunity cost of capital. Since we assume the project is not perfectly correlated with the company evaluating it, we cannot use the company's cost of capital. Therefore, we seek another approach. We want to find another asset whose current value is readily observable and that has payouts that are perfectly (or highly) correlated with our project. We need to find a good comparable. After a long search, we come up with the security diagrammed in Exhibit 15.4. In the good state of nature, its price increases by a factor u=1.7857, and in the bad state its price falls to d = .7143 of its starting value. Its payouts are strictly proportional (one-fourth of the project payouts), and the market values the security at $28. The key is that this is a perfectly correlated *priced* security. Without knowing its market price, we could not proceed. At this price, the market-required rate of return on the security is

$$\$28 = \frac{.5(\$50) + .5(\$20)}{1+r} = \frac{\$35}{1+r}.$$

$$r = 25\%.$$

Now that we have estimated the required rate of return (the opportunity cost) for our risky project, we can compute its NPV.

$$\text{NPV} = \frac{\text{expected cash flows}}{1+\text{risk-adjusted rate}} - \text{investment outlay.}$$

$$= \frac{.5\big($200\big)+.5\big($80\big)}{1+.25} - $118.$$

$$= -$6.$$

Given this set of facts, our decision is obvious. We do not undertake the project, due to its negative NPV. Because NPV is a familiar methodology, we usually accept without question that the opportunity cost of capital is a reasonable approximation, even though it is based on the search for a comparable security. Keep this in mind, because our ability to understand option pricing as a practical decision-making tool depends on exactly the same leap of faith—finding a comparable security.

Next, suppose we complicate the picture by introducing a one-year license that allows management to wait one year, and then undertake the project if the good state of nature occurs or allow the license to expire if the bad state occurs. The license provides flexibility—the *option to defer*.[1] Let us say the risk-free rate of interest is 8 percent. Now the decision tree is more complex, as shown in Exhibit 15.5. Note that the option to defer (implied by the license) dramatically alters the shape of payouts. Instead of paying $118 now to receive either $200 or $80, we can wait to see if the state of nature is favorable, then go ahead and invest, for a net of $72.56; or we can decide to abandon the project in the bad state of nature. An analogous situation is an R&D project. We invest a small sum now to find out if a product or an idea is going to turn out to be good or bad. If it is good, we invest more and proceed. If it is bad, we stop. Without the license to defer, the optimal (inflexible) NPV decision was to stop today, and its payout was $0.

How shall we value the license that provides a flexibility option

---

[1] For an excellent presentation of the option to defer, using this example, as well as other asset options, see L. Trigeorgis, and S. Mason, "Valuing Managerial Flexibility" *Midland Corporate Finance Journal* 5, no. 1 (Spring 1987): 14–21. Also, see A. Dixit and R. Pindyck, *Investment Under Uncertainty* (Princeton, N.J.: Princeton University Press, 1994).

Exhibit 15.5 **DECISION TREE WITH AN OPTION TO DEFER**

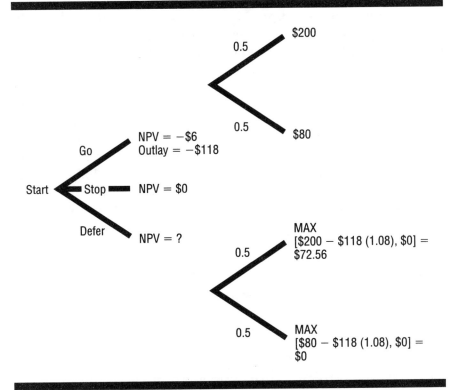

to defer? We will illustrate both the decision-tree and the option-pricing approaches. The problem with the decision-tree approach is that we do not know the appropriate discount rate. The 25 percent rate defined from our NPV comparable is inappropriate, because the comparable security is not even approximately correlated with the payouts from the flexibility option. But let us use it anyway, just for the heck of it. The decision-tree analysis would compute the NPV as

$$NPV = \frac{.5\left(\$72.56\right) + .5\left(\$0\right)}{1.25} = \$29.02.$$

Next, we turn to the option-pricing approach. It combines the desirable features of both the NPV and DTA approaches. From the NPV approach, it borrows the idea that we must find a comparable (perfectly correlated security) to correctly evaluate risk, and from the DTA approach it uses decision nodes (not rigid event nodes) to model flexibility.

The option-pricing approach proceeds to solve the problem by creating a portfolio of observable securities whose prices (and required rates of return) are known and whose payouts exactly mimic the payouts of our decision tree. Since the market prices of the comparable securities are known, we can value the option to defer. The mimicking portfolio, whose payouts are diagrammed in Exhibit 15.6, consists of m shares of the comparable stock, S, and borrowing B dollars at the risk-free rate, r_f. The payouts in the good state $72.56 and the bad state ($0) exactly replicate the payouts in the decision tree, given the option to defer (Exhibit 15.5). We can solve for the value of m and the number of units of the riskless bond, B, because we have two equations and two unknowns.

$$m(uS) - (1 + r_f)B = \$72.56$$
$$m(dS) - (1 + r_f)B = \$0$$

Given that uS = $50, dS = $20, and r_f = .08, we have

$$B = \$44.79 \text{ and } m = 2.42 \text{ shares}$$

Exhibit 15.6 **PAYOUTS OF A MIMICKING PORTFOLIO**

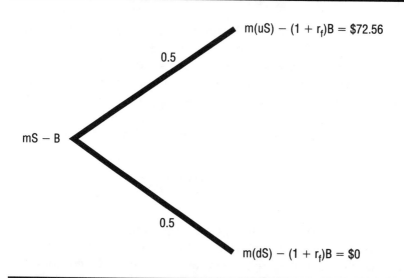

Thus, a mimicking portfolio, with 2.42 shares of the comparable security and borrowing $44.79, has exactly the same payouts as the flexible option to defer. Since the mimicking portfolio has the same payouts, it has the same value.

$$mS - B = 2.42(\$28) - \$44.79$$
$$= \$22.97$$

Going back to Exhibit 15.5, this means that if the license to defer cost less than $22.97, we would purchase it. Then, if the favorable state of nature occurred, we would proceed with the project, paying $118 (1.08) = $127.44 and receiving a cash flow stream worth $200. But if the unfavorable state turned up, we would simply decide not to go forward with the project.

If we compare the option-pricing value of the option to defer, $22.97, with the DTA value, $29.02, we see that the DTA overvalued the option because it used the 25 percent discount rate taken from the NPV analysis—but the NPV payouts did not mimic the payouts on the flexibility option. Naively applied, the DTA was comparing apples and oranges. The DTA would have given the same answer as the option-pricing approach had it used a discount rate of roughly 58 percent:

$$Value = \frac{expected\ cash\ flow}{1 + risk\text{-}adjusted\ rate}.$$

$$= \frac{.5(\$72.56) + .5(\$0)}{1.58}.$$

$$= \$22.97.$$

Alternatively, we could have used certainty-equivalent probabilities and discounted at the risk-free rate. The certainty-equivalent probabilities are

$$Value = \frac{expected\ cash\ flow}{1 + risk\text{-}adjusted\ rate}.$$

$$= \frac{.5(\$72.56) + .5(1-p)(\$0)}{1.08}.$$

$$p = .342.$$

Finally, the value of the flexibility provided by the option to defer is the difference between the NPV computed using only event nodes, and the value with the option to defer. Recall that the NPV was –$6 and the value with the option to defer was $22.97; therefore, the option to defer is worth $28.97.

To summarize this section, we have shown that the option-pricing approach is superior to both the naive application of the NPV technique and DTA. It combines the use of decision nodes with the concept of using risk-adjusted comparables to correctly evaluate decisions that involve flexibility. Next, we describe the broad categories of asset options and give real-world analogues for each.

A Taxonomy of Asset Options

Ordinary NPV analysis tends to understate a project's value because it fails to capture adequately the benefits of operating flexibility and other strategic factors such as follow-on-investment. To identify potential operating flexibility and strategic factors, we will classify asset options into five mutually exclusive (but not exhaustive) categories and discuss some potential implications.

Abandonment option   The option to abandon (or sell) a project—for example, the right to abandon an open pit coal mine—is formally equivalent to an American put option on the stock. Exhibit 15.7 is a decision tree with an abandonment option attached to it. If the bad outcome turns up at the end of the first period, the decision maker may decide to abandon the project and realize the expected liquidation value. Then, the expected liquidation (or resale) value of the project may be thought of as the exercise price of the put. When the present value of the asset falls below the liquidation value, the act of abandoning (or selling) the project is equivalent to exercising the put. Because the liquidation value of the project sets a lower bound on the value of the project, the option to liquidate is valuable. A project that can be liquidated is therefore worth more than the same project without the possibility of abandonment.

Option to defer development   The option to defer an investment outlay to develop a property is formally equivalent to an American call option on the stock. For example, the owner of a lease on an undeveloped oil reserve has the right to "acquire" a developed reserve by paying a lease-on-development cost. However, the owner can

Exhibit 15.7 **DECISION TREE WITH AN ABANDONMENT OPTION**

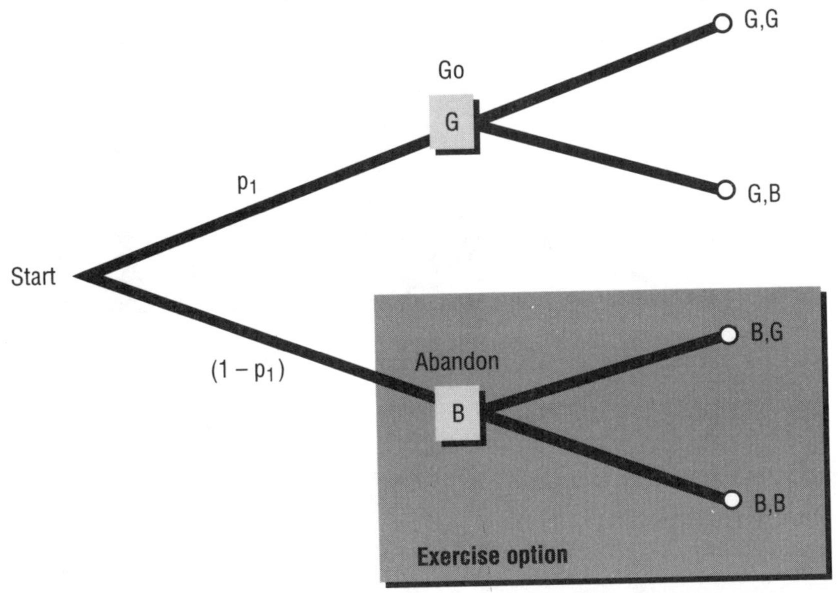

defer the development process until oil prices rise. In other words, the managerial option implicit in holding an undeveloped reserve is in fact a deferral option. The expected development cost may be thought of as the exercise price of the call. The net production revenue less depletion of the developed reserve is the opportunity cost incurred by deferring the investment. If this opportunity cost is too high, the decision maker may want to exercise the option (that is, develop the reserve) before its relinquishment date. Exhibit 15.8 illustrates this type of option. Because the deferrable investment option gives management the right, but not the obligation, to make the investment to develop the property, a project that can be deferred is worth more than the same project without the flexibility to defer development.

Option to expand   The option to expand the scale of a project's operation is formally equivalent to an American call option on the stock. For example, management may choose to build production capacity in excess of the expected level of output so that it can

Exhibit 15.8 **DECISION TREE WITH AN OPTION TO DEFER**

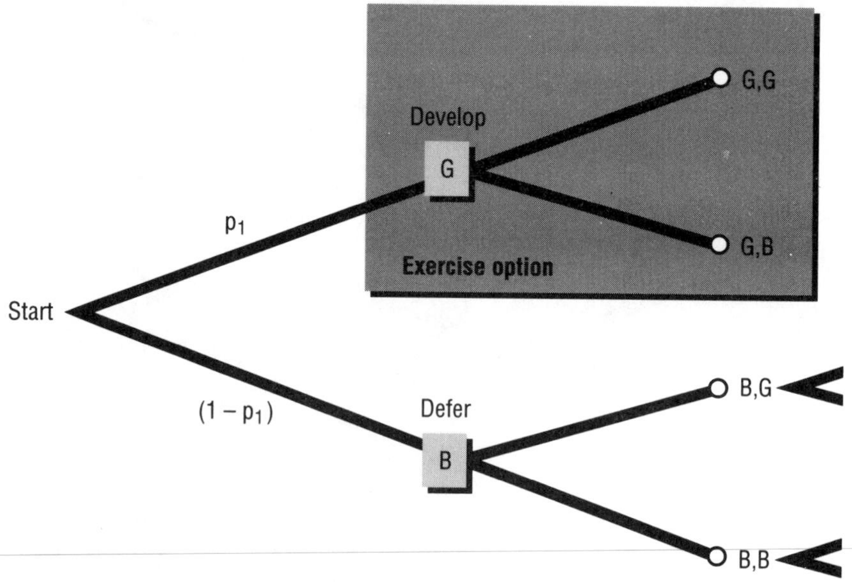

produce at a higher rate if the product is more successful than was originally anticipated. Exhibit 15.9 illustrates this type of option. Because the expansion option gives management the right, but not the obligation, to make additional follow-on investment (for example, to increase the production rate) if project conditions turn out to be favorable, a project that can be expanded is worth more than the same project without the flexibility to expand.

The option to expand is difficult to evaluate in practice because its decision tree is complex. For example, the option to expand can be exercised today by building excess capacity or next year by building excess capacity then, and so it goes.

Option to contract   The option to contract the scale of a project's operation is formally equivalent to an American put option on stock. Many projects can be engineered in such a way that output can be contracted in the future. For example, a project can be modularized. Foregoing planned future expenditures on the project is equivalent to the exercise price of the put. Exhibit 15.10 illustrates this type of option. Because the contraction option gives manage-

Exhibit 15.9 **DECISION TREE WITH AN OPTION TO EXPAND**

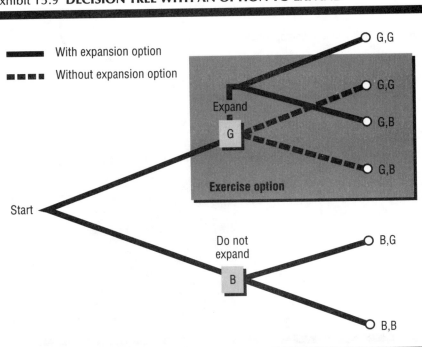

ment the right to reduce the operating scale if project conditions turn out to be unfavorable, a project that can be contracted is worth more than the same project without the flexibility to contract.

Switching options   This is the most general class of asset option. The option to switch project operations is in fact a portfolio of options that consists of both call and put options. For example, restarting operations when a project is currently shut down is equivalent to an American call option. Similarly, shutting down operations when unfavorable conditions arise is equivalent to an American put option. The cost of restarting (or shutting down) operations may be thought of as the exercise price of the call (or put). A project whose operation can be dynamically turned on and off (or switched between two distinct locations, and so on) is worth more than the same project without the flexibility to switch. A flexible manufacturing system (FMS) with the ability to produce two products is a good example of this type of option. (See Exhibit 15.11.)

Exhibit 15.10 **DECISION TREE WITH AN OPTION TO CONTRACT**

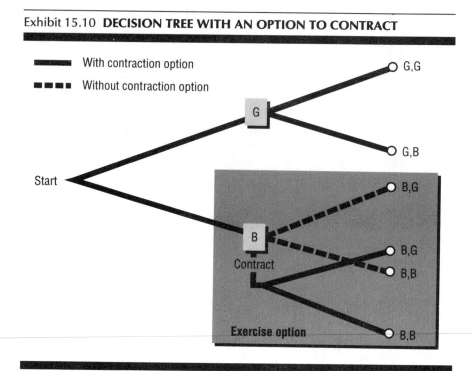

Asset Options in Practice

Drawing from our experience with clients, we now briefly describe four case histories that illustrate four types of options. Names of corporations and data are, of course, disguised to ensure confidentiality. We make explicit comparisons among different valuation approaches to show the usefulness of the option-pricing approach. Finally, we discuss some conclusions and lessons learned from each application.

Most asset option-pricing applications are limited to those situations in which the option value depends on the market price of a world commodity, such as oil, coal, copper, nickel, gold, or zinc. When we have observable price data about the underlying risky asset, option pricing is feasible. Without the priced comparable security, it is guesswork at best.

Oil extraction A major North American energy client, OILCO, planned to sell an interest in an important heavy oil asset. Deferral options were important. The asset was unique in having poten-

Exhibit 15.11 **DECISION TREE WITH SWITCHING OPTIONS**

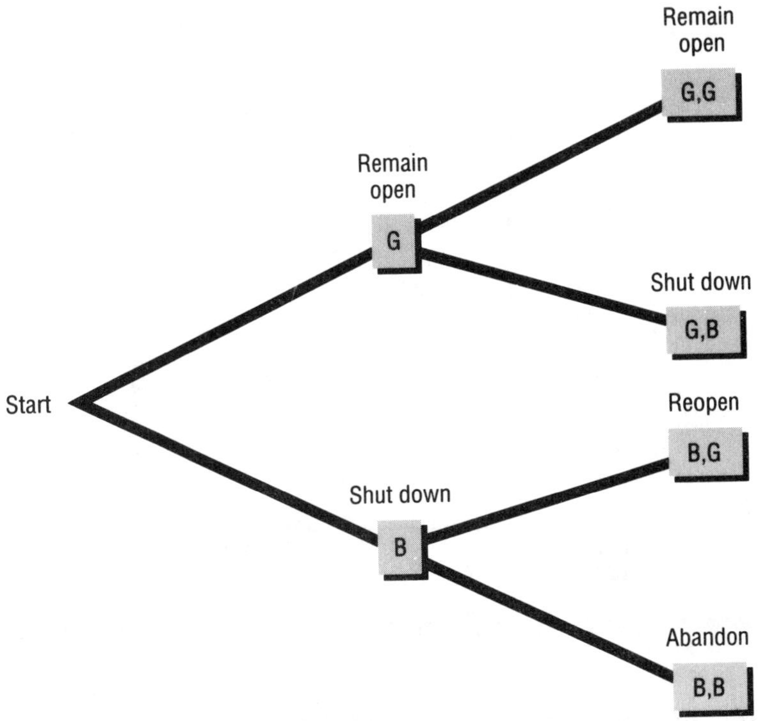

tial expansion opportunities that could be phased in over time to significantly increase capacity with minimal geological risk. Conventional NPV approaches and assumptions considerably understated the value of OILCO's operations to an investor. The lack of industry consensus about the future behavior of oil prices led to greatly divergent NPVs. Specifically, two major operating flexibilities were present: the option of deferring a debottlenecking program and the option of deferring an expansion program. These two options added significant value to OILCO's operation, an increase of 21 percent over its conventional NPV (see Exhibit 15.12).

The option premiums that the company identified placed upper bounds on the asset's market value under a given set of oil price and macroeconomics assumptions. The option-pricing approach also provided decision rules on when to time investments.

Exhibit 15.12 **AFTER-TAX VALUATION OF OILCO OPERATIONS,** $ MILLIONS

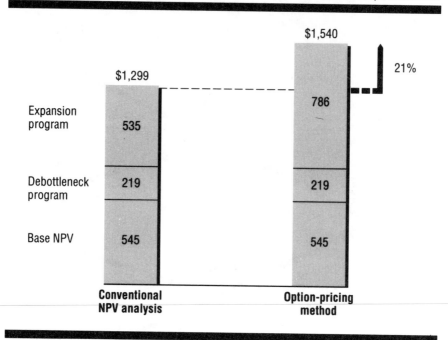

Specifically, the OPM indicated that OILCO should initiate its expansion program as soon as the oil price rose above $20 per barrel. Since, in practice, it might not be possible to time investments in this optimal manner, a rational investor sharing the same expectations as OILCO would in reality be prepared to pay only some portion of the option premium. However, the option valuation provided a reasonable starting point for negotiations to sell the property.

Kryptonite mining   Kryptonite (not the real name of the mineral) is a globally traded commodity product. Kryptonite Mining Limited was the world's leading producer of kryptonite, supplying over one-third of the free world's demand. It had four production sites, each with a different layout of operating mines and different extraction technology. The random movement of spot kryptonite prices had been extremely volatile in the past four years. Our study focused on developing a valuation method for each site as well as providing some guidance regarding the shut-down/re-open decision—

a switching option. Initial estimates of Kryptonite Mining's NPV based on analysts' forecasts of kryptonite prices measured only up to 45 percent of Kryptonite Mining's current market value of equity (see Exhibit 15.13). A scenario-based NPV analysis allowing for no explicit operational flexibilities increased this estimate to 71 percent of equity value. Finally, the option-pricing valuation with shut-down/re-open and abandonment options gave us a valuation of Kryptonite Mining's equity of 116 percent of its current market value.

The shut-down, re-open, and abandonment option values as fractions of the corresponding site option-pricing values ranged between 5 and 15 percent for a spot price range of $1.75/ounce to $2.25/ounce. These option values were much higher for lower spot prices and much lower for higher spot prices.

A major benefit of the analysis was that it provided insight into the economics of when to open up and shut down each site. Given

Exhibit 15.13 **VALUATION OF KRYPTONITE MINING LIMITED,** $ MILLIONS

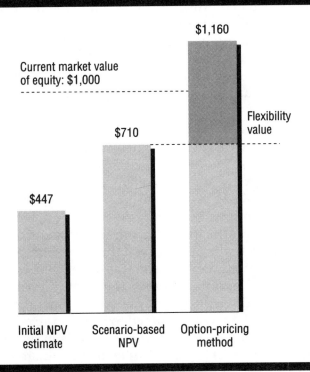

that a mine was open, it was optimal to keep it open even when the marginal revenue from a ton of output was less than the marginal cost of extraction. The intuitive explanation is that the fixed cost of closing an operation might be incurred needlessly if the commodity price rose in the near future. The opposite result applies to a closed mine. Due to the cost of reopening it, the optimal decision might be to keep it closed until the commodity price rose substantially above the marginal cost of production.

Pharmaceutical R&D   Drug & Company was a leading manufacturer of human and animal health care products. It needed to value a new drug research and development project.

Four development stages were involved: (1) initial R&D, with a 20 percent chance of success; (2) preclinical testing, with a 50 percent chance of success; (3) testing I, with a 40 percent chance of success; and (4) testing II, with a 90 percent chance of success. Exhibit 15.14 illustrates the decision tree with abandonment options. Using the traditional NPV approach—that is, neglecting the staged-abandonment option—this R&D project was valued at $18.3 million. By contrast, the OPM, taking account of the staged abandonment option, gave a valuation of $33.5 million, 83 percent more than its traditional NPV. Exhibit 15.14 also shows the value increment from the abandonment options. This analysis ascribed put-option values to a multistage research program that could be abandoned at various phases of development.

Mineral lease   MINCO was deciding on the correct bid for a mineral lease. A very careful NPV analysis indicated a value that was 50 percent lower than the anticipated winning bid. At current prices, the project would have only marginal profitability if developed immediately. However, the NPV analysis did not account for the value of an implicit option to defer development for up to five years—that is, to wait for better prices before making capital outlays to develop the project. Given the very high production rate that was anticipated once the site was developed, analysis showed that the deferral option increased the NPV estimate by up to 100 percent, depending on the variance of mineral prices and on whether or not they were assumed to be mean-reverting.

Mean reversion played an important role in developing a realistic model, because mineral prices tend to fluctuate around a long-term average. When prices rise rapidly, they are driven down as

Exhibit 15.14 **ANALYSIS OF A MULTISTAGED PHARMACEUTICAL R&D PROJECT,** $ MILLIONS

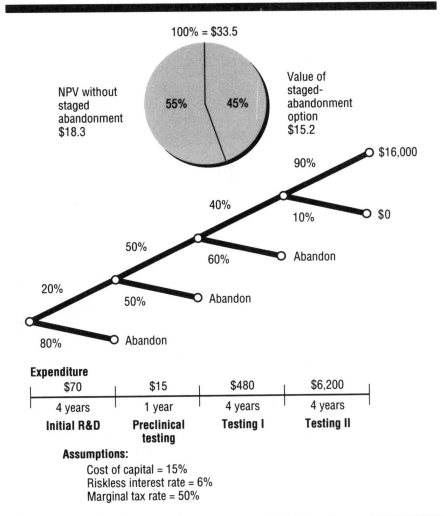

100% = $33.5

NPV without staged abandonment $18.3

55%   45%

Value of staged-abandonment option $15.2

90% ——O $16,000

40%

10% O $0

50%

60% O Abandon

20%

50% O Abandon

80% O Abandon

Expenditure			
$70	$15	$480	$6,200
4 years	1 year	4 years	4 years
Initial R&D	**Preclinical testing**	**Testing I**	**Testing II**

Assumptions:
Cost of capital = 15%
Riskless interest rate = 6%
Marginal tax rate = 50%

marginal suppliers open up production and as users switch to substitutes. And when prices fall, producers shut down and users move away from alternate sources. Therefore, mean reversion tends to reduce the value of the option.

It is easy to see from the examples that asset options can substantially alter the value of a business. The fact that the options exist, however, does not mean that they are optimally managed. One of the important outcomes of understanding asset options is that this understanding can provide new insight into managing flexibility.

LIABILITY OPTIONS

So far we have discussed flexibility options on the assets side of the balance sheet. Now we turn to options implicit in various sources of funding. These liability options are important because they affect the company's weighted average cost of capital.

Plain vanilla approaches to valuation describe the WACC as the simple weighted average of the after-tax opportunity costs of debt and equity. But hybrid securities that have option features are often used as sources of capital. We looked at a random sample of one hundred companies listed on the New York Stock Exchange and found that forty-three of them had convertible securities outstanding. The yield to maturity on convertible securities is usually much lower than on straight debt with the same maturity and quality. But the yield on convertible securities is a particularly bad estimate of their actual cost of capital.

The objective of this section is to show how option pricing can be used to compute the true opportunity cost for callable, convertible debt and preferred stock, and to illustrate with a few examples that employ McKinsey's convertible securities pricing model (CSPM). Of course, a wide variety of instruments on the liabilities side of the balance sheet have option features. A non-exhaustive list includes the equity of a leveraged company, warrants, callable or convertible debt and preferred stock, variable-rate loans with caps or floors, guaranteed lines of credit, operating leases, and executive stock options. All of these instruments affect the cost of capital and, therefore, the value of equity. The first part of our analysis will show how to value callable and convertible debt. Then we will discuss how its cost of capital is estimated. Finally, we will give a few real-world examples and discuss the complications involved.

Valuing Callable Debt

A callable bond can be repurchased by the issuing company at a fixed price for a predetermined period of time. Nearly all fixed-coupon bonds are callable. Exhibit 15.15 shows the terms for American Medical Intl. callable, convertible 9½s due 2001 whose

Exhibit 15.15 **TERMS FOR AMERICAN MEDICAL 9-½S DUE 2001**
(DATA FROM FALL 1988)

Rating	Baa1	
Amount authorized	$125.0 million	
Amount outstanding	$124.9 million	
Issued	11/5/81	
Due	11/15/2001	
Interest dates	5/15, 11/15	
CALL TERMS	Year	Price
	1987	$104.75
	1988	103.80
	1989	102.85
	1990	101.90
	1991	100.95
	1992 on	100.00
Conversion price	$24.38/share	

face value is $100. A callable bond is equivalent to a straight bond plus a call option. Since the option limits the potential capital gain of investors who hold the bond, they require a higher return on callable bonds than on equivalent noncallable bonds.

If interest rates fall low enough, it is to the company's advantage to call the bonds, pay the call premium, and then refund them at a lower rate. The variability of interest rates is crucial for pricing callable bonds. For example, assume a three-year callable bond, which pays a 12 percent coupon, has a $100 face value and can be called for $104 from Year 1 onward. The current market rate of interest is 10 percent, but it can move upward by a factor of 1.2 or down by .85 with equal probability. Exhibit 15.16 models the term structure of interest rates (the yield curve) used in our example.

Exhibits 15.17 and 15.18 show the valuation of a straight 12 percent (default-free) bond and its callable equivalent, given the assumed term structure. Note that in every state of nature where the market value of the bond exceeds its call price, it should be called. The effect is to reduce the value of the bond to investors (from $104.46 to $103.54), and therefore to increase its cost of capital to the company from 10.20 percent to 10.56 percent pretax.

Exhibit 15.16 SIMPLIFIED TERM STRUCTURE OF INTEREST RATES

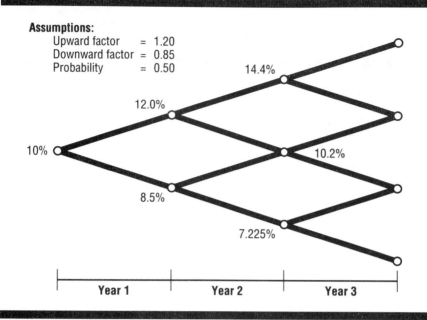

Assumptions:
Upward factor = 1.20
Downward factor = 0.85
Probability = 0.50

14.4%
12.0%
10%
10.2%
8.5%
7.225%

Year 1 | Year 2 | Year 3

Exhibit 15.17 VALUATION OF A STRAIGHT 12 PERCENT BOND

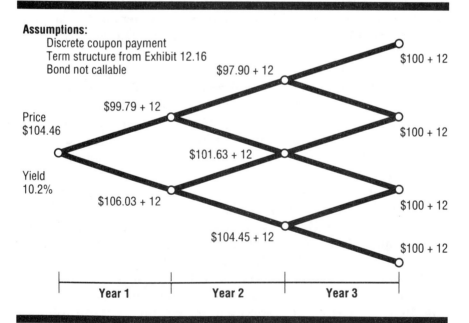

Assumptions:
Discrete coupon payment
Term structure from Exhibit 12.16
Bond not callable

$100 + 12
$97.90 + 12
$99.79 + 12
Price
$104.46
$100 + 12
$101.63 + 12
Yield
10.2%
$106.03 + 12
$100 + 12
$104.45 + 12
$100 + 12

Year 1 | Year 2 | Year 3

486

Exhibit 15.18 **VALUATION OF A CALLABLE BOND**

Assumptions:

Discrete coupon payment
Term structure from Exhibit 15.16
Bond callable at $104 in Year 1

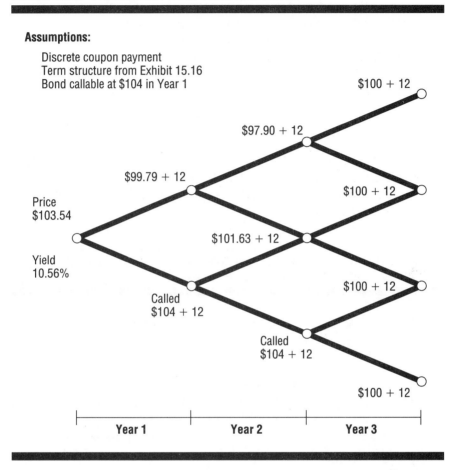

Price
$103.54

Yield
10.56%

$100 + 12

$97.90 + 12

$99.79 + 12

$100 + 12

$101.63 + 12

Called
$104 + 12

$100 + 12

Called
$104 + 12

$100 + 12

| Year 1 | Year 2 | Year 3 |

Valuing Callable, Convertible Securities

Convertible bonds allow their owners to convert them into another security at a predetermined exchange ratio for a fixed interval of time. For example, the American Medical 9-½s, described in Exhibit 15.15, could be converted into common stock at a price of $24.38 per share anytime during their life. The actual common stock price at the time of our data collection was $14.75. When exercising conversion rights, the bondholder gives up, as the exercise price, the present value of the expected bond payments. For American

Medical, the bondholders would give up the bond payments in return for 4.102 shares (per $100 of face value on the bond). Thus, convertible bonds have a changing exercise price.

Exhibit 15.19 shows a numerical example of the valuation of a callable, convertible bond. The following set of assumptions details the interest rate environment, the way the value of the company varies through time, and the provisions of the callable, convertible bond.

- The constant risk-free rate is 8 percent per year.
- The company is worth $400,000 right now (no senior debt).
- There is a 60 percent probability that company value will increase by 50 percent, and a 40 percent probability that it will decrease by 50 percent.

Exhibit 15.19 **VALUATION OF A HYPOTHETICAL COMPANY AND ITS CALLABLE, CONVERTIBLE BOND,** $ THOUSANDS

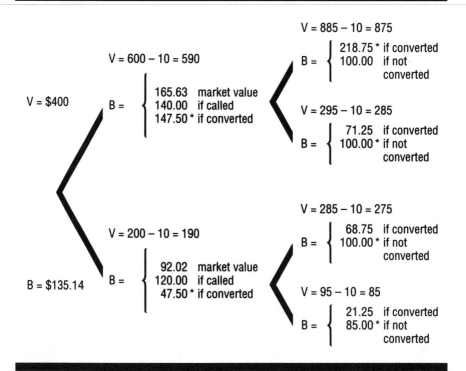

* Optimal decision.

- Two securities are outstanding: 150 shares of stock and 100 callable, convertible bonds, which can be converted at a ratio of one-half share per bond.
- If bonds are converted, bondholders will own $50/(150 + 50)$ = 25 percent of the company.
- Each $1,000-face-value bond pays $100 per period coupon.
- Anytime before maturity, stockholders can call the bonds for $1,400.
- The company pays no dividends.
- The first bond coupon has just been paid.

To value the callable, convertible bonds, we start with their final payouts, determine the optimal action, and compute their value at the end of Year 1 conditional on the value of the company, as illustrated in Exhibit 15.19. For example, given that the value of the company has gone up the first year, the final value of the company can be $875 thousand or $285 thousand, ex coupon. If it is $875 thousand, the bondholders receive $218.75 thousand if they convert, and $100 thousand otherwise. Obviously, they will convert. If the company value is $285 thousand, they will not convert, preferring to receive the $1,000 face value per bond rather than the conversion value of $712.50. With these facts in hand, we can determine the market value of the bond at the end of Year 1.

$$B = \frac{.58\big($218.75\big) + .42\big($100\big)}{1.08} + \frac{$10}{1.08} = $165.63.$$

Note that the payouts are multiplied by their respective hedging (or certainty equivalent) probabilities

$$p = \frac{r_f - d}{u - d} = \frac{1.08 - .5}{1.5 - .5} = .58,$$

and then discounted at the risk-free rate.

Since the market value of the bond is greater than the $1,400 call price, shareholders will exercise their right to call. When they do this, bondholders, who would not voluntarily convert, are forced to do so at a value of 0.25 ($590) = $147.50. Thus, we see that the Year-1 value of the callable, convertible bond, given that the company value goes up, is $147.50.

By working backward from the final set of payouts, we find that the current market value of the bond is $135.14. Similar calculations can be performed to show that the present value of the same bond, if callable but not convertible, is $101.30. The value of the conversion feature is $33.84 per bond.

Whenever the entity approach for valuing a company is used, the market value of equity is estimated by first valuing the whole company—the entity—and then subtracting the market value of debt to estimate the value of equity. Having a good estimate of the market value of convertible securities is often crucial. In our example, the best estimate of the market value of equity is the value of the company, $400,000, less the market value of callable, convertible debt, $135,140. The value of equity is $264,860. Had we used the face value of the debt, $100,000, we would have overestimated the equity value by 13.3 percent.

The Cost of Capital for Callable, Convertible Securities

In 1966, Eugene Brigham surveyed the chief financial officers of 22 companies that had issued convertible debt. Of them 68 percent said they had used convertible debt because they believed their stock price would rise over time and that convertibles would provide a way of selling common stock at a price above the existing market. Another 27 percent said that their company had wanted straight debt but had found conditions to be such that a straight bond issue could not be sold at a reasonable rate of interest.

The problem with these responses is that neither reason makes much sense. Convertible bonds are not "cheap debt." Because convertible bonds are riskier, their true cost of capital is greater (on a before-tax basis) than the cost of straight debt. Also, convertible bonds are not equal to deferred sale of common stock at an attractive price. The uncertain sale of shares at $28, for example, each at some unknown future date, can hardly be compared directly with a current share price of $25.

The risk of convertible debt is higher than that of straight debt and lower than that of equity, so its true opportunity cost lies between these limits. The yield to maturity on convertible debt (often lower than on the company's senior debt) has nothing to do with its opportunity cost, because convertible debt has an option embedded in it, and options are much riskier than debt.

Three broad categories of information are needed to value a callable, convertible bond and to determine its cost of capital:

1. *The interest rate environment.* Ideally, we would capture the entire term structure and its expected variability. However, our model can handle only one random variable at a time, and the variability of the company's common stock is the most important element. Consequently, the interest rate environment is captured by the yield to maturity on a Treasury bond with the same maturity as the convertible bond.

2. *Characteristics of the bond.* We need to know the amount outstanding, the face value, the number of months to maturity, the conversion price, the number of months until the first coupon date, the time between coupons, the annual coupon rate, and the call provisions (the call prices and their timing).

3. *Characteristics of the common stock.* Since the bond is convertible into common stock, we need to know the current stock price, the equity beta, the expected dividend per share, the ex dividend dates, the number of shares outstanding, the equity volatility, and the amount of senior debt outstanding.

Exhibit 15.20 shows our estimate of the value and the before-tax cost of capital for a sample of seven callable, convertible bonds. The results were provided by McKinsey's in-house convertible securities pricing model. In every case, the before-tax cost of capital for the callable, convertible bond is higher than the coupon rate, and in all but one case (Baker Hughes) the difference is substantial.

The after-tax cost of the bond depends on the percentage of its opportunity cost that is actually tax deductible. Thus, an estimate of its after-tax cost is

$$\text{After - tax } K_{CV} = K_{CV}\left[1 - \frac{\text{coupon rate}}{K_{CV}}(\text{tax rate})\right].$$

For example, if American Medical's tax rate were 39 percent, the after-tax cost of the 9-½s would be

$$\text{After - tax } K_{CV} = .180\left[1 - \frac{.095}{.180}(.39)\right] = 14.3\%.$$

Exhibit 15.20 **COST OF CAPITAL FOR SEVEN CALLABLE, CONVERTIBLE BONDS**

Company	Common Stock		Convertible Bond	
	Price	Beta	Coupon rate	Cost of capital
American Medical Int'l.	$14.88	1.15	9.50%	18.00%
Baker Hughes	16.75	1.21	9.50	10.40
Bally	17.00	1.35	6.00	26.10
Bank of Boston	25.75	1.06	7.75	19.90
General Instrument	31.00	1.40	7.25	12.40
Humana	22.25	1.11	8.50	11.60
Loral	39.38	1.04	10.75	14.60

Company	Callable, Convertible Bond			
	Exercise price	Market price	Model price	Percent difference
American Medical Int'l.	$24.38	$ 932.50	$ 798.84	−14.3%
Baker Hughes	47.13	977.50	913.86	−6.5
Bally	28.99	760.00	622.47	−18.1
Bank of Boston	23.42	1,135.00	1,103.67	−2.8
General Instrument	40.57	1,015.00	1,066.07	+5.0
Humana	37.80	935.00	902.29	−3.5
Loral	44.25	1,020.00	969.16	−5.0

Source: McKinsey analysis.

SUMMARY

Option pricing is analogous with flexibility in decision making, because the holder of an option can exercise the option at his or her discretion to take advantage of an opportunity. Viewed broadly, options can affect every arena of management. We have illustrated only a few applications. On the assets side of the balance sheet are options to defer, expand, contract, abandon, or switch projects on and off. Net present value analysis, rigidly applied, often undervalues assets because it fails to account for the rich set of flexibility options involved in business decisions. On the liabilities side, options can have a significant impact on the cost of capital. We analyzed callable, convertible debt and saw that the true opportunity cost is often substantially higher than the coupon rate. Convertible debt is not a free lunch. It is neither cheap debt nor cheap equity.

Valuing options is a complex task, generally beyond the capability of an analyst with a pocket calculator. Although PC-based programs are available for standard situations, it is usually advisable to seek the advice of an expert, especially when asset options (with their extreme complexity) are involved.

REVIEW QUESTIONS

1. Consider the following strategies:
   - *Money Spread:* purchase a call (or put) above and sell a call (or put) below the current underlying asset price.
   - *Strip:* purchase two puts and one call of the same maturity on the same asset.
   - *Strap:* purchase two calls and one put of the same maturity on the same asset.
   - *Straddle:* purchase a put and a call on the same asset.

   Graph the possibilities of the value of each strategy versus the underlying asset value at the maturity of the options. Discuss the rationale of each strategy.

2. Suppose that a stock is quoted at $50, and a 90-day put with $40 strike price written on the stock is worth $3.05; 90-day T-Bills yield 7.1 percent. Assume that the stock does not pay dividends, and Federal Reserve policy appears to be relatively stable over the 90-day period. Value the corresponding call option.

3. A mining firm in the United States wants to borrow 60 percent of the market value of its only asset, an open pit copper mine in Southeast Asia. Geologists expect the mine to tap out its reserve in three years at the rate of 150 tons next year, 100 million the next year, and the remainder of the 300-million-ton reserve in the third year. The copper ore mine mouth net operating profit less adjusted taxes is currently $0.10 per ton mined. Copper price percentage changes vary with a standard deviation of 20 percent per year; this represents the only uncertainty of any importance to the mine. What is the value of the mine if it lasts the next three years? If the mine can be abandoned at a salvage value of $0.09 per ton of ore remaining, how far must the net copper yield fall for the firm to abandon its stake and revert its franchise to the domestic government? What is the value of the mine with an abandonment option? How much can the firm borrow?

4. An Australian bank issued 20 billion JPY fixed rate 7 percent coupons maturing in five years based on LIBOR. Currently LIBOR is 6.50 percent with an estimated volatility of 15 percent per annum. Estimate the risk-adjusted rate on the note and the risk-adjusted spread on par.

5. The same Australian bank wants to investigate the issuance of a companion note, this time based on floating LIBOR with a 45 basis point margin. Estimate the risk-adjusted yield and compare with the fixed-rate note in the previous question.

6. Finally, the Australian bank desires to swap JPY denominated fixed-rate borrowing into USD LIBOR floating-rate borrowing. Construct a swap diagram to illustrate the transaction. Comment on the cash flows that face the bank and the swap counterparty. How can the counterparty migrate its risk? Value the swap and compare the fixed, floating, and swapped alternatives. This transaction has been labeled by some the reverse sushi swap.

7. Thrift institutions can offset long positions in mortgages by investing in mortgage-backed securities strips (SMBS) that are weighted in the direction of coupon interest away from principal repayment. Effectively, these SMBSs are high coupon, premium securities with a prepayment option. Similarly, pension funds can offset long-term future service liabilities by investing in MBS strips that are more heavily weighted in the direction of the principal repayment and away from coupon interest. These SMBSs are low coupon, deep discount securities with a prepayment option.

   Consider a $1,000 mortgage pool with a 10 percent coupon, and a five-year maturity. Assume a simplified term structure of interest rates with spot one year rate starting at 7 percent and volatility of 15 percent per year. Divide the pool into two strips: an SMBS with one-quarter of the interest, two-thirds of the principal; another SMBS with three-quarters of the interest, one-third of the principal.

   Value the straight bond, the bond if zeroed, the bond if stripped, and the two combo bonds.

16

Valuing Banks

The banking and thrift industries have been going through a decade of change catalyzed by the globalization of financial markets; privatization; deregulation, which has enhanced competition among financial institutions; the growing popularity of nonbank substitutes that channel individual savings into corporate investment; greater interest-rate volatility; and changes in tax laws. These powerful forces have led banks and savings and loans (S&Ls) to take greater risks in order to enhance their perceived profitability. The pitfalls have been numerous, and nearly every financial institution has experienced some difficulty. Bank managers have created large lending positions in less-developed countries (LDCs), in leveraged-buyout situations and in commercial real estate; S&L managers have over-extended mortgage credit and engaged in risky land speculation.

The inevitable result is massive restructuring in the banking and thrift industries. In the fourth quarter of 1988, the Bank of New York successfully completed its hostile takeover of Irving Trust. Many commercial banks have adopted a "poison pill" defense against potential takeover. In 1991 Chemical Bank and Manufacturers Hanover agreed to merge. In 1994 the Bank of America offered to buy Continental Illinois, and the Mellon Bank bought Dreyfus. These events suggest that a substantial level of internal restructuring and "friendly" acquisitions or divestitures will occur as the industry consolidates.

Valuation is an important tool for understanding restructuring.

Managers who focus on value creation, rather then being misled by accounting models of their businesses, will have a competitive advantage. Banks that restructure themselves to maximize value for their shareholders are less subject to takeover attempts and regulatory pressure. They are also in the best position to acquire other financial institutions in order to create value through superior management skills.

THE DIFFICULTY OF VALUING BANKS

Valuing banks is conceptually difficult. For an outsider, determining the quality of the loan portfolio, measuring the amount of current accounting profits attributable to interest-rate mismatch (for example, the difference between long-term rates earned on loans and short-term rates paid on deposits), and understanding which business units are driving the bank's profit potential are all hard to do.

For an insider attempting to value a bank, the major issue is transfer pricing. As illustrated in Exhibit 16.1, most banks can be separated into three basic business units (although most have dozens of distinct businesses): a retail bank, which may have only twenty cents in loans for each dollar in deposits; a wholesale bank, with only twenty cents in deposits for each dollar in loans; and a treasury that stands between them and carries on activities of its own, such as securities trading. The excess funds generated by the retail bank can be loaned to the marketplace or to the wholesale bank. If loaned internally, the rate credited to the retail bank and the rate paid by the wholesale bank are crucial transfer prices. If the price credited to the retail bank is set too high, it will appear to be more profitable, and vice versa. It is critical to establish the correct transfer price in order to determine where the bank should allocate its marginal resources—to the retail bank or the wholesale bank.

This short chapter focuses mainly on the issue of how to value banks. It does not present all the answers to bank valuation. First, we discuss the practical reasons why it is easier to use an equity approach than an entity approach to valuing banks. Second, we cover the issues involved in an outsider's approach. And finally, we turn to the problems of an insider's approach.

Exhibit 16.1 **BUSINESS-UNIT STRUCTURE OF BANKS**

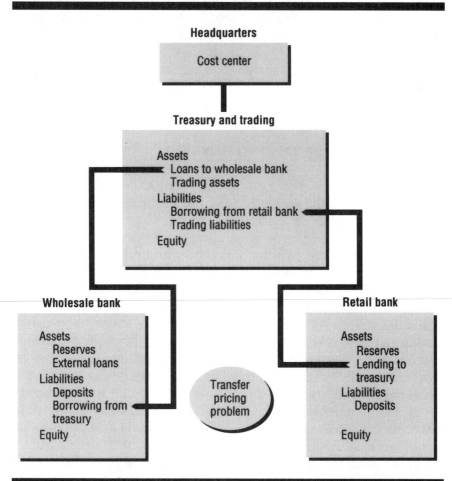

THE EQUITY APPROACH TO VALUING BANKS

Throughout the book we have recommended and used the entity approach to valuing companies. (The entity approach discounts the after-tax free cash flow from operations at the weighted average cost of capital to first obtain the estimated entity value, then it subtracts the market value of debt to estimate the equity value.) Banks are the exception that proves the rule. Although the equity and entity approaches are mathematically equivalent, the equity approach to valuing banks is more appropriate and easier to use. Therefore, we recommend that for banks you forecast free cash flow to equity holders and discount it at the cost of equity.

In addition to being easier to use, there is a conceptual reason for using the equity approach for valuing banks. The deposit franchise given by the government to the bank potentially allows the bank to create value on the liabilities side of its balance sheet. If the cost of issuing deposits (e.g., interest expense, check clearing, and tellers) is less than the cost of raising an equivalent amount of funds with equal risk in the open market, then a positive spread that creates value for shareholders is created. Thus, liabilities management is part of the business operations of the bank and is not purely financing. If it was pure financing, there would be no spread. The bank would be paying market rates for funds received, and no value would be created for shareholders (aside from the tax shield of interest expenses). For banks, the equity approach treats liabilities management as part of business operations—and it is. Therefore, the equity approach makes more sense for banks.

The entity method is more difficult to use for banks because a main source of financing is noninterest-bearing customer deposits raised through the retail bank, not borrowing in capital markets. The cost of capital for these deposits can be very difficult to estimate. Furthermore, the retail bank is legitimately a separate business in its own right, unlike the treasury function of most corporations. These facts make it difficult, if not impossible, to value the bank's equity by first valuing its assets (that is, its lending function) by discounting interest income less administrative expenses at the weighted average cost of capital; then subtracting the present value of its deposit business (interest expenses plus consumer bank administrative costs, discounted at the cost of debt). Still another problem with the entity approach for banks is that the spread between the interest received on loans and the cost of capital is so low that small errors in estimating the cost of capital can result in huge swings in the value of the entity.

The equity approach is the straightforward approach to valuing banks. To implement it, you need to know:

1. How to define free cash flow to shareholders; and
2. How to use the "spread" or the "income" model.

Defining Free Cash Flow to Shareholders

Free cash flow to shareholders is net income plus noncash charges, less cash flow needed to grow the balance sheet. The value of equity is not simply net income discounted at the cost of equity, because not all of net income can be paid to shareholders. In fact, only dividends can be paid to shareholders.

Exhibit 16.2 shows the definition of free cash flow to shareholders of a bank. The best way to think about it is to keep your eye on actual cash in and cash out. Cash flow from the income statement is reasonably straightforward except for the fact that depreciation and provisions for credit losses are not cash flow. Their only effect is to reduce taxes. We find it easier, however, to treat

Exhibit 16.2 **FREE CASH FLOW TO SHAREHOLDERS OF A BANK (THE EQUITY APPROACH)**

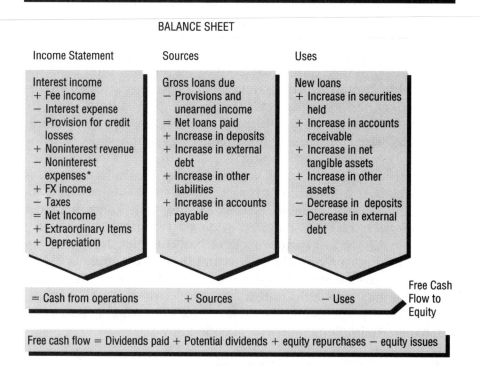

* Includes depreciation.

loan loss provisions as though they are an actual cash flow. We have little choice in the matter, because actual cash flows regarding the nonpayment of loans are not a matter of public record. Balance sheet cash flow starts with cash in, as loans are repaid. Actual cash received is gross loans due, less provisions (and unearned income) resulting in net loans paid. To this number we must add increases in deposits and external debt, and sale of new equity, all sources of funds. On the uses side, new loans, increases in deposits with banks and in securities held represent the main cash outflows.

When cash from operations is combined with sources and uses from the balance sheet, the result is free cash flow to shareholders, which is mathematically identical to dividends that *could* be paid to shareholders. This is usually not the same as actual dividends in a given, year because management deliberately smoothes dividend payments across time. This topic is discussed in greater detail later in the chapter when we cover valuing banks from the outside.

Using the Spread or Income Model

The language of banking often expresses income as "spreads" earned on balances—that is, the difference between the rate paid on borrowings and the rate received on loans and investments. Consequently, as a first step it is useful to show the equivalence between the traditional computation of earnings as reported in financial statements for nonfinancial companies, which for lack of a better phrase we shall call the *income model*, and the *spread model* that is common practice in banking.

The balance sheet and income statement for the hypothetical bank in Exhibit 16.3 show the traditional income model computation of net income. We assume that loans earn 12 percent, cash reserves at the Federal Reserve Bank earn nothing, deposits pay 5 percent, and the tax rate is 40 percent. Note that the income model, based on the financial statements, computes net income as $8.38.

The spread model is an alternative, but equivalent, approach for computing net income. It starts with the assumption that an opportunity cost of money (call it the money rate, MR) is charged to the wholesale bank and credited to deposits. For the sake of argument, suppose it is 8 percent in our example. The spread model calculates net income by adding spreads times balances. It then adds a credit for the equity component of the bank's financing, since the spreads used assume that investments are 100 percent

Exhibit 16.3 **FINANCIAL STATEMENTS FOR ABC BANK, ILLUSTRATING THE INCOME MODEL,** $ MILLIONS

Balance sheet		Income statement	
Assets		Interest income, 12% ($933) =	$111.96
Cash reserves	$ 120	− Interest expense, 5% ($1,000) =	−50.00
Loans	933	− Other expenses	−48.00
	1,053	Net profit before tax	13.96
Liabilities		− Taxes at 40%	−5.58
Deposits	1,000	Net income	$ 8.38
Equity	53		
	$1,053		

from borrowings. Likewise, income is reduced for reserves at the Fed, since they do not earn interest. Exhibit 16.4 illustrates the spread model net income calculation.

The spread model gives the same answer as the income model, but should be used with care. For example, the MR used in the equity credit is not equivalent to the cost of equity: it is merely an accounting convention necessary to provide the right answer.

VALUING BANKS FROM THE OUTSIDE

Banks remain among the most difficult companies to value, because in spite of the multitude of regulatory and reporting requirements imposed on them, it is hard to determine the quality of their loan portfolio, to figure out what percentage of their accounting profits results from interest-rate mismatch gains, and to understand which business units are creating or destroying value.

Exhibit 16.5 illustrates an outsider's valuation of a money center bank using publicly available information. The method was to forecast free cash flow to equity holders and discount it at the cost of equity, business unit by business unit. The analysis raises numerous issues. Can the businesses that appear to be destroying value be turned around, and if so, how long will it take? If the

Exhibit 16.4 **INCOME CALCULATED FOR ABC BANK USING THE SPREAD MODEL,** $ MILLIONS

Definition		Calculation	
(Spread on loans) × (Loan balance)		(12% − 8%) ($933)	= $37.32
+ (Spread on deposits) × (Deposit balance)	+	(8% − 5%) ($1,000)	= +30.00
+ (Equity credit) × (Equity)	+	(8%) ($53)	= +4.24
− (Reserve debit) × (Reserves)	−	(8%) ($120)	= −9.60
− Expenses			−48.00
= Net profit before tax			13.96
− Taxes at 40%			−5.58
Net income			$ 8.38

losing businesses cannot be turned around, can they be sold to someone else for whom they would have greater value? For example, if the government bond trading and corporate trust units were sold for only one dollar each, the equity value of the bank would quadruple. Can corporate overhead be cut? If so, by how much? For the value creating units, one must examine ways to improve them further and to secure their competitive advantage, or to sell them if they would have higher value to someone else.

Exhibit 16.5 shows the power of valuation for coming to grips with the strategic issues facing a money center bank, as well as showing the potential for creating value. But great care should be used before taking action. Let's turn to some of the conceptual problems involved in getting the valuation right.

Understanding Mismatch Gains and Losses

Normally, the term structure of interest rates is upward sloping, as shown in Exhibit 16.6. A bank that lends 3-year money and borrows 1-year money will earn a mismatch profit equal to the difference between the longer- and shorter-term rates of interest. However, much of this profit is illusory, because the 1-year funds must be rolled over twice at future 1-year spot rates that are expected to be higher than today's 1-year rate. The mismatch profit

Exhibit 16.5 **AN OUTSIDER'S ESTIMATE OF SOURCES OF VALUE FOR A LARGE BANK,** $ MILLIONS

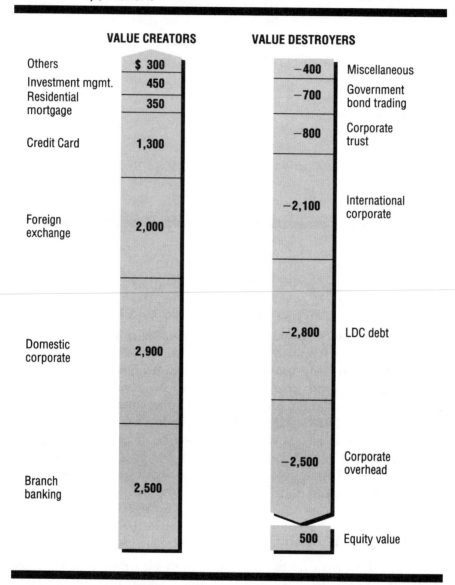

VALUE CREATORS

Others	$ 300
Investment mgmt.	450
Residential mortgage	350
Credit Card	1,300
Foreign exchange	2,000
Domestic corporate	2,900
Branch banking	2,500

VALUE DESTROYERS

−400	Miscellaneous
−700	Government bond trading
−800	Corporate trust
−2,100	International corporate
−2,800	LDC debt
−2,500	Corporate overhead
500	Equity value

Source: McKinsey analysis.

Exhibit 16.6 **THE SLOPE IN THE TERM STRUCTURE, WHICH CREATES MISMATCH PROFITS**

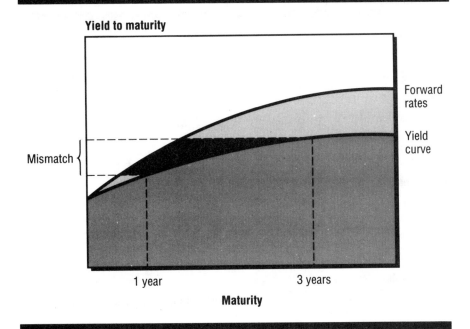

observed in today's market should not, in most circumstances, be forecasted to persist over time.

To illustrate how spreads would be expected to change over time, suppose a bank lends $1 million of 3-year fixed-rate money and borrows $900,000 of 1-year CDs, which are rolled over each year for 3 years. The assumed term structure is as follows:

Maturity	Yield	1-year forward rate
1 year	8.0%	8.0%
2 years	9.0	10.0
3 years	9.5	10.5

Exhibit 16.7 shows the forecasted income statements and balance sheets for three units of a bank: the wholesale bank that lends $1 million, the retail bank that raises $900,000 in 1-year CDs, and the treasury. To keep the example as simple as possible, we have

Exhibit 16.7 **FINANCIAL STATEMENTS FOR THREE UNITS OF A BANK,
ILLUSTRATING HOW CURRENT ACCOUNTING PROFITS OVERSTATE
LONG-TERM CASH FLOW**

Balance sheets
$ Thousands

Income statements
$ Thousands

Wholesale bank

					Year 1	Year 2	Year 3
Loans	$1,000.00	Borrowing from		Interest income	95.00	95.00	95.00
		treasury	$950.00	Interest expense	90.25	90.25	90.25
		Equity	50.00	Wholesale bank profit			
	$1,000.00		$1,000.00		4.75	4.75	4.75

Retail bank

Lending to		CDs	$900.00	Interest income	76.00	95.00	99.75
treasury	$950.00	Equity	50.00	Interest expense	72.00	90.00	94.50
	$950.00		$950.00	Retail bank profit			
					4.00	5.00	5.25

Treasury (mismatch)

Lending to wholesale		Borrowing from retail		Interest income	90.25	90.25	90.25
bank	$950.00	bank	$950.00	Interest expense	76.00	95.00	99.75
	$950.00		$950.00	Treasury profit	14.25	-4.75	-9.50

Total bank

Loans	$1,000.00	CDs	$900.00	Interest income	95.00	95.00	95.00
		Equity	100.00	Interest expense	72.00	90.00	94.50
	$1,000.00		$1,000.00	Total bank profit	23.00	5.00	0.50

assumed no reserve requirements and no taxes. The wholesale bank is match-funded with 3-year money that costs 9.5 percent; therefore, it earns 9.5 percent on $1 million and pays 9.5 percent on $950,000, for an annual profit $4,750. Its spread, however, is 0 percent—not a good deal. The retail bank is forecasted to earn the expected 1-year spot rate (8 percent, then 10 percent, and finally 10.5 percent), which is assumed to be equal to the 1-year forward rate. The retail bank pays the expected 1-year spot rate on CDs. It, too, has a 0-percent spread.

In Exhibit 16.7 both the wholesale and retail banks are perfectly match-funded; therefore, all of the mismatch profits appear in the treasury. In the first year, the treasury lends at the 3-year rate (to the wholesale bank) and borrows at the 1-year rate (from the retail bank) for a net profit of $14,250. In the second and third years, however, it loses money, because it still earns the 3-year fixed rate, 9.5 percent, but pays the 1-year spot rate, 10 percent in Year 2 and 10.5 percent in Year 3. The mismatch profits of the treasury are reflected in the bank as a whole.

If one were to build a valuation model that forecasted profits to be $23,000 perpetually (that is, a 23 percent return on equity), the bank would appear profitable. The reality is that the bank ROE is 5 percent or less in the second year and .5 percent or less in the third year. Its high mismatch profits in the first year are an illusion, which is discovered only when the forecast of profit over time takes into account the fact that short-term rates are forecasted to rise.

The key to handling the problem of mismatch gains or losses is to build a good forecast that takes into account:

- The way spreads are forecasted to change across time with changing interest rate environments.
- The inflow of funds from loans being paid off and the outflow of funds at new rates as new loans are made.
- The substitution between interest-bearing and noninteresting-bearing deposits as interest rate environments change.
- The portion of mismatch profits that is sustainable because forward rates tend to be higher than their corresponding realized spot rates.

It is not easy to build all of these variables into your forecast. Even if you decide not to do so, it helps to understand the illusion of mismatch profits.

Determining the Quality of Loans

Determining the quality of loans is the most difficult problem for an outsider's valuation, and very little information is available to help solve it. Take loans to LDCs or commercial real estate as an example. Although they are sometimes sold in secondary markets for 50 cents on the dollar, this kind of markdown must be viewed with healthy cynicism. The loans that banks keep are probably worth more than those they choose to sell in the secondary market.

The market value of the loan portfolio constantly changes with changes in interest rates and with changes in the credit-worthiness of debt in the bank's loan portfolio. It is usually possible to find out what percentage of the portfolio is represented by LDC, LBO, or commercial real estate lending. These can then be marked to market (at least approximately) as market conditions change.

An Example of Valuing a Bank from the Outside

Using publicly available data and Value Line's forecasts of assets, net income, loan loss provisions, and debt balances, we valued Citicorp. The income model was used, and there was no attempt to forecast the effect of the term structure of interest rates on expected cash flows. Our intent is to illustrate how forecasts of the income statement and balance sheet are converted into cash flows to equity—not to provide a detailed (or accurate) forecast. Exhibit 16.8 shows that the total equity value less the market value of preferred stock outstanding results in the discounted cash flow value of Citicorp's common stock outstanding. The difference between the DCF estimate and the market value of common stock is roughly 12 percent. The cost of equity, 12.8 percent, uses a BARRA beta of 1.29, an assumed market risk premium of 5.4 percent, and a 10-year T-bond rate of 5.8 percent. A perpetuity model was used to estimate the continuing value.

Exhibits 16.9, 16.10, and 16.11 show the income statement, the balance sheet, and free cash flow statement, respectively. Exhibit 16.11 also shows a statement of retained earnings, a part of the model that requires more discussion. The discounted cash flow value of equity is the present value of cash flow to equity holders. Normally, one would say that dividends is the same thing as free cash flow, but caution is required. Free cash flow is the cash that *could* be paid as dividends in a given year, not the actual dividends that forecasted to be paid. The difference between the two is primarily a matter of timing. To build a spreadsheet, however, one must decide what to do with the cash difference between actual and potential dividends. There are two ways of handling the problem. Usually, surpluses of cash are carried as "excess marketable securities" and deficits as "unscheduled debt." Either way, there is no effect on the value of the company, because investments in

Exhibit 16.8 **OUTSIDE-IN EQUITY METHOD VALUATION OF CITICORP, JANUARY 1994,** $ BILLIONS

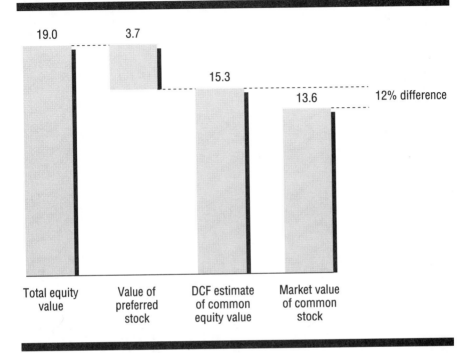

Source: Annual reports; Compustat; Value Line forecasts; McKinsey analysis.

marketable securities have zero net present value. In our banking model we have adopted a different approach in order to keep calculation of key ratios, such as equity as a percent of total assets, as simple as possible. Our solution is to assume that free cash flow in excess of forecasted dividends paid is also disbursed to shareholders in the year it is generated. In Exhibit 16.11, for example, 1994 forecasted dividends are $379 million, yet potential dividends add another $1.176 billion to equity free cash flows. Consequently, the statement of retained earnings in Exhibit 16.11 starts with the beginning retained earnings, adds net income, and subtracts dividends paid, adjustments to retained earnings, and potential dividends, in order to arrive at end-of-period retained earnings. This process allows us to keep the ratio of equity to total assets at the BIS guideline, and helps to keep the financial statements reasonable to the eye of a line manager.

Exhibit 16.9 **CITICORP, INCOME STATEMENT FORECAST**, $ MILLIONS

Income Statement	1988	1989	1990	1991	1992	Forecast 1993	Forecast 1994	Forecast 1995
Interest Revenue								
Interest & Fees on Loans	20,575	23,220	24,526	20,440	18,476	17,890	18,256	19,048
Interest on Deposits with Banks	1,362	1,533	1,474	886	1,029	1,023	1,033	1,044
Interest on Funds Sold and Repos	1,234	4,133	2,107	637	1,393	1,489	1,702	1,784
Interest & Dividends on Investments	1,234	1,265	1,359	1,081	875	997	984	1,211
Interest on Trading Securities	2,206	1,425	1,517	1,310	2,010	2,550	2,970	3,333
Other Interest Income	0	0	0	0	0	0	0	0
	26,611	31,576	30,983	24,354	23,783	23,949	24,946	26,420
Interest Expense								
Interest on Deposits—Customer	(10,612)	(12,830)	(14,486)	(11,116)	(10,458)	(10,534)	(10,856)	(11,380)
Interest on Deposits—Banks	0	0	0	0	0	0	0	0
Interest on ST Debt	(5,783)	(8,222)	(6,235)	(3,369)	(3,474)	(3,523)	(3,906)	(3,984)
Interest on LT Debt	(2,611)	(2,747)	(2,741)	(2,289)	(2,220)	(2,007)	(2,034)	(2,108)
Other Interest Expense	0	(418)	(336)	(315)	(175)	(176)	(180)	(184)
	(19,006)	(24,218)	(23,798)	(17,089)	(16,327)	(16,240)	(16,975)	(17,656)
Net Interest Revenue	7,605	7,358	7,185	7,265	7,456	7,709	7,971	8,764
Provision for Credit Losses	(1,330)	(2,521)	(2,662)	(3,890)	(4,146)	(2,637)	(2,182)	(2,200)
Net Interest Revenue after Provision	6,275	4,837	4,523	3,375	3,310	5,072	5,789	6,564
Noninterest Revenue								
Commissions & Fees	3,887	4,374	5,024	4,815	5,084	5,004	5,157	5,315
Trading Securities—Gain(Loss)	277	256	271	457	326	377	439	385
Investment Securities—Gain(Loss)	108	180	52	330	12	145	143	147
Other Income	435	1,113	1,398	1,174	1,738	1,755	1,773	1,791
	4,707	5,923	6,745	6,776	7,160	7,281	7,511	7,638

Exhibit 16.9 Continued

Income Statement	1988	1989	1990	1991	1992	Forecast 1993	Forecast 1994	Forecast 1995
Noninterest Expense								
Admin & General Expense	(5,868)	(6,217)	(7,024)	(7,368)	(6,555)	(6,755)	(6,962)	(7,255)
Commissions & Fees Paid	0	0	0	0	0	0	0	0
Other Expense	(3,113)	(3,481)	(4,075)	(3,729)	(3,502)	(3,609)	(3,719)	(3,800)
Total Operating Expenses	(8,981)	(9,698)	(11,099)	(11,097)	(10,057)	(10,364)	(10,681)	(11,055)
Income before Except, Tax and Approp	2,001	1,062	169	(946)	413	1,989	2,619	3,147
Foreign Exchange Income(Loss)	616	471	657	709	1,005	1,136	1,159	1,207
Exceptional Income & Provisions	90	0	0	0	0	0	0	0
Income before Tax and Approp	2,707	1,533	826	(237)	1,418	3,125	3,778	4,354
Appropriations to Untaxed Reserves	0	0	0	0	0	0	0	0
Shareholders' Profit before Tax	2,707	1,533	826	(237)	1,418	3,125	3,778	4,354
Income Tax	(1,009)	(1,035)	(508)	(677)	(696)	(1,281)	(1,549)	(1,785)
Shareholders' Profit after Tax	1,698	498	(318)	(914)	722	1,844	2,229	(2,894)
Minority Interest	0	0	0	0	0	0	0	0
Net Items—Total	0	0	0	0	0	0	0	0
Net Income	1,698	498	318	(914)	722	1,844	2,229	2,569
Extraordinary Items	180	0	140	457	0	0	0	0
Transfer to Retained Earnings	1,858	498	458	(457)	722	1,844	2,229	2,569

Exhibit 16.9 Continued

Income Statement	Forecast 1996	Forecast 1997	Forecast 1998	Forecast 1999	Forecast 2000	Forecast 2001	Forecast 2002	Forecast 2003
Interest Revenue								
Interest & Fees on Loans	20,297	21,626	22,823	23,863	24,950	26,087	27,275	28,518
Intterest On Deposits with Banks	1,054	1,065	1,075	1,086	1,097	1,108	1,119	1,130
Interest on Funds Sold and Repos	1,901	2,025	2,158	2,300	2,451	2,611	2,782	2,965
Interest & Dividends on Investments	1,163	1,115	1,187	1,264	1,347	1,434	1,528	1,627
Interest on Trading Securities	3,736	4,181	4,639	5,085	5,515	5,915	6,273	6,576
Other Interest Income	0	0	0	0	0	0	0	0
	28,151	30,013	31,883	33,598	35,359	37,155	38,977	40,816
Interest Expense								
Interest on Deposits—Customer	(12,127)	(12,922)	(13,769)	(14,672)	(15,633)	(16,658)	(17,751)	(18,914)
Interest on Deposits—Banks	0	0	0	0	0	0	0	0
Interest on ST Debt	(4,236)	(4,504)	(4,789)	(5,001)	(5,223)	(5,454)	(5,696)	(5,949)
Interest on LT Debt	(2,205)	(2,356)	(2,533)	(2,706)	(2,871)	(3,044)	(3,225)	(3,414)
Other Interest Expense	(191)	(212)	(246)	(270)	(282)	(293)	(303)	(311)
	(18,759)	(19,994)	(21,337)	(22,648)	(24,009)	(25,450)	(26,975)	(28,588)
Net Interest Revenue	9,392	10,020	10,546	10,950	11,350	11,705	12,002	12,229
Provision for Credit Losses	(2,264)	(2,326)	(2,455)	(2,566)	(2,683)	(2,806)	(2,933)	(3,067)
Net Interest Revenue after Provision	7,129	7,694	8,091	8,383	8,666	8,899	9,069	9,161
Noninterest Revenue								
Commissions & Fees	5,663	6,034	6,430	6,852	7,301	7,780	8,290	8,833
Trading Securities—Gain(Loss)	303	353	408	467	530	596	664	734
Investment Securities—Gain(Loss)	152	161	172	183	195	208	222	236
Other Income	1,809	1,827	1,845	1,863	1,882	1,901	1,920	1,939
	7,926	8,375	8,855	9,365	9,908	10,484	11,096	11,742

Exhibit 16.9 Continued

Income Statement	Forecast 1996	Forecast 1997	Forecast 1998	Forecast 1999	Forecast 2000	Forecast 2001	Forecast 2002	Forecast 2003
Noninterest Expense								
Admin & General Expense	(7,557)	(7,867)	(8,383)	(8,933)	(9,518)	(10,142)	(10,807)	(11,516)
Commissions & Fees Paid	0	0	0	0	0	0	0	0
Other Expense	(3,875)	(3,944)	(4,203)	(4,478)	(4,772)	(5,085)	(5,418)	(5,773)
Total Operating Expenses	(11,432)	(11,811)	(12,586)	(13,411)	(14,290)	(15,227)	(16,225)	(17,289)
Income before Except, Tax and Approp	3,622	4,258	4,361	4,338	4,284	4,157	3,939	3,615
Foreign Exchange Income(Loss)	1,283	1,364	1,437	1,501	1,567	1,637	1,709	1,785
Exceptional Income & Provisions	0	0	0	0	0	0	0	0
Income before Tax and Approp	4,906	5,622	5,798	5,839	5,851	5,793	5,648	5,400
Appropiations to Untaxed Reserves	0	0	0	0	0	0	0	0
Shareholders' Profit before Tax	4,906	5,622	5,798	5,839	5,851	5,793	5,646	5,400
Income Tax	(2,011)	(2,305)	(2,377)	(2,394)	(2,399)	(2,375)	(2,316)	(2,214)
Shareholders' Profit after Tax	2,894	3,317	3,421	3,445	3,452	3,418	3,332	3,186
Minority Interest	0	0	0	0	0	0	0	0
Net Items—Total	0	0	0	0	0	0	0	0
Net Income	2,894	3,317	3,421	3,445	3,452	3,418	3,332	3,186
Extraordinary Items	0	0	0	0	0	0	0	0
Transfer to Retained Earnings	2,894	3,317	3,421	3,445	3,452	3,418	3,332	3,186

Exhibit 16.10 **CITICORP, BALANCE SHEET FORECAST**, $ MILLIONS

Balance Sheet	1988	1989	1990	1991	1992	Forecast 1993	Forecast 1994	Forecast 1995
Assets								
Excess Marketable Securities	0	0	0	0	0	3,085	1,826	0
Cash and Due from Banks	4,818	6,332	7,098	5,326	5,138	5,241	5,347	5,684
Short-Term Investments	6,441	7,659	4,071	4,550	6,381	6,576	6,777	7,221
Deposits With Banks	10,706	13,813	7,546	6,692	6,550	6,615	6,682	6,748
Gross Loans–Customers	152,372	162,397	158,571	152,837	141,073	143,974	146,935	156,568
Less: Provisions and Unearned Income	(7,380)	(7,014)	(6,714)	(5,201)	(5,222)	(5,329)	(5,439)	(5,796)
Net Loans–Customer	144,992	155,383	151,857	147,636	135,851	138,645	141,496	150,773
Trading Securities	3,924	9,018	7,518	12,064	17,085	19,897	23,172	26,986
Investment Securities	15,217	14,699	14,075	14,713	15,056	14,820	15,273	15,739
Accounts Receivable	3,448	4,251	3,801	2,917	2,721	2,740	2,854	3,023
Investments–Permanent	0	0	501	904	563	593	625	658
Net Tangible Fixed Assets	3,337	3,351	4,010	3,659	3,819	3,846	4,006	4,243
Intangible Assets	1,081	972	910	595	489	489	489	489
Foreign Exchange Assets	0	0	0	0	0	0	0	0
Customer Acceptances	3,839	3,606	2,165	1,567	1,802	1,838	1,875	1,912
Other Assets	9,863	11,559	13,434	16,297	18,246	18,373	19,138	20,269
Total Assets	207,666	230,643	216,986	216,922	213,701	222,758	229,559	243,746

Exhibit 16.10 Continued

Balance Sheet	1988	1989	1990	1991	1992	Forecast 1993	Forecast 1994	Forecast 1995
Liabilities and Provisions								
Deposits—Customers	124,072	137,922	142,452	146,475	144,175	148,582	153,123	163,162
Deposits—Banks	0	0	0	0	0	0	0	0
Short-Term Borrowings	37,579	39,278	22,604	21,566	22,189	24,596	25,091	26,675
Long-Term Borrowing	19,268	19,605	19,062	19,221	16,067	15,828	16,499	17,003
Additional Borrowing	0	0	0	0	0	0	0	739
Accounts Payable	0	0	0	0	0	0	0	0
Foreign Exchange Liabilities	0	0	0	0	0	0	0	0
Acceptances Outstanding	3,856	3,619	2,276	1,604	1,866	1,903	1,941	1,980
Other Liabilities	12,987	20,103	20,823	18,530	18,187	18,461	18,943	19,332
	197,762	220,527	207,217	207,396	202,484	209,471	215,597	228,892
Minority Interests	0	0	0	0	0	0	0	0
Shareholders' Capital and Reserves								
Preferred Capital—Total	1,630	1,880	1,579	2,177	3,248	3,923	3,923	3,923
Share Capital(Common Equity)	346	352	363	372	392	392	392	392
Share Premium(Capital Surplus)	2,901	3,016	3,187	3,277	3,598	3,598	3,598	3,598
Treasury Stock	(424)	(421)	(405)	(389)	(389)	(389)	(389)	(389)
Equity Reserves								
Net Unrealized Capital Gains	0	0	0	0	0	0	0	0
Retained Earnings	5,593	5,458	5,204	4,314	4,368	5,764	6,438	7,330
Revaluation Reserves	0	0	0	0	0	0	0	0
Transfers and Other Movements	(142)	(169)	(159)	(225)	0	0	0	0
Total Stockholders' Equity	9,904	10,116	9,769	9,526	11,217	13,288	13,962	14,854
Total Liabilities & Equity	207,666	230,643	216,986	216,922	213,701	222,758	229,559	243,746

Exhibit 16.10 Continued

Balance Sheet	Forecast 1996	Forecast 1997	Forecast 1998	Forecast 1999	Forecast 2000	Forecast 2001	Forecast 2002	Forecast 2003
Assets								
Excess Marketable Securities	0	(0)	0	0	0	0	0	394
Cash and Due from Banks	6,044	6,427	6,711	7,008	7,319	7,644	7,983	8,338
Short-Term Investments	7,695	8,199	8,737	9,310	9,920	10,570	11,264	12,002
Deposits With Banks	6,816	6,884	6,953	7,022	7,093	7,164	7,235	7,306
Gross Loans—Customers	166,834	177,772	185,872	194,341	203,196	212,454	222,134	232,256
Less: Provisions and Unearned Income	(6,176)	(6,580)	(6,880)	(7,194)	(7,522)	(7,864)	(8,223)	(8,597)
Net Loans—Customer	160,658	171,191	178,991	187,147	195,674	204,590	213,912	223,659
Trading Securities	31,428	36,600	42,090	47,983	54,221	60,727	67,407	74,148
Investment Securities	16,771	17,871	19,043	20,291	21,621	23,039	24,550	26,159
Accounts Receivable	3,221	3,434	3,648	3,844	4,045	4,251	4,459	4,670
Investments—Permanent	693	730	769	810	854	899	947	998
Net Tangible Fixed Assets	4,520	4,819	5,120	5,395	5,678	5,966	6,259	6,554
Intangible Assets	489	489	489	489	489	489	489	489
Foreign Exchange Assets	0	0	0	0	0	0	0	0
Customer Acceptances	1,951	1,990	2,029	2,070	2,111	2,154	2,197	2,241
Other Assets	21,597	23,026	24,460	25,776	27,127	28,505	29,903	31,314
Total Assets	261,882	281,661	299,040	317,146	336,152	355,998	376,605	398,272

516

Exhibit 16.10 Continued

Balance Sheet	Forecast 1996	Forecast 1997	Forecast 1998	Forecast 1999	Forecast 2000	Forecast 2001	Forecast 2002	Forecast 2003
Liabilities and Provisions								
Deposits—Customers	173,860	185,259	197,405	210,348	224,139	238,834	254,493	271,179
Deposits—Banks	0	0	0	0	0	0	0	0
Short-Term Borrowings	28,363	30,160	31,495	32,889	34,347	35,871	37,464	39,129
Long-Term Borrowings	18,054	19,397	20,862	22,149	23,490	24,898	26,368	27,894
Additional Borrowing	4,016	7,611	8,539	9,460	10,252	10,787	10,932	10,932
Accounts Payable	0	0	0	0	0	0	0	0
Foreign Exchange Liabilities	0	0	0	0	0	0	0	0
Acceptances Outstanding	2,020	2,060	2,101	2,143	2,186	2,230	2,275	2,320
Other Liabilities	19,730	20,135	20,550	20,972	21,403	21,844	22,293	22,751
	246,041	264,623	280,952	297,962	315,818	334,464	353,824	374,205
Minority Interests	0	0	0	0	0	0	0	0
Shareholders Capital and Reserves								
Preferred Capital—Total	3,923	3,923	3,923	3,923	3,923	3,923	3,923	3,923
Share Capital(Common Equity)	392	392	392	392	392	392	392	392
Share Premium(Capital Surplus)	3,598	3,598	3,598	3,5968	3,598	3,598	3,598	3,598
Treasury Stock	(389)	(389)	(389)	(389)	(389)	(389)	(389)	(389)
Equity Reserves								
Net Unrealized Capital Gains	0	0	0	0	0	0	0	0
Retained Earnings	8,317	9,513	10,565	11,660	12,810	14,010	15,257	16,543
Revaluation Reserves	0	0	0	0	0	0	0	0
Transfers and Other Movements	0	0	0	0	0	0	0	0
Total Stockholders' Equity	15,841	17,037	18,089	19,184	20,334	21,534	22,781	24,067
Total Liabilities & Equity	261,882	281,661	299,040	317,146	336,152	355,996	376,805	396,272

Exhibit 16.11 **CITICORP, CASH FLOW FORECAST,** $ MILLIONS

Cash Flows	1988	1989	1990	1991	1992	Forecast 1993	Forecast 1994	Forecast 1995
Net Interest Revenue	7,605	7,358	7,185	7,265	7,456	7,709	7,971	8,764
Net Noninterest Revenue	(4,274)	(3,775)	(4,354)	(4,321)	(2,897)	(3,083)	(3,170)	(3,417)
Provision for Credit Losses	(1,330)	(2,521)	(2,662)	(3,890)	(4,146)	(2,637)	(2,182)	(2,200)
Net Income before Exceptional Items & Appropriations	2,001	1,062	169	(946)	413	1,989	2,619	3,147
Foreign Exchange Income	616	471	657	709	1,005	1,136	1,159	1,207
Exceptional Income & Provisions	90	0	0	0	0	0	0	0
Appropiations to Untaxed Reserves	0	0	0	0	0	0	0	0
Pretax Income	2,707	1,533	826	(237)	1,418	3,125	3,778	4,354
Income Taxes	(1,009)	(1,035)	(508)	(677)	(696)	(1,281)	(1,549)	(1,785)
Income before extraordinary items	1,698	498	318	(914)	722	1,844	2,229	2,569
Net Items—Total	0	0	0	0	0	0	0	0
Extraordinary Items	160	0	140	457	0	0	0	0
Cash from Operations	1,858	498	458	(457)	722	1,844	2,229	2,569
Increase in Assets	(4,059)	(22,977)	13,657	64	3,221	(9,057)	(6,800)	(14,187)
Increase in Liabilities	3,005	22,765	(13,310)	179	(4,912)	6,987	6,126	13,295
Cash Flow before Financing	804	286	805	(214)	(969)	(227)	1,555	1,676
Minority Interest	0	0	0	0	0	0	0	0
Equity cash flow	804	286	805	(214)	(969)	(227)	1,555	1,676

Exhibit 16.11 Continued

Cash Flows	1988	1989	1990	1991	1992	Forecast 1993	Forecast 1994	Forecast 1995
Incr in Equity & Adj to RE	(238)	347	(95)	662	1,194	675	0	0
Dividends Paid	(566)	(633)	(710)	(448)	(225)	(313)	(379)	(617)
Potential Dividends	0	0	0	0	0	(134)	(1,176)	(1,060)
	0	0	0	0	0	0	0	0

Statement of Retained Earnings	1988	1989	1990	1991	1992	Forecast 1993	Forecast 1994	Forecast 1995
Beginning Retained Earnings	4,526	5,593	5,458	5,204	4,314	4,368	5,764	6,438
Net Income	1,858	498	458	(457)	722	1,844	2,229	2,569
Dividends Paid	(566)	(633)	(710)	(448)	(225)	(313)	(379)	(617)
Adjustments to retained earnings	(225)	0	(2)	15	(443)	0	0	0
Potential Dividends	0	0	0	0	0	(134)	(1,176)	(1,060)
Ending Retained Earnings	5,593	5,458	5,204	4,314	4,368	5,764	6,438	7,330

Exhibit 16.11 Continued

Cash Flows	Forecast 1996	Forecast 1997	Forecast 1998	Forecast 1999	Forecast 2000	Forecast 2001	Forecast 2002	Forecast 2003
Net Interest Revenue	9,392	10,020	10,546	10,950	11,350	11,705	12,002	12,229
Net Noninterest Revenue	(3,506)	(3,436)	(3,731)	(4,045)	(4,382)	(4,743)	(5,130)	(5,547)
Provision for Credit Losses	(2,264)	(2,326)	(2,455)	(2,586)	(2,683)	(2,806)	(2,933)	(3,067)
Net Income before Exceptional Items & Appropriations	3,622	4,258	4,361	4,338	4,284	4,157	3,939	3,615
Foreign Exchange Income	1,283	1,364	1,437	1,501	1,567	1,637	1,709	1,785
Exceptional Income & Provisions	0	0	0	0	0	0	0	0
Appropiations to Untaxed Reserves	0	0	0	0	0	0	0	0
Pretax Income	4,906	5,622	5,798	5,839	5,851	5,793	5,648	5,400
Income Taxes	(2,011)	(2,305)	(2,377)	(2,394)	(2,399)	(2,375)	(2,316)	(2,214)
Income before extraordinary items	2,894	3,317	3,421	3,445	3,452	3,418	3,332	3,186
Net Items—Total	0	0	0	0	0	0	0	0
Extraordinary Items	0	0	0	0	0	0	0	0
Cash from Operations	2,894	3,317	3,421	3,445	3,452	3,418	3,332	3,186
Increase in Assets	(18,136)	(19,778)	(17,380)	(18,106)	(19,006)	(19,846)	(20,607)	(21,668)
Increase in Liabilities	17,150	18,582	16,328	17,010	17,856	18,645	19,360	20,381
Cash Flow before Financing	1,908	2,121	2,370	2,350	2,303	2,218	2,086	1,899
Minority Interest	0	0	0	0	0	0	0	0
Equity cash flow	1,908	2,121	2,370	2,350	2,303	2,218	2,086	1,899

Exhibit 16.11 Continued

Cash Flows	Forecast 1996	Forecast 1997	Forecast 1998	Forecast 1999	Forecast 2000	Forecast 2001	Forecast 2002	Forecast 2003
Incr in Equity & Adj to RE	0	0	0	0	0	0	0	0
Dividends Paid	(695)	(796)	(821)	(827)	(829)	(820)	(800)	(765)
Potential Dividends	(1,213)	(1,325)	(1,549)	(1,523)	(1,474)	(1,397)	(1,286)	(1,134)
	0	0	0	0	0	0	0	0

Statement of Retained Earnings	1996	1997	1998	1999	2000	2001	2002	2003
Beginning Retained Earnings	7,330	8,317	9,513	10,565	11,660	12,810	14,010	15,257
Net Income	2,894	3,317	3,421	3,445	3,452	3,418	3,332	3,186
Dividends Paid	(695)	(796)	(821)	(827)	(829)	(820)	(800)	(765)
Adjustments to retained earnings	0	0	0	0	0	0	0	0
Potential Dividends	(1,213)	(1,325)	(1,549)	(1,523)	(1,474)	(1,397)	(1,286)	(1,134)
Ending Retained Earnings	8,317	9,513	10,565	11,660	12,810	14,010	15,257	16,543

Note that dividend policy has no effect on the company's value in our model. This result is consistent with the accepted theory of finance as taught at most business schools. If dividend payout is increased, the adjustments line takes up the slack in the statement of retained earnings. Even if actual dividends paid exceed net income, the adjustments line will change sign and the effect will be equivalent to borrowing unscheduled debt. Either way, there is no effect on equity free cash flow, because it is the sum of actual total dividends and adjustments.

VALUING BANKS FROM THE INSIDE

The main objective of an insider's valuation is to value the bank's business units and to use the results for restructuring or value-based management. Even with complete information, this is a difficult problem because of transfer pricing and shared costs. We will discuss valuation from the inside by focusing on issues concerning the retail bank, the wholesale bank, and the treasury.

The Retail Bank

Most retail banks are in the business of collecting deposits: noninterest-bearing demand deposits; interest-bearing demand deposits; money market accounts; and certificates of deposit. For each dollar in deposits there *might* be 20 cents in external consumer loans, and the remaining 80 cents is lent to the treasury at a transfer price we call the money rate. The first of several issues central to valuing the retail bank is the correct money rate to use. Next is the value of "deposit stability." Conceptual issues concerning capital structure and the cost of equity are also important.

The money rate for the retail bank   The usual economic principle for transfer pricing is to use the market price. But what is the correct opportunity cost for deposits? Logically, it should be the market rate for securities that have the same duration—that is, the same sensitivity of market value to changes in interest rates. Determining the duration of demand deposits and deciding how to match-fund them are tricky topics for two reasons. First, most banks confuse the length of time a dollar stays in a demand deposit (that is, its maturity) with the sensitivity of balance values to changes in interest rates (that is, their duration). A propensity exists to choose a money rate that eliminates fluctuations in net interest income rather than to choose a rate that stabilizes shareholder value. Second, one has to decide whether to match-fund to immunize demand deposits or to immunize the entire retail bank against changes in interest rates. In the example that follows, we have chosen to immunize the entire business unit.

Exhibit 16.12 illustrates how the choice of a money rate affects the stability of net income versus shareholder value. To keep this example simple, we have assumed that the retail bank has deposits that pay no interest but will be withdrawn in Year 5. Reserves at the Federal Reserve Bank will be recovered at the same time. The initial situation assumes the market rate is 10 percent and loans to the treasury earn 10 percent, so that their market value equals their book value. Reserves and deposits are like zero-coupon notes, so their market value is less than book.

The bank can choose to match-fund deposits at the five-year rate, the time interval equal to their maturity, or the shorter three-year rate. The five-year rate keeps net income constant for five years, but fails to immunize shareholders' wealth. Equity value declines from $795.14 to $696.50 when interest rates rise from 10 percent to 15 percent after 3 years. This happens because the value of assets falls faster than the value of deposits. This problem is alleviated when deposits are match-funded with three-year money, because the interest rate credited to loans to the treasury rises from 10 percent to 15 percent in Year 4. Consequently, loans to the treasury decline less in value when interest rates rise and the value of equity remains unchanged (immunized against changes in interest rates).

If you wish to centrally manage all interest-rate risk in the treasury, the correct money rate to use for match-funding deposits is the rate that immunizes the value of equity in the retail bank against changes in interest rates. To find this rate, you must take into account the sensitivity of balance levels to changes in interest rates, the ratio of fixed to variable costs into business unit, and the duration of external loans held by the retail bank.

The value of deposit stability   In valuing retail banks, the issue often arises of whether deposit-taking units should receive a credit for deposit stability. The logic for a credit is that depositors understand and value the FDIC insurance attached to demand deposits. When banks get into trouble (for example, when their credit rating

---

Exhibit 16.12 **EXAMPLE OF HOW CHOICE OF MONEY RATE AFFECTS STABILITY OF NET INCOME VS. EQUITY VALUE**

Initial situation:
Reserves and deposits are paid off in 5 years
Current interest rate is 10%

Book value balance sheet

Reserves	$240.00	Deposits	$2,000.00
Loans to		Equity	128.00
treasury	1,888.00		
	$2,128.00		$2,128.00

Market value balance sheet

Reserves	$149.02	Deposits	$1,241.84
Loans to		Equity	795.14
treasury	1,888.00		
	$2,037.02		$2,037.02

Match-fund deposits with 5-year loan:
Interest rate rises to 15%

Market value balance sheet

Reserves	$119.32	Deposits	$944.36
Loans to		Equity	696.50
treasury	1,571.54		
	$1,690.86		$1,690.86

Year	Net income
1	$188.80
2	188.80
3	188.80
4	188.80
5	188.80

Result
Net income constant
Equity value varies

Match-fund deposits with 3-year loan:
Interest rate rises to 15%

Market value balance sheet

Reserves	$119.32	Deposits	$994.36
Loans to		Equity	797.42
treasury	1,672.46		
	$1,791.78		$1,791.78

Year	Net income
1	$188.80
2	188.80
3	188.80
4	283.20
5	283.20

Result
Net income varies
Equity value constant

---

is downgraded), customers usually do not withdraw their deposits and place them in "safer" institutions. As a result, FDIC-insured deposits tend to be stable. Troubled institutions that have fewer insured deposits have to pay higher yields to obtain short-term funding. For example, the Bank of America, with its large deposit base, was able to retain its FDIC-insured deposits during troubled times; but Continental Illinois, without a large deposit base, had to pay relatively higher yields to keep itself funded during a time of crisis.

The benefit of FDIC insurance to a retail bank is directly related to the lower cost of funds that banks have to pay, compared with nonbank institutions, for similar duration liabilities. The lower the credit rating of the bank, the higher the benefit of FDIC insurance to it. The cost of FDIC insurance is deducted directly from the cash flow of the retail bank. The value of FDIC insurance is the difference between the indirect benefit and the direct cost.

FDIC insurance is a put option. (See Chapter 15 for a description of put options.) In the event of bank default, insured depositors receive the face value of their deposits, rather than the fraction of the face value they might otherwise receive following bankruptcy or reorganization. The maturity date of the FDIC "put option" is the interval until completion of the next audit of the bank's assets. Since the FDIC charges a uniform fee, riskier banks receive a subsidy. The value of the subsidy depends primarily on:

- The market value of the bank's assets.
- The variability of the market value of the bank's assets.
- The *total* debt of the bank.
- The proportion of total debt represented by insured deposits.

Although the procedure is somewhat crude, it is possible to obtain cross-sectional estimates of the per-dollar value of the deposit insurance premium by using a put option pricing model. Exhibit 16.13 shows some estimates obtained by Ronn and Verma (1986) for a cross section of banks in 1983.[1] The highest value was 72.41 basis points per dollar of FDIC-insured deposits for the troubled First Pennsylvania Corp., while the average value was 8.08 basis points. Since normal discounted cash flow methods cannot capture the value of deposit stability, the retail bank should be credited with a value equal to its insured deposit balance times an estimate of the average annual deposit insurance premium.

Capital structure   Exhibit 16.14 shows a simplified balance sheet of a hypothetical retail banking unit. Two broad approaches exist for deciding how much equity should be allocated to the retail banking unit. Since most retail banks have required reserves as a

---

[1] E. Ronn, and A. Verma, "Pricing Risk-Adjusted Deposit Insurance: An Option-Based Model," *Journal of Finance* (September 1986): 871–895.

Exhibit 16.13 PER-DOLLAR VALUE OF FDIC DEPOSIT INSURANCE, 1983

Bank	Market value of assets, $ millions	Face value of total debt, $ millions	Ratio of assets to debt	Average annual deposit ins. premium,%
First Pennsylvania	$ 3,857	$ 3,866	.998	.7241%
Crocker National Corp.	15,247	15,195	1.003	.2666
Continental Illinois	22,289	22,073	1.010	.1944
Wells Fargo	22,200	21,911	1.013	.1838
Manufacturers Hanover	34,626	34,313	1.009	.1269
BankAmerica	74,642	73,714	1.013	.1035
First Interstate	37,039	36,405	1.017	.0856
Chase Manhattan	36,184	35,674	1.014	.0577
Bankers Trust	20,996	20,266	1.036	.0568
Citicorp	66,129	63,407	1.143	.0440
Chemical, New York	32,754	31,718	1.033	.0270
Security Pacific	29,699	28,682	1.035	.0162
Mellon	19,864	19,122	1.039	.0157
NCNB	10,301	9,890	1.042	.0129
Bank of Boston	10,690	10,231	1.045	.0106
Morgan, J. P.	28,913	26,981	1.072	.0001
Average				.0808%

Source: Ronn and Verma, 1986.

Exhibit 16.14 BALANCE SHEET OF A RETAIL BANKING UNIT, $ MILLIONS

Assets		Liabilities	
Reserves	180	Demand deposits	1,000
Consumer loans	100	Money market accounts	500
Small business loans	100	Certificates of deposit	300
Loans to treasury	1,420+	Equity	?
	?		?

buffer against unanticipated account withdrawals, they would carry less equity than the regulatory requirement. We assume, therefore, that the regulators determine the percentage of equity to be carried on the balance sheet. We could compute equity either as a percentage of total assets, or as a percentage of external assets only (reserves, consumer loans, and small business loan). If we adopt the former approach, then equity is a percentage of a major intercompany account, namely loans to the treasury. This philosophy overallocates equity, because the total equity of all business units will exceed total equity in the bank. To avoid this aggregation problem, it is better to allocate equity to external assets only. Given the numbers in Exhibit 16.14, and assuming book equity must be 5 percent of external assets, equity in the retail bank would be $19 million and loans to the treasury would be $1.439 billion.

The cost of equity   As always, the cost of equity is the rate of return investors would require for other investments of equivalent risk. Preliminary thinking would indicate that no good market comparable exists for the retail banking unit as we have structured it because no stand-alone banks exist with 80 percent of their assets invested in "loans to treasury" (or in government securities that return the money rate, the bank's transfer price). We have deliberately chosen the money rate to immunize the value of shareholders' equity against changes in market rates of interest. Consequently, even though in our allocation scheme the book equity of the retail banking unit is only about 1 percent of total assets, it has very little interest-rate risk. Furthermore, reserves serve as a buffer to protect against account withdrawals and loan defaults.

Further thought leads to the realization that the major risk borne by equity in the retail bank is the portion of loan default risk correlated with the economy, a risk that affects only the external assets of the retail bank. Since equity is roughly 5 percent of external assets (that is, the amount required by regulation in our hypothetical example), equity risk will be roughly the same as for comparable retail banks that have a low ratio of loans to deposits.

The Wholesale Bank

The primary business activity of the wholesale bank is making loans. For each dollar of loans, there might be only 20 cents in deposits; therefore, the wholesale bank funds itself by borrowing from the bank's treasury. Once again, the critical issue is how to determine the correct transfer price or money rate the wholesale bank must pay for the funds it uses. Once this issue has been resolved, we can turn to capital structure and the cost of equity.

The money rate for the wholesale bank   The opportunity cost of funds for a loan portfolio depends on those factors that affect its systematic risk: (1) duration, the sensitivity of its value to changes in interest rates; and (2) the portion of its credit or default risk that cannot be diversified away. Diversifiable credit risk does not affect the opportunity cost of funds; rather, it is reflected in the computation of the expected cash flow to the loan portfolio. To illustrate, suppose we are evaluating the opportunity cost of capital for the low-quality loan in Exhibit 16.15. We lend $1,000 in return for promised payments of $200 per year plus repayment of the principal, $1,000, at the end of the fifth year. The *promised* yield to maturity is 20 percent; however, the cumulative default rate rises each year until only 80 percent of loans of this type reach maturity without defaulting. Asquith, Mullins, and Wolff (1989) indicate that actual cumulative default rates on five- to nine-year-old portfolios of original issue junk bonds were between 19 and 26 percent.[2] We need to figure out the *expected* yield to maturity. This can be done by finding the rate that equates the expected cash flow with the amount we lend out.

Exhibit 16.15 **EXPECTED PAYOUTS FOR A LOW-QUALITY LOAN**

Year	Cumulative default rate	Promised payments	Assumptions
1	1%	$ 200	• $1,000 lent at year 0
2	2	200	• When the loan defaults, nothing can be recovered
3	5	200	
4	10	200	
5	20	1,200	

[2] P. Asquith, D. Mullins Jr., and E. Wolff, "Original Issue High Yield Bonds: Aging Analysis of Defaults, Exchanges, and Calls," *Journal of Finance* 44, No. 4. (1989): 923–952.

$$\$1.000 = \frac{.99(\$200)}{1+y} + \frac{.98(\$200)}{\left(1+y\right)^2} + \frac{.95(\$200)}{\left(1+y\right)^3} + \frac{.9(\$200)}{\left(1+y\right)^4} + \frac{.8(\$1,200)}{\left(1+y\right)^5}.$$

In our formula, the expected yield, y, turns out to be approximately 15.8 percent. Thus, the expected yield is 420 basis points lower than the promised yield.

Once the difference between the expected and promised yields has been clarified, the choice of the appropriate money rate to charge the wholesale bank for borrowing from the treasury becomes a matter of taste. If expected cash flow estimates forecast charge-offs, then the MR should be the expected yield for loan portfolios of equivalent credit risk and duration. Alternately, if expected charge-offs are not computed (and by default, all payments are assumed to be made as promised), then the MR should be the promised yield to maturity for loan portfolios of equivalent credit risk and duration.

A commonly used source of data for yields on loan portfolios of equivalent credit risk and duration is market prices of publicly traded debt issues. However, a certain amount of skepticism is appropriate when drawing comparisons, because the covenants on publicly held debt issues are often different from bank debt covenants. Consequently, a direct comparison of yields may be inappropriate unless they are adjusted for the effect of differences in covenants.

Capital structure As with the retail bank, the dominating consideration is that the equity for all of the pieces of the bank should aggregate to equal the total bank equity. Therefore, we recommend that book equity in the wholesale bank be determined as a percentage of its external assets (usually equal to total assets).

Cost of equity Because each loan portfolio is match-funded with a money rate that accounts for both credit risk and interest-rate (duration) risk, and because the ratio of equity to total assets will be close to the regulatory requirement, the cost of equity for the wholesale bank will be less than for the bank as a whole. Business risk is the primary risk left in the wholesale bank after match-funding; hence, its cost of equity will be close to the unlevered cost of equity for the entire bank, which, of course, is an estimate of business risk for the entire bank.

Treasury and Headquarters

The bank treasury borrows from the retail bank and lends to the wholesale bank. It also handles the bank's trading business and is responsible for centralized risk management. And, for the sake of argument, we will assume it is responsible for solving the shared-cost problem. To organize our discussion of these issues, we cover, in turn, the mismatch problem, centralized risk management, the cost of equity, and the shared-cost problem. We will not discuss the treasury's capital structure except to say that, as before, equity will be allocated to the treasury based on the amount of external assets it holds.

Mismatch profits and losses   The philosophy we have adopted is to match-fund the retail and wholesale banks as closely as possible for credit and interest-rate (duration) risk. The business reason for doing so is to provide business-unit managers with guidelines that lead directly to positive net present value decisions. For example, a loan officer must earn an all-in-rate (fees plus interest) that exceeds a money rate that is adjusted both for credit and duration risk.

To the extent that the risk and duration of deposits is less than for loans, the treasury unit will record a mismatch profit. We have already illustrated, in Exhibit 16.7 and the accompanying discussion, that mismatch profits can be illusory. Recall that the key to handling mismatch gains or losses is to build a good cash flow forecast that takes into account (1) the way spreads are forecasted to change across time with changing interest-rate environments; (2) the inflow of funds from loans being paid off and the outflow of funds at new rates as new loans are made; (3) the substitution between interest-bearing and noninterest-bearing deposits as interest-rate environments change; and (4) the portion of mismatch profits that are sustainable because forward rates tend to be higher than their corresponding realized rates.

Centralized risk management   Although current mismatch profits or losses may be illusory because they will not persist across time, the fact that they fluctuate with unexpected changes in the term structure of interest rates means that mismatch creates risk for shareholders. Financial futures positions can be used to offset this mismatch risk. A bank or savings and loan that lends long term and borrows short term can hedge against the risk of an increase in interest rates by taking an offsetting short position in financial futures. This form of risk management is best implemented by the treasury unit, which has a centralized point of view.

The cost of equity   The recommended transfer-pricing mechanism collects interest-rate risks in the treasury unit. If the treasury does nothing to hedge these risks, then the cost of equity will generally be higher for the treasury than for the bank as a whole. To the extent that risks are hedged, the cost of equity will be lower.

The shared-cost problem   Most banks try to use cost accounting systems to push all overhead costs down to the business-unit level. It is better, we believe, to allocate only those costs that the business units would incur were they standing alone. Unallocated headquarters costs should be kept at headquarters as a cost center. Furthermore, business units should be encouraged to compare costs of providing services via outsourcing with internal costs. This provides a means of checking to be sure that internally provided services are cost-efficient.

The shared-cost problem arises from the fact that multiple business units may use the same resource. For example, a teller may provide services for noninterest-bearing checking, money market accounts, coupon clipping, and mortgage loan payments. If all these activities are within the same business unit—for example, retail banking—no problem results for valuation at the business-unit level. However, if the costs are shared between business units—for example, retail banking and the trust department—then an effort should be made to allocate the costs on the basis of services used.

SUMMARY

At the outset we said this short chapter would not present all the answers. Still, by raising the issues we hope to catalyze an ongoing discussion among banking managers. We firmly believe that valuation is a useful tool in the banking industry and that for planning purposes it should supplement and even replace more arcane and myopic performance standards, such as growth in net income or return on equity.

However, difficult and unresolved issues are present in valuing banks. From an outsider's point of view, banks are particularly opaque businesses because of blind pool risk in their loan portfolios and because adequate information is not available concerning their actual hedging practices. From an insider's perspective, a variety of transfer-pricing schemes are possible. We have discussed an approach that match-funds each business unit for interest-rate and credit risk, thereby collecting these risks in a centralized treasury operation where they can be explicitly managed. One of the by-products of this approach is that each match-funded unit, as well as the treasury, has no good market comparables that can be used to estimate the cost of equity. Consequently, some guesswork is involved in this area and the answers are soft, requiring us to use ranges rather than point estimates. Nevertheless, the most relevant differences among banking business units are reflected in their expected free cash flow to shareholders, and this is adequately captured in the value process.

REVIEW QUESTIONS

1. What is so different about banks that the entity method of valuation is difficult and may even be inappropriate to use?
2. If the entity method does not apply to banks, formulate a method that does, and relate it to the entity method.
3. The following is a simplified balance sheet for a bank with associated yields on items:

Community Bank

Assets		Rate
Cash Reserves	150	7%
Loans	850	11%
Total Assets	1000	
Liabilities		
Deposits	950	4%
Equity	50	
Total Liabilities	1000	

The bank does not earn income on the Federal Reserve cash balance. Cash noninterest expenses are $40. The tax rate is 40 percent. Formulate income using the income and spread models.

4. Define free cash flow to equity holders of a bank.
5. Value Neighborhood Bank System, Inc., using the equity method. Here is a very simplified version of Neighborhood Bank System's balance sheet, income statement, and average rates for 1994.

Income Statement

	1994 Amount	Rate
Interest Income	66.919	8.11%
– Interest Expense	(25.221)	3.52%
Net Interest Income	41.698	4.59%
+ Other Income	5.120	
– Other Expenses	(26.498)	
Net Profit Before Tax	20.320	
– Taxes	(7.721)	38.00%
Net Income	12.598	

Balance Sheet

	1994 Amount	Rate
Cash Reserves	32.411	
Investment Securities	378.520	6.93%
Net Loans	446.135	9.12%
Net Premises, Other Assets	25.526	
Less: Provision for Credit Losses	(6.281)	
TOTAL ASSETS	876.311	
Interest Bearing Deposits	552.892	3.29%
Noninterest Bearing Deposits	98.587	
Other Short Term Liabilities	6.102	
Federal Funds Purchased	57.300	4.00%
Term Borrowings	105.550	4.49%
LIABILITIES	820.431	
SHAREHOLDERS' EQUITY	55.880	13.48%
TOTAL	876.311	

Depreciation is $1.434 million for 1994. Beta for the firm's equity is 1.20.

Proof of the Equivalence of Two Formulas for Estimating Continuing Value

This appendix proves the equivalence of the two recommended continuing-value formulas: the free cash flow perpetuity formula and the value-driver formula. The two formulas are as follows:

$$\text{Continuing value} = \frac{\text{FCF}}{\text{WACC} - g} = \frac{\text{NOPLAT}(1 - g/r)}{\text{WACC} - g}.$$

Since the denominators are identical, we only need to prove that free cash flow can be expressed by the following equation:

$$\text{FCF} = \text{NOPLAT}(1 - g/r),$$

where

FCF   = free cash flow.
NOPLAT = net operating profits less adjusted taxes.
g   = growth rate in NOPLAT.
r   = rate of return on net new capital invested.

First, let us define free cash flow as the company's operating profits less the net new capital invested.

$$FCF = NOPLAT - In,$$

where

In = net increase in invested capital over and above replacement capital.

As long as the return on existing capital employed remains constant, a company's NOPLAT in any period equals last period's NOPLAT, plus the return in earns on last period's net investment in new capital.

$$NOPLAT_T = NOPLAT_{T-1} + (r \times In_{T-1}).$$

This equation can be rearranged to show that the change in NOPLAT equals the rate of return on new investment times the amount of new investment.

$$NOPLAT_T - NOPLAT_{T-1} = (r \times In_{T-1}).$$

Dividing both sides by last year's NOPLAT calculates the growth rate in NOPLAT.

$$g = \frac{NOPLAT_T - NOPLAT_{T-1}}{NOPLAT_{T-1}} = \frac{r \times In_{T-1}}{NOPLAT_{T-1}}.$$

$$g = r \times \frac{In}{NOPLAT}.$$

Solving for the amount of investment required to increase NO-PLAT at the rate, g, and substituting for the first definition of free cash flow gives the free cash flow calculation in terms of the key value drivers.

$$\text{In} = \text{NOPLAT} \times \frac{g}{r}.$$

$$\text{FCF} = \text{NOPLAT} - \left(\text{NOPLAT} \times \frac{g}{r} \right).$$

$$\text{FCF} = \text{NOPLAT} \left(1 - \frac{g}{r} \right).$$

The ratio g/r can be called the net investment rate, as it represents the ratio of net new investment to NOPLAT, which is consistent with a growth rate of g and a rate of return r.

APPENDIX B

Sources of
Valuation Data

U.S. COMPANIES

Source	Brief description
Public Companies: Printed Data	
Moody's Manuals	Historical financials, detailed descriptions of securities outstanding, bond ratings
Standard & Poor's Stock Reports	Financial information, business segment descriptions, current information on company activities
Standard & Poor's Industry Reports	Discussion of industry trends, including company-specific information
Value Line Investment Survey	Financial information on 1,700 public companies, including forecasts
SEC filings:	
• 10-K	Detailed annual financial information
• 10Q	Quarterly financial information
• Proxy statement	Details regarding security issues
• 13D	
• Insider trading	Historical data on transactions by insiders
Annual report	Audited annual report to shareholders
Wall Street Transcript	Summaries of analyst reports, CEO speeches

Dun & Bradstreet:
- Business Rankings   Ranking by sales of both public and private companies within SIC codes
- Million Dollar Directories   Listings of both public and private companies within SIC codes
- Corporate affiliations   Listing of divisions, product lines, and subsidiaries with SIC codes

Magazine indexes:
- F&S index   List of recent articles about a company
- Business Periodicals Index   List of recent articles about a company
- *The Wall Street Journal* Index   List of *The Wall Street Journal* cites of a company

Analysts' reports   Detailed studies often containing forecasts

Newspaper articles   Miscellaneous data
Trade journals   Miscellaneous data

Public Companies: Computer-Readable Data
Datext   Compact-disk-based information on 10,000 publicly held companies, organized by groups (Technology, Industrial, Service, Consumer, Corp-Tech, and Commercial Bank); contains financials, subsidiaries, directors, stock reports, recent articles, comparable financials

Dialog:
- Disclosure   Historical financials, officers, subsidiary list, annual report
- Moody's Corporate Profiles   Condensed financials, institutional holdings
- Media General   Weekly prices, dividends, ratios
- Investext   Analysts' reports
- Predicast   Financial abstracts
- Newspaper Index   Index of newspaper articles
- Business Wire   News summaries

Dow Jones:
- Stock quotes   Recent stock quotes
- Current news   News wire service
- Media General   Summary data on prices, dividends, shareholdings
- Disclosures   Historical financials, ratios, ownership information, analysts' reports
- *The Wall Street Journal*   Search for routine articles from *The Wall Street Journal*

Nexis:
- Full text   Text of articles on a company
- Exchange   Search capability

Privately Held Companies: Printed Data
Dun & Bradstreet Reports   Brief financial and nonfinancial profiles
                                       on private companies; includes sales,
                                       SIC, and number of employees

Standard & Poor's Corporate Register   List of officers, products, SIC
Thomas Register   CEO, SIC, sales, number of employees

Privately Held Companies: Computer-Readable Data
Dialog   See description under "Public compa-
                                       nies"
Nexis   See description under "Public compa-
                                       nies"
Dun & Bradstreet Credit Rating   Credit rating, special events, financials,
                                       officers
Newsnet   TRW business profiles

Industry Sources: Printed Data
U.S. Industrial Outlook   Description of two-digit and three-digit
                                       SIC industry groups; industry sales
                                       forecasts
Standard & Poor's Industry Surveys   Industry overviews by S&P analysts
Value Line Investment Surveys   Industry analysis and forecasts of sales
                                       growth, operating margins, tax rates,
                                       capitalization
Wall Street Transcript   Panel discussions of industry outlook
Dun & Bradstreet   Key business ratios and industry norms
Moody's Industry Review   Comparative statistics for major compa-
                                       nies within an industry classification
Predicast   Summary of industry data, employ-
                                       ment, capital expenditures, etc.
Encyclopedia of Associations   Listing of industry associations that can
                                       be contacted for further data, lobby-
                                       ing efforts, etc.

Industry Sources: Computer-Readable Data
Dialog:
- Predicast   Sales growth rates
- Trade & Industry Index   Abstracts of trade journal articles
- Investext   Abstracts of market/industry studies
- Arthur D. Little/on-line   A.D. Little industry reports
- Encyclopedia of Associations   Industry associations
Nexis   See description under "Public com-
                                       panies"
Dow Jones   See description under "Public com-
                                       panies"

Other Sources

U.S. Government	Specific department publications
Yellow Pages	Phone book
Statistical Abstracts	Summary of government data (for example, Federal Reserve, Commerce Department)

NON-U.S. COMPANIES

BARRA International   Produces individual company betas using a Goldman Sachs monthly rate of return database. The betas are computed using BARRA methodology that incorporates regression toward the mean and a multifactor approach. Currently available are

- The World Book, containing 2,500 companies from the *Financial Times* list
- Separate, more complete, country books:
  - United Kingdom, with 1,300 companies
  - Japan, with 1,800 companies
  - West Germany, with 250 companies
  - Australia

Although BARRA produces betas, it unfortunately does not provide information on the number of shares outstanding, market risk premiums, or line-of-business breakdowns of company assets. For more information contact: BARRA International, 65 London Wall, London EC2M STU, England. Phone: 01-920-0131.

London Business School, London, England   Has a share price database and a risk measurement service. The share price database is updated annually and contains monthly rate of return data for over 4,500 U.K. companies from 1975 to present (with some as early as 1955). It also contains indexes (dividend yields, earnings yields, exchange rates, interest rates on government bonds, and the *Financial Times* A Classified Index), shares outstanding, dividends, earnings, and adjustments (for splits, script, and rights). The LBS risk measurement service produces quarterly updates of total volatility and betas that are adjusted for thin trading and for regression toward the mean. For more information contact: London Business School, Sussex Place, Regent's Park, London NW1 4SA, England. Phone: 01-262-5050.

Karlsruhe Universität, Karlsruhe, West Germany   Has the most complete source of German data. Under the direction of Professor Herman Göppl, the Karlsruhe Kapitalmarktdatenbank has been produced. It has 7 stock market indexes, monthly rates of return for 234 German stocks, 13 foreign stocks listed in Germany, 62 call and put options, 44 warrants, and 300 government bonds. Although no commercial service for betas yet exists, the computer programs are available and the institute is willing to produce data under contract. For more information contact: Professor Herman Göppl, Institut fur Entscheidungstheorie und Unternehmensforschung, Universität Karlsruhe, Postfach 6980 D-7500 Karlsruhe 1, West Germany. Phone: 721-608-3427.

Morgan Stanley Capital International, New York, New York, USA   Provides stock market return indexes for 19 countries as well as European and World indexes. They also have P/E, price-to-cash-earnings, and price-to-book ratios; limited balance sheet information; shares outstanding; earnings and dividends per share. Their sample contains roughly 1,700 of the largest companies in the world (1970 to present). For more information contact: Morgan Stanley, Inc., 1633 Broadway, New York, New York 10019. Phone: 212-765-3114.

Compass   Very large database with heavy product/service offering orientation but with some financial information, covering
- All significant U.K. companies
- Major European companies (Euro-Compass)

Datastream   Online database service providing
- Equity data for
  - All U.K. quoted companies
- Foreign companies quoted in
  - Canada
  - France (190 companies)
  - Germany (4,000 companies)
  - Hong Kong
  - Japan
  - Netherlands
  - Switzerland
  - U.S.
- Company accounts information for
  - Quoted companies
  - 40,000 unquoted U.K. companies

Extel   Authoritative card-based five-year summary (for main market, USMA, third market, and major unquoted companies) of financial statements and
- Capital and restructuring transactions
- Acquisitions and disposals
- Dividends

Hoppenstat   German database of company financial information.

ICC   Archive service for company accounts, public documents, and brokers' reports.

Investex   Online brokers' reports, including all major U.K. brokers (and some foreign) and covering all major U.K. and most major foreign corporations.

Japan Company Handbook   Useful reference for Japanese companies in first and second section with summary financial information.

M&A Database   Based on M&A magazine data, covers all major transactions, most smaller U.K. deals, and many smaller U.S. deals.

Topic   Real-time stock exchange information.

World Scope   CD-ROM system with financial information on major global and U.S. corporations.

SUMMARY OF VALUATION DATA SOURCES

Country	Indexes			Betas		Individual security returns			
	Market portfolio	Industry	Risk-free rate	CAPM	APM	Stock	Bonds	Options	Shares outstanding
Austria	MS	X	X	X	X	X	X	X	MS
Australia	MS	X	X	B	X	X	X	X	MS
Belgium	MS	X	X	X	X	X	X	X	MS
Canada	MS	X	—	—	X	D	X	X	MS
Denmark	MS	X	X	X	X	D	X	X	MS
France	MS	X	X	X	E	D	X	X	MS
Germany	MS	X	K	B,K	E	E,K,D	K	K	MS
Hong Kong	MS	X	X	X	X	D	X	X	MS
Italy	MS	X	X	X	X	X	X	X	MS
Japan	MS	X	RR	B	RR	RR,D	X	X	MS
Mexico	MS	X	X	X	X	X	X	X	MS
Netherlands	MS	X	E	E	E	E,D	X	X	MS
Norway	MS	X	X	X	X	X	X	X	MS
Singapore	MS	X	X	X	X	X	X	X	MS
South Africa	MS	X	X	X	X	X	X	X	MS
Spain	MS	X	X	B	X	X	X	X	MS
Sweden	MS	X	X	X	X	X	X	X	MS
Switzerland	MS	X	X	X	X	D	X	X	MS
United Kingdom	LBS,MS	LBS	LBS	LBS,B	E	LBS,D	X	X	LBS,MS
United States	MS	X	CRSP	B	A	CRSP,C,D	CRSP	Berk	CRSP,MS

A = Alcar
B = BARRA International
Berk = University of California, Berkeley
C = Compuserve
CRSP = Center for Research in Securities Prices, University of Chicago Graduate School of Business
D = Datastream
E = Erasmus University
K = Universität Karlsruhe
LBS = London Business School Financial Services
MS = Morgan Stanley Capital International
RR = Roll and Ross, Inc., Culver City, California
X = No known data source

Index